W9-BRM-813

Silver Burdett Ginn
Mathematics

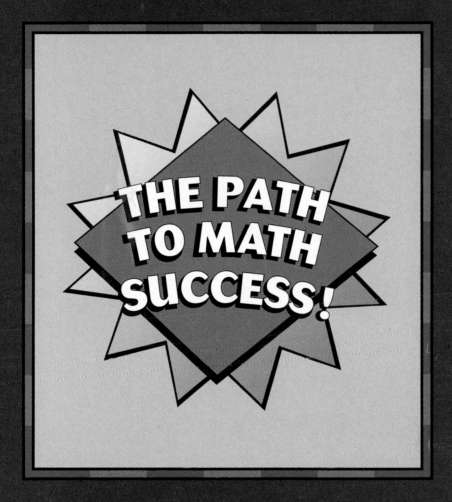

THE PATH TO MATH SUCCESS!

Silver Burdett Ginn

Parsippany, NJ

Atlanta, GA • Deerfield, IL • Irving, TX • Needham, MA • Upland, CA

Program Authors

Francis (Skip) Fennell, Ph.D.
Professor of Education and Chair, Education Department

Western Maryland College
Westminster, Maryland

Joan Ferrini-Mundy, Ph.D.
Professor of Mathematics

University of New Hampshire
Durham, New Hampshire

Herbert P. Ginsburg, Ph.D.
Professor of Psychology and Mathematics Education

Teachers College, Columbia University
New York, New York

Carole Greenes, Ed.D.
Professor of Mathematics Education and Associate Dean,
 School of Education

Boston University
Boston, Massachusetts

Stuart J. Murphy
Visual Learning Specialist

Evanston, Illinois

William Tate, Ph.D.
Associate Professor of Mathematics Education

University of Wisconsin-Madison
Madison, Wisconsin

Acknowledgments appear on page 538, which constitutes an extension of this copyright page.

ISBN 0-382-40120-4

3 4 5 6 7 8 9 10 WC 05 04 03 02 01 00 99

Silver Burdett Ginn

299 Jefferson Road, P.O. Box 480
Parsippany, NJ 07054-0480

Grade Level Authors

Mary Behr Altieri, M.S.
Mathematics Teacher
1993 Presidential Awardee

Lakeland Central School District
Shrub Oak, New York

Jennie Bennett, Ed.D.
Instructional Mathematics Supervisor

Houston Independent School District
Houston, Texas

Charles Calhoun, Ph.D.
Associate Professor of Elementary
 Education Mathematics

University of Alabama at Birmingham
Birmingham, Alabama

Lucille Croom, Ph.D.
Professor of Mathematics

Hunter College of the City University
 of New York
New York, New York

Robert A. Laing, Ph.D.
Professor of Mathematics Education

Western Michigan University
Kalamazoo, Michigan

Kay B. Sammons, M.S.
Supervisor of Elementary Mathematics

Howard County Public Schools
Ellicott City, Maryland

Marian Small, Ed.D.
Professor of Mathematics Education

University of New Brunswick
Fredericton, New Brunswick, Canada

Contributing Authors

Stephen Krulik, Ed.D.
Professor of Mathematics Education

Temple University
Philadelphia, Pennsylvania

Donna J. Long
Mathematics/Title 1 Coordinator

Metropolitan School District of
 Wayne Township
Indianapolis, Indiana

Jesse A. Rudnick, Ed.D.
Professor Emeritus of Mathematics
 Education

Temple University
Philadelphia, Pennsylvania

Clementine Sherman
Director, USI Math and Science

Dade County Public Schools
Miami, Florida

Bruce R. Vogeli, Ph.D.
Clifford Brewster Upton Professor of
 Mathematics

Teachers College, Columbia University
New York, New York

Contents

Chapter 1: Understanding Place Value

Chapter Theme: Earth and Beyond

Chapter 3 — Using Data and Statistics

Chapter Theme: Inventions

Chapter 4 — Multiplying Whole Numbers

Chapter 5 — Dividing by One-Digit Divisors

Chapter Theme: Transportation

Chapter 6 · Dividing by Two-Digit Divisors

Chapter 7

Geometry

Chapter Theme: Shapes and Forms

Chapter 8 — Multiplying and Dividing Decimals

Chapter Theme: Using Money

Chapter 9 Fraction Concepts

Chapter 10 Working With Fractions

Chapter Theme: Food

Gazpacho

6 green onions
6 ripe tomatoes
1 clove of garlic
1 green pepper
1 slice of bread
2 tbsp olive oil
pinch of salt

Chapter 11

Measurement

 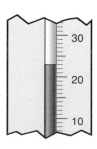  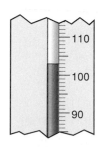 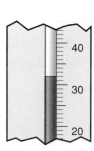

Chapter 12

Ratio, Percent, and Probability

Understanding Place Value

Chapter Theme: EARTH AND BEYOND

·················**Real Facts**···················

The solar system consists of the sun and the objects that revolve around it, including the planets. Earth, Mars, Mercury, and Venus are the closest planets to the sun. They are called the inner planets.

Average Distances From the Sun	
Planet	**Distance**
Earth	149,600,000 km
Mars	227,900,000 km
Mercury	57,900,000 km
Venus	108,200,000 km

- Understanding place value can help you compare numbers. Which place should you look at first to help you arrange the planets in order from closest to farthest from the sun? Explain why.

- Which planet is about twice as far from the sun as Venus? Which planet is about half as far from the sun as Venus?

·················**Real People**···················

Meet John Dobson, a very unusual astronomer. He travels around cities, setting up his equipment on the sidewalk. Everyone who walks by is invited to see the stars!

Astronomers use very large numbers when talking or writing about distances between Earth and other planets or the stars. They must keep track of place value when writing such big numbers!

One Billion Stars

*One billion is an enormous number.
Here's your chance to find out just how big it is.*

Learning About It

There are billions and billions of stars in our galaxy. How big is one billion?

Work with your partner. Find out how many sheets of grid paper it would take to draw one billion stars.

Step 1 Outline a grid that is 25 squares wide and 40 squares long. Draw a star in every square. Count each star or multiply the number of rows by the number of columns. How many stars will fit on a grid?

Step 2 Copy the chart below. Look for patterns to complete your chart to find how many sheets of grid paper you will need to draw one billion stars.

What You Need

For each pair:
  grid paper
  calculator (optional)

Sheets of Grid Paper	Total Stars
1	1,000
10	10,000
100	
	1,000,000
10,000	10,000,000
100,000	

Step 3 A ream of paper has 500 sheets and is about 2 inches thick. Complete a chart like the one at the right to help you find how many reams of paper you would need for one billion stars.

> **Hint** One billion is written as 1,000,000,000.

Reams	Sheets of Paper	Total Stars
1	500	500,000
2	1,000	1,000,000
20	10,000	10,000,000
200	100,000	100,000,000
	1,000,000	

Science Connection ➤
We live in a galaxy with
billions of stars.

Think and Discuss Look back at the chart you made
in Step 2. Describe any patterns you see.

Practice

1. Look back at Step 3. If all the reams of grid paper
   showing a billion stars are piled in a stack, about how
   tall will the stack be?

2. A sheet of paper is 11 inches long. If you put sheets
   of grid paper showing one billion stars end to end,
   would the line of paper be about as long as your
   school or the 173-mile distance between Chattanooga
   and Clarksville, Tennessee? Tell how you decided.
   Hint 12 in. = 1 ft and 5,280 ft = 1 mi

3. **Journal Idea** Write a paragraph describing something
   that is measured in billions.

Critical Thinking Corner

Number Sense

Time for a Billion

If you drew a dot in every square of a 25 by 40
grid every second for 24 hours a day and 365
days a year, would it take more or less than two
years to draw one billion dots?

What a Place!

*Understanding place value can help you
read and write very large numbers.*

Learning About It

There are nine known planets in our solar system.
Saturn, the sixth planet from the sun, travels more than
five billion miles in its orbit. A **place-value** chart can
help you learn how to read and write large numbers.

Saturn's orbit 5,553,580,000 miles

period	BILLIONS			MILLIONS			THOUSANDS			ONES		
place value	hundred billions	ten billions	billions	hundred millions	ten millions	millions	hundred thousands	ten thousands	thousands	hundreds	tens	ones
			5,	5	5	3,	5	8	0,	0	0	0
						1,	2	3	4,	5	6	7

The value of the 3 in 5,553,580,000 is
3,000,000. It is in the millions place.

 THERE'S ALWAYS A WAY!

A number can be expressed in
different ways.

- **Standard form:** 5,553,580,000

- **Word form:** five billion, five hundred fifty-three million,
  five hundred eighty thousand

- **Short word form:** 5 billion, 553 million, 580 thousand

- **Expanded form:** 5,000,000,000 + 500,000,000 +
  50,000,000 + 3,000,000 + 500,000 + 80,000

Word Bank

place value
standard form
word form
short word form
expanded form

Think and Discuss When reading large numbers,
it is useful to think of periods of three digits starting
at the right. Explain why you think this is true.

Try It Out

Write the value of each underlined digit.

1. 25,<u>4</u>52
2. <u>8</u>21,553
3. <u>1</u>,845,932
4. 6,0<u>5</u>3,827

5. Write the expanded and word forms for Exercises 1–4.

Practice

Write the value of the digit 7 in each number.

6. 3,743
7. 67,236
8. 756,809
9. 575,432

10. 74,294,523
11. 432,148,675
12. 6,452,809,765
13. 357,503,236,954

Write a number that has the digit 5 in the place listed.
Use the digit 5 only once in each number.

14. hundreds
15. tens
16. ten thousands

17. hundred billions
18. ten millions
19. hundred millions

Write two other forms for each number.

20. 712,004
21. 3,619,963
22. 344,598,000
23. 3,671,910,000

24. fifty-two million, one hundred fourteen thousand

Problem Solving

25. A science store is having a contest to guess the number of marbles in a jar. I guessed 75, but I was off by 20. My friend guessed 90, but she was off by 5. How many marbles are in the jar? What strategy did you use to find your answer?

26. Look at the photo of a quipu. What number does a string with three knots at the bottom, four knots in the middle, and five knots at the top represent?

Review and Remember

Write a fact family for each set of numbers.

27. 7, 8, 15
28. 8, 10, 18
29. 5, 9, 14

30. 4, 8, 12
31. 3, 7, 10
32. 2, 12, 14

▲ Social Studies Connection
In the 1400s, Incas in Peru used quipus (KEE pooz) to keep records. The structure of the knots and their locations on the strings were based on the decimal system.

For Extra Practice, see Set A, page 34.

Next in Line

You can use what you know about place value to compare and order numbers.

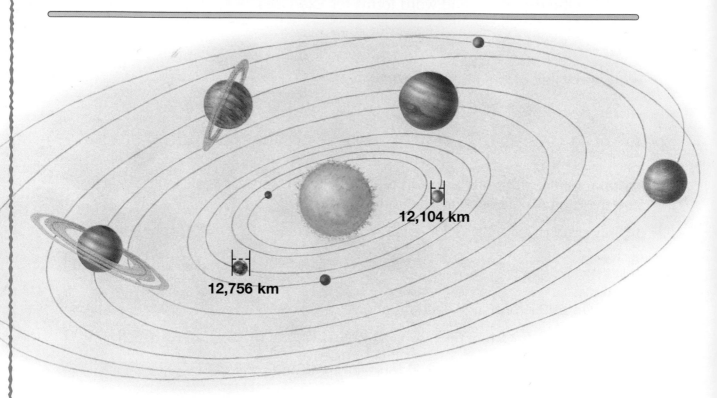

12,104 km

12,756 km

Learning About It

Each of the nine planets in our solar system has a different diameter—the width across the widest part. Earth has a diameter of 12,756 km. Venus, the next planet closer to the sun, has a diameter of 12,104 km. Compare the diameters of Earth and Venus to see which is greater.

Diameters of Planets

Planet	Diameter (in kilometers)
Earth	12,756
Mars	6,794
Mercury	4,878
Venus	12,104

Step 1 Start at the left. Compare digits in the same place. The ten thousands and thousands digits are the same.

Step 2 Compare the next digits to the right. 7 > 1, so 12,756 > 12,104.

1 2 , 7 5 6 km

1 2 , 1 0 4 km

Since 12,756 > 12,104, the diameter of Earth is greater than the diameter of Venus.

Connecting Ideas

You can use what you have learned about comparing numbers to put numbers in order.

The table below lists the planets and their average distances from the sun.

Average Distances From the Sun (in kilometers)	
Earth	149,600,000
Mars	227,900,000
Mercury	57,900,000
Venus	108,200,000

Science Connection ▲
Early Spanish astronomers used an astrolabe to observe the position of a star.

Follow the steps to write the distances in order from greatest to least.

Step 1 Start at the left. Compare digits in the same place.

1 49,600,000
2 27,900,000
57,900,000
1 08,200,000

2 > 1, so
227,900,000 is the greatest number.

Step 2 When two digits are the same, compare the next digits to the right.

1 4 9,600,000
1 0 8,200,000

4 > 0, so
149,600,000 > 108,200,000.

Step 3 Write the numbers in order from greatest to least.

Mars 227,900,000 km
Earth 149,600,000 km
Venus 108,200,000 km
Mercury 57,900,000 km

Think and Discuss Look at the illustration on page 6. Use the information in Step 3 above to identify the four planets nearest to the sun.

Try It Out

Compare. Write >, <, or = for each ●.

1. 23,878 ● 26,799

2. 162,033 ● 162,303

3. 99,992,881 ● 100,234,710

4. 62,334,010 ● 62,333,001

5. 23,368,892 ● 23,368,492

6. 1,885,340,211 ● 1,885,340,211

Order each set of numbers from least to greatest.

7. 1,997   1,836   1,979

8. 23,004   322,008   32,008

9. 913,771   91,374   912,722

10. 8,056   8,566   8,605   8,065

Practice

Compare. Write >, <, or = for each ●.

11. 10,198 ● 1,203   **12.** 1,444 ● 1,447   **13.** 35,271 ● 35,271

14. 108,655,544 ● 108,553,222   **15.** 10,000,000 ● 100,000,000

16. 791,539,406 ● 791,539,406   **17.** 543,904,286 ● 548,904,286

Order each set of numbers from least to greatest.

18. 1,276   1,726   1,627   **19.** 152,275   152,475   152,175

20. 33,881   33,188   33,818   **21.** 5,415,362   5,113,944   6,013,455

22. 42,721   42,822   4,823   **23.** 2,334,556   2,344,566   2,343,655

24. 718,049   98,764   984,336   **25.** 31,672,582   31,672,852   31,672,558

26. Using Algebra These numbers are arranged from greatest to least. They follow a pattern. Write the missing number in the pattern.

655,898   655,896   __?__   655,892

Problem Solving

27. The table below shows the populations of five countries. List the countries in order from greatest to least according to their populations.

28. Look at your order of population in Problem 27. Where would these countries fit if they were added to the list: Colombia—36,200,251; France—58,109,160; Mozambique—18,115,250?

INTERNET ACTIVITY
www.sbgmath.com

Country	1995 Population
Canada	28,434,545
Egypt	62,359,623
Mexico	93,985,848
Philippines	73,265,584
Turkey	63,405,526

29. Create Your Own Use what you know about ordering and comparing numbers to write a word problem for your classmates to solve. Use three or more numbers. Choose numbers that have the same number of digits.

30. Find the mystery number and explain what strategy you used.

- Its thousands digit is half its tens digit.
- Its hundreds digit is 3 times its ones digit.
- Its tens digit is 8.
- Its ones digit is one fourth its tens digit.

Review and Remember

Using Algebra Find each ■.

31. $9 + 8 = $ ■

32. $16 - 9 = $ ■

33. $14 \div 7 = $ ■

34. $8 \times $ ■ $ = 56$

35. $4 \times 6 = $ ■

36. $12 - $ ■ $ = 9$

37. ■ $\times 5 = 30$

38. $27 \div $ ■ $ = 9$

Time for Technology

Using the MathProcessor™ CD-ROM

Using the Graphing Tool
You can link spreadsheets and graphs to organize and display data.

- Open a spreadsheet ▦. Link it to a bar graph 📊.

- Key into the spreadsheet the data from the Diameters of Planets table on page 6. To resize columns, grab the solid line between columns with the cross-hatch cursor ✛ and drag the line right or left.

- Use writing spaces to label the graph.

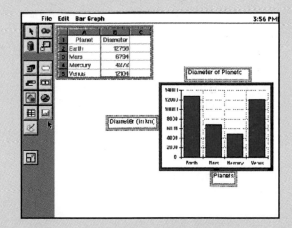

- You may wish to save this screen for use with Time for Technology on page 111.

Around Here Somewhere

Knowing the place value of a number helps you decide quickly how to round it to the nearest ten, hundred, or thousand.

Learning About It

Every year, the fifth-grade class takes a trip to Washington, D.C. Included in the trip is a visit to a space museum. The estimated cost this year is $3,840. To the nearest hundred dollars, about how much money will this year's class need?

Round $3,840 to find out.

1 Year Ago
$3,360

This Year
$3,840

EINSTEIN
PLANETARIUM

African American Historical Attractions Guide

THERE'S ALWAYS A WAY!

● **One way** to round is to use a number line.

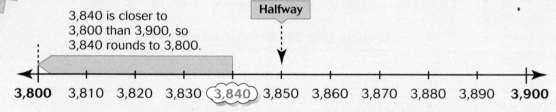

3,840 is closer to
3,800 than 3,900, so
3,840 rounds to 3,800.

Halfway

3,800 3,810 3,820 3,830 3,840 3,850 3,860 3,870 3,880 3,890 3,900

● **Another way** to round is to use rounding rules.

Step 1 Find the rounding place.	**Step 2** Look at the digit one place to the right. If the digit is less than 5, the digit in the rounding place stays the same. If the digit is 5 or greater, the digit in the rounding place increases by 1.
$3,**8**40	$3,8**4**0 4 < 5, so $3,840 rounds to $3,800.

The fifth-grade class needs about $3,800 for its trip.

Think and Discuss What is $3,840 rounded to the nearest thousand? to the nearest ten? Tell what method you used.

Try It Out

Round each number to the underlined place.

1. 200,<u>0</u>95
2. <u>3</u>,308
3. 23,<u>4</u>72
4. 12<u>1</u>,988
5. 5<u>9</u>7

6. 13,<u>2</u>76
7. <u>5</u>,896
8. 99,<u>9</u>65
9. 712,<u>0</u>29
10. <u>2</u>,968,115

Practice

Round each number to the nearest million.

11. 6,183,198
12. 7,827,292
13. 10,984,183
14. 2,456,789

15. 7,145,498
16. 5,924,300
17. 16,634,845
18. 828,999,834

Round each number to the underlined place.

19. <u>4</u>30
20. 1,<u>5</u>50
21. 23,<u>0</u>27
22. 929,<u>8</u>99

23. <u>1</u>21,200
24. 864,<u>9</u>32
25. 2,9<u>9</u>1,643
26. 473,<u>7</u>18,125

27. 84,<u>1</u>75
28. 2,3<u>9</u>6,733
29. 8,<u>3</u>54,687
30. 3<u>5</u>6,764,159

Problem Solving

31. **What If?** Last year a videodisc cost $174.99. To which place would you round this cost to cover a price increase when you buy a new one?

32. **Using Estimation** Look back at the cost of the trip to Washington for last year. About how much did the cost of the trip increase since last year?

Review and Remember

Using Mental Math Find each answer.

33. $16 - 7$
34. $23 + 10$
35. 9×6
36. $36 \div 9$
37. $18 + 13$

Money $ense

A Nice Piece of Change!

Paige rounded the prices of the items shown to estimate the total cost. Then she gave the clerk that estimated amount. How much change should she get back? Explain.

$2.60

$19.65

$1.99

For Extra Practice, see Set C, page 35.

Developing Skills for Problem Solving

First read for understanding and then focus on whether the data is exact or estimated.

READ FOR UNDERSTANDING

Did you know that there are 88 different constellations, or groupings of stars in the sky? Orion is a constellation made up of 24 stars. Of the 24 stars, three form his belt and eight form his shield. Scientists estimate that one star in Orion is about 320 light-years away from Earth.

1 How many constellations are there in the sky?

2 How many stars make up the constellation Orion?

3 About how far from Earth is one of Orion's stars?

THINK AND DISCUSS

 MATH FOCUS

Exact and Estimated Data Exact data represents an amount that can be counted. Estimated data represents an amount that has been rounded or that cannot be counted or measured.

▲ **Science Connection**
The constellation Orion

Reread the paragraph at the top of the page.

4 List the words that tell you a number is an estimate.

5 Is the distance from Earth to Orion exact? Explain.

6 Not including the stars that make up his belt and shield, how many stars make up Orion? Did you use exact or estimated data?

7 Give an example from everyday life of an amount that can be counted.

Show What You Learned

Answer each question. Give a reason for your choice.

The Big Dipper, often thought of as a constellation, is really part of a constellation called Ursa Major, or Big Bear. Ursa Major was first observed thousands of years ago by peoples of the ancient world.

Ursa Major consists of 20 major stars. Seven of these stars make up the Big Dipper. Dubhe, one star in Ursa Major, is about 75 light-years from Earth.

▲ The constellation Ursa Major, with the Big Dipper in green

1 Which of these phrases best describes the distance that Dubhe is from Earth?

a. exactly 75 light-years from Earth

b. about 75 light-years from Earth

c. much more than 75 light-years from Earth

2 Which of these numbers are estimates?

a. 20 stars and 7 stars

b. 75 light-years and thousands of years ago

c. both of the above

3 Which of the following best describes the difference in the number of major stars in Ursa Major and the Big Dipper?

a. exactly 13 stars

b. about 13 stars

c. less than 13 stars

4 Which of the following represents when peoples of the ancient world first observed Ursa Major?

a. 8,000 years ago

b. 6,000 years ago

c. cannot tell from information given

Ulugh Beg was an astronomer born in Persia in 1393. He used a curved object more than 130 feet long to study stars. In 1437 he produced a book that gave the positions of 992 stars. With data from his observatory, he computed the length of the year as 365 days 5 hours 49 minutes 15 seconds, an accurate value for the 1400s.

5 **Explain** List all the numbers used above that are estimates. Tell how you know.

6 **Explain** List all the numbers that are exact. Tell how you know.

▲ Philosophers observing the stars; from a fifteenth-century manuscript

✔ Checkpoint
Whole-Number Place Value

Match each number form with its name. (pages 4–5)

1. 325,000

2. 325 thousand

3. 300,000 + 20,000 + 5,000

4. three hundred twenty-five thousand

Word Bank

expanded form
standard form
word form
short word form

Write the value of each underlined digit. (pages 4–5)

5. 723,176

6. 25,355

7. 37,719,827

8. 5,255,366,177

9. 451,728,013

10. 63,521,423

11. 12,688,276

12. 162,773,261

Write each number in expanded form and word form. (pages 4–5)

13. 2,085

14. 198,073

15. 4,550,972,119

16. 977,348,002

17. 64,037

18. 216,709,856

19. 18,514,655

20. 781,463,112

Order each set of numbers from greatest to least. (pages 6–9)

21. 991   189   909

22. 13,242   11,221   13,144

23. 722   702   72

24. 109,817   109,871   109,877

Round each number to the underlined place. (pages 10–11)

25. 8,347

26. 4,096

27. 3,305

28. 19,632

29. 728,340,109

30. 87,843,366

31. 165,253

32. 8,237,613,526

33. 4,352,183

34. 118,239,430

35. 234,572,038

36. 234,662,929,348

Problem Solving

37. Write the least possible nine-digit number that can be created using the digits 1–9 exactly one time. Write the greatest possible nine-digit number that can be created using the digits 1–9 exactly one time.

38. Here are the diameters of four planets: Jupiter—142,800 km; Neptune—49,500 km; Saturn—120,400 km; Uranus—51,800 km. Order them from least to greatest.

39. Use this number to answer each question.

6832104845761819133948658321 90183

  a. If a code used only every third digit, what would the number be? every fourth digit?

  b. Compare the numbers you created in **a.** Which number is greater?

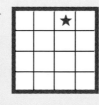

What do you think?

Rounding up when planning for the cost of purchases is often a good idea. Why?

40. Tina and her friends collect stamps. One collection has 11,082 stamps, another has 4,826 stamps, a third has 600 stamps, and a fourth has 7,132 stamps. Amahn has the largest collection. Ella's collection has fewer stamps than Tina's but more than Jeanne's collection. Order the collections from least to greatest and label the owner of each.

Journal Idea

Describe a situation in which the data would be an estimate. Then describe a situation in which the data would be exact. Explain your reasoning.

Critical Thinking Corner

Visual Thinking

Maze Puzzle

Stephen has made up puzzles with unusual star paths. To discover what some of these are, trace each grid and draw a path that starts and ends at the star. You can move vertically (↕) or horizontally (↔). Pass through each box once, without lifting your pencil. Do not pass through the shaded areas; they are uncharted.

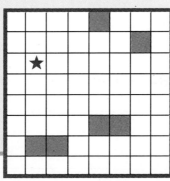

Create your own star-path puzzle. Make sure that it has a solution, and then trade with a classmate!

Taking a Part of One

What you know about numbers to billions will help you understand numbers between 0 and 1.

Learning About It

A decimal is a number with one or more digits to the right of the decimal point. Decimals represent wholes and parts of wholes.

What You Need

For each pair:
  grid paper
  ruler or straightedge

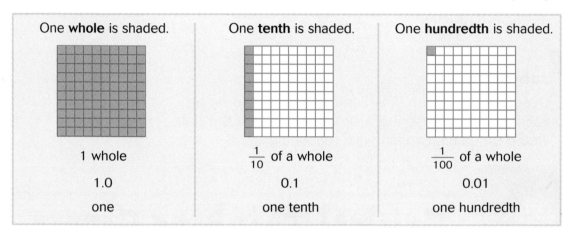

One **whole** is shaded.	One **tenth** is shaded.	One **hundredth** is shaded.
1 whole	$\frac{1}{10}$ of a whole	$\frac{1}{100}$ of a whole
1.0	0.1	0.01
one	one tenth	one hundredth

Work with a partner. Explore decimal values.

Step 1 Copy the chart below. Use the information above to complete your chart. Use grid paper for your models.

Sketch of Decimal Model	Number of Shaded Squares	Word Name of Decimal	Standard Form of Decimal Number
	100	one whole	1.0
	10	one tenth	
	1		0.01

Step 2 One tenth (0.1) and 10 hundredths (0.10) have the same value. Use grid paper to show why this is true.

Step 3 Look at the grid shown. The shaded part stands for one thousandth (0.001). It is $\frac{1}{1,000}$ of the whole grid.

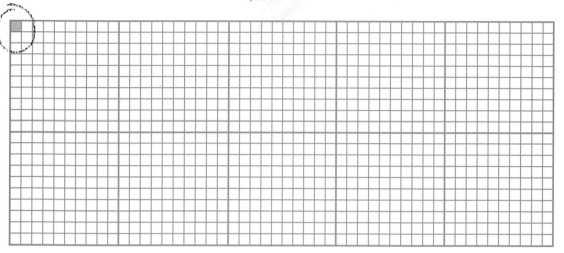

Step 4 Outline three 20 x 50 grids.

- Shade 3 tenths (0.3) on one grid.

- Shade 30 hundredths (0.30) on another.

- Shade 300 thousandths (0.300) on the third grid.

Think and Discuss Do 0.3, 0.30, and 0.300 have the same value? Explain your reasoning.

Try It Out

Use grid paper to show these numbers.

1. 0.25   **2.** 0.8   **3.** 0.78   **4.** 0.521   **5.** 0.896

Practice

What part is shaded?

6. 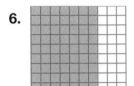   **7.**   **8.** 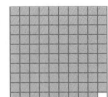   **9.**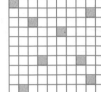

10.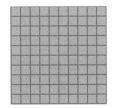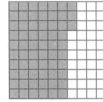

Use grid paper or make your own grid to show each number.

11. 0.2   **12.** 0.5   **13.** 0.75   **14.** 0.50   **15.** 0.80

16. 0.500   **17.** 0.555   **18.** 0.850   **19.** 1.2   **20.** 2.5

21. How many thousandths are in one tenth? one hundredth?

Problem Solving

22. Jeanne shaded grid paper to show 0.456. Lien shaded 0.500. How many more thousandths did Lien shade?

23. Juan has 20 quarters and 14 dimes. He wants to buy magnets for his friends. A magnet costs $1.25. What is the greatest number of magnets Juan can buy? Do you think your answer is reasonable? Explain.

Review and Remember

Using Algebra Find each n.

24. $25 \div 5 = n$ **25.** $7 \times n = 56$ **26.** $10 \times 0 = n$

27. $81 \div 9 = n$ **28.** $6 \times n = 48$ **29.** $72 \div n = 8$

◀ **Math Note**

You can use *n* or any other letter to show a missing number.

Critical Thinking Corner

Number Sense

Base-Ten Blocks Show Decimals

You can also use base-ten blocks to show decimals to thousandths.

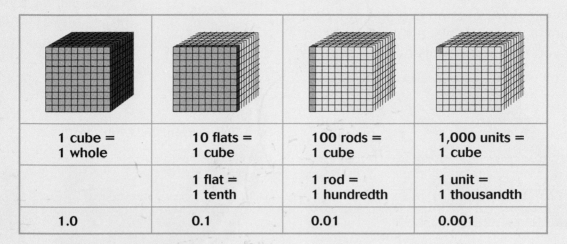

1 cube = 1 whole	10 flats = 1 cube	100 rods = 1 cube	1,000 units = 1 cube
	1 flat = 1 tenth	1 rod = 1 hundredth	1 unit = 1 thousandth
1.0	0.1	0.01	0.001

The blocks shown represent the decimal **1.235**.

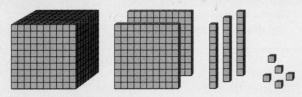

What decimal is represented by each set of blocks?

1.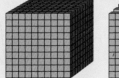

2.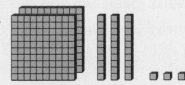

3.

4.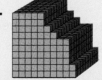

Tell or draw how you would model these numbers using base-ten blocks.

5. 0.01   **6.** 3   **7.** 0.5   **8.** 1.425   **9.** 3.006

For Extra Practice, see Set D, page 35.

Beside the Point

Knowing decimal place values will help you read and write decimals.

Learning About It

Quillayute, WA, gets an average of 2.654 m of rainfall a year. A place-value chart can help you understand this decimal number.

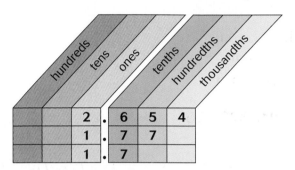

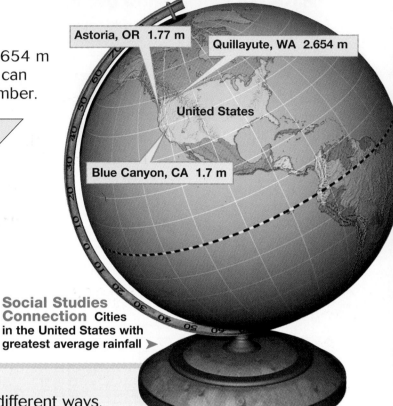

Astoria, OR 1.77 m

Quillayute, WA 2.654 m

United States

Blue Canyon, CA 1.7 m

The value of the 5 in 2.654 is 0.05. It is in the hundredths place.

Social Studies Connection Cities in the United States with greatest average rainfall ▶

THERE'S ALWAYS A WAY!

A number can be shown in different ways.

- **Standard form:** 2.654
- **Word form:** two and six hundred fifty-four thousandths
- **Short word form:** 2 and 654 thousandths

Another Example

Standard Form	1.77
Word Form	one and seventy-seven hundredths
Short Word Form	1 and 77 hundredths

Think and Discuss Annual rainfall in Blue Canyon, CA, is 1.7 m. Tell how to show this with grid paper.

▶ **Math Note**

When you read or write a decimal number, remember to use the word *and* to stand for the decimal point.

Try It Out

Write the word form for each decimal.

1. 2.8   **2.** 0.19   **3.** 0.089   **4.** 4.465   **5.** 2,350.75

Practice

Write each number in standard form.

6. two tenths

7. seventeen hundredths

8. nine hundred ninety thousandths

9. nine and eight thousandths

Write the value of each underlined digit.

10. 5.1<u>3</u>1

11. 4.<u>9</u>90

12. 4.9<u>9</u>

13. 6.47<u>8</u>

14. 9.10<u>2</u>

15. 3.<u>5</u>6

16. <u>2</u>.175

17. 0.0<u>9</u>2

Make a place-value chart. Show each decimal on the chart. Then write the word name for each decimal.

18. 0.66

19. 0.21

20. 33.2

21. 51.7

22. 0.891

23. 0.225

24. 322.406

25. 5,012.739

Problem Solving

26. Explain How are 0.66 and 0.066 different? How are they alike?

27. What If? Suppose you removed the zero in 0.45. Would the value change? What if you removed the zero in 1.708 or 1.780? Use models or drawings to explain your answers.

28. Buenaventura, Colombia, is the wettest inhabited place in the world. If it rained one meter more than the recorded annual rainfall of 6.743 m, would the amount of rainfall be 7.743 m? Tell how you decided.

Science Connection Rain forests in Colombia have recorded annual rainfall as great as 6.743 meters each year. ➤

Review and Remember

Using Algebra Compare. Use >, <, or = for each ●.

29. 9 × 7 ● 10 × 8

30. 4 × 6 ● 3 × 6

31. 6 × 9 ● 8 × 7

32. 5 × 5 ● 6 × 6

33. 10 × 8 ● 9 × 8

34. 7 × 10 ● 8 × 8

Making the Point

Very small numbers are usually expressed as decimals.

Bishop, CA
0.142 m

Las Vegas, NV
0.106 m

Yuma, AZ
0.067 m

Bakersfield, CA
0.145 m

Learning About It

The data in the illustration show some of the driest places in the United States. Did Bakersfield or Bishop, CA, have less rain? To find out, compare the amount of rainfall in the two cities.

Step 1 Line up the decimal points.	**Step 2** Start at the left. Compare digits in the same places. The tenths digits and the hundredths digits are the same.	**Step 3** Compare the next digits to the right.
0.145 0.142	0.145 0.142	0.145 0.142 2 < 5, so 0.142 < 0.145

Since 0.142 < 0.145, Bishop gets less rain than Bakersfield.

Connecting Ideas

You just compared decimals. You also need to compare decimals when you put them in order.

Follow these steps to order Bishop, CA; Las Vegas, NV; and Yuma, AZ, from driest to wettest.

Step 1 Start at the left. Compare digits in the same place.	Step 2 When digits in a place are the same, compare digits to the right.	Step 3 Order the numbers.
0.1**4**2 0.1**0**6 0.0**6**7	0.1**4**2 0.1**0**6	Yuma, AZ 0.067 m Las Vegas, NV 0.106 m Bishop, CA 0.142 m
0.067 < 0.106 or 0.142, so Yuma is the driest.	0 < 4, so 0.106 < 0.142, so Las Vegas is drier than Bishop.	

More Examples

A. Order 3.118, 5.62, and 4.1 from least to greatest.

3.118 < 4.1, since 3 < 4
4.1 < 5.62, since 4 < 5

3.118 < 4.1 < 5.62

B. Order 2.785, 2.914, and 2.641 from greatest to least.

2.914 > 2.785, since 9 > 7
2.785 > 2.641, since 7 > 6

2.914 > 2.785 > 2.641

Think and Discuss Explain how comparing and ordering whole numbers is like comparing and ordering decimals.

Try It Out

Compare. Write >, <, or = for each ⬤.

1. 4.26 ⬤ 4.88   **2.** 0.08 ⬤ 0.10

3. 0.5 ⬤ 0.05   **4.** 0.847 ⬤ 0.849

5. 0.40 ⬤ 0.400 **6.** 0.250 ⬤ 0.25

Order from least to greatest.

7. 0.2   0.510   0.07

8. 0.09   67.3   0.15

9. 0.9   0.6   0.4   0.72

10. 0.24   0.6   0.2   0.725

Science Connection Al Roker is a weathercaster who uses computer graphics to give weather forecasts on TV.

23

Practice

Compare. Write >, <, or = for each ●.

11. 0.331 ● 0.332　　　　**12.** 6.200 ● 6.2　　　　**13.** 1.989 ● 1.981

14. 0.16 ● 0.4　　　　　**15.** 0.30 ● 0.3　　　　　**16.** 8.5 ● 6.9

17. 0.331 ● 0.17　　　　**18.** 0.950 ● 0.95　　　　**19.** 44.41 ● 44.07

20. 5.600 ● 5.6　　　　　**21.** 0.011 ● 0.11　　　　**22.** 2.267 ● 2.261

Order from least to greatest.

23. 0.15　0.008　0.9　　　　　　**24.** 4.42　0.11　5.25

25. 1.00　0.35　0.50　　　　　　**26.** 0.5　0.98　0.009

27. 1,543　1.543　15.43　　　　　**28.** 0.24　0.6　0.725

29. 1.87　0.613　1.22　3.0　　　　**30.** 0.7　0.12　0.86　0.012

31. 0.8　0.002　0.49　0.881　　　**32.** 2.2　5.091　0.1　0.01

33. Explain Why is 20.0 greater than 0.2?

Problem Solving

Use the table to answer
Problems 34–36.

Rainfall in St. Louis, Missouri (1996)	
Month	Rainfall
May	13.7 cm
June	7.9 cm
July	11.9 cm
August	6.5 cm
September	9.6 cm

34. Which month had the most rainfall? the least?

35. Which month had 11.9 cm of rainfall?

36. What are the three wettest months?

37. Aswan, Egypt, gets 0.5 mm of rainfall each year. Minya, Egypt, gets 5.1 mm of rain. What is the difference in rainfall in the two cities?

▲ **Kid Connection** Children at the Herzog Elementary School in St. Louis, MO, collect information about rainfall for station KSDK.

INTERNET ACTIVITY
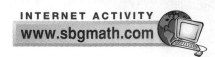
www.sbgmath.com

Use the graph below to answer Problems 38 and 39.

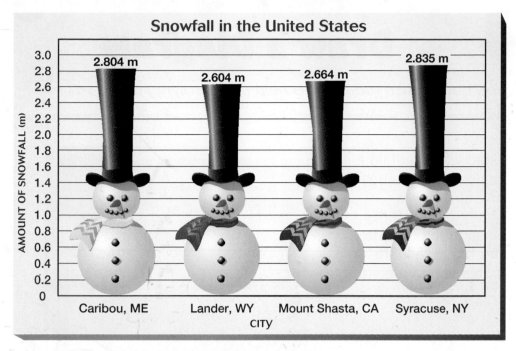

Snowfall in the United States

38. Order the locations shown in the graph from the greatest amount of snowfall to the least amount of snowfall.

39. **What If?** Suppose a fifth location having 2.634 m of snowfall were added to the group. Where would it fall on the ordered list?

40. **Language Arts Connection** A call number is part of the Dewey Decimal System, which is a way of arranging nonfiction books according to subject areas. Write the call numbers of the books below in order from least to greatest.

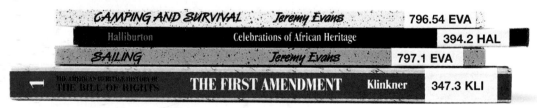

Review and Remember

Write the place-value name and the value of each underlined digit.

41. 1,2<u>3</u>4
42. 3,48<u>7</u>
43. <u>6</u>79
44. <u>9</u>,961

45. 2<u>5</u>
46. <u>2</u>3,814
47. <u>7</u>93
48. <u>3</u>,216

49. 6,<u>6</u>62
50. <u>5</u>6
51. 1,3<u>5</u>2
52. <u>1</u>0,376

For Extra Practice, see Set F, page 36.

Problem Solving
Draw a Diagram

You can draw a diagram to help make solving problems easier.

Claudia and Pablo want to build a simple telescope, using two tubes. Five inches of the small tube extend out of the big tube. Three inches of the small tube fit inside the big tube. The big tube is the same length as the small tube. How long is each tube?

 ## UNDERSTAND

What do you need to find?

You need to find the length of each tube.

 ## PLAN

How can you solve the problem?

You can **draw a diagram** and label the lengths you know. Then you can use the diagram to help you find the length of each tube.

 ## SOLVE

The diagram shows that one tube extends 5 in. out of the other tube. Add 3 in. to 5 in. to find the length of the small tube, which is 8 in. Since the big tube is the same length as the small tube, it is also 8 in. long.

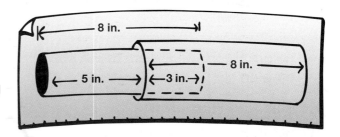

 ## LOOK BACK

Use the diagram. Explain how you can find the total length of the telescope.

Using the Strategy

Use the diagram on page 26 to solve Problems 1–2.
Draw diagrams to solve Problems 3–6.

1 **What If?** Suppose 4 inches of the small tube were pushed inside the big tube. What would the total length of the telescope be?

2 **What If?** Suppose the small tube were pushed completely inside the big tube. How long would the telescope be?

3 A model uses a long and a short strip of cardboard. The long strip is 3 times the short strip. The short strip is 12 in. long. How long are the two strips when placed end to end?

4 Terry has pictures of constellations 2 in. wide and 4 in. long. She wants to put them in a photo album 8 in. wide by 12 in. long. How many pictures can she fit on a page?

5 Carole lives 12 blocks north of Brian. Sue lives 4 blocks south of Brian. Lien lives north of Sue halfway between Carole and Sue. How far does Lien live from Brian?

6 A rock climber slides down 1 foot for every 15 feet she climbs. How many feet will she actually have moved by the time she reaches a height of 42 feet?

Mixed Strategy Review

Try these or other strategies to solve each problem.
Tell which strategy you used.

Problem Solving Strategies

- *Work Backwards*
- *Find a Pattern*
- *Make a Table*
- *Guess and Check*

Use the sign at the right to solve Problems 7–8.

7 A group arrives at the museum on Tuesday. They have time to see a 45-minute movie and then spend an hour and a half looking at exhibits before the museum closes. At what time do they begin watching the movie?

8 The museum is empty at 8:00 A.M. on Saturday. Three people enter in the first hour, 4 enter in the second hour, 6 enter in the third hour, and 9 enter in the fourth hour. If the pattern continues, how many people will enter in the fifth hour? the last hour?

AIR AND SPACE MUSEUM

Open Weekdays
8:00 A.M. to 6:00 P.M.

Open Weekends
10:00 A.M. to 5:00 P.M.

Closed Wednesdays

Rounding Up and Down

You can round decimals the same way you round whole numbers. Just keep track of the decimal point!

Learning About It

For more than 40 years, men and women have been using rockets to explore space. America's space-shuttle launch system is about 56.08 meters tall. About how many meters tall to the nearest tenth is the launch system?

Round 56.08 to the nearest tenth to find out.

THERE'S ALWAYS A WAY!

• **One way** is to use a number line.

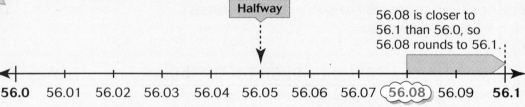

Halfway

56.08 is closer to 56.1 than 56.0, so 56.08 rounds to 56.1.

| 56.0 | 56.01 | 56.02 | 56.03 | 56.04 | 56.05 | 56.06 | 56.07 | 56.08 | 56.09 | 56.1 |

• **Another way** is to use rounding rules.

Step 1 Find the rounding place.	**Step 2** Look at the digit one place to the right. If the digit is less than 5, the digit in the rounding place stays the same. If the digit is 5 or greater, the digit in the rounding place increases by 1.
56.08	56.08
	8 > 5, so 56.08 rounds to 56.1.

More Examples

A. To the nearest dollar, $6.65 rounds to $7.

B. To the nearest hundredth, 2.964 rounds to 2.96.

Think and Discuss When rounding decimals, you do not have to change digits to the right of the rounding place to 0. Use what you know about place value to tell why.

Try It Out

Round each number to the underlined place.

1. 0.9<u>8</u>7
2. 0.<u>9</u>76
3. 0.3<u>7</u>2

4. 0.6<u>7</u>4
5. 1.<u>9</u>45
6. <u>8</u>.166

7. <u>4</u>.592
8. 7.5<u>5</u>3
9. 10.<u>9</u>64

For Exercises 10–11, use a number line to illustrate your work.

10. Round 0.16 to the nearest tenth.

11. Round 0.64 to the nearest tenth.

▲ **Science Connection** Shannon Lucid, an American astronaut, is shown checking a wheat-growing experiment on Russia's space station *Mir*. She was in space for a record 188 days.

Practice

Round each number to the underlined place.

12. 0.<u>8</u>3
13. 33.<u>2</u>6
14. 61.<u>0</u>42
15. 71.<u>6</u>39

16. 0.<u>4</u>89
17. 0.<u>2</u>45
18. 424.<u>6</u>2
19. 726.<u>0</u>629

20. 0.6<u>2</u>5
21. 198.<u>9</u>9
22. <u>0</u>.555
23. 1,2<u>2</u>9.04

24. <u>2</u>.725
25. 0.6<u>9</u>2
26. 157.<u>0</u>33
27. 5<u>7</u>6.79

Problem Solving

28. Analyze You rounded a number to the nearest hundredth and got 3.50. Name a possible starting number.

29. Using Mental Math Mark spent $16.00 on model rocket supplies and $2.00 for a gift for his sister. The tax was $1.08. He gave the store clerk $20.00. What was his change?

30. Journal Idea Explain some ways that people use rounding in their everyday lives.

Review and Remember

Compare. Write >, <, or = for each ⬤.

31. 1,235 ⬤ 299
32. 312 ⬤ 1,001
33. 9,911 ⬤ 8,999

34. 612 ⬤ 612
35. 99 ⬤ 101
36. 3,019 ⬤ 3,109

37. 819 ⬤ 891
38. 210 ⬤ 21
39. 1,617 ⬤ 1,716

For Extra Practice, see Set G, page 36.

Problem Solving

★★★★★ **Preparing for Tests**

Practice What You Learned

Choose the correct letter for each answer.

1 One toy car is 0.03 m long. Another is 0.13 m long. A third is 0.25 m long. Which number sentence can be used to show the combined length of the two shortest cars?

A. 0.13 − 0.30 = ■
B. 0.13 + 0.25 = ■
C. 0.03 + 0.25 = ■
D. 0.03 + 0.13 = ■

Tip

When reading a problem, decide what information is necessary to solve the problem.

2 On Monday the number of cards at a gift shop was 134 cards. Each day during the week 5 cards were sold. How many cards were left at the end of the fourth day?

A. 20
B. 129
C. 114
D. 109
E. Not Here

Tip

Use one of these strategies to solve this problem.
• *Find a Pattern*
• *Act It Out*
• *Make a Table*

3 Mark lives 22 miles from Sally along a straight road. Juan lives between them, and his house is 14 miles from Mark. How far does Sally live from Juan?

A. 8 mi
B. 12 mi
C. 36 mi
D. 44 mi
E. Not Here

Tip

Using the *Draw a Diagram* strategy can help you solve this problem.

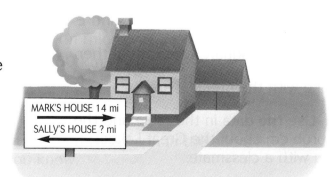

MARK'S HOUSE 14 mi
SALLY'S HOUSE ? mi

4 Sid is taller than Betty, but shorter than Walt. Pete is taller than Sid. Which of the following is a reasonable conclusion?

A. Sid is the tallest.
B. Walt is the tallest.
C. Walt is taller than Pete.
D. Betty is the shortest.

5 Jack had a board that was 8 feet long. He cut seven 10-inch pieces from the board. Which is the best estimate of the length of the board that was left?

A. Less than 1 ft
B. About 2 ft
C. About 3 ft
D. More than 3 ft
E. Not Here

6 Gil and 2 classmates divide 18 pens equally among them. How can you find the number of pens each person gets?

A. Subtract 2 from 18.
B. Multiply 18 by 2.
C. Multiply 18 by 3.
D. Divide 18 by 2.
E. Not Here

7 For a science project, the fifth grade collected about 40 pictures of spiders, 28 pictures of bees, 12 pictures of wasps, and about 60 pictures of butterflies. Which best describes the total number of pictures?

A. Exactly 140
B. About 100
C. About 150
D. More than 200

8 Lucy and Paul drove in separate cars to a campground. Lucy drove 74.1 mi in the morning and 31.5 mi in the afternoon. Paul drove 35.2 mi in the morning and twice that far in the afternoon. Which number sentence shows how far Paul drove in the afternoon?

A. $74.1 - 35.2 =$ ■
B. $35.1 + 35.2 =$ ■
C. $35.2 + (2 \times 35.2) =$ ■
D. $2 \times 35.2 =$ ■
E. Not Here

9 The weights of four cartons in pounds are 32, 41, 18, and 29. Which is the best estimate for the total weight of the cartons?

A. 100 pounds
B. 120 pounds
C. 140 pounds
D. 150 pounds

10 This graph shows the number of teenage volunteers at a hospital.

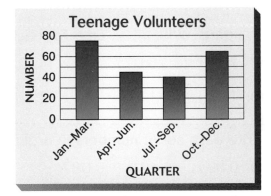

To the nearest ten, which is the number of volunteers from January through June?

A. 90
B. 120
C. 150
D. 200

✓ Checkpoint

Decimal Place Value

Vocabulary

Write the missing words that complete each sentence.

1. A __?__ chart can help you understand decimal numbers.

2. A decimal written as *one tenth* is said to be written in __?__ .

3. If the number is written as 0.1, it is said to be written in __?__ .

Concepts and Skills

Write the decimal that names the shaded part. (pages 16–19)

4.

5.

6.

Write the standard form or word form for each. (pages 20–21)

7. 501.023

8. six and thirty-two hundredths

9. 414.406

10. 0.87

11. 8 and 73 thousandths

12. fifty-two and seven tenths

Compare. Write >, <, or = for each ⬤. (pages 22–25)

13. 26.77 ⬤ 26.077

14. 0.660 ⬤ 0.66

15. 0.2 ⬤ 0.082

16. 11.010 ⬤ 11.01

17. 222.22 ⬤ 22.222

18. 987.65 ⬤ 9,876.5

Write each set of numbers in order from greatest to least. (pages 22–25)

19. 0.837   0.473   0.087

20. 56.93   573.9   834.93

21. 28.348   73.382   58.394

22. 6,493.0   6,490.01   6,493.32

Round each number to the underlined place. (pages 28–29)

23. 0.8<u>2</u>7

24. 17.<u>3</u>44

25. 1,030.5<u>4</u>6

26. 582.<u>7</u>31

27. <u>9</u>.801

28. 13.09<u>1</u>

29. $6<u>5</u>.14

30. $4<u>4</u>9.99

31. $2,04<u>9</u>.76

Problem Solving

Use the price list for Problems 32 and 33.

32. Order the items from most expensive to least expensive.

33. Round each price to the nearest dollar.

Price List

Galaxy baseball hat	$16.95
Space pen	$ 5.95
Constellation T-shirt	$21.45
How to Use a Telescope video	$21.75

Use the number 4,500,986,422.753 to answer Problems 34–35.

34. What digit is in the hundredths place?

35. What is the result if the number is rounded to the ten-thousands place? to the tenths place?

What do you think?

Why is using a number line helpful when rounding a number?

Journal Idea

Round 6.68 and 6.73 to the nearest tenth. What do you notice? Give the greatest number (to hundredths) and the least number (to hundredths) that round to 6.7. Explain.

You Decide

Activity

And the Winner Is...

The table lists four of last year's leading NBA players. Select a player for your personal sports award. Explain what the award is for and why you chose that player.

Player	Field Goals	Free Throws	Total Points
Barkley, C.	554	379	1,561
Ewing, P.	730	420	1,886
Richmond, S.	668	375	1,867
Robinson, G.	636	397	1,755

 You might wish to include this work in your portfolio.

Extra Practice

Set A (pages 4–5)

Write each number in standard form and expanded form.

1. seven thousand, eight hundred ninety-two

2. four hundred thousand, seven hundred two

3. two million, three hundred sixty-six thousand

4. one hundred twenty-seven billion, twenty-nine million

Write the word form for each number. Then write the value of each underlined digit.

5. 3<u>4</u>8

6. 2<u>6</u>,918

7. <u>1</u>9,621

8. 98,72<u>5</u>

9. 81,<u>3</u>92

10. 34,<u>6</u>12

11. <u>6</u>,381,410

12. <u>6</u>12,833,410

13. Greenland is the largest island in the world. Its area is about eight hundred forty thousand square miles. Write the area in standard form.

14. A newspaper reported the attendance at the opening day of a new museum as 102,35. What is wrong with this number?

Set B (pages 6–9)

Compare. Write >, <, or = for each ●.

1. 395 ● 892

2. 632 ● 635

3. 981 ● 918

4. 4,698 ● 4,695

5. 3,205 ● 3,250

6. 36,895 ● 36,995

For Exercises 7–12, order the numbers from least to greatest.

7. 580   750   612

8. 48,000   47,681   49,361

9. 30,800   30,080   30,008

10. 29,751   27,951   29,571

11. 88,252   89,150   98,010

12. 13,015   10,038   9,070

13. The distances from the sun to four planets are 778,300,000 km, 4,496,600,000 km, 5,900,100,000 km, and 149,600,000 km. Order the distances from least to greatest. Use the clues at the right to match the planet with its distance from the sun.

- Pluto is farthest from the sun.
- Earth is closer to the sun than Neptune.
- Jupiter is between Earth and Neptune.

Extra Practice

Set C (pages 10–11)

Round each number to the underlined place.

1. 3<u>5</u>4   **2.** <u>6</u>89   **3.** 8,1<u>2</u>6   **4.** 5,<u>4</u>72

5. 3,8<u>7</u>1   **6.** 28,<u>9</u>42   **7.** 7<u>6</u>1,385   **8.** 6,<u>8</u>75,941

9. 32,3<u>9</u>6   **10.** <u>3</u>02,419   **11.** <u>5</u>6,010,145   **12.** 123,6<u>5</u>2

13. Explain Write a rule to explain how to round a number.

14. Using Estimation Karen reads about 22 pages an hour of her book on planets. About how many pages might she read in three hours?

Set D (pages 16–19)

What part is shaded?

1. 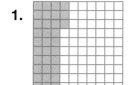   **2.** 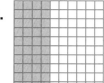   **3.** 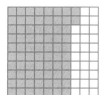   **4.**

Set E (pages 20–21)

Name the place of each underlined digit.

1. 8.9<u>1</u>   **2.** 2.<u>0</u>04   **3.** <u>5</u>6.179   **4.** 69.73<u>6</u>   **5.** 4,43<u>0</u>.27

6. 9.<u>3</u>81   **7.** 24.0<u>1</u>   **8.** <u>1</u>41.501   **9.** <u>2</u>5,763   **10.** <u>5</u>17,432

11. 2<u>2</u>,584,901   **12.** <u>4</u>56,122,981   **13.** 7<u>0</u>,356,184,350

Write a number with the digit 6 for each place value listed. Use the digit 6 only one time in each number.

14. tens   **15.** thousands   **16.** tenths   **17.** hundredths

18. A television weather reporter announced that the amount of rainfall for the week was two tenths of an inch. Write the number in standard form, as it would appear on the screen.

Performance Assessment

Show What You Know About Place Value

1 Study these whole numbers. Then answer each question.

13,184   5,020
74,056

a. Write the least number in as many ways as you can.

b. Round the greatest number to the nearest ten thousand.

Self-Check Are you sure that you identified the least and greatest numbers?

2 Study these decimal numbers. Then answer each question.

4.098   4.099
4.90

a. Write the least number in as many ways as you can.

b. Round the greatest number to the nearest whole number.

3 Use the tables below to answer each question.

Research Grants Awarded to Scientific Organizations
$34,000
$14 million
two hundred thousand dollars
$6,945
$17,056
nine hundred twenty dollars

Population Growth Rates
one and forty-four hundredths
2.02
0.78
sixty-three hundredths
1.67
two and nineteen hundredths

a. Write the whole numbers in standard form.

c. Write the decimals in standard form.

b. Order the whole numbers from greatest to least.

d. Order the decimals from least to greatest.

Self-Check Did you make sure you ordered the whole numbers and decimals in the order indicated?

For Your Portfolio

You might wish to include this work in your portfolio.

9. If $n \div 8 =$

   A. 17
   B. 64
   C. 72
   D. 74

10. Which dec
point *A* on

  4.7   4.8

   A. 4.81
   B. 4.9
   C. 5.01
   D. 5.1

11. Houses on
State Stree
even numb
is number
number of

   A. 102
   B. 104
   C. 105
   D. 106

12. Which poin
the ordere

   A. *H*
   B. *I*
   C. *J*
   D. *K*

Extension

Writing a Check

A person writes a check to tell a bank to send money from his or her account to another person or business. One person's check may look different from another person's check, but all checks have the same basic information.

On a check, the amount is written two ways—in numbers and in words. This helps a banker double-check the amount. Any two-word amount between 21 and 99 is written with a hyphen.

   twenty-one   forty-seven   ninety-nine

The decimal part of the amount—the cents—is written as a fraction with 100 as the denominator. If there are no cents, the amount can be written as $\frac{00}{100}$, $\frac{no}{100}$, or $\frac{xx}{100}$.

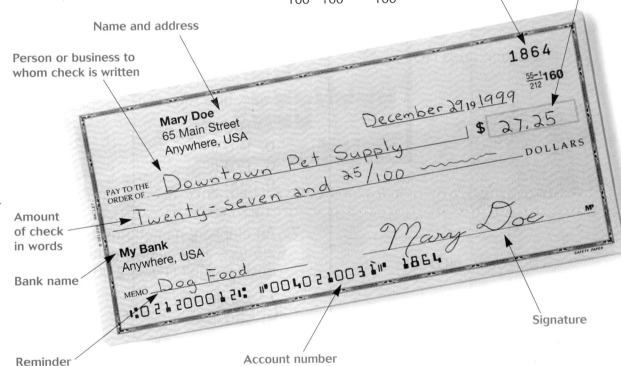

Try writing these amounts in words as you would on a check. Make up a name for the person or business to whom each check is written.

1. $53.75	**2.** $19.95	**3.** $6.34	**4.** $75.60
5. $166.50	**6.** $214.83	**7.** $925.62	**8.** $439.15
9. $845.78	**10.** $2,881.27	**11.** $1,762.71	**12.** $12,500.00

Choose the cor

Numb

1. Casey had
Friday eve
the bushes
bushes dic

A. $\frac{2}{5}$

B. $\frac{4}{10}$

C. $\frac{1}{2}$

D. $\frac{3}{5}$

2. Which frac
equal $\frac{1}{2}$?

A. $\frac{2}{5}$

B. $\frac{3}{6}$

C. $\frac{4}{8}$

D. $\frac{5}{10}$

3. Which num
than 4,643

A. 4,543
B. 4,567
C. 4,639
D. 4,645

4. Which of th
when round
and 200 wl
nearest hur

A. 239
B. 244

Chapter 2
Adding and Subtracting Whole Numbers and Decimals

Chapter Theme: FUN AND FITNESS

Real-World Math

·····················**Real Facts**·····················

Officials and coaches at the Olympics use math to compare the scores of athletes. The table below shows the points earned by the top four platform divers at the 1996 Olympics.

1996 Olympic Women's Platform Diving				
Place	First	Second	Third	Fourth
Athlete	F. Mingxia	A. Walter	M. E. Clark	B. Ruehl
Points	521.58	479.22	472.95	455.19

• Estimate the difference between the numbers of points scored by A. Walter and M. E. Clark.

• If B. Ruehl had scored 60 more points, would she have placed ahead of any of the other athletes? If so, which ones?

·····················**Real People**·····················

Meet Becky Ruehl, one of the best divers in the world. At the 1996 Olympic Games in Atlanta, Georgia, Becky finished fourth in the women's 10-meter platform final. Quite a triumph for a teenager!

The swimmers in the photo at the right hope that one day they will also compete in the Olympics.

Think an
make it e

Try It O

Find each

1. 36 +

3. $n + 0$

Practic

Find each

5. (48 +

7. 238 +

Using Me

9. 0 + 35

12. 21 +

Problem

15. **Using**
and Ar
a pool.
20 tile
many t
model'
you ad
your ar

16. Mark p
ribbon
How m
make?
be? Ex
used to

Review an

Write the p

17. 2<u>5</u>4

22. 27,<u>1</u>84

41

Using Algebra

Swish!

Mental math shortcuts can help you add and subtract mentally.

Learning About It

Who will win the most-valuable-player award in the tournament? Does Carolyn, Denise, or Sandy have the highest point total? Here is an easy way to find Denise's total.

$$12 + 17 + 13 = 12 + (17 + 13)$$
$$= 12 + 30$$
$$= 42$$

Compatible numbers are numbers that are easy to compute mentally. Add these numbers first.

Denise scored a total of 42 points.

You can also do mental math by using **compensation**. Change one number to make it easier to add or subtract. Adjust another number.

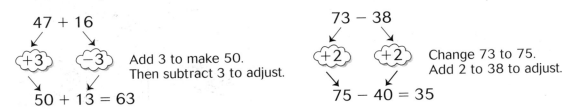

$47 + 16$

$(+3)$ (-3) Add 3 to make 50. Then subtract 3 to adjust.

$50 + 13 = 63$

$73 - 38$

$(+2)$ $(+2)$ Change 73 to 75. Add 2 to 38 to adjust.

$75 - 40 = 35$

Think and Discuss Which mental math strategy would you use to determine the most valuable player?

My scores for 3 games:
$16 + 11 + 14 = ?$

My scores for 3 games:
$12 + 17 + 13 = ?$

My scores for 3 games:
$7 + 15 + 13 = ?$

CAROLYN

DENISE

SANDY

Learni

Matt, Sha
After me
that the t
sections
different

Associati

The way in
does not
Do the worl

Commuta

The order
does not

Identity

When 0 is
the sum is

More Exa

A. $(n + 5)$

Try It Out

Use mental math to find each sum or difference.

1. $9 + 25 + 1$ **2.** $7 + 13 + 19$ **3.** $80 + 36 + 20$ **4.** $150 - 50$

5. $264 + 96$ **6.** $93 - 17$ **7.** $48 + 97$ **8.** $48 + 13 + 52$

Practice

Use mental math to find each sum or difference.

9. $12 + 29$ **10.** $34 - 19$ **11.** $9 + 17 + 11$

12. $99 + 21$ **13.** $35 + 67$ **14.** $26 + 24$

15. $43 + 98$ **16.** $92 + 18 + 8$ **17.** $40 + 52 + 60$

18. $23 + 78 + 77$ **19.** $57 - 32$ **20.** $998 + 302$

21. $350 + 500 + 150$ **22.** $33 + 55 + 15 + 12$ **23.** $2 + 14 + 56 + 44$

Problem Solving

24. What If? Suppose in four games you score 6 points, 13 points, 14 points, and 17 points. How many points would you score in all?

25. Robert scored eight points in each of four games. Then he scored 10 points in the fifth game. How many points has he scored so far this season?

26. Explain Samantha was saving her baby-sitting money to treat her family to tickets for a basketball tournament. She earned $12 one month, $15 another month, and $18 a third month. The tickets cost $60. How much more does she need? Explain how you got your answer.

▲ **Health and Fitness Connection**
Playing team sports is a good way to stay physically fit. Keeping track of points scored is a good way to stay mentally fit.

INTERNET ACTIVITY
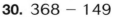
www.sbgmath.com

Review and Remember

Find each answer.

27. 9×9 **28.** $56 \div 7$ **29.** 7×9 **30.** $368 - 149$ **31.** $1.2 + 2.08$

32. $72 \div 9$ **33.** $25 \div 5$ **34.** 8×8 **35.** $499 + 8.76$ **36.** $911 - 78.2$

For Extra Practice, see Set B, page 78.

They're All Related

Using Algebra

*Addition and subtraction are related because
one operation "undoes" the other.*

Learning About It

An input/output relationship follows a rule.
For each input, there is only one output.

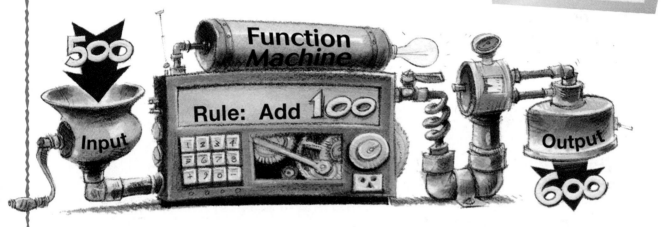

If you know the input for the machine above, you can
add to find the output. If you know the output, you can
subtract to find the input. Subtraction "undoes" addition,
so addition and subtraction are **inverse operations**.

An input/output table can also be used to show the
same relationship.

The input is 736.
What is the output?

If the input is 736,
the output is 836.

Rule: Add 100

Input	Output
500	600
736	836
x	850

Look at the table above. How would you find *x*? You can
subtract to find *x* because addition and subtraction are
inverse operations.

$$850 - 100 = x$$
Since $850 - 100 = 750$, $x = 750$

Think and Discuss Create a rule so that the output is
the same as the input.

Try It Out

Find each input or output.

Rule: Subtract 16

	Input	Output
1.	48	■
2.	103	■
3.	94	■

Rule: Add 51

	Input	Output
4.	■	115
5.	9	■
6.	25	■

Rule: Subtract 28

	Input	Output
7.	253	■
8.	■	56
9.	■	74

Practice

Follow or find the rule to complete each input/output table.

Rule: Add 22

	Input	Output
10.	33	■
11.	86	■
12.	15	■

Rule: Subtract 11

	Input	Output
13.	91	■
14.	■	67
15.	119	■

16. Rule: ___?___

	Input	Output
	24	50
17.	■	28
18.	309	■

Choose a Method Use mental math or paper and pencil to find each x. Tell which method you used.

19. $x + 5 = 10$ **20.** $x + 76 = 100$ **21.** $13 - x = 7$ **22.** $x - 83 = 423$

23. $80 - 40 = x$ **24.** $88 + x = 108$ **25.** $232 - x = 30$ **26.** $100 - x = 50$

Problem Solving

27. What is the output for this machine?

$$(50) + \boxed{400} - \boxed{100} = \triangle$$

28. You have four inputs: 600; 900; 1,000; 30,000. The rule is *Add 22*. What are the four outputs?

29. Create Your Own Design your own function machine. Use addition, subtraction, or both for your rule. Trade machines with a classmate and solve.

Review and Remember

Write the place-value name of each underlined digit.

30. 1.6<u>2</u>3   **31.** 10.27<u>6</u>   **32.** <u>2</u>1,268   **33.** 1,8<u>4</u>6   **34.** 7.<u>6</u>35

35. 46<u>5</u>.1   **36.** <u>2</u>5,025   **37.** 120.3<u>6</u>2   **38.** 3,<u>6</u>72   **39.** 0.67<u>6</u>

For Extra Practice, see Set C, page 78.

Developing Skills for Problem Solving

First read for understanding and then focus on estimated and exact answers.

READ FOR UNDERSTANDING

Mandy, Zach, Linda, and Keith are starting out on a 15-mile hiking trail at 8:00 A.M. Mandy and Linda must be back at 1:00 P.M. to catch a bus to a movie. Zach and Keith need to be back for lunch between 11:30 A.M. and 1:30 P.M.

1 How long is the trail?

2 What time must Mandy and Linda be back?

THINK AND DISCUSS

Is an Estimate Enough? Whether or not an estimate or an exact answer is needed depends on the situation.

Reread the paragraph at the top of the page.

3 Do Zach and Keith have to know exactly how much time they have to hike, or can they use an estimate?

4 Since Mandy and Linda have to be back at an exact time, how many miles per hour do they need to hike?

5 Give two examples from everyday life—one when an estimate is enough and one when an exact answer is needed.

Show What You Learned

Answer each question. Give a reason for your choice.

Red Trail to Picnic Area

5.3 miles long
difficult trail

Blue Trail to Picnic Area

7.5 miles long
easy trail

Two groups of girls are hiking to a picnic site. The younger girls take the Blue Trail. They hike at an average speed of 3 miles per hour. The older girls take the Red Trail and hike at an average speed of 1 mile per hour.

1 Which of the following is needed to calculate about how long it will take to hike the Red Trail?

  a. an estimate of the trail length and the exact hiking speed

  b. an estimate of the hiking speed and the exact trail length

  c. the exact trail length and the exact hiking speed

  d. an estimate of the trail length and an estimate of the hiking speed

2 Which of the following describes how long it will take the girls to hike the Red Trail?

  a. $5 + 1 = 6$

  b. $5.3 \div 1 = 5.3$

  c. $7.5 \div 3 = 2.5$

  d. $5.3 \times 3 = 15.9$

3 Which best describes how long it will take to hike the Blue Trail?

  a. Multiply the length of the trail by the hiking speed.

  b. Divide the length of the trail by the hiking speed.

  c. Add the length of the Red Trail and the Blue Trail.

4 Which number sentence best describes how long it will take to hike the Blue Trail?

  a. $3 + 7.1 = 10.1$

  b. $7.5 \div 3 = 2.5$

  c. $5.3 + 7.1 = 12.4$

5 **You Decide** If the older girls start hiking on the Red Trail at 6 A.M., about what time will they arrive at the picnic area? Decide if an estimate or an exact answer is necessary. Explain how you found your answer.

6 The groups decide to meet at the picnic area for lunch at 12:00 noon. What information do you need to find the time at which each group should start hiking so that they will reach the picnic area at exactly the same time? Explain.

Packing Up and Heading Out

Sometimes you can solve a problem by estimating.

Learning About It

Felicia and her family are planning a camping trip, and they need to buy a few supplies. About how much will these supplies cost? Estimating the sum is the quickest way to find out.

$194

$49

$129

You can round to the nearest hundred.

$194	rounds to	$200
129		100
+ 49		+ 0
		$300

The amount needed will be about $300.

You can get a closer estimate by rounding to the nearest ten.

$194	rounds to	$190
129		130
+ 49		+ 50
		$370

The amount needed will be closer to $370.

The backpack, lantern, and binoculars will cost about $370.

More Examples

A. Estimate to the greatest place.

1,684	rounds to	2,000
+ 347		+ 300
		2,300

B. Estimate to the nearest thousand.

7,324	rounds to	7,000
− 3,676		− 4,000
		3,000

You can get a closer estimate by rounding to the nearest hundred.

7,324	rounds to	7,300
− 3,676		− 3,700
		3,600

Connecting Ideas

Knowing how to estimate whole-number sums and differences can help you estimate decimal sums and differences.

The weight of a stove is important when packing camping gear that you will carry when hiking. Estimate the difference between the weight of the heaviest and the lightest stoves by rounding the weights to the nearest whole number.

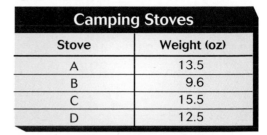

Camping Stoves	
Stove	Weight (oz)
A	13.5
B	9.6
C	15.5
D	12.5

$$
\begin{array}{r} 15.5 \\ -\ 9.6 \end{array}
\quad \text{rounds to} \quad
\begin{array}{r} 16 \\ -\ 10 \\ \hline 6 \end{array}
$$

There is about a 6-ounce difference in the weights of the stoves.

Another Example

Estimate by rounding to the nearest tenth.

$$
\begin{array}{r} 0.566 \\ +\ 0.470 \end{array}
\quad \text{rounds to} \quad
\begin{array}{r} 0.6 \\ +\ 0.5 \\ \hline 1.1 \end{array}
$$

Think and Discuss Why might you want to know whether an estimate is greater than or less than your exact answer?

Try It Out

Estimate each sum or difference.

1. 78 + 36   **2.** 349 + 854   **3.** 648 − 191   **4.** 2,098 + 7,498

5. 298 + 567   **6.** 1,173 − 385   **7.** 1,652 + 8,541   **8.** 3,250 − 628

Estimate by rounding to the nearest whole number or dollar.

9. 2.55 + 6.75   **10.** 15.32 − 7.052   **11.** $11.98 − $7.62   **12.** $15.45 + $12.60

13. 7.68 + 4.95   **14.** 19.86 − 9.49   **15.** 48.07 − 21.75   **16.** $88.45 − $38.80

17. Discuss Can an estimate ever be wrong? Explain your reasoning.

Practice

Estimate by rounding to the greatest place.

18. 38
     − 21

19. 8.62
     + 3.81

20. 7,996
     − 796

21. 1,513
     + 4,405

22. 6.2
     + 3.38

23. 407
     − 298

24. 91.78
     − 4.28

25. 8,044
     − 2,757

◄ **Math Note**

Remember the rules for rounding. If the digit to the right of the rounding place is 5 or greater, increase the digit in the rounding place by 1; otherwise, keep the digit the same.

26. 44 + 98

27. 102 − 48

28. 443 + 347

29. 6,950 + 4,350

30. 10,734 − 8,284

31. $5.13 − $2.98

32. 0.894 + 0.183

33. $4,643.85 + $5,326.29

34. 9.89 − 7.95

35. 19,346 + 31,447

36. 0.295 − 0.045

37. 7.50 − 2.62

Using Estimation Compare. Write >, <, or = for each ●.

38. 45 + 99 ● 35 + 85

39. 80 − 14 ● 68 − 16

40. 375 + 80 ● 700 − 295

41. 412 − 282 ● 125 + 125

42. 87 + 93 ● 101 + 79

43. 685 − 80 ● 600 + 90

44. 554 + 328 ● 628 + 205

45. 67 − 28 ● 99 − 28

46. 556 + 585 ● 986 + 128

47. 191 + 75 ● 225 + 86

Using Algebra Find each pattern. Then write a rule. Finally, use your rule to write the next three terms of each sequence.

48. 0.12, 0.24, 0.36, 0.48, ▪, ▪, ▪

49. 12.0, 10.9, 9.8, 8.7, ▪, ▪, ▪

50. ▪, ▪, ▪, ▪, ▪, ▪, ▪

Social Studies Connection ➤
A Nenet woman feeds young reindeer at a winter camp. Nenets are a nomadic tribe of reindeer herders who wander across the Siberian Arctic.

Problem Solving

For Problems 51 and 52, use the price tags on the items shown at the right.

51. **Using Estimation** If you were going to the store to buy shin guards, socks, and a soccer ball, about how much money would you need?

52. You decide to buy three pairs of socks, a soccer ball, and shin guards. Not including sales tax, how much money will you spend?

53. Kim has $50.00 to spend. Does she have enough money to buy jeans for $29.95 and a shirt for $14.79? Explain.

54. **Analyze** The travel agent told Arthur to take luggage weighing no more than 75 pounds. He had three suitcases weighing 24.5 lb, 31.3 lb, and 26.75 lb. Is Arthur's luggage under the weight limit, or does he need to lighten his bags? Explain.

55. **What If?** Suppose you open your book on travel and see that the sum of the two facing page numbers is 37. What are the two page numbers? Explain the strategy used to find your answer.

56. Order the following sums and differences from least greatest. Explain your thinking.
    a. $1,535 + 465$ **b.** $2,941 - 587$
    c. $8,025 - 4,661$ **d.** $2,104 + 204$

57. Four students live on Main Street. Alan lives 6 blocks east of the school. Joyce lives 2 blocks west of the school. Myra lives 1 block west of Alan. Paul lives 4 blocks east of Joyce. How many blocks is it from Paul's house to Myra's? Tell which strategy you used to solve the problem.

Review and Remember

Using Algebra Find each n.

58. $8 + n = 16$

59. $n - 10 = 20$

60. $88 + n = 108$

61. $n - 12 = 16$

62. $17 + n = 17$

63. $n + 97 = 298$

64. $n - 35 = 65$

65. $n - 0 = 28$

66. $(650 - 50) + 20 + n = 650$

67. $12 + 13 + n = 50 + 50$

68. $40 + 8 - 5 = n + 8$

69. $85 - (5 + 40) - n = 15$

For Extra Practice, see Set D, page 78.

Estimate Up Front

Front-end estimation is another way to estimate.

Learning About It

How many more people rode the roller coaster on Saturday than on Sunday? Look at the sign in the drawing below. You can use the **front digit**—the digit in the greatest place—to estimate. This is called **front-end estimation**.

Step 1 Estimate by subtracting front digits.	**Step 2** Adjust the estimate by looking at the digits to the right.
$\begin{array}{r} 384 \\ -\ 207 \end{array} \longrightarrow \begin{array}{r} 300 \\ -\ 200 \\ \hline 100 \end{array}$	$\begin{array}{r} 384 \\ -\ 207 \\ \hline >100 \end{array}$ Since 84 > 7, the exact answer will be > 100.

About 100 more riders rode on Saturday.

More Examples

A. $\begin{array}{r} 3.6 \\ +\ 4.8 \end{array}$ about 1

$7 + 1 = 8$

B. $\begin{array}{r} 561 \\ +\ 261 \end{array}$ about 100

$700 + 100 = 800$

C. $\begin{array}{r} 8.29 \\ -\ 3.70 \end{array}$ Since 29 < 70, the exact answer will be < 5.

<5

Think and Discuss For $9.37 - 6.62$ will the exact answer be greater than or less than 3? Explain your thinking.

Try It Out

Estimate, using front-end estimation. Then adjust to find a closer estimate.

1. $6{,}734 - 3{,}544$

2. $3.78 - 2.90$

3. $3.925 - 0.524$

4. $1.327 + 4.652$

5. $342 + 287$

Daily Riders

Saturday.........384

Sunday..........207

Practice

Estimate each sum or difference, using front-end estimation. Then adjust to find a closer estimate.

6. $137 + 753$ **7.** $7.3 + 5.3$ **8.** $701 + 978$ **9.** $299 - 158$

10. $3.39 + 6.99$ **11.** $836 + 171$ **12.** $316 + 249$ **13.** $5.70 - 1.42$

14. $1.27 + 5.4$ **15.** $5,640 - 4,522$ **16.** $4.72 - 2.84$ **17.** $21.863 - 10.033$

Problem Solving

Estimate. Tell what method you used.

18. Wednesdays are group days at the amusement park. Last Wednesday groups of 125, 183, and 203 students went to the park. About how many students went?

19. The amusement park has a supply of 11,850 tickets and needs 36,000 for the month. About how many more tickets need to be ordered?

20. Journal Idea Describe a situation in which front-end estimation is helpful and reasonably accurate.

Review and Remember

Compare. Write $>$, $<$, or $=$ for each ⬤.

21. 231 ⬤ 231

22. 5,837 ⬤ 5,241

23. 9,655 ⬤ 9,566

24. 100,285 ⬤ 101,874

25. 8.74 ⬤ 9.1

26. 0.26 ⬤ 0.260

Critical Thinking Corner

Number Sense

Clustering

Clustering is another way to estimate sums. Clustering works when the numbers are all close to the same number.

With $25.73 + 23.89 + 26.36 + 27.01$, the numbers all cluster around 25. So the sum is about 4×25 or 100.

How would you use clustering to estimate the sum of $22.0 + 21.4 + 19.42 + 18.6$?

22.0
21.4
19.42
18.6

For Extra Practice, see Set E, page 79.

Problem Solving
Write an Equation

To solve some problems, you can write an equation.

José skates from home to school, from school to the park, and from the park to karate lessons. The drawing shows how long it takes him to skate from place to place. How long does José spend skating from home to karate lessons?

 ## UNDERSTAND

What do you need to find?

You need to find the total time José spends skating from home to karate lessons.

 ## PLAN

How can you solve the problem?

You can **write an equation**. An equation is a number sentence with a variable, such as *t*.

 ## SOLVE

Let *t* = the total time José spends skating from home to karate lessons.

Write, in words, how long José skates.

13 min + 9 min + 15 min = total time

Now, write an equation using the variable *t*. Then solve for *t*.

$$13 + 9 + 15 = t$$
$$37 = t$$

José spends 37 minutes skating from home to his karate lessons.

 ## LOOK BACK

Check your work. Be sure the equation describes the problem.

Using the Strategy

Using Algebra Write an equation to solve each problem.

1 Directions for getting to the dog show are "Drive 3 miles along Spring St. Turn right onto Route 202 and drive 17 miles to Exit 16. Turn left off the exit ramp and follow Park Rd. for 5 miles to the dog show." What was the total distance to the dog show?

2 Marcus and Cheryl traveled from New York to Philadelphia to Pittsburgh to Chicago. Use the drawing below. What was the total distance traveled?

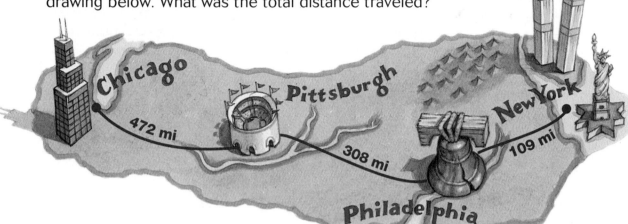

Chicago 472 mi Pittsburgh 308 mi Philadelphia 109 mi New York

3 A talent show is supposed to last 50 minutes. The band will play for 16 minutes, and the chorus will sing for 20 minutes. A quartet will perform for 10 minutes. How much time is left for the juggler?

4 **Create Your Own** Write a problem about your everyday life that can be solved by using the sentence $6 \times 55 = x$. You may wish to exchange problems with a classmate.

Mixed Strategy Review

Try these or other strategies to solve each problem. Tell which strategy you used.

THERE'S ALWAYS A WAY!

Problem Solving Strategies

- Guess and Check
- Make a List
- Write an Equation
- Draw a Diagram
- Find a Pattern
- Make a Table

5 You and a classmate make a game called Pick the Numbers. The board has the numbers from 1 to 25. On your turn, you have to pick two consecutive whole numbers with a sum of 31. What are the numbers?

6 **Analyze** There is a train ride that goes through a rectangular park. The length of the train ride is 9 miles less than the perimeter of the park. If the park is 4 miles long and 3 miles wide, how long is the train ride?

✓ Checkpoint
Mental Math and Estimation

Use words from the Word List to complete the story.

1 Adds Up!

Ms. Bell's fifth-grade class was trying to add 16 + 28 + 4. Andrew wanted to add the 16 and the 4 because they were _____ 1. _____ and would add easily to 20. He wasn't sure he could.

"Sure," chimed in Maria, "we can change the order of the 28 and the 4, using the ___2.___ ."

Enrique said, "If I were you, I would add (16 + 28) + 4." Tara disagreed. She wanted to add 16 + (28 + 4).

"You're both right," said Maria, "you're using the ___3.___ ."

Frank wanted to add 0. "You could," said Ms. Bell, "but, according to the ___4.___ , adding 0 won't change the answer."

Some students used ___5.___ to estimate the answer. Others used ___6.___ and found easier numbers to find the exact answer. The students all knew that addition and subtraction were ___7.___ , because one operation "undoes" the other.

There sure are lots of ways to add numbers!

Word Bank

Associative Property
Commutative Property
compatible numbers
compensation
front digits
Identity Property
inverse operations

Using Algebra Use properties to help you find each *n*. (pages 42–43)

8. $17 + 0 = n$ **9.** $55 + 8 = n + 55$ **10.** $8 + (2 + 3) = (n + 2) + 3$

Use mental math to find each sum. (pages 44–45)

11. $8 + 15 + 22$ **12.** $6 + 9 + 14$ **13.** $24 + 19 + 11$ **14.** $15 + 27 + 15$

Using Algebra Use mental math or paper and pencil to find each *x*. (pages 46–47)

15. $x - 8 = 12$ **16.** $144 - 23 = x$ **17.** $x + 37 = 49$

Round each number to estimate. (pages 50–53)

18. 68 + 13

19. 25 − 17

20. 125 − 92

21. 562 + 156

22. 748 + 256

23. 469 − 271

Estimate using front-end estimation. Then adjust to find a closer estimate. (pages 54–55)

24. 136 + 347

25. 792 − 431

26. 7,622 + 3,458

27. 3,567 − 2,382

What do you think?

How can compatible numbers help you add mentally?

Mixed Practice

Estimate. Tell why you chose the method you did.

28. 22 + 19

29. 38 + 26 + 22

30. 175 − 62

31. 657 + 90 + 323

32. 2,548 − 2,156

33. 3,578 + 1,765

Problem Solving

34. Weekly cassette-tape sales in November were 192 tapes, 71 tapes, 57 tapes, and 366 tapes. Estimate the sales for November.

35. Alex sold her skateboard for $63 and her kneepads for $12. If she had $16, about how much money does she have now?

Journal Idea

Write an addition problem where only an estimate is needed and another where an exact answer is needed.

Critical Thinking Corner

Visual Thinking

Straw Figures

Look at the picture at the right. There are eight rectangles. How can you move two straws to make only four rectangles?

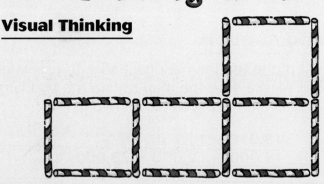

Launching Some Fun

*You can use basic facts to
add and subtract greater whole numbers.*

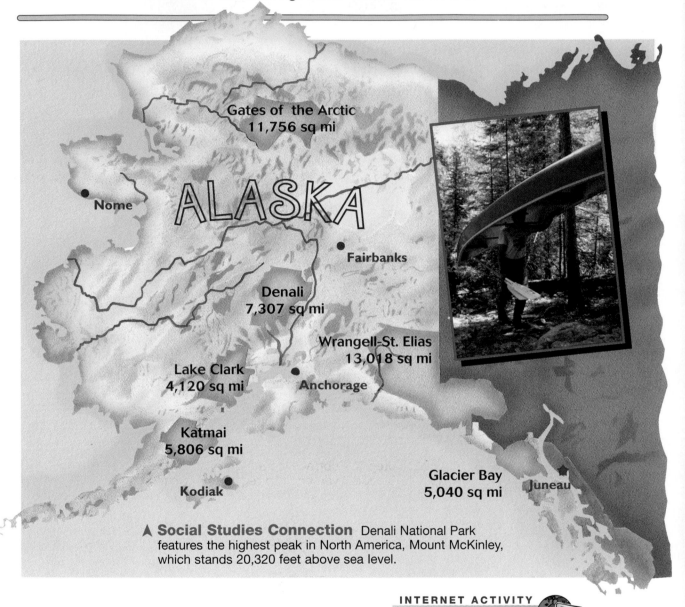

Gates of the Arctic
11,756 sq mi

Nome

ALASKA

Fairbanks

Denali
7,307 sq mi

Wrangell-St. Elias
13,018 sq mi

Lake Clark
4,120 sq mi

Anchorage

Katmai
5,806 sq mi

Kodiak

Glacier Bay
5,040 sq mi

Juneau

▲ **Social Studies Connection** Denali National Park
features the highest peak in North America, Mount McKinley,
which stands 20,320 feet above sea level.

INTERNET ACTIVITY
www.sbgmath.com

Learning About It

On the list of the top ten national parks, the six largest in
area are in Alaska! Use the map to find the two largest
parks. What is the total area of the two parks?

$$13{,}018 + 11{,}756 = n$$

Estimate first: $13{,}000 + 12{,}000 = 25{,}000$

Then add to find the exact answer.

● **One way** to add is to use paper and pencil.

Step 1 Add the ones. Regroup if you can. 14 ones = 1 ten 4 ones	**Step 2** Add the tens. Regroup if you can.	**Step 3** Add the hundreds. Regroup if you can.	**Step 4** Continue to add.
1 $$\begin{array}{r} 13{,}018 \\ +\ 11{,}756 \\ \hline 4 \end{array}$$	1 $$\begin{array}{r} 13{,}018 \\ +\ 11{,}756 \\ \hline 74 \end{array}$$	1 $$\begin{array}{r} 13{,}018 \\ +\ 11{,}756 \\ \hline 774 \end{array}$$	1 $$\begin{array}{r} 13{,}018 \\ +\ 11{,}756 \\ \hline 24{,}774 \end{array}$$

● **Another way** is to use a calculator.

Press: (1)(3)(0)(1)(8)(+)(1)(1)(7)(5)(6)(=)

Display: 24774

Place a comma in your answer when you write it: 24,774

The total area of the two parks is 24,774 square miles.
Since the answer is close to the estimate, it is reasonable.

Connecting Ideas

Using basic facts can help when you are subtracting greater numbers.

Find **762 − 395 = n**

Step 1 Subtract the ones. Decide if you need to regroup.	**Step 2** Subtract the tens. Decide if you need to regroup.	**Step 3** Subtract the hundreds.
512 $$\begin{array}{r} 76\!\!\!/2 \\ -\ 395 \\ \hline 7 \end{array}$$	15 6̶ 5̶12 $$\begin{array}{r} 76\!\!\!/2 \\ -\ 395 \\ \hline 67 \end{array}$$	15 6̶ 5̶12 $$\begin{array}{r} 76\!\!\!/2 \\ -\ 395 \\ \hline 367 \end{array}$$

More Examples

A.
1 1 1
$$\begin{array}{r} 6{,}578 \\ 135 \\ +\ 5{,}902 \\ \hline 12{,}615 \end{array}$$

B.
11
5 1 12
$$\begin{array}{r} 3{,}6\!\!\!/2\!\!\!/2 \\ -\ 1{,}487 \\ \hline 2{,}135 \end{array}$$

C.
3 10 3 12
$$\begin{array}{r} \$4\!\!\!/0{,}74\!\!\!/2 \\ -\ \$18{,}633 \\ \hline \$22{,}109 \end{array}$$

$$\begin{array}{r} \$22{,}109 \\ +\ \$18{,}633 \\ \hline \$40{,}742 \end{array}$$
You can add to check.

Think and Discuss Which method would you use to add 79,486 and 56,792? Explain why.

Try It Out

Estimate first. Then find each sum or difference.

1. 3,525
   + 1,927

2. 75,050
   + 7,850

3. 2,127
   − 429

4. 37,451
   − 21,340

5. 2,632 + 867 + 803

6. 418 + 10,251 + 4,136

7. 83,588 − 47,564

8. 35,089 + 88,145

9. 63,713 − 45,608

10. 26,390 + 67,987

▼ **Science Connection** Denali National Park is home to grizzly bears. The grizzly bear is the largest North American carnivore. A grizzly's paw can grow to be larger than 12 in. long!

Practice

Add or subtract. Estimate to be sure each answer is reasonable.

11. 8,157
    + 65

12. 7,577
    − 642

13. 9,092
    + 4,160

14. 63,835
    − 43,632

15. $1,070
    + 2,678

16. 25,685
    − 4,372

17. 36,489
    − 516

18. 5,457
    + 380

19. 640 + 187 + 389

20. 3,476 + 275 + 652

21. 4,723 + 3,982 + 728

22. 4,261 − 302

23. 2,118 − 364

24. 44,426 − 43,386

25. 26,391 + 37,298

26. 40,280 + 6,321

27. 86,040 − 56,972

Using Algebra Find the missing digits.

28.
$$\begin{array}{r} 7,98\blacksquare \\ +\ 4,\blacksquare 95 \\ \hline \blacksquare 2,976 \end{array}$$

29.
$$\begin{array}{r} 55,72\blacksquare \\ -\ 36,\blacksquare 07 \\ \hline 1\blacksquare,316 \end{array}$$

30.
$$\begin{array}{r} 18,8\blacksquare 8 \\ -\ 1\blacksquare,632 \\ \hline 3,26\blacksquare \end{array}$$

31.
$$\begin{array}{r} 4\blacksquare,589 \\ +\ 22,1\blacksquare 4 \\ \hline \blacksquare 2,743 \end{array}$$

32.
$$\begin{array}{r} 3\blacksquare,095 \\ -\ \ \blacksquare 75 \\ \hline 29,92\blacksquare \end{array}$$

33.
$$\begin{array}{r} 4,\blacksquare 67 \\ +\ 2,03\blacksquare \\ \hline 6,7\blacksquare 3 \end{array}$$

34.
$$\begin{array}{r} 6,1\blacksquare 2 \\ +\ \blacksquare,936 \\ \hline 10,\blacksquare 08 \end{array}$$

35.
$$\begin{array}{r} 37\blacksquare,931 \\ -\ 144,\blacksquare 67 \\ \hline \blacksquare 31,7\blacksquare 4 \end{array}$$

Problem Solving

36. There are many adventure trips available throughout the national parks of Alaska. The River Wilderness canoe trip costs $85 for four days. The Wrangell-St. Elias river raft trip is a trip of 5 days costing $410. What is the difference in the cost of these two trips?

Use the table at the right for Problems 37–38.

37. **Social Studies Connection** Indian reservations and trust lands cover a great deal of land. What is the total number of acres in the four states listed?

38. **Using Estimation** About how many more acres of federal Indian reservations and trust lands are in Florida than in the other three states combined?

39. The annual numbers of visitors to three national parks are listed.

> Blue Ridge Parkway: 16,928,600
> Golden Gate Recreation Area: 14,695,800
> Great Smoky Mountains: 8,628,200

In a year, how many more tourists visit the Blue Ridge Parkway than the Great Smoky Mountains?

Federal Indian Reservations and Trust Lands

State	Acres
Alaska	86,773
Nebraska	23,792
Texas	4,726
Florida	153,874

Review and Remember

Round each number to the underlined place.

40. 5,3<u>9</u>9

41. 10,<u>3</u>12

42. 1<u>2</u>,290

43. 63,<u>0</u>74

44. 1,<u>8</u>26,281

45. 324,<u>5</u>08

46. 1<u>2</u>6,871

47. 9,391,<u>9</u>57

48. 44,7<u>3</u>9,931

49. 12<u>3</u>,985,281

50. <u>7</u>87,759

51. <u>9</u>21,298

For Extra Practice, see Set F, page 79.

Box It Out!

Grid paper can help you learn to add or subtract decimals.

Learning About It

In figure-skating competitions, a skater is given a technical score and an artistic score. The judges add the two scores to obtain a total score. In a junior competition, a judge gave a skater a technical score of 4.4 and an artistic score of 3.7. What was the skater's total score from that judge?

$$4.4 + 3.7 = n$$

Decimal grids can help you add decimals.

 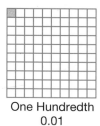

One Whole	One Tenth	One Hundredth
1.0	0.1	0.01

What You Need

For each group:
  grid paper
  colored pencils
  scissors
  tape

Work with a group.

Step 1 Outline ten 10 by 10 decimal grids on your grid paper.

Step 2 Shade 4 whole grids and 0.4 of one grid to show 4.4 grids. With a different color, shade 3.7 grids. Use your scissors to cut out the whole grids, the 0.4 part, and the 0.7 part.

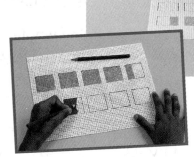

Step 3 Add the 0.4 part and the 0.7 part by taping the two decimal parts together. Compare the taped piece to one whole decimal grid. Use your scissors to cut off any extra tenths.

Step 4 To find the sum of 4.4 and 3.7, count the number of whole decimal grids (including the one you taped together) and the number of tenths you have left over.

Think and Discuss How could you use grids to show 4.4 − 3.7?

Practice

Use grid paper to find each sum.

1. 1.8 + 2.5

2. 2.53 + 1.4

3. 1.96 + 3.42

4. 2.18 + 1.05

5. 3.24 + 2.78

6. 1.89 + 2.35

7. 1.59 + 3.8

8. 4.17 + 2.39

9. Look at the answer to Exercise 1. Then find the sum of 18 and 25. How do the two answers compare?

For each set of shaded grids, write the correct addition sentence.

10.

11.

Use grid paper to find each difference.

12. 3.6 − 1.3

13. 1.8 − 0.3

14. 3.48 − 2.98

15. Look at the answer to Exercise 12. Then subtract 13 from 36. How do the answers compare?

16.  **Journal Idea** Describe how adding whole numbers and adding decimals are alike. How are they different?

▲ **Kid Connection** At the 1996 World Championship Figure Skating Competition, Michelle Kwan received an average technical score of 5.8 and an average artistic score of 5.9.

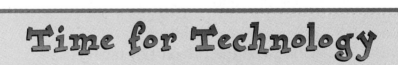

Time for Technology

Surf the Net

More on Sports

You can use the Internet to find information about sports. Explore one of the sites listed. Follow links to other related sites. Share your findings with the class.

www.espn.com

www.nba.com

www.foxsports.com

Fishy Facts

Adding decimals is like adding whole numbers except that you need to place a decimal point in the answer.

Learning About It

Lucy and Max go fishing every chance they get. This time they will attach weights, called sinkers, to their lines. Sinkers help hold the bait at a certain depth to catch fish. If the sinkers weigh 4.73 grams and 3.54 grams, how much weight will Lucy and Max add to their lines?

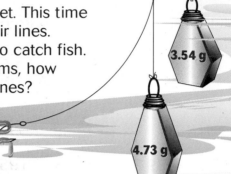

3.54 g

4.73 g

$$4.73 + 3.54 = n$$
Estimate first: $5 + 4 = 9$

Then find the exact answer.

Step 1 Line up the decimal points.	**Step 2** Add the hundredths. Regroup if you can.	**Step 3** Add the tenths. Regroup if you can. 12 tenths = 1 one 2 tenths	**Step 4** Add the ones. Place the decimal point in your answer.
		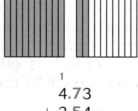	
4.73 + 3.54	4.73 + 3.54 ——— 7	1 4.73 + 3.54 ——— 27	1 4.73 + 3.54 ——— 8.27

They will add 8.27 grams of weight to their lines.
The answer 8.27 is close to the estimate of 9.

More Examples

A. 5.20   Use a 0 to
    + 3.18   hold the
    ———   hundredths
    8.38   place.

B.   0.98
    + 0.07
    ———
    1.05

C.   0.675   Use 0's to hold
    + 0.400   the hundredths
    ———   and thousandths
    1.075   places.

Think and Discuss Explain why it is important to line up the decimal points before adding decimals.

Try It Out

Estimate. Then find each exact sum.

1. 3.58
    + 7.41

2. 2.90
    + 7.82

3. 39.67
    + 21.46

4. 384.10
    + 92.03

5. 0.38 + 7.2

6. 5.12 + 8.76 + 9.01

7. 987.23 + 99.37 + 7.98

Practice

Add.

8. 772.09
    + 48.78

9. 957.47
    + 70.62

10. 28.39
    + 52.66

11. 125.2
    + 97.98

12. 9.4 + 3.76

13. 7.03 + 2.61

14. 201.5 + 18.92

15. 810.08 + 59.95

16. 26.95 + 1.35

17. 3.71 + 7.29

18. 10.28 + 9.2

19. 447.49 + 84.1 + 60.42

20. 271.2 + 66.3

21. 8.02 + 83.48

22. 12.17 + 0.01 + 0.64

23. 202.7 + 6.43

24. 437.8 + 91.9

25. 615.04 + 31.7 + 18.3

26. 529.36 + 28.71

Problem Solving

27. A leader attaches a hook to a fishing line. Max needs to replace the leaders on his fishing lines. He wants leaders that are 10 in., 9.5 in., and 11.75 in. in length. How many inches of leader line will he use?

28. **Science Connection** Estimate and then find the actual total of the record weights of fish listed in the table at the right.

29. **Predict** Will the sum of 52.061 and 49.74 be greater than or less than 100? Explain.

Some World-Record Weights	
Fish	**Weight**
Bass	10.09 kg
Catfish	43.99 kg
Perch	2.15 kg
Salmon	42.18 kg
Trout	19.10 kg
Whitefish	5.92 kg

Review and Remember

Compare. Use >, <, or = for ●.

30. 0.2 ● 0.09

31. 6.53 ● 6.53

32. 5.05 ● 5.050

33. 8.270 ● 8.218

34. 4.01 ● 37.1

35. 0.46 ● 0.460

36. 0.31 ● 0.299

37. 2.10 ● 2.01

38. 302.8 ● 320.9

For Extra Practice, see Set G, page 79.

Subtracting Decimals

Tune In!

You can use what you know about adding decimals to subtract decimals.

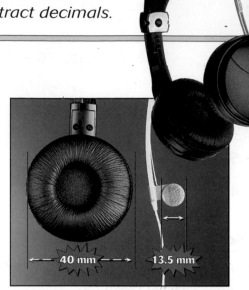

Learning About It

People still use large headphones in recording studios. Small earphones are popular for home use. What is the difference in the diameters of headphones and earphones?

$$40 - 13.5 = n$$

Estimate first: $40 - 14 = 26$

Then find the exact answer.

Step 1 Line up the decimal points. Use zeros to hold places, if needed.	**Step 2** Subtract the tenths. Decide if you need to regroup.	**Step 3** Subtract the ones.	**Step 4** Subtract the tens. Place the decimal point in your answer.
40.0 − 13.5	9 3 10 10 4̸0̸.0̸ − 13.5 ‾‾‾‾5	9 3 10 10 4̸0̸.0̸ − 13.5 ‾‾6.5	9 3 10 10 4̸0̸.0̸ − 13.5 ‾‾26.5

The difference in the diameters of the headphones and earphones is 26.5 mm—close to the estimate of 26.

Think and Discuss Use examples to explain how to subtract a decimal from a whole number and a decimal from a decimal.

Try It Out

Estimate first. Then subtract.

1. 32.86
    − 10.74

2. 73.45
    − 53.52

3. 344.75
    −   0.12

4. 10.4
    − 5.28

5. 9.62 − 1.15

6. 5.02 − 0.78

7. 19.87 − 13.017

Practice

Subtract.

8. 83.5
– 3.2

9. 72.69
– 66.40

10. 75.77
– 8.42

11. 1.79
– 0.09

12. 4.6 – 0.8

13. 3.9 – 2.46

14. 47.83 – 16.45

15. $12.13 – $7.26

16. $1.05 – $0.69

17. $50.90 – $35.67

18. $29.76 – $13.14

19. 18.17 – 6.56

20. 805.79 – 64.81

21. 64.0 – 53.2

22. 426.1 – 30.2

23. 211.8 – 3.64

24. 7.21 – 4.9

25. 1.98 – 0.899

26. 321.80 – 24.90

Problem Solving

27. Florida has 35 Spanish-language radio stations. Texas has 120. There are 292 Spanish-language stations in the rest of the United States. What is the total number of these stations in the country?

28. Deena has saved $5.00, $3.50, $3.00, and $4.75 from baby-sitting. She wants to buy a CD for $18.99, tax included. How much more money does she need to buy the CD?

Review and Remember

Using Estimation Estimate each sum or difference.

29. 56 + 78

30. 92 + 22

31. 433 – 179

32. 571 + 368

33. 764 – 491

34. 386 + 210

35. 871 – 594

36. 2,307 + 2,512

Money $ense

To Coin a Phrase...

Al had four coins and wanted more.
Beth had eight, lost two, found four.
Chuck had a hundred in his store.
Dot had twenty coins galore.

Each person had the same amount of money. They each had only one kind of coin. Which coin and how many coins did each have?

For Extra Practice, see Set H, page 80.

Cycling Through Decimals!

You can use what you have learned to add and subtract thousandths.

Learning About It

Carlos and Brant crossed the finish line so close together that a photograph of the finish was the only way to determine who took second and third places. Look at the scoreboard to find out who was second and by how much time.

53.261 − 53.214 = n

Estimate first: **53 − 53 = 0**

Then subtract to find the exact answer.

| Carlos | 53.214 s |
| Brant | 53.261 s |

THERE'S ALWAYS A WAY!

● **One way** to subtract is to use paper and pencil.

Step 1 Line up the decimal points. Use zeros to hold places, if needed.	**Step 2** Subtract the thousandths. Decide if you need to regroup.	**Step 3** Subtract the hundredths and tenths. Decide if you need to regroup.	**Step 4** Subtract the whole numbers. Place a decimal point in the answer.
53.261 − 53.214	53.2⁵¹61 − 53.214 7	53.2⁵¹61 − 53.214 047	53.2⁵¹61 − 53.214 0.047

● **Another way** to subtract is to use a calculator.

Press: ⑤ ③ . ② ⑥ ① − ⑤ ③ . ② ① ④ =

Display: 0.047

Carlos came in second place by 0.047 of a second!
Since the answer is close to the estimate, it is reasonable.

More Examples

A.
$$\begin{array}{r} \overset{71517}{\cancel{8}\cancel{6}.\cancel{7}} \\ -\ 29.8 \\ \hline 56.9 \end{array}$$

B.
$$\begin{array}{r} \overset{1}{3.40} \\ +\ 9.78 \\ \hline 13.18 \end{array}$$

Think and Discuss Without adding, how can you tell that the sum of 24.813 and 4.5 will have a 3 in the thousandths place?

◀ Math Note

Remember that you can use zeros as placeholders so that numbers have the same place values.

Try It Out

Estimate first. Then find the exact sum or difference.

1. 1.389 + 5.42   **2.** 17.76 − 5.01   **3.** 3.5 − 1.86

Practice

Find each sum or difference.

4. 6.35 + 7.14   **5.** 21.4 − 20.1   **6.** 17.54 − 3.62

7. 9 + 3.001   **8.** 0.984 + 2.3   **9.** 7.6 − 3.24

10. 16.8 − 0.35   **11.** 6.3 − 5.02   **12.** 136 − 21.3

Problem Solving

13. In a cycling race, the winner's time was 11.782 s. The third-place time was 12.092 s. What is the difference between the two times?

14. Using Estimation Use the picture to estimate the distance from the ground to the top of the handlebars of the bicycle.

15. Willa can buy a bike at a store for $329.99 plus $19.80 tax. She can buy one from a catalog for $316.49 plus $34.50 for shipping and handling. Which is the lower cost?

22.5 in.

12.5 in.

Review and Remember

Using Algebra Compare. Write >, <, or = for each ●.

16. 36 ÷ 6 ● 20 − 15   **17.** 54 ÷ 9 ● 4 × 2   **18.** 6 × 8 ● 8 × 6

19. 81 ÷ 9 ● 49 ÷ 7   **20.** 80 ÷ 8 ● 42 ÷ 7   **21.** 6 × 9 ● 1 × 54

Go Figure!

*You can make smart choices about the
method of computation you use to find an answer.*

Learning About It

You can use mental math, paper and pencil,
or a calculator to add or subtract. The
method of calculation you choose depends
on the numbers you are using.

Mental Math

You can use mental math when numbers
are easy to compute. Use compensation
to find this sum.

$$4{,}305 \longrightarrow 4{,}305 - 5 = 4{,}300$$
$$+\ 4{,}295 \longrightarrow 4{,}295 + 5 = \underline{4{,}300}$$
$$8{,}600$$

So $4{,}305 + 4{,}295 = 8{,}600$.

Paper and Pencil

You might use paper and pencil to find an
answer if the numbers are small or if you
only need to regroup a few times.

$$\begin{array}{r} 7.26 \\ +\ \ 4.32 \\ \hline 11.58 \end{array}$$

Calculator

 You might use a calculator to find an answer
when the numbers are greater numbers or
when you need to regroup many times.

$$\begin{array}{r} \$8{,}925.33 \\ -\ \ 2{,}897.79 \end{array}$$

Press: (8)(9)(2)(5)(.)(3)(3)(-)(2)(8)(9)(7)(.)(7)(9)(=)

Display: (*6027.54*)

Place a dollar sign and a comma in your answer: $6,027.54

Think and Discuss Why is it important to estimate the answer, no matter which method you use?

Try It Out

Choose a Method Use mental math, paper and pencil, or a calculator to add or subtract. Tell which method you used.

1. $500 + 308$ 2. $3.22 + 2.11$ 3. $28.373 - 4.217$ 4. $7,490 + 1,911$

5. $2,114 + 701$ 6. $24 + 32$ 7. $4,001 + 3,282$ 8. $4,090 - 1,040$

Practice

Choose a Method Use mental math, paper and pencil, or a calculator to add or subtract. Tell which method you used.

9. $\begin{aligned} 43.21 \\ + 55.41 \end{aligned}$

10. $\begin{aligned} 82{,}349.87 \\ - 32{,}495.00 \end{aligned}$

11. $\begin{aligned} 5{,}086{,}000 \\ + 3{,}100{,}000 \end{aligned}$

12. $\begin{aligned} 4{,}325 \\ + 4{,}315 \end{aligned}$

13. $394.7 + 193.4$ 14. $4,002 + 4,002$ 15. $65.43 - 54.32$

16. $23.2 + 15.7$ 17. $878.2 - 780.002$ 18. $1,497 - 1,493$

19. $0.84 - 0.587$ 20. $723.4 + 850.32$ 21. $\$76.25 - \$14.31$

Problem Solving

22. Vickie and her cousin Hannah were playing a computer game. Vickie scored 3,056 points, and Hannah scored 1,686 points. How many more points did Vickie score?

23. **Create Your Own** Use the number 3,958 to create three problems—one in which using mental math is most appropriate, one for using the calculator, and one for using paper and pencil.

▲ **Science Connection** Ravi J. K. Mehta is a computer programmer who used his love of computer games to start his own computer-game company.

Review and Remember

What part of each figure is shaded?

24.   25.   26.   27. 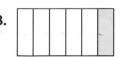   28. [figure: rectangle divided into 6 parts]

For Extra Practice, see Set J, page 80.

Practice What You Learned

Choose the correct letter for each answer.

1 Cathy is arranging four pictures on a shelf. She puts the boat between the airplane and the dog. Then she puts the cat in the leftmost position. Which picture is third from the left?

A. Airplane
B. Boat
C. Cat
D. Dog

Tip

Use one of the strategies to solve this problem.
• *Draw a Diagram*
• *Use Logical Reasoning*

2 On a trip to the zoo, Terry spent $32. Mike spent $4 less than Terry. Which number sentence could you use to find the total, *t*, that both people spent?

A. $t = 32 + (32 + 4)$
B. $t = 32 + (32 - 4)$
C. $t = 32 - (32 + 4)$
D. $t = 32 - (32 - 4)$
E. Not Here

Tip

To check your answer, do the computation and see if your answer choice makes sense.

3 Sam is putting a braid border around a rectangular rug with a 24-ft *perimeter*. Which of these is most reasonable for the longer dimension of the rug?

A. 2 feet
B. 4 feet
C. 8 feet
D. 24 feet

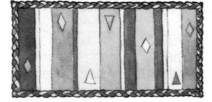

Tip

Make a Diagram to help you solve this problem. Draw several rectangles that have perimeters of 24 feet.

4 The pictograph shows the numbers of different kinds of trees planted.

Trees Planted in Our Town

Maple	🌳🌳🌳🌳🌳🌳🌳🌿
Spruce	🌳🌳🌳🌳🌳🌳
Elm	🌳🌳🌳🌿
Pine	🌳🌳🌳🌳🌳🌳🌳🌿
Other	🌳🌳🌳🌳🌳🌿

Key: 🌳 = 20 trees

How many more pine trees than spruce trees were planted?

A. 15
B. 20
C. 25
D. 30
E. Not Here

5 The house numbers on Lyle's side of the street are 420, 422, 424, and 426. Which set would most likely be the numbers of the houses across the street?

A. 410, 412, 414, 416
B. 421, 423, 425, 427
C. 429, 430, 431, 432
D. 428, 430, 434, 436

6 Harriet has $72.00 in her savings account. She plans to save about $5 a week for 20 weeks. Which is a reasonable amount for Harriet to have in her account after 3 weeks?

A. About $170
B. About $150
C. About $90
D. About $70
E. Not Here

7 Art has $20.00. He pays $6.50 admission to an amusement park and another $4.75 on lunch. He plans to spend the rest of his money on rides, which cost $2.45 each. Which is the best estimate for the number of ride tickets Art can buy?

A. 7
B. 5
C. 3
D. 2

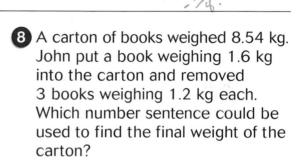

8 A carton of books weighed 8.54 kg. John put a book weighing 1.6 kg into the carton and removed 3 books weighing 1.2 kg each. Which number sentence could be used to find the final weight of the carton?

A. $8.54 + 1.6 + 3.6 = $ ■
B. $8.54 + 1.6 - (3 \times 1.2) = $ ■
C. $(8.54 + 1.6) \times 3 - 1.2 = $ ■
D. $8.54 - 1.6 + (3 \times 1.2) = $ ■

9 In a dart game, Doris scored 132, 186, and 214 points. To the nearest hundred, what is the best estimate of her point total for the three games?

A. 300
B. 400
C. 500
D. 600

10 Fran had 24 tomatoes and 15 cucumbers from her garden. She gave half the tomatoes and about half of the cucumbers to her neighbor. How many tomatoes did she have left?

A. About 12
B. Exactly 12
C. About 20
D. Exactly 20

✔ Checkpoint

Adding and Subtracting Whole Numbers and Decimals

Vocabulary

Write the missing words that complete each sentence.

1. One way to estimate is to use only the ___?___ .

2. ___?___ are numbers that are easy to compute mentally.

3. The ___?___ states that the way in which addends are grouped does not change the sum.

4. Addition and subtraction are ___?___ .

> **Word Bank**
>
> Associative Property
> Commutative Property
> compatible numbers
> compensation
> front digits
> Identity Property
> inverse operations

Concepts and Skills

Add or subtract. (pages 60–63)

5. $912 + 344$

6. $45,690 - 388$

7. $10,421 + 7,347$

8. $23,850 - 2,433$

9. $1,733 + 2,984$

10. $25,619 - 13,302$

11. $27,019 + 15,984$

12. $13,988 + 10,752 + 3,462 + 1,641$

Using Estimation Estimate the sum or difference. Then find the exact answer. (pages 66–71)

13. $3.98 + 1.23$

14. $7.15 + 9.08$

15. $6.8 + 3.92$

16. $8.3 - 5.1$

17. $5.5 + 4.13$

18. $9.95 - 6.32$

19. $6.45 + 3.83$

20. $17.2 - 3.5$

Compare. Write > or < for each ⬤.

21. $5.63 - 1.76$ ⬤ $12.38 - 10.16$

22. $15.9 - 3.45$ ⬤ $12.624 + 0.563$

23. $16.454 + 3.911$ ⬤ $28.5 - 4.664$

24. $18.582 - 12.799$ ⬤ $5.458 + 2.197$

Choose a Method Use mental math, paper and pencil, or a calculator to add and subtract. Tell which method you used. (pages 72–73)

25. $2,900 + 1,304$

26. $290 + 3,865$

27. $8,365 - 2,905$

28. $1.45 + 3.76$

29. $10.91 - 8.44$

30. $13.26 - 12.3$

31. $13,000 - 288$

32. $65.18 + 12$

33. $32.9 - 14.85$

Mixed Practice

Add or subtract.

34. $205.64 + 34.02$

35. $346.12 - 125.8$

36. $135,932 - 35,693$

37. $18,501 + 2,659$

38. $23.9 - 13.47$

39. $174.19 - 100.42$

40. $14.85 + 2.3$

41. $4.03 + 2.61$

42. $25.52 + 30.89$

Problem Solving

43. If Winona's family walks 2.5 miles on Friday, 3.75 miles on Saturday, and 4.25 miles on Sunday, how many miles do they walk in all?

44. **Analyze** Mark has $2.00 to buy fruit bars. He wants to buy two bars for $0.79 each and one bar for $0.53. Does he have enough money?

45. A farmer plans to buy 135.5 acres of land to enlarge his 239.49 acre farm. To the nearest acre, how large will his farm be then?

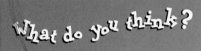

What do you think?

What are the two important things to remember when adding or subtracting decimals?

Journal Idea

Write a paragraph explaining how to find the sum of 3.2 and 4.85 by using grid paper. Include drawings.

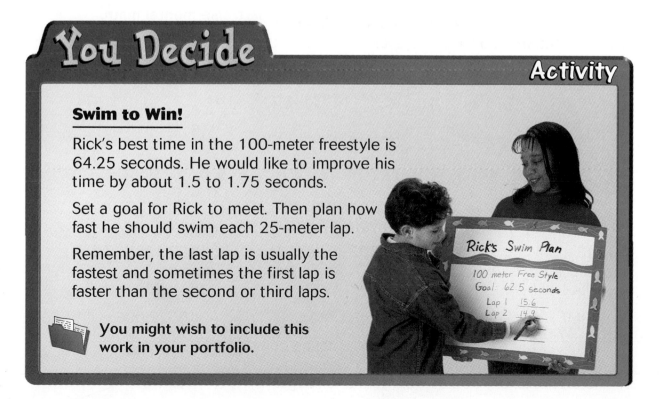

You Decide

Activity

Swim to Win!

Rick's best time in the 100-meter freestyle is 64.25 seconds. He would like to improve his time by about 1.5 to 1.75 seconds.

Set a goal for Rick to meet. Then plan how fast he should swim each 25-meter lap.

Remember, the last lap is usually the fastest and sometimes the first lap is faster than the second or third laps.

You might wish to include this work in your portfolio.

Rick's Swim Plan

100 meter Free Style
Goal: 62.5 seconds
Lap 1   15.6
Lap 2   14.9

Extra Practice

Set A (pages 42–43)

Using Algebra Use the properties and mental math strategies to find n.

1. $8 + (n + 12) = (8 + 48) + 12$
2. $20 + n = 5 + 20$
3. $446 + 0 = n$
4. $726 + 173 = n + 726$
5. $13 + 28 + 37 = n$
6. $98 + 22 = n$
7. $n + (5 + 43) = (65 + 5) + 43$
8. $257 + 15 + 13 = n$
9. $0 + n = 249$

Set B (pages 44–45)

Use compatible numbers or compensation.

1. $1 + 52 + 99$
2. $56 - 44$
3. $3 + 97 + 19$
4. $91 + 17 + 83$
5. $95 - 28$
6. $69 + 31 + 11$

7. A wall map was made from three pieces of cardboard—17 in. long, 25 in. long, and 13 in. long. How long was the wall map?

Set C (pages 46–47)

Using Algebra Follow the rule to complete each chart. Use mental math.

Rule: Add 5

	Input	Output
1.	35	■
2.	■	19
3.	95	■

Rule: Subtract 20

	Input	Output
4.	■	33
5.	■	45
6.	92	■

Rule: Add 10

	Input	Output
7.	■	181
8.	310	■
9.	58	■

Set D (pages 50–53)

Round each number to the greatest place to estimate.

1. $348 + 75$
2. $0.202 + 4.84$
3. $7,423 - 7,349$
4. $2,129 + 7,341$
5. $11.2 - 0.38$
6. $5,545 - 908$
7. $284.5 + 42$
8. $55,482 + 2,628$
9. $522,006 - 11,553$

10. Last year the Boonton Animal Shelter found homes for 796 cats and dogs. They found 385 homes for cats. About how many homes were found for dogs?

Extra Practice

Set E   (pages 54–55)

Estimate by using front-end estimation.

1. 520 + 433   **2.** 6,008 − 3,200   **3.** 836 − 271   **4.** 1,306 + 891

5. 822 − 315   **6.** 1,397 + 2,492   **7.** $29 + $13   **8.** $5.34 − $2.88

9. In 1994 about 8,628,170 people visited Great Smoky Mountain National Park, 4,364,320 visited the Grand Canyon, and 3,962,120 visited Yosemite. About how many people visited these parks that year?

10. On her camping trip, Lily drove 36.3 miles, bicycled 8.7 miles, and hiked 3.4 miles. About how many miles did she travel altogether?

Set F   (pages 60–63)

Add or subtract.

1. 3,435 + 8,357   **2.** 1,208 − 249   **3.** 76,372 + 26,175

4. 21,890 + 16,019   **5.** 6,296 − 1,821   **6.** 12,490 + 423,314

7. 54,266 − 25,854   **8.** 33,281 − 14,267   **9.** 96,603 − 29,111

10. Before a family left on a trip, they found that their odometer read 33,897 miles. After the trip it read 35,065 miles. How many miles did they travel?

Set G   (pages 66–67)

Find each sum.

1. 2.011 + 3.37   **2.** 5.06 + 8.13   **3.** 84.01 + 12.73   **4.** 7.242 + 3.1

5. $67.19 + $13.98   **6.** 29.63 + 4.21   **7.** 0.02 + 0.08   **8.** 31.99 + 6.03

9. 104.13 + 8.746   **10.** 56.03 + 9.72   **11.** 14.873 + 1.59   **12.** 83.96 + 42.81

13. 73.988 + 121.8   **14.** 391.83 + 8.17   **15.** 0.67 + 89.9   **16.** 0.039 + 0.390

17. It costs $9.95 for adults and $7.25 for children to go on a fishing trip. How much will it cost for Mr. Barnes and his eight-year-old son, Brian, to go?

Performance Assessment

Show What You Know About Whole Numbers and Decimals

Use the spinners for Questions 1 and 2.

What You Need

2 six-part spinners

1 **a.** Spin the whole number spinner twice. Find the sum and difference of the numbers you get.

Whole Numbers

4,578   143
8,908   780
12,562   1,055

b. Which two numbers would give you the sum nearest 1,000?

2 **a.** Spin the decimal spinner twice. Find the sum and difference of the numbers you get.

Decimal Numbers

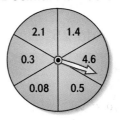

2.1   1.4
0.3   4.6
0.08   0.5

b. Which three decimals would give you the sum nearest 2?

Self-Check When adding or subtracting, did you remember to regroup when necessary?

3 The table shows the number of points five players scored playing a video game.

a. How many more points does Dave need to be in first place?

b. How many more points does Cathy need to score to reach one million points?

c. If Rose scores 752,481 more points, what will her total score be?

d. Write the two scores that are closest together.

Self-Check Did you remember to check your numbers against the numbers in the chart?

Top Five Video Scores	
Player	**Score**
Amie	456,584
Will	426,321
Cathy	406,816
Dave	388,652
Rose	368,043

 **For Your Portfolio**

You might wish to include this work in your portfolio.

Extension

Roman Numerals

The movie industry has experienced many important "firsts." Copyright dates for movies are shown as Roman numerals. Some of these are given in the table.

The Roman numeral system was created by the Romans about 500 B.C. It uses seven Roman letters as symbols to represent numbers.

	MOVIE FIRSTS	
Type	Movie	Date
Movie	The Great Train Robbery	MCMIII
Color Movie	The Toll of the Sea	MCMXXII
Talkie	The Jazz Singer	MCMXXVII
Full-Length Cartoon	Snow White and the Seven Dwarfs	MCMXXXVII

$$I = 1 \qquad C = 100$$
$$V = 5 \qquad D = 500$$
$$X = 10 \qquad M = 1,000$$
$$L = 50 \qquad \overline{V} = 5,000$$

To read and write Roman numerals, keep in mind these two simple rules.

Rule I The values of the Roman numeral symbols are added from left to right.

$$CCCLXVII = 300 + 50 + 10 + 5 + 2 = 367$$

Rule II You cannot have more than three of any one symbol in a row. For example, 4 is not IIII. Instead, you write a lesser number before a greater number and subtract the lesser from the greater.

$$IV = 5 - 1 = 4 \qquad\qquad IX = 10 - 1 = 9$$

1 Find the dates of the movie firsts in the table.

2 Write each as an Arabic numeral.

   a. CVIII   **b.** XCII   **c.** MLXVI

3 Write each as a Roman numeral.

   a. 1925   **b.** 473   **c.** the current year

4 **Create Your Own** Make up your own number system. Start by creating symbols for the numbers 1–10.

▲ **Social Studies Connection**
The symbols for Arabic numerals are believed to have been invented by peoples of India. Arabic numerals came into common use about 1500. A license plate with Arabic numbers and letters is shown here.

Chapter 3

Using Data and Statistics

Chapter Theme: INVENTIONS

·············Real Facts·················

Statistics show that most successful inventions are ones that we need! The dog washer shown here was invented by the student on page 85, one of several participants in a recent Silver Burdett Ginn Invention Convention. To protect an invention from being copied, an inventor must obtain a patent.

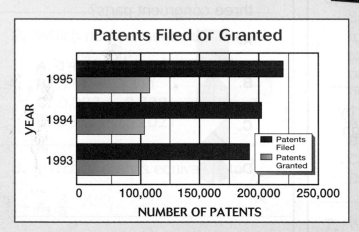

Patents Filed or Granted

Legend:
- Patents Filed
- Patents Granted

YEAR: 1995, 1994, 1993
NUMBER OF PATENTS: 0, 100,000, 150,000, 200,000, 250,000

- In which year were the most patents filed?

- Using the data in the graph, about how many more patents were filed in 1995 than in 1993? Explain.

··············Real People···················

Meet Martine Kempf. She invented Katalavox to make life easier for people with disabilities. Katalavox allows people to control a wheelchair, turn on lights, dial a phone, and more—all by voice command. This is an invention that is definitely needed!

A Brighter Smile!

A line plot and a frequency table are two ways to organize and display the results of a survey.

◄ **About 3000 B.C.**
The toothbrush was probably first used in Egypt around this time. It was in the form of a "chew stick."

◄ **About 1500 A.D.**
The bristles from the Siberian hog were used to make early toothbrushes.

Today Most modern toothbrushes have plastic bristles. ►

Learning About It

Work with a group.

Researchers for companies use **surveys** to find out what customers want. Decide on a topic to research and conduct a survey.

Word Bank

survey
line plot
frequency table

Step 1 Decide which students and how many students to survey.

Step 2 Develop a set of questions. The following question was used for a toothbrush survey of 14 people: What color toothbrush do you have?

Step 3 Collect and organize data.

Toothbrush Colors

```
X
X       X
X       X       X
X       X       X       X
X       X       X       X
Purple  Red     Blue    Other
```

Toothbrush Colors	
Response	**Number**
Purple	5
Red	4
Blue	3
Other	2

A **line plot** shows each response by marking *X*'s on a line above the choice.

A **frequency table** shows the total responses for each choice as a number.

Step 4 Analyze the data you collected. Draw one conclusion from your data. The toothbrush survey shows that more students had purple toothbrushes than any other color toothbrush.

Think and Discuss What other ways might you have collected and displayed your data?

Practice

Use the data you collected for Exercises 1–2.

1. **Discuss** Tell why you chose the method that you did to organize your data.

2. Based on the results of your survey, think of another question you would want to ask. Write the question. Then tell why.

Use the line plot and the frequency table below for Exercises 3–6.

Toothbrushing Habits

```
              X
              X
              X          X
       X      X          X
       X      X          X
       X      X          X
    _____
      Once    Twice    More than
     a day    a day   twice a day
```

Toothbrushing Habits	
Response	**Number**
Once a day	3
Twice a day	6
More than twice a day	5

3. How many people were surveyed?

4. How many more people brushed twice a day than once a day?

5. **Analyze** What question do you think the researcher asked?

6. **Journal Idea** What is the same about the line plot and frequency table? What is different? Explain.

7. **Create Your Own** Collect data. Then use your data to make a line plot. Have a classmate write one statement about the data.

Two-Wheelers

You can show two different sets of related data on the same graph with a double bar graph.

Learning About It

Bar graphs are used to show data that can be counted. A **double bar graph** uses two different shaded or colored bars to compare two sets of data.

This graph gives information about the costs of three different bicycles during two different years. The key shows which colored bars represent which years. The **axes** represent the brand and the cost.

Compare the heights of the two bars for each brand of bicycle.

- Bicycles D and S cost less in 1990 than in 1994.

- Bicycle B cost more in 1990 than in 1994.

Compare the bars for each year.

- Bicycle B was the most expensive in both years.

- Bicycle D was the least expensive in both years.

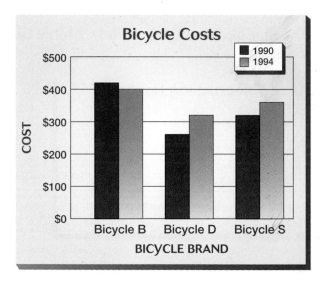

> **Word Bank**
>
> double bar graph
> axis (*pl.*, axes)

The 1827 velocipede was a bicycle with no pedals.

The "ordinary" was the most popular bicycle in the 1880s.

Connecting Ideas

You have learned how to read double bar graphs. You can use what you know to make a double bar graph.

The steps below show how to make a double bar graph using the data in the table.

Equipment Donated		
Equipment	Grade 5	Grade 6
Helmets	15	12
Water bottles	16	16
Air pumps	4	3
Reflector strips	30	24

Step 1 Draw the horizontal and vertical axes.

Step 2 Label the vertical axis.

Step 3 Choose a scale and label the horizontal axis. Think: Since the numbers range from 3 to 30, use an interval of 5 for the scale. Start with 0 where the axes intersect. Stop at 35.

Step 4 Draw, label, and shade the bars. Be sure all Grade 5 bars are one color and Grade 6 bars are a second color.

Step 5 Make a key. Title your graph. Make sure the colors in the key match the colors of the bars.

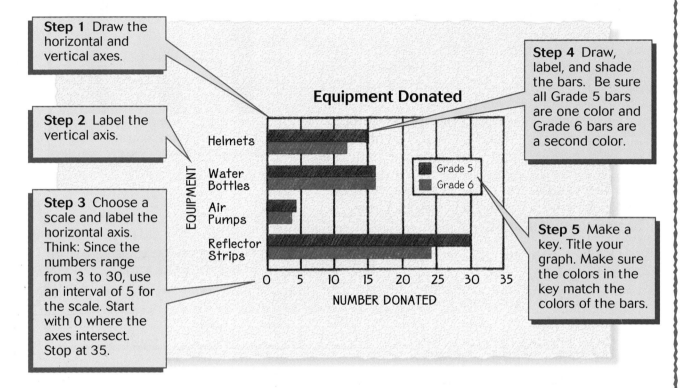

Think and Discuss Look at Step 3. Would an interval of 20 be useful? Tell why or why not. What intervals might be useful if the range were from 2 to 500? Explain.

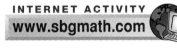

INTERNET ACTIVITY
www.sbgmath.com

Today's bicycle comes in a variety of styles, sizes, and colors.

This HPV, or *human-powered vehicle*, is the latest version of the bicycle.

Try It Out

Use the graph at the right for Exercises 1–5.

1. What are the labels for each axis?

2. What does each pair of bars represent?

3. What does the key tell you?

4. What does the title tell you about the graph?

5. Which helmet was the most expensive? least expensive? Tell how you know.

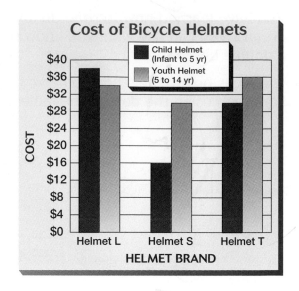

Use the data in the table at the right to make your own double bar graph. Then answer Exercises 6–8.

6. What is the title of your graph?

7. What labels did you use for the axes?

8. What interval did you use for the hours of bicycle repairs? Tell why.

Hours of Bicycle Repairs						
Kind of Bike	Mon.	Tues.	Wed.	Thurs.	Fri.	Sat.
Racing	5	7	3	7	4	8
Mountain	7	10	5	2	11	14

Practice

Use the bar graph at the right to answer Exercises 9–12.

9. What does each bar represent?

10. In which store is the difference in cost between the backpacks the greatest?

11. **Analyze** What is the difference in cost between the types of backpacks at Life Outdoors?

12. **Explain** If you bought a canvas backpack and a nylon one at Camp Out, would you spend more or less than if you bought them at Sports Plus? Explain your answer.

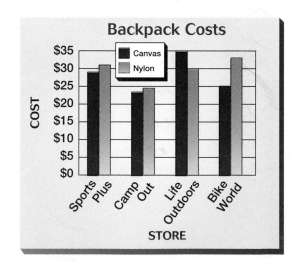

All-terrain wheelchair ➤

All-Terrain Wheelchairs		
Model	Brand X	Brand Y
A-Frame	$2,395	$2,500
T-Tube	$2,250	$2,235
Chrome	$2,050	$2,055

Use the table above for Exercises 13–16.

13. Make a double bar graph from the data in the table. Include a key.

14. What information is shown in the key?

15. What does each bar represent?

16. What does the graph show?

Problem Solving

Use the graph at the right for Problems 17–20.

17. What was the total number of riders in the 9–12 age group?

18. What was the total number of riders using racing bikes?

19. How many ages are represented by each age group? Might this make a difference in the number of riders shown in the graph? Explain your reasoning.

20. Analyze In which class of bicycles was there the greatest difference between the number of riders in the two age groups? Tell how you know.

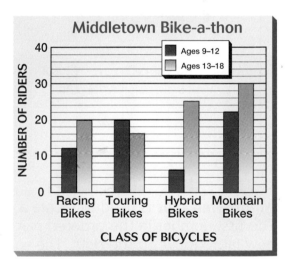

Review and Remember

Find each answer. Estimate to make sure your answer is reasonable.

21. 12,987 − 987

22. 234 × 3

23. 9,835 − 1,290

24. 1,265 + 10,478

25. 555 ÷ 5

26. 8,745,753 − 999,701

27. 532.7 − 62.48

28. 621 × 4

29. 4.735 + 16.85

For Extra Practice, see Set A, page 120.

Using Algebra

Get to the Point

You can use ordered pairs to locate points on a grid.

Learning About It

The fifth graders at West School placed a grid over a map of the United States to help locate the states where several inventions originated.

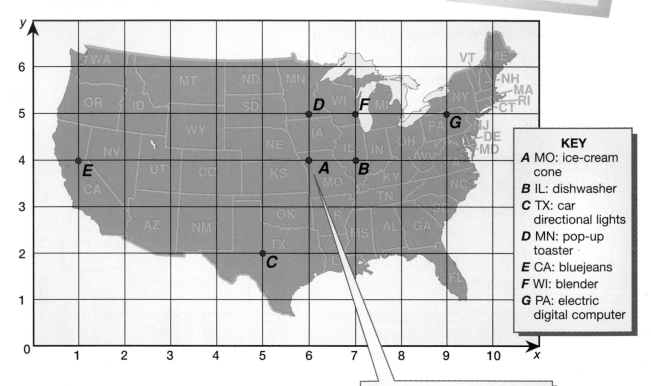

KEY

A MO: ice-cream cone
B IL: dishwasher
C TX: car directional lights
D MN: pop-up toaster
E CA: bluejeans
F WI: blender
G PA: electric digital computer

The ordered pair (6, 4) helps locate Missouri, the state where ice-cream cones were invented. The two numbers 6 and 4 are called **coordinates**.

An **ordered pair** is used to locate a point. The first number in the ordered pair tells how far to move to the right. The second number tells how far to move up.

The point named by the ordered pair (6, 4) is 6 units to the right and 4 units up. On the grid above, (6, 4) is point *A*.

Find the invention at (5, 2).

- Start at 0.

- Move 5 spaces to the right. Then move 2 spaces up. The invention at (5, 2), point *C*, is the car directional lights.

Write the ordered pair for point *B*, which shows where the dishwasher was invented.

- Start at 0.

- Count 7 spaces to the right. Point *B* is 7 spaces to the right of 0.

- Count 4 spaces up. Point *B* is 4 spaces above 0.

- Write the ordered pair (7, 4).

Connecting Ideas

Use what you have learned about locating and naming points on a coordinate grid to plot points on a coordinate grid.

Work with your partner.

Step 1 Draw a horizontal axis and a vertical axis on grid paper. Number each axis from 0 to 10 as shown on the grid at the right.

Step 2 Locate, mark, and label these points.

point *A* (1, 2)

point *B* (2, 4)

point *C* (3, 6)

point *D* (4, 8)

point *E* (5, 10)

Step 3 Look for patterns in the ordered pairs. What do you notice?

- Compare the first numbers in the pairs.

- Compare the second numbers in the pairs.

- Compare the first number to the second number in each ordered pair.

Step 4 On your graph, connect the points *A*, *B*, *C*, *D*, and *E* in order. Describe how your graph looks.

Think and Discuss If the pattern continued, what would the next point be? Explain.

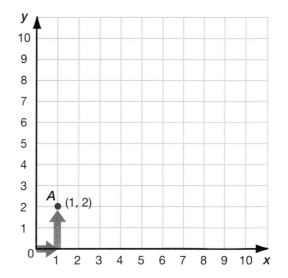

▲ **Kid Connection** Lizzie Gray, a fifth-grade student from Ohio, invented the "Flip-o-Matic." This is a music stand that allows you to use your foot to turn the pages of your music.

To locate (1, 2) on the grid
- Start at 0.
- Move 1 space to the right.
- Move 2 spaces up.

Try It Out

Use the map and the key at the right for Exercises 1–8. Write the ordered pair that locates the state that is home to each invention.

1. adhesive bandage

2. peanut butter

3. traffic signal

4. telephone

Name the invention from the state located by each ordered pair.

5. (7, 13)   6. (1, 10)

7. (3, 8)   8. (6, 11)

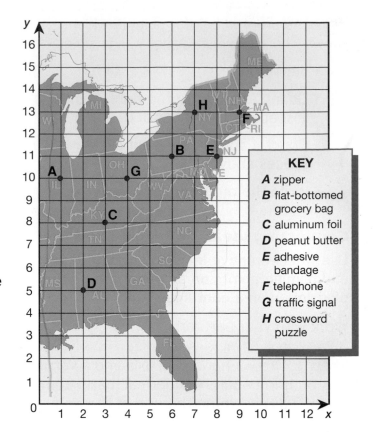

KEY

A zipper
B flat-bottomed grocery bag
C aluminum foil
D peanut butter
E adhesive bandage
F telephone
G traffic signal
H crossword puzzle

Practice

Use grid paper for Exercises 9–16.

9. Graph the ordered pairs (3, 1), (3, 4), and (5, 1). Name the ordered pair that would form a rectangle.

10. **Analyze** Is it important which coordinate is written first in an ordered pair? Tell why or why not.

Graph each ordered pair. Label the points *A*, *B*, *C*, *D*, *E*, and *F*.

11. *A* (1, 8)   12. *B* (2, 3)   13. *C* (8, 4)

14. *D* (5, 0)   15. *E* (0, 5)   16. *F* (3, 2)

Use the grid at the right for Exercises 17–30. Write the ordered pair for each point.

17. *A*   18. *B*   19. *C*   20. *D*

21. *E*   22. *F*   23. *G*   24. *H*

Name the point located by each ordered pair.

25. (11, 1)   26. (6, 5)   27. (5, 2)

28. (10, 10)   29. (3, 9)   30. (9, 6)

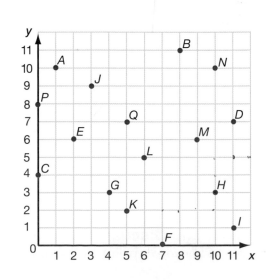

Problem Solving

31. Carol draws a path starting at (6, 2). She moves 4 spaces to the right, 3 spaces up, and 2 spaces to the right.

    a. On what point does she stop?

    b. If each space is 1 cm, how long is her path?

32. Use straight lines to print your first name on grid paper. Write directions to draw it, using ordered pairs. Have a classmate use the directions to draw your name.

Review and Remember

Give the place and the value of the 8 in each number.

33. 12,789   **34.** 0.098   **35.** 78.97

36. 187,904   **37.** 16.81   **38.** 8,976,345

39. 1.286   **40.** 0.82   **41.** 1,381,309

▲ Garrett Morgan, inventor of the automatic traffic signal; a sketch of Morgan's invention

Critical Thinking Corner

Visual Thinking

Using Patterns

Using Algebra Draw the next three figures in each pattern, or use cubes. Then write a rule that relates the number of squares in each figure to its position in the pattern.

Finally, use the rule to tell the number of squares in the tenth figure in each pattern.

1.

2.

Hint Make a table to find the rule.

Position Number	Number of Squares
1	1
2	4
3	9
⋮	⋮

For Extra Practice, see Set B, page 120.

Developing Skills for
Problem Solving

First read for understanding and then focus on interpreting line graphs without numbers.

READY FOR UNDERSTANDING

Cars have changed a lot over time. One thing, though, has not changed. Nearly everyone loves to travel! The line graph at the right tells a story about a car trip.

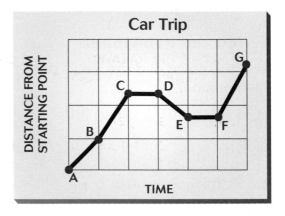

Car Trip

1. What does the line on the graph represent?

2. At what point is the car furthest from the starting point?

THINK AND DISCUSS

 MATH FOCUS

Understanding Line Graphs A line graph shows change over time. How a line slants and how steep the line is are visual clues to interpreting the graph.

3. Between points *A* and *B*, the line rises. Is the car moving away from or nearer to the starting point?

4. Between points *C* and *D*, the line does not rise or fall. Has time passed? Is the car moving?

5. Between points *D* and *E*, the line falls. Is the car moving further away from or closer to the starting point?

6. Do you think it is always necessary to have numbers on a graph to learn something from the graph? Why or why not?

7. **You Decide** Write a story telling what the line graph tells you about the trip.

Show What You Learned

Answer each question. Give a reason for your choice.

Miguel's mother belongs to a car pool. On her days to drive, she takes Miguel and some of his classmates from her home to their school. The graph shows one of these trips. Use the graph at the right for Problems 1–5.

1 Which point shows Miguel's home?

    a. Point *A*

    b. Point *D*

    c. Point *E*

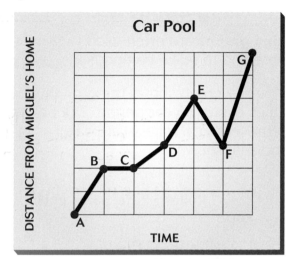

Car Pool

2 Which of the following best describes what happened between points *F* and *G*?

    a. The car stopped.

    b. The car continued moving until it reached the school.

    c. The car went back home.

3 Which of the following describes what may have happened from point *B* to *C*?

    a. Miguel and his mother waited for a classmate.

    b. Miguel's mother stopped for gas.

    c. Both of the above

4 **Explain** What happened between points *E* and *F*? Tell how you know.

5 Besides the events described in Questions 1–4, what are two other events that occurred during this trip?

▲ **1914** Ford Model T Speedster   ▲ **1957** Thunderbird   ▲ **1992** Blitz Electric Car

Roll-a-Long

Using Algebra

Understanding line graphs can help you draw conclusions about trends and changes over time.

Learning About It

Line graphs are often used to show changes over time and to make comparisons.

This line graph shows the growth of roller skate sales over a 5-year period. The points on the graph represent total roller-skate sales as of January 1 of the year shown.

Word Bank

line graph

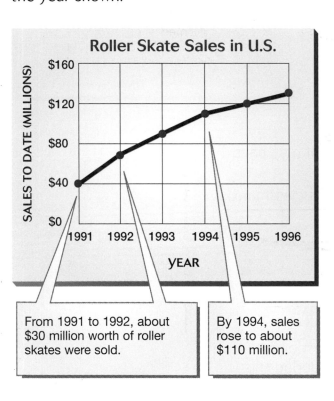

Roller Skate Sales in U.S.

SALES TO DATE (MILLIONS)

$160
$120
$80
$40
$0

1991 1992 1993 1994 1995 1996

YEAR

From 1991 to 1992, about $30 million worth of roller skates were sold.

By 1994, sales rose to about $110 million.

▲ **1760** The earliest roller skate consisted of wooden wheels attached along the center of the skate.

▲ **1879** The four-wheel skate had wooden wheels and ball bearings.

- About $10 million worth of skates were sold during 1994.

- By 1995, $120 million worth of roller skates had been sold.

Think and Discuss By which year had about $90 million worth of roller skates been sold? Explain how you know.

▲ **Today** The in-line skate is fast, sleek, and very quiet.

Try It Out

Use the graph on page 98 for Exercises 1–5.

1. By what year had about $130 million worth of roller skates been sold?

2. Between which two years was the greatest increase in roller skate sales?

3. What can be said about the increase in sales from 1992 to 1993 and from 1993 to 1994? Explain your answer.

4. About how many millions of dollars worth of roller skates were sold from 1991 to 1996?

5. **Analyze** Did sales increase faster from 1991 to 1992 or from 1995 to 1996? Explain your answer.

▲ **Kid Connection** Jeff Meredith invented wheel covers for roller skates. With this invention you can skate indoors or outdoors.

Practice

Use the graph below for Exercises 6–9.

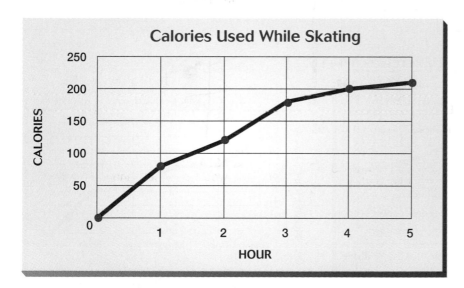

6. How many hours are represented in the graph?

7. About how many calories were burned after 2 hours of skating?

8. About how many more calories had been burned after 4 hours than after 1 hour? after 5 hours than after 2 hours?

9. During which hour did the skater burn the most calories? the fewest? What do you notice about the line on the graph in each case?

Use the graph below for Exercises 10–12.

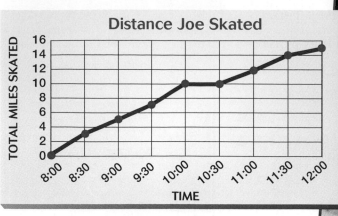

Distance Joe Skated

10. About how many miles did Joe skate between 9:30 and 10:00?

11. What happened between 10:00 and 10:30? How do you know?

▲ **Health and Fitness Connection**
Skating is both fun and good for you.

12. In which hour intervals did Joe skate the greatest number of miles? About how many miles did he skate each of those hours?

13. Do you think a table or a line graph gives you a better idea of changes over time? Explain.

Problem Solving

Use the graphs below for Exercises 14–16.

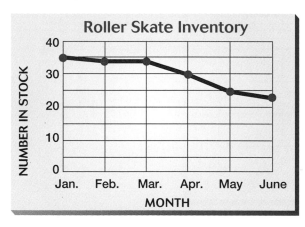

Roller Skate Inventory

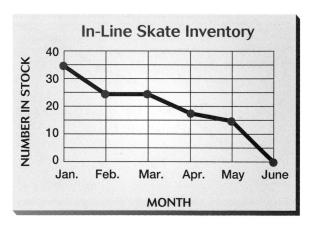

In-Line Skate Inventory

14. Compare the in-line skate and the roller skate inventories in January. Then compare the inventories in June. Describe your findings.

15. Between which two months did the greatest number of roller skates sell? in-line skates? How many of each sold during these months?

16. What If? Suppose 20 more pairs of roller skates were sold in May. How would the graph change?

Irma and her friends skated from one end of the park to the other. Use the graph for Problems 17–18.

17. Between which two times did Irma stop to take a rest? How can you tell from the graph?

18. Explain Irma dropped her water bottle during the trip. She went back to look for it and then continued on after she found it. How is this shown on the line graph?

19. You Decide Suppose you want a snack. You can buy juice—$0.55, fruit—$0.25, or nuts—$0.39. What would you buy and how much change would you get from $5?

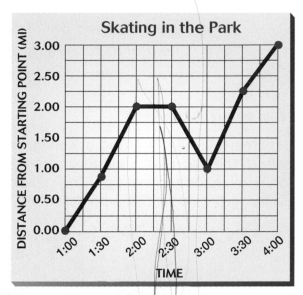

Skating in the Park

Review and Remember

Find each sum or difference.

20.	**21.**	**22.**	**23.**	**24.**
2.34 + 0.99	13.8 − 1.23	21.131 − 2.77	4.87 + 3.11	23.5 + 4.61

25.	**26.**	**27.**	**28.**	**29.**
5.66 − 3.4	25.256 + 1.35	6.78 − 1.97	90.1 + 21.9	10.01 − 9.94

Money $ense

It Makes Cents!

For lunch, Gina is having soup, a large salad, a small glass of milk, and a piece of pie. She doesn't want any pennies as change, so she plans to give the cashier the money shown. How much change should she receive?

Guest Check
soup $0.95
salad   4.25
milk   0.65
pie   1.20
subtotal $7.05
tax   0.34
Total:

For Extra Practice, see Set C, page 121.

Super Saucer

You have learned how to read line graphs. Sometimes it is helpful to make a graph to interpret a set of data.

Learning About It

In the early 1900s, a group of college students realized that the empty pie tins from the Frisbie Pie Company made fascinating flying devices. This is how the flying disc was accidentally invented.

What You Need

For each student:
  straightedge
  grid paper

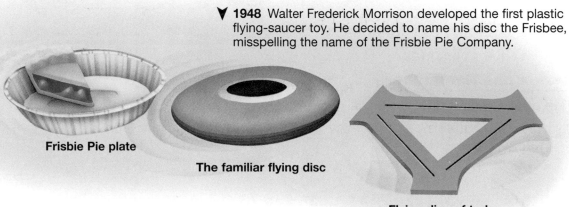

▼ **1948** Walter Frederick Morrison developed the first plastic flying-saucer toy. He decided to name his disc the Frisbee, misspelling the name of the Frisbie Pie Company.

Frisbie Pie plate

The familiar flying disc

Flying disc of today

To raise money, Central Middle School sells flying discs printed with the school's name. The table and graph show the sales history of the flying discs.

Flying Disc Sales	
Year	Money Raised to Date
1990	$150
1991	$375
1992	$400
1993	$500
1994	$655
1995	$800

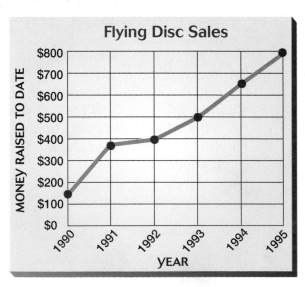

Notice that the titles and labels of the table and graph are the same. The data displayed is also the same. The table shows the data by using numbers, and the graph shows the data with points connected by lines.

Work with your partner. Follow these steps to make a line graph of the number of flying discs printed from 9:00 A.M. to 12:00 P.M.

Disc Printing	
Time	Number of Discs
9:00	0
10:00	10
11:00	30
12:00	45

Step 1 Draw and label each axis.

Step 2 Use a scale with intervals of 10 for the vertical axis. Because the numbers range from 0 to 45, begin with 0 and stop at 50.

Step 3 Mark points on the line graph as you do on a coordinate graph. Start at 0, move right to the time, and then move up to the number of discs printed by that time.

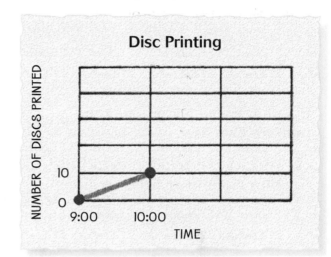

Step 4 Connect the points in order.

Step 5 Title your graph.

Think and Discuss Would it be useful to mark intervals of 1 on the vertical axis? intervals of 25? Why or why not?

Practice

Use the table below for Exercises 1–2.

1. The fifth grade is packing flying discs in bags to sell at the football game. Make a line graph of the data. Put the time on the horizontal axis and the number of bags packed on the vertical axis.

2. Explain why you chose the intervals you did for the vertical axis.

3. **Create Your Own** Collect your own data about one of the following topics. Create a line graph to display your data. Tell one thing your graph shows.

   • The hours spent watching television in a week

   • The growth of a plant over a month

   • The hours spent using a computer in a week

   • The hours spent reading in a week

Disc Packing					
Time	12:00	12:30	1:00	1:30	2:00
Number of bags	0	7	7	16	20

Checkpoint

Reading and Making Graphs

Make a line plot using the data in Exercise 1. Then answer the question. (pages 86–87)

1. Several students were asked how many compact discs they owned. Three students owned 4 CDs; six owned 5 CDs; eight owned 6; and five students owned 7 CDs. How many students were surveyed?

Use the double bar graph at the right for Exercises 2–4. (pages 88–91)

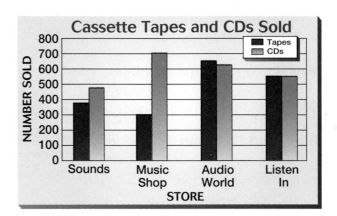

2. Which store sold the most CDs? How many did it sell?

3. About how many cassette tapes did Audio World sell?

4. Which store sold the same number of CDs and cassette tapes? How do you know?

Use the table for Exercises 5–6. (pages 88–91)

5. Make a double bar graph. Be sure to include a key.

6. Compare the pairs of bars. Write a statement about what the graph shows.

Kinds of Recordings Owned		
Audio Device	Fifth Graders	Teachers
Cassette tape	13	25
Record	3	30
CD	25	12

Using Algebra Use the grid for Exercises 7–18. Name the point or write the ordered pair for each location. (pages 92–95)

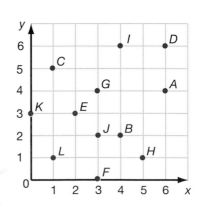

7. (2, 3)　　8. (6, 4)　　9. D

10. C　　11. G　　12. (3, 0)

13. (4, 6)　　14. B　　15. H

16. K　　17. (3, 2)　　18. L

Use the line graph for Exercises 19–23.
(pages 98–101)

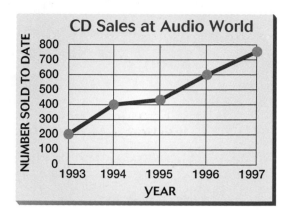

CD Sales at Audio World

19. How many CDs were sold by 1994?

20. By 1997, about how many CDs had been sold?

21. Between which two years did sales increase the least?

22. About how many CDs were sold between 1995 and 1996?

23. Between which two years was the greatest increase in sales?

Problem Solving

24. Sarah used a line graph to display information about the number of CDs she owned by different artists. Is a line graph a good choice to display this data? Why or why not?

25. The cost of a CD, including tax, is $18.01. Cassette tapes cost $9.53 including tax. If you bought one of each, how much change should you receive from $30.00?

What do you think?

Explain how a double bar graph helps you to compare data at a glance.

Journal Idea

When is it better to use a bar graph instead of a line graph? Explain your reasoning.

Critical Thinking Corner

Logical Thinking

What's Wrong?

Kenneth and Jan live on a straight road exactly 5 miles apart. One day, Kenneth rides his bike 3 miles toward Jan's house. At the same time, Jan rides her bike 1 mile toward Kenneth's house. They are now exactly 4 miles apart. What's wrong with the last statement?

Problem Solving
Make a Graph

Making the appropriate graph provides an easy way to interpret data and help solve a problem.

One hundred adults and 100 students were surveyed about inventors. The results are shown in the table at the right. Which group could identify the most inventors?

Who Invented It		
Invention	Number of Correct Answers	
	Adults	Students
Telephone	88	88
Propeller airplane	87	59
Rocket engine	85	51
Compact disc	62	81

 UNDERSTAND

What do you need to find?

You need to find which group could identify the most inventors.

 PLAN

How can you solve the problem?

The data may be easier to interpret if you **make a graph**. Choose the most appropriate graph. Then use the graph to solve the problem.

	Line Graph Since the data is not data over time, a line graph is not a good choice.
	Pictograph Since the data is not multiples, a pictograph is not a good choice.
	Bar Graph A double bar graph makes it easy to compare the two groups.

 SOLVE

Make a double bar graph. Compare the pairs of bars where adults identified more inventors with the pairs of bars where students identified more. This shows that the adults identified more inventors.

 LOOK BACK

Why does a double bar graph make it easy to compare the two groups?

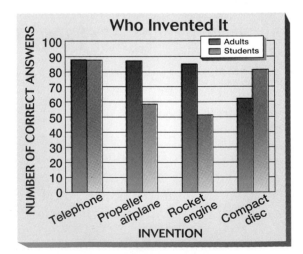

Using the Strategy

Make an appropriate graph to represent the data about computer boxes. Then use your graph to solve Problems 1–2.

1 In which interval of 1 hour were the greatest number of computer boxes packed?

2 In which hour were the fewest computer boxes packed? Why do you think so?

Computer Boxes Packed	
Time	Cumulative Total
9:00	0
10:00	20
11:00	60
12:00	83
1:00	88
2:00	120

Make an appropriate graph to represent the data about CDs purchased. Then use your graph to solve Problems 3–4.

3 **Explain** Would you say that the two age groups prefer the same kinds of music? How do you know?

4 **Analyze** Compare the data for the two age groups. Write a story about what is similar and what is different about their purchases.

CDs Purchased		
Type	Ages 9–10	Ages 13–17
Rock	37	38
Country	8	28
Classical	9	10
Jazz	12	30
Reggae	32	9

Mixed Strategy Review

Try these or other strategies to solve each problem. Tell which strategy you used.

THERE'S ALWAYS A WAY!

Problem Solving Strategies

- Draw a Diagram
- Write an Equation
- Find a Pattern
- Work Backwards

5 The first auto race, which was 50 miles long, was held in Chicago in 1895. The winning car, a Duryea, traveled at an average speed of 9 miles per hour. About how long did it take the car to finish the race?

6 **What If?** Cars are lined up black, black, red, black, black, red. If this pattern continues, what will be the color of the thirty-fourth car?

▲ **Social Studies Connection** The first successful gasoline-powered car, built by J. Frank Duryea

107

Using Algebra

It's a Shoe-In!

You have used several graphs in this chapter. Now you will learn ways to change how data in a graph looks.

Learning About It

Today, sneakers are so common that we forget they were invented long ago.

South and Central Americans covered their feet with rubbery tree sap.

Modern sneakers come in many styles and with many types of soles.

The graphs below show data about sneakers worn by fifth graders. Compare the graphs. What do you notice?

Graph A

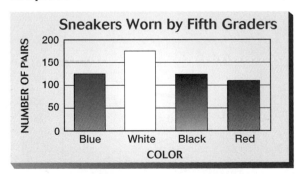

In this graph, you can easily see that more than 100 students wore red sneakers.

Graph B

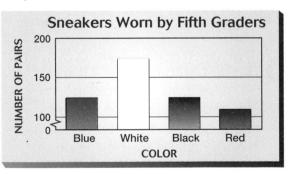

This graph shows the data by using a broken axis. It makes it appear that very few students wore red sneakers.

Sometimes the same information can appear to look different because of how the graph is made. Why do you think a graph might be made to look a particular way?

Connecting Ideas

You have learned that using a broken axis can change a graph's appearance. Changing the scale can also change how a graph looks.

Compare the graphs below. What do you notice about the lines? about the intervals on the scales?

Graph A

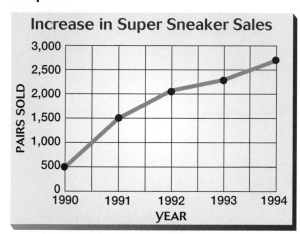

A shoe store produced Graph A to convince people that Super Sneaker sales have increased greatly.

Graph B

A competitor used the same data to create Graph B.

The interval of 500 in Graph A makes it look as if there were a greater increase in sales than the interval of 1,000 in Graph B.

Think and Discuss Look again at Graph B. What do you think the competitor was trying to show about Super Sneaker sales? Explain.

Try It Out

Use the graph at the right.

1. What does this graph seem to show about the sale of shoes of various sizes?

2. How many more pairs of size 5 shoes were sold than pairs of size 6 shoes?

3. **What If?** Suppose the number of different-sized shoes sold is about the same. How would you change the graph?

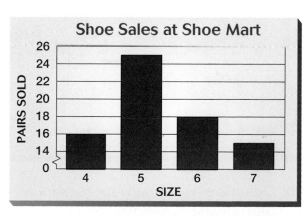

Practice

Use the graph at the right for Exercises 4–6.

4. About how many students preferred each of the different colors of sneakers?

5. What does this graph seem to show about the favorite colors of sneakers in this fifth-grade class?

6. **Describe** How would you change this graph to show that almost no students prefer red sneakers? Explain your answer.

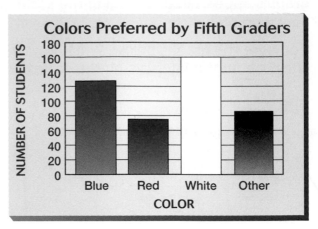

Problem Solving

Use the data in the table for Problems 7–9.

7. Draw a bar graph that shows that Our Brand and the competitors' brands cost about the same.

8. Draw a bar graph that shows that Competitor B's price is much more expensive.

9. **Describe** How are the graphs you constructed in Problems 7 and 8 different?

Sneaker Costs	
Our Brand	$38
Competitor A	$43
Competitor B	$58
Competitor C	$50

Use the pictograph for Problems 10–11.

10. **Describe** How many more pairs of blue sneakers and white sneakers were sold than the other colors? Tell how you found your answer.

11. **Using Mental Math** How many more pairs of white sneakers were sold than blue sneakers? than black sneakers?

Choose a Method Use mental math, paper and pencil, or a calculator to solve each problem.

12. Tara bought two pairs of socks for $8.25. One pair cost twice as much as the other. How much did she pay for each pair?

13. A store had 12 pairs of sneakers of one brand. It received 48 more pairs and then sold 16. How many pairs does the store now have?

Review and Remember

Find each answer.

14. 134
× 7

15. 4,289
+ 6,472

16. 25.08
− 12.92

17. 723
× 8

18. 25.2
− 9.35

19. 625
832
+ 756

20. 9,824
576
+ 1,275

21. 39.92
16.3
+ 68.78

22. 25.2
− 9.3

23. 1,879
+ 99

24. 181 × 4

25. 448 ÷ 4

26. 123 × 8

27. 2.85 + 3.6

28. 2)264

29. 9.2 − 8.3

30. 9 × 891

31. 65.1 − 0.28

Time for Technology

Using the MathProcessor™ CD-ROM

Changing a Graph

Sometimes the same information can appear to look different because of how a graph is made.

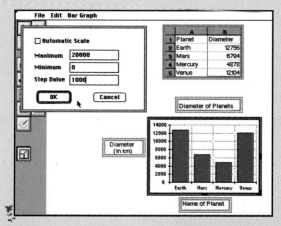

- Open or remake the spreadsheet and graph from Time for Technology on page 9.

- Click on the graph. Click ⊞ to open the scaling window.

- Click in the box by Automatic Scale. The *X* disappears.

- Explore what happens to the graph as you change the values in the scaling window. Click OK to enter values and change the graph.

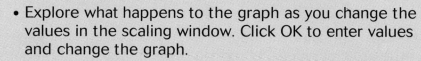

For Extra Practice, see Set D, page 121.

Got the Blues?

You have learned that data can be organized in many ways.
Making a stem-and-leaf plot is another way to organize information.

About 1750 Sturdy canvas was first used on covered wagons.

1849 Levi Strauss created the first jeans from canvas. His first customers were miners.

Today Jeans are usually made of denim.

Learning About It

Bluejeans are sometimes sold by waist size measured in inches. The bluejeans in stock at an army-navy store are listed below.

31, 32, 41, 44, 33, 21, 22, 32, 36, 37, 42, 29

A **stem-and-leaf plot** provides a concise way to organize many numbers by their front digits. This allows for easy interpretation of numerical data.

Before making a plot, it is useful to list the data in order from least to greatest.

21, 22, 29, 31, 32, 32, 33, 36, 37, 41, 42, 44

Word Bank

stem-and-leaf plot
stem
leaves

Stem	Leaves
2	1 2 9
3	1 2 2 3 6 7
4	1 2 4

Record the tens digits in order from least to greatest (20, 30, 40) to the left of the vertical line.

For each tens digit, record the ones digits from least to greatest to the right of the vertical line.

Think and Discuss Use the stem-and-leaf plot. What can you conclude about the sizes of bluejeans that are in stock? Explain your answer.

Try It Out

Use the stem-and-leaf plot on page 112 for Exercises 1–2.

1. How can you tell from the plot how many bluejeans are in stock?
2. How many bluejeans have a 32-inch waist?
3. List the following data from least to greatest: 36, 57, 25, 35, 36, 58, 49, 46.
4. Make a stem-and-leaf plot for the data in Exercise 3.

Practice

Use the stem-and-leaf plot on page 112 for Exercises 5–6.

5. How many bluejeans have a waist of 31 inches or greater? How do you know?
6. How many bluejeans have a waist of less than 30 inches?
7. List the following data from least to greatest: 11, 24, 39, 32, 37, 18, 19, 10, 22, 47, 49, 18, 22, 34, 5.
8. Make a stem-and-leaf plot for the data in Exercise 7.

Problem Solving

Make a stem-and-leaf plot using the data shown at the right. Use the plot for Problems 9–10.

Number of Times Each Student Wore Jeans in One Month

28, 20, 11, 9, 6, 21, 28, 15, 16, 17, 11, 11, 5, 21, 2, 9, 22, 15, 6, 12, 15, 17, 20, 21

9. How can you tell from the stem-an-leaf plot the number of students who wore bluejeans more than 10 times in a month?
10. How does the stem-and-leaf plot show that two or more students wore jeans the same number of times?
11. **Journal Idea** Find a set of data with at least 15 numbers. Display the data in a stem-and-leaf plot and describe something you learned from the plot.

Review and Remember

Find each answer.

12. 127.8 + 6.1
13. 784.27 − 622.17
14. 13.205 + 6.013
15. 1.704 − 1.521
16. 127.43 + 32.78
17. 32 × 4
18. 96 ÷ 12
19. 44 × 3
20. 42 ÷ 6
21. 6 × 80
22. 77 ÷ 11
23. 111 × 9
24. 63 ÷ 7
25. 19 × 5
26. 76 ÷ 4

For Extra Practice, see Set E, page 122.

Sticky Stuff

Graphs are one way to look at data. Another way is to look at the range, mode, and median.

Learning About It

▲ Science Connection
Velcro was invented in 1958 by George de Mestral. He was inspired by observing the hooks on the burs of the burdock plant.

A fifth-grade class is looking for as many different uses as possible for Velcro. Fifteen students do a scavenger hunt to answer the question, "How many uses of Velcro can you find?"

Here are the responses of the 15 students.
1, 2, 2, 2, 2, 3, 3, 4, 5, 5, 6, 6, 6, 8, 8

Statistics is the science of working with data. The **range**, **mode**, and **median** are all statistical measures that can be read from a line plot.

The **range** is the difference between the greatest and the least numbers. 8 − 1 = 7, so the range is 7.

> **Word Bank**
>
> range
> mode
> median

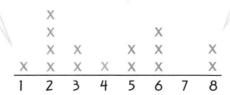

The **mode** is the number that occurs most often. The mode is 2, because it occurs most often.

The **median** is the middle number when the numbers are arranged in order. There are 15 numbers. The middle number is the eighth number, or 4.

More Examples

A. 1, 2, 2, 2, 3, 3, 4, 4, 4, 5, 6

range: $6 - 1 = 5$
modes: 2 and 4
median: 3

> 2 and 4 both occur three times, so there are two modes.

B. 9, 12, 12, 13, 13, 13, 15, 16, 17

range: $17 - 9 = 8$
mode: 13
median: 13

> Sometimes the mode and the median are the same.

Think and Discuss What can you say about the data collected if the range is a large number?

Try It Out

Find the range, median, and mode for each set of data.

1. 10, 12, 11, 14, 11, 11, 15   **2.** 5, 8, 1, 2, 3, 2, 1   **3.** 96, 100, 88, 88, 95

Practice

Find the range, median, and mode for each set of data.

4. 76, 77, 69, 80, 77   **5.** 2, 1, 7, 9, 7, 5, 4   **6.** 35, 32, 21, 55, 55

Problem Solving

The table shows how many times students used sticky materials in one week. Use the table for Problems 7–8.

7. **Describe** Find the range, median, and mode. Tell how you found each number.

8. **Explain** Suppose you used sticky materials six times a week. Are there more people in this survey who used sticky materials more times or fewer times than you? Explain.

9. **Analyze** The range of four numbers is 12. Three of the numbers are 28, 35, and 37. What is the fourth number? Tell what strategy you used to find your answer.

Use of Sticky Materials	
Students	Times Used in 1 Week
Jorge	9
Bill	5
Lee	7
Elena	9
Joyce	9
Aisha	10
Darryl	5

Review and Remember

Using Algebra Compare. Write >, <, or = for each ●.

10. 3×8 ● $21 \div 1$

11. $10.31 + 5.06$ ● 9×2

12. $14.6 - 2.3$ ● $8.1 + 4.5$

13. $33.8 - 10.2$ ● $45.9 - 23.1$

14. 2×3 ● $18 \div 3$

15. $16.5 - 3.3$ ● $18.8 - 5.4$

For Extra Practice, see Set F, page 122.

Problem Solving
Ways to Represent Data

Choosing the right way to organize and display data will make it easier to interpret data and solve problems.

A school is buying a clock that will hang above the cafeteria doors. Students are being surveyed on their preference for a digital or an analog clock. Based on this survey, should the school buy a digital or an analog clock?

 ### UNDERSTAND
What do you need to find?

You need to find out whether the school should buy a digital or an analog clock.

 ### PLAN
How can you solve the problem?

You might organize the data in a table or you might make a double bar graph.

 ### SOLVE

Both a table and a double bar graph are shown. By looking at both the table and the graph, you can tell that Grades 1 and 2 do not have much of a difference in their preferences. All other grades, except for Grade 5, prefer a digital clock. So the school should buy a digital clock.

Clock Preferences		
	Digital	**Analog**
Grade 1	13	14
Grade 2	15	13
Grade 3	20	11
Grade 4	25	6
Grade 5	12	20
Grade 6	21	11

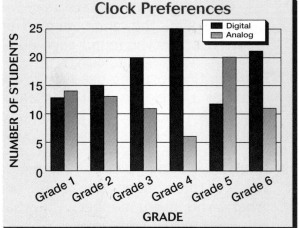

 ### LOOK BACK

Did you find it easier to use a table or a graph? Why?

▲ Sundials have been used to tell time since about 1500 B.C.

▲ This 1800s clock is at the Musee d'Orsay in Paris, France.

▲ A modern digital clock does not need sunlight or hands that move to show the time.

Show What You Learned

Organize and display the data for Problems 1–7. Explain your choices.

1 Answers to the question, "How many years have you owned your watch?"
Student A—7 yr   Student B—6 yr,
Student C—2 yr   Student D—1 yr,
Student E—2 yr   Student F—0 yr

2 Watch sales for December:
Digital with stopwatch—$3,654
Pocket watch—$1,879
Analog with date and time—$2,959
Necklace watch—$1,987

3 The total number of multiplication facts a fifth grader memorized by the end of the month: September, 10; October, 15; November, 28; December, 36; January, 40; February, 45; March, 48; April, 50; May, 53; June, 100

4 The school principal is looking for ways to reduce late arrivals at school. She asked each student to keep a record of the number of late arrivals for one month. Here are the records of 10 students: 0, 6, 4, 1, 3, 0, 0, 7, 0, 2

5 Five students were asked, "How many digital and analog clocks do you have in your home?" The responses were as follows.
Student A: 4 analog, 3 digital   Student B: 2 analog, 6 digital
Student C: 7 analog, 5 digital   Student D: 4 analog, 5 digital
Student E: 2 analog, 4 digital   Student F: 5 analog, 3 digital

6 Scores on a telling-time test: 64, 72, 80, 92, 100, 92, 80, 72, 88, 64, 92, 94, 98, 88, 68, 78, 76, 100, 100, 96, 98

7 **Create Your Own** Survey students about preferences for such things as food, music, and colors. After displaying your data, write a few sentences about it.

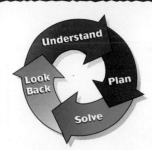

Problem Solving

Practice What You Learned

Choose the correct letter for each answer.

1 Monday through Friday the temperatures were 28°F, 29.5°F, 31°F, 32.5°F, and 34°F. If this pattern continues, what will the temperature be next Tuesday?

Tip

Use *Find a Pattern* to help you solve this problem.

A. 37°F
B. 38.5°F
C. 40°F
D. 41.5°F
E. Not Here

2 Here are the ages of a group of children at a day care center: 5, 3, 6, 4, 6, 5, 4, 6, 3, 2, 7, 4, 5, 6, 5, 3, 2. How many children are younger than the *median* age of the group?

Tip

The median is the middle number when the numbers are arranged in order.

A. 5
B. 6
C. 7
D. 8
E. Not Here

3 Barb makes a display of 6 rows of videos in a store window. She puts 12 boxes in the bottom row, 10 boxes in the next row, 8 boxes in the next, and so on. There are 2 videos on top. How many videos does Barb use for this display?

Tip

Use one of these strategies to solve this problem.
• *Draw a Diagram*
• *Find a Pattern*

A. 32
B. 36
C. 42
D. 43
E. Not Here

4 On his weekend job, Will made $97.50 on Saturday. At the end of the day on Sunday, he had a total of $204.50 for the two days. Which is the best estimate for the amount Will made on Sunday?

A. Less than $75
B. About $85
C. About $100
D. More than $150

5 The average of the ages of four brothers is 16. The youngest brother is 8 years old, and the oldest is 22. Which could be the ages of the other two brothers?

A. 10 and 16   **C.** 15 and 19
B. 12 and 18   **D.** 18 and 20

6 Jill is 4 years older than Pat. Bob is 2 years older than Pat. If you know that Pat is 12 years old, which number sentence can you use to find the sum, s, of the three ages?

A. $s = 2 + 4 + 12$
B. $s - (12 - 4) + (12 - 2) + 12$
C. $s = (12 + 4) + (12 - 2) + 12$
D. $s = (12 + 4) + (12 + 2) + 12$

7 The youth group washed cars to raise money for charity. They made more than $400 the first day, $250 the second day, and less than $200 the third day. Which is a reasonable amount for how much more they made the first day than the second day?

A. Exactly $150
B. Less than $150
C. More than $150
D. More than $650

8 Suki bought a book for $7.95 and 2 notebooks. She gave the clerk $20 and received $9 change. Which is the best estimate for the price of each notebook?

A. Less than $1.00
B. $1.50
C. $2.00
D. $2.50

Use this graph for Problems 9 and 10.

The graph shows the distance Greg and his brother drove to a campground.

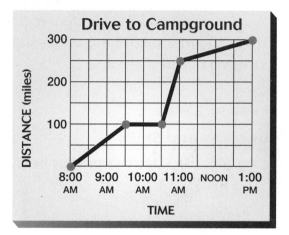

9 Choose the best interpretation of the graph.

A. They drove to the campground without stopping.
B. The campground is 300 miles from their starting point.
C. They drove to the campground and stayed for 3 days.
D. They stopped twice on their way to the campground.

10 After leaving for their camping trip, how far did George and his brother drive before they stopped for a rest break?

A. 300 miles   **C.** 150 miles
B. 250 miles   **D.** 100 miles

Checkpoint

Analyzing Data and Graphs

Vocabulary

Use the words at the right to complete each sentence.

A __1.__ is used to organize and display data. The __2.__ represents the tens digits in order from least to greatest. The __3.__ are the ones digits placed to the right of the vertical line.

The difference between the greatest and the least numbers of a set of data is called the __4.__. The __5.__ is the middle number when the numbers are arranged in order. The number that occurs most often is called the __6.__.

Word Bank

leaves
median
mode
range
stem
stem-and-leaf
  plot

Concepts and Skills

Using Algebra Use the graphs below. (pages 108–111)

Graph A

Graph B

7. How does the difference in the intervals on the vertical scales affect the way the two graphs look?

8. Which graph would you use if you were the Super Can Company? a Super Can competitor? Why?

Make a stem-and-leaf plot to organize each set of data. (pages 112–113)

9. 13, 25, 12, 19, 36, 28, 34, 36

10. 58, 46, 58, 43, 69, 42, 54, 62

Find the range, median, and mode for each set of data. (pages 114–115)

11. 13, 25, 48, 25, 16

12. 95, 13, 5, 88, 71, 54, 88, 1, 5

13. 30, 47, 48, 48, 48, 22, 23, 34, 49, 34, 23

What do you think?

Why is it helpful to list your data from least to greatest when finding the range, median, and mode?

Problem Solving

14. Describe Marcie's newest invention is a high-bouncing ball. In five bounces, the ball reached heights of 2 ft, 5 ft, 5 ft, 7 ft, and 9 ft. Describe what each measure—range, median, and mode—tells you about the data.

15. Susan kept track of the weight of her dog, Smokey, when she began feeding it a new dog food. What would be the best type of graph to display this data? Why? Use the table to create the graph.

Smokey's Weight	
Week	Pounds
1	9
2	12
3	15
4	20

Journal Idea

Explain why someone would display data in a graph instead of listing it in a table.

You Decide

Activity

Different Views of the Same Data

Work with a partner to conduct a survey of 30 friends or classmates. Collect data about favorites, such as favorite pets, favorite school subjects, or favorite school lunch.

Create one graph that appears to show little difference among the data and a second graph that shows a greater difference.

You might wish to include this work in your portfolio.

Extra Practice

Set A (pages 88–91)

Use the graph at the right for Exercises 1–4.

1. What is the label on the horizontal axis? the vertical axis?

2. How many fifth graders own a blue bicycle? How many sixth graders own a blue bicycle?

3. Which color bicycle is owned by the same number of fifth and sixth graders? How many in each grade own one?

4. How many sixth graders have a bicycle of a color other than red, blue, or white? Is this more or less than the number of fifth graders?

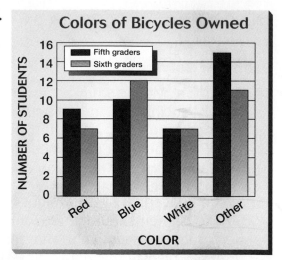

Colors of Bicycles Owned

Use the table for Exercises 5–6.

5. Use the table to make a double bar graph.

6. What interval did you use for the number of hours? Explain your choice.

Bike-Riding Times		
Day of the Week	**Paul**	**Karyn**
Monday	2 hours	$1\frac{1}{2}$ hours
Wednesday	1 hour	3 hours
Friday	$2\frac{1}{2}$ hours	$2\frac{1}{2}$ hours

Set B (pages 92–95)

Using Algebra Use the grid to name the point at each location or to write the ordered pair for each point.

1. (1, 3)   2. (6, 5)   3. (7, 0)   4. (1, 6)

5. B   6. O   7. A   8. F

9. J   10. (4, 2)   11. K   12. (5, 3)

13. Write ordered pairs that, if connected, would form a rectangle that is 3 units long and 2 units high.

14. Write ordered pairs that, if connected, would form a square 5 units on a side.

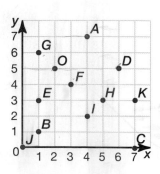

Extra Practice

Set C (pages 98–101)

Use the graph at the right for Exercises 1–3.

1. How many times around the rink did Sandy skate between 8:00 and 12:00?

2. During which half-hour interval did Sandy skate around the rink the greatest number of times?

3. **Using Algebra** What do you notice about the line between 9:30 and 10:00? Explain what this means.

Set D (pages 108–111)

Using Algebra Use the graphs below for Exercises 1–3.

Graph A   **Graph B**

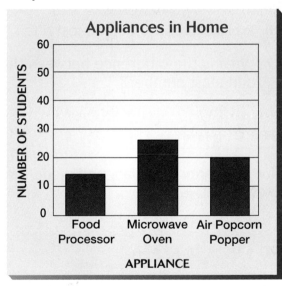

1. Which graph would you use to show that there are many more students who have a microwave oven than a food processor? Why?

2. What is the difference in the vertical scale in the two graphs?

3. How could Graph B be changed to show even less difference in the number of appliances owned?

Extra Practice

Set E (pages 112–113)

Record the following data about bluejean lengths in a stem-and-leaf plot. Then use the stem-and-leaf plot to answer each question.

32, 50, 48, 37, 38, 55, 42, 58, 48, 31

1. What numbers make the stem? the leaves?

2. How many pairs of bluejeans are longer than 40 inches?

3. How many pairs of bluejeans are represented?

4. Could you make this stem-and-leaf plot into a bar graph? Why or why not?

Use the stem-and-leaf plot at the right for Exercises 5–7.

5. How many numbers are represented? Explain how you know.

6. Which number occurs most often?

7. What is the difference between the greatest number and least number?

Stem	Leaves
0	1 4 6 8
1	0 0 3 8
2	1 1 7 9
3	3 3 3 6
4	4 4 5
5	2 6 8

Set F (pages 114–115)

Find the range, median, and mode for the data in Exercises 1–9.

1. 12, 12, 15, 9, 17

2. 98, 96, 98, 100, 92

3. 2, 5, 7, 7, 8, 8, 6

4. 26, 35, 19, 25, 38, 12, 12

5. 34, 37, 30, 29, 37

6. 5, 6, 3, 2, 6

7. 125, 168, 118, 118, 118, 212, 100

8. 21, 19, 16, 16, 15, 17, 20

9. Use the stem-and-leaf plot at the right. Find the range, median, and mode of the data.

Stem	Leaves
1	7 8
2	1 4 4 4 4
3	0 0 8 9
4	1 3 7 9
5	1 2

Chapter Test

Use the graph for Exercises 1–6.

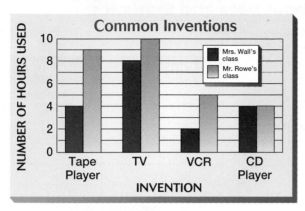

1. How many classes were polled?

2. How many hours did students watch a VCR in Mrs. Wall's class? in Mr. Rowe's class?

3. How many more hours did the students in Mr. Rowe's class listen to a tape player than did the students in Mrs. Wall's class?

4. Which invention was used the same number of hours by both classes?

5. Which invention was used the most?

6. How many more hours were spent watching TV than using a VCR?

Name the point or the ordered pair.

7. (3, 2)

8. (0, 1)

9. (5, 3)

10. B

11. E

12. C

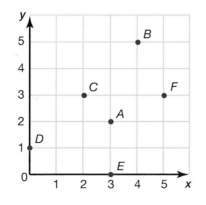

Use the graph for Exercises 13–18.

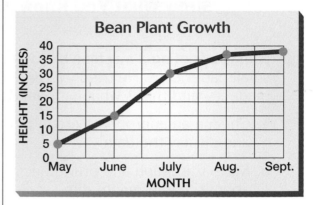

13. How tall was the bean plant in July?

14. Between which months did the greatest increase occur?

15. How much did the bean plant grow between May and June?

16. Between which two months was there very little growth?

17. About how much did the bean plant grow over the four months?

18. How might the graph be changed to make it appear that there was very little growth?

Solve.

19. Find the range, median, and mode of 77, 78, 88, 88, 85.

20. Albert is graphing weekly in-line skate sales at stores in his town. What type of graph would be the best? Why?

 Self-Check

For Exercises 7–12, did you proofread the ordered pairs carefully?

Performance Assessment

Show What You Know About Data and Statistics

1 Sam is inventing a machine that will pick up small paper clips. He tried five different magnets, and this is what happened.

   a. Choose an appropriate graph to organize and display the data.

   b. Make the graph and draw conclusions about the information the graph displays.

   Self-Check Did you remember to display all of the data in the table?

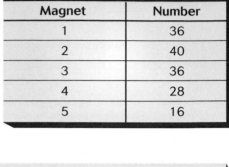

Paper Clips Picked Up	
Magnet	Number
1	36
2	40
3	36
4	28
5	16

2 Sharice invented a new shape of greenhouse. She tracked the growth of one particular plant in the greenhouse for 4 weeks.

   a. During which week did the plant show the most growth?

   b. About how much did the plant grow from Jan. 5 to Jan. 26?

   Self-Check Did you use the correct dates when answering the questions?

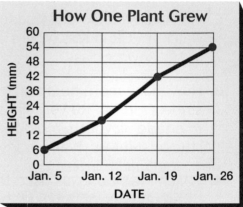

3 These are the heights of five plants grown in the greenhouse for 5 weeks.

   5.8 cm, 0 cm, 6.4 cm, 4.5 cm, 6.4 cm

   a. Find the median and mode of the heights.

   b. Another plant 4.5 cm tall is added to this data group. What is the mode now? Explain your answer.

   Self-Check Did you check to make sure you used the correct plant heights for finding the median?

 For Your Portfolio

You might wish to include this work in your portfolio.

Extension

Exploring Circle Graphs

Circle graphs are used to represent data as parts of a whole. The parts can be easily compared.

This circle graph represents pizza toppings that 20 students in one fifth-grade class prefer. The graph is split into sections, or wedges, that each represent one topping. The size of the wedge indicates the number of students who prefer that topping.

Pizza Topping Preferences

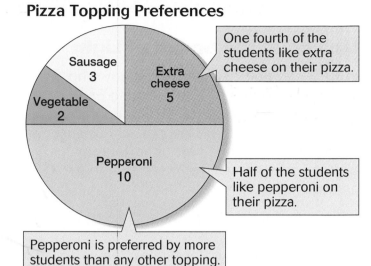

Sausage 3

Vegetable 2

Extra cheese 5

Pepperoni 10

One fourth of the students like extra cheese on their pizza.

Half of the students like pepperoni on their pizza.

Pepperoni is preferred by more students than any other topping.

Students in Mr. Alaveda's class are writing reports about inventions and inventors. Each student picked an invention from the table at the right.

Use the circle graph at the right to answer each question.

1. How many students are in the class?

2. Which invention was picked by the most students?

3. What fraction represents the part of the class that chose to write about the telephone?

4. How many papers will be written altogether about the telephone and Velcro? What fraction represents this part of the class?

Inventors and Their Inventions		
Date	Invention	Inventor
1876	telephone	Alexander G. Bell
1884	lantern	Michael Harvey
1887	ironing board	Sarah Boone
1903	airplane	Orville & Wilbur Wright
1938	ballpoint pen	Ladislas Biro
1939	helicopter	Igor Sikorski
1957	Velcro	George de Mestral
1971	cellular car phone	Henry T. Sampson

Inventions Picked by Class

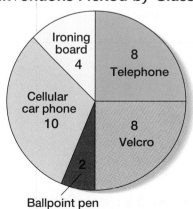

Ironing board 4

Cellular car phone 10

8 Telephone

8 Velcro

2

Ballpoint pen

Using Math in Science

*Use **graphing** to **compare and order** the speed at which light travels through different materials.*

Moving at the Speed of Light

Write a short story about Ray, a boy who travels on a beam of light reaching Earth from outer space. He travels through all kinds of materials. The last part of Ray's trip should be the fastest part of his journey. Before you start writing your story, do the activity below.

What You Need

For each pair:
  data table
  graph paper
  pencil
  colored pencil (optional)

Explore

Step 1 The table below shows the speed at which light travels through different materials. Study the data shown.

Material	Speed of Light
None (vacuum)	300,000 km/s
Water	225,000 km/s
Air	299,000 km/s
Glass	197,000 km/s
Diamond	124,000 km/s
Ice	229,000 km/s

  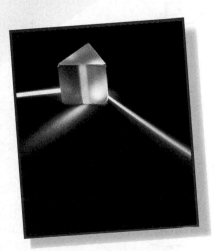

▲ Light passing through a diamond (left), water (center), and glass (right).

Step 2 On a sheet of graph paper, make a bar graph of the data in the table on page 126. Label the *y*-axis *Speed in km/sec* and label the *x*-axis *Material*, as shown in the picture at the right.

Step 3 Use your completed graph to compare and order the speeds at which light travels through the six materials. List the materials in order of the speed that light travels through each material, from slowest to fastest.

Step 4 Now use the data in your table and graph to help you answer the questions below. Then write your story about Ray.

Analyze

1. Through which material is the speed of light slowest? fastest?

2. How much faster does light travel through a vacuum than through ice?

3. Imagine that Ray travels from inside a diamond mountain into a river. How will the speed at which Ray travels change?

4. What will happen to Ray's speed as he leaves Earth's surroundings and ventures into outer space (a vacuum)? Explain.

 For Your Portfolio

Write about what you discovered. Explain how graphing helped you organize and understand your data. Include your story about Ray.

Explore Further!

Predict As light moves from one material into another, the speed of the light changes, and the light bends. The greater the change in speed, the greater the bending of the light. Which will cause greater bending of light—passing from a diamond into water or passing from glass into a vacuum? Explain.

Cumulative Review

★ ★ ★ ★ ★ **Preparing for Tests**

Choose the correct letter for each answer.

Operations	Patterns, Relationships, and Algebraic Thinking

1. Alan scored 3 times as many goals as Lee scored. If Alan scored 27 goals, how many did Lee score?

   A. 3   **C.** 30
   B. 9   **D.** 81

2. Which is the sum of 1.08, 0.76, and 23.012?

   A. 23.196   **C.** 24.960
   B. 24.852   **D.** 31.690

3. Denise and her dad went on a 5-day canoeing trip. The first 3 days, they paddled 4 miles, 3 miles, and 5 miles. Then they returned home and paddled the same number of miles each day. How far did they paddle each day of the return trip home?

   A. 4 mi   **C.** 6 mi
   B. 5 mi   **D.** 12 mi

4. Ben had to get 34 copies of a 13-page booklet made. The copies cost $0.03 per page. How much did the copies cost?

   A. $4.42
   B. $10.25
   C. $12.26
   D. $13.26
   E. Not Here

5. Which of the following makes this number sentence true?

$$3 \times (2 + \blacksquare) = 24$$

   A. 6   **C.** 10
   B. 8   **D.** 12

6. Manuel and Jessie are setting up chairs for a concert. The first row has 8 chairs; the second row—9 chairs; the third row—11 chairs; and the fourth row—14 chairs. If this pattern continues, how many chairs will there be in the *seventh* row?

   A. 18   **C.** 29
   B. 23   **D.** 36

7. Which number sentence best represents this problem?

Tara bought 3 plants for $1.29 each and 3 clay pots for $2.29 each.

   A. ($1.29 + $2.29) + 3
   B. (3 + $1.29) × (3 + $2.29)
   C. (3 × $1.29) + (3 × $2.29)
   D. 3 × ($1.29 × $2.29)

8. Which expression has the same value as 4 × (3 + 2)?

   A. 4 + 5
   B. 7 + 6
   C. (4 × 3) + (4 × 2)
   D. (4 + 3) × (4 + 2)

Geometry and Spatial Reasoning	Probability and Statistics

9. The sides of triangle *EFG* are equal. What is the perimeter of the triangle?

45 in.

A. 135 in.
B. 90 in.
C. 45 in.
D. 20 in.

10. Which plane figure forms the base of a rectangular prism?

A. Trapezoid
B. Rectangle
C. Circle
D. Triangle

11. Which shape appears to be similar but **NOT** congruent to Figure 1?

A.

B.

C.

D.

12. Which of the following is the number of sides a *pentagon* has?

A. 5
B. 6
C. 8
D. 10

13. In a total of 80 spins, on which shape is it likely that the spinner will land most often?

A. ♥
B. ▲
C. ●
D. ★

Use the bar graph below to answer Questions 14–16.

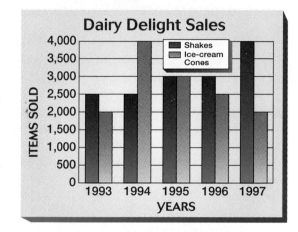

14. In which year did Dairy Delight sell more ice-cream cones than shakes?

A. 1993   C. 1995
B. 1994   D. 1996

15. About how many more shakes than ice-cream cones did Dairy Delight sell in 1997?

A. 1,000   C. 2,000
B. 1,500   D. 2,500

16. About how many ice-cream cones were sold over the 5 years?

A. 28,500
B. 15,500
C. 13,500
D. 12,500

Chapter 4

Multiplying Whole Numbers

Chapter Theme: ANIMALS

REAL-WORLD Math

·················· **Real Facts** ··················

Caring for animals is a big responsibility. Staff members at Ohio's Cincinnati Zoo know that feeding animals is a big part of their responsibility. Here is a weekly grocery bill.

Weekly Food Expenses at the Cincinnati Zoo					
apples	$309	grain	$683	celery	$75
bananas	$402	hay	$2,464	grapes	$281
collard greens	$19	papayas	$110	fish	$961
green beans	$170	kale	$29	onions	$10
sweet potatoes	$196	spinach	$22	corn	$100
white potatoes	$18	lettuce	$363	pears	$18
bean sprouts	$5	meat	$626	carrots	$212
alfalfa sprouts	$6	oranges	$90		

- How much is spent on bananas in 6 weeks?

- On which food does the zoo spend about as much in 1 week as it does on meat in 4 weeks?

- What would be the total cost of feeding the animals for 2 months?

··············· **Real People** ···············

Meet Lisa Marie Stevens, a zoo curator in Washington, D.C. Like staff members at the Cincinnati Zoo, she is responsible for the care and feeding of all kinds of animals, from tiny marmosets to 4-ton elephants! The students in the photograph at the right are learning about calculating a proper diet for animals.

Think Smarter

 Using Algebra

You can save time by using multiplication properties.

Learning About It

At a dog show, dogs can be set up in different ways. The arrays to the right are arranged differently, but the number of paw prints in each array is the same.

Commutative Property

The order of the factors does not change the product.

factors   product

$3 \times 5 = 15$
$5 \times 3 = 15$

Associative Property

The way in which the factors are grouped does not change the product.

Do the work in parentheses first.

$3 \times (4 \times 2) = 3 \times 8 = 24$
$(3 \times 4) \times 2 = 12 \times 2 = 24$

Identity Property

When 1 is one of two factors, the product is the other factor.

$1 \times 15 = 15$
$15 \times 1 = 15$

Zero Property

When 0 is a factor, the product is 0.

$0 \times 7 = 0$
$7 \times 0 = 0$

The Distributive Property combines multiplication and addition.

Distributive Property

Think of one factor as the sum of two addends. Then multiply each addend by the other factor and add the products.

$3 \times 14 = 3 \times (10 + 4)$
$= (3 \times 10) + (3 \times 4)$
$= \quad 30 \quad + \quad 12$
$= \quad 42$

Think and Discuss Find $6 \times 78 \times 32 \times 799 \times 0$. Why is it helpful to look at all of the factors before beginning to multiply?

Try It Out

Find each *n*. Name the property that you used.

1. $6 \times (4 \times 3) = (6 \times 4) \times n$

2. $5 \times 9 = n \times 5$

3. $6 \times n = 6$

4. $45 \times (n \times 6) = (45 \times 12) \times 6$

5. $4 \times (10 + 3) = n$

6. $0 \times 238 = n$

Practice

Find each *n*. Use multiplication properties to help you.

7. $17 \times n = 17$

8. $6 \times 20 = n \times 6$

9. $(3 \times 2) \times 7 = 3 \times (2 \times n)$

10. $(17 \times n) \times 4 = 0$

11. $n = (10 + 7) \times 5$

12. $(2 \times 8) \times 4 = 4 \times (n \times 2)$

Compare. Write >, <, or = for each ⬤.

13. $3 \times 8 \times 5$ ⬤ $8 \times 3 \times 2$

14. $34 \times 0 \times 100$ ⬤ 4×8

15. 3×19 ⬤ $(3 \times 10) + (3 \times 9)$

16. $1 \times 2 \times 3 \times 100$ ⬤ $101 \times 3 \times 2$

17. $417 \times 16 \times 3$ ⬤ $16 \times 0 \times 417$

18. 45×3 ⬤ 9×15

Problem Solving

19. Analyze If guide-dog trainers walk each dog for 15 minutes twice a day, how much time is needed to walk ten dogs every week?

20. You Decide At least 4 hours a week must be spent giving your puppy obedience training. You can spend 30 minutes a day on Monday, Wednesday, and Friday, or 60 minutes a day on Tuesday, Thursday, and Saturday. Make a weekly schedule and explain your plan.

Review and Remember

Compare. Write >, <, or = for each ⬤.

21. 345 ⬤ 344

22. 2,670 ⬤ 2,076

23. 582.6 ⬤ 592.8

24. 1,808 ⬤ 1,080

25. 15.08 ⬤ 15.8

26. 1,482 ⬤ 1,582

27. 97.600 ⬤ 97.6

28. 4,308.0 ⬤ 4,308.1

▲ Guide dogs are trained to help blind people live independently.

For Extra Practice, see Set A, page 160.

Developing Skills for Problem Solving

*First read for understanding and
then focus on which operation to use.*

READ FOR UNDERSTANDING

Thomas has been doing research on how fast birds fly. Some of his notes are shown on the notebook at the right.

1 How fast does a blackbird fly?

2 How fast does a mallard fly?

3 How fast does a swan fly?

4 How fast does a quail fly?

> A blackbird flies 30 miles per hour.
>
> A swan flies 55 miles per hour.
>
> A quail flies 57 miles per hour.
>
> A mallard flies 65 miles per hour.

THINK AND DISCUSS

Choose the Operation Clues in a problem help you decide which operation to use. You add to combine groups, subtract to compare groups, multiply to combine equal groups, and divide to separate into equal groups.

▼ The mallard is probably the best-known duck in the United States.

Reread the paragraph and the information in the notebook at the top of the page.

5 Which operation would you use to find the number of miles a swan can fly in 5 hours? Tell how you decided.

6 Which operation would you use to find out about how many times faster a mallard can fly than a blackbird? Tell how you decided.

▼ Swans were brought to the United States in the 1800s.

7 A swan flies for 3 hours, stops for 1 hour, and flies for 2 more hours. How many miles does the swan fly? Tell how you found your answer.

8 What can help you decide which operation to use?

Show What You Learned

Answer each question. Give a reason for your choice.

Sarah is interested in how much sea animals weigh. She recorded her data in a table like the one at the right.

Sea Animal	Weight
Great white shark	55,000 lb
Giant octopus	125 lb
Giant clam	600 lb
Dolphin	400 lb

1 How would you find the combined weights of the giant octopus and the giant clam?

　a. Multiply the weights.

　b. Add the weights.

　c. Subtract the weight of the giant octopus from the weight of the giant clam.

2 How would you find how much heavier the giant clam is than the dolphin?

　a. Multiply the giant clam's weight by the dolphin's weight.

　b. Add the weights of the dolphin and the giant clam.

　c. Subtract the weight of the dolphin from the weight of the giant clam.

3 Which number sentence would you use to find how much heavier the giant clam is than the dolphin?

　a. $600 \times 400 = h$

　b. $600 + 400 = h$

　c. $600 - 400 = h$

4 How would you find the weight of four giant octopuses?

　a. Multiply the weight of the giant octopus by 3.

　b. Multiply the weight of the giant octopus by 4.

　c. Divide the weight of the giant octopus by 4.

5 How would you find the weight of four giant octopuses?

　a. $170 \times 4 = x$

　b. $170 - 125 = x$

　c. $125 \times 4 = x$

6 **Explain** A sea turtle's average weight is twice that of the giant octopus. Write a number sentence that represents the weight of a sea turtle. Tell why you chose the operation you did.

7 **Create Your Own** Use the data in the table at the top of the page to write a problem. Tell which operation you would use to solve it.

▲ Sea turtles can weigh between 100 pounds and 1,500 pounds.

Using Algebra

Math Can Fly!

You can use basic facts and patterns of zeros to help you multiply mentally.

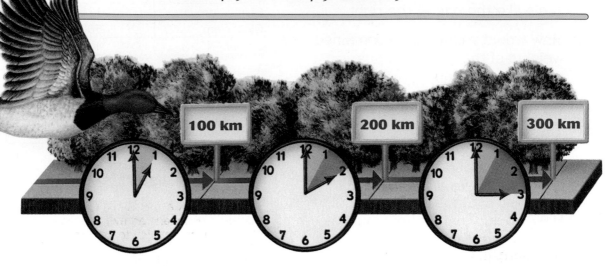

Learning About It

A canvasback duck cannot fly at all when it is growing new feathers. But when it is migrating, it can fly about 100 kilometers per hour. How far can a canvasback duck travel if it flies for three hours at that speed?

$$3 \times 100 = n$$

Basic facts and patterns of zeros can help you multiply by 10, 100, and 1,000.

$$3 \times 1 = 3 \qquad \} \text{ Basic Fact}$$
$$3 \times 10 = 30$$
$$3 \times 100 = 300 \qquad \} \text{ Patterns of Zeros}$$
$$3 \times 1,000 = 3,000$$

The basic fact $3 \times 1 = 3$ and the pattern of zeros make it easy to see that the product of 3×100 is 300.

A canvasback duck can fly 300 kilometers in three hours.

Did You Know?

Airplane wings are modeled after birds' wings. Both are curved on top and flat or slightly curved up on the bottom.

More Examples

A. $8 \times 1 = 8$
$8 \times 10 = 80$
$8 \times 100 = 800$
$8 \times 1,000 = 8,000$

B. $1 \times 15 = 15$
$10 \times 15 = 150$
$100 \times 15 = 1,500$
$1,000 \times 15 = 15,000$

C. $60 \times 1 = 60$
$60 \times 10 = 600$
$60 \times 100 = 6,000$
$60 \times 1,000 = 60,000$

Connecting Ideas

You just learned to look for patterns to multiply by 10, 100, or 1,000. Patterns can also help you multiply when a factor is a multiple of 10, 100, or 1,000.

If a dolphin swims at a speed of 40 kilometers per hour, how far can it swim in two hours?

$2 \times 40 = n$ $2 \times 4 = 8$

Since there is one zero in the factors 2 and 40, place a zero at the end of the product of 2×4.

$2 \times 40 = 80$

A dolphin can swim 80 kilometers in two hours.

▲ Social Studies Connection
Carvings like these were made by the Maya Indians of Central America. Historians believe that the Maya were the first to use the idea of zero.

More Examples

A. $9 \times 3 = 27$
$9 \times 30 = 270$
$9 \times 300 = 2,700$
$9 \times 3,000 = 27,000$

B. $5 \times 6 = 30$ ⟵
$5 \times 60 = 300$
$5 \times 600 = 3,000$
$5 \times 6,000 = 30,000$

If the product of a basic fact has a zero, be sure to include that zero when you multiply by a multiple of 10, 100, or 1,000.

Think and Discuss   How can you use what you know to find 8×500? $8 \times 5,000$?

Try It Out

Find each product. Use patterns to help you.

1. 7×100 **2.** $1,000 \times 8$ **3.** 5×90 **4.** 9×50

5. 50×3 **6.** 60×100 **7.** 490×10 **8.** $1,000 \times 400$

9. 100×90 **10.** 5×80 **11.** 200×50 **12.** 300×9

13. How can you tell that 6×400 equals 60×40 without multiplying?

Fine Arts Connection ➤
John James Audubon is famous for his detailed paintings of birds. He is known to have done at least 435 bird paintings.

Practice

Find each product.

14. 200
× 70

15. 900
× 40

16. 500
× 7

17. 6,000
× 30

18. 4,000
× 50

19. 820
× 100

20. 100
× 38

21. 760
× 100

22. 4,450
× 100

23. 1,090
× 1,000

24. 10 × 5

25. 10 × 54

26. 43 × 100

27. 10 × 788

28. 50 × 10

29. 4 × 50

30. 7 × 80

31. 70 × 8

32. 200 × 7

33. 700 × 6

34. 8 × 300

35. 3 × 4,000

36. 9 × 8,000

37. 50 × 30

38. 40 × 90

39. Look at Exercises 30 and 31 above. What do you notice about their products? Why does this happen?

Using Algebra Complete each input/output table.

Rule: Multiply by 300

	Input	Output
40.	5	▪
41.	70	▪
42.	▪	240,000
	9,000	2,700,000

Rule: Multiply by 50

	Input	Output
43.	8	▪
44.	▪	2,000
45.	▪	15,000
46.	6,000	▪

Rule: Divide by 20

	Input	Output
47.	▪	2
48.	600	▪
49.	1,200	▪
50.	▪	140

51. Rule: ___?___

	Input	Output
	7	1,400
	12	2,400
52.	22	▪
53.	44	▪

54. Rule: ___?___

	Input	Output
	7	28,000
	4	16,000
55.	▪	24,000
56.	90	▪

57. Rule: ___?___

	Input	Output
	5	5,000
58.	▪	9,000
59.	3	▪
60.	▪	40,000

Problem Solving

61. Dry dog food comes in bags of different sizes. An animal shelter uses half a pound of dry dog food each day for every small dog. How much dry dog food does the shelter need to feed 30 small dogs for 4 weeks?

62. A store sells 10-lb bags of dog food for $9.50, 20-lb bags for $18.50, and 40-lb bags for $30.00. A shelter uses 980 lb of dry dog food in four weeks. What is the least expensive way to buy a 4-week supply without having any left over?

Use the graph to answer Problems 63–66.

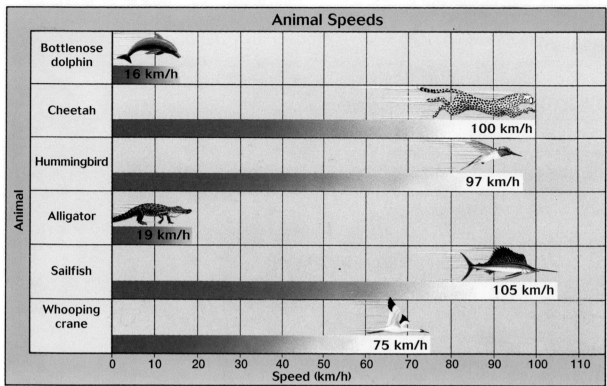

Animal Speeds

63. How many kilometers can a bottlenose dolphin travel in 10 hours?

64. What is the difference in the travel speed of an alligator and a whooping crane?

65. What is the difference in the distance a sailfish and a bottlenose dolphin can travel in three hours?

66. **Create Your Own** Use information in the graph to create a problem of your own.

67. **Journal Idea** Do you think the bar graph shown above is the best way to show animal speeds? Could you have used a line graph? What problems might you have using a pictograph? Write your answers in one or two short paragraphs.

Review and Remember

Add or subtract.

68. 2.2 + 3.3

69. 123.5 + 120.9

70. 26.05 + 105.15

71. 1,239 − 982

72. 981.5 − 908.4

73. 0.609 − 0.019

74. 5,360 + 476.3

75. 3,014 − 2,619

76. 17.83 − 12.09

77. 2.763 − 1.884

78. 5.043 + 50.43

79. 143 + 1.43

For Extra Practice, see Set B, page 160.

Protecting the Puffins

Sometimes you can solve a problem by estimating the product.

Learning About It

Puffin decoys are sometimes used to lure live puffins to safe breeding areas. Your school decides to make 126 puffin decoys. If each decoy takes 12 pounds of clay, about how much clay does the school need to order?

126 decoys

× **12 lb**

To estimate, find the rounding place and look at the digit to the right. Round each factor to the nearest 10.

$$\begin{array}{r} 126 \\ \times\ 12 \end{array}$$ rounds to $$\begin{array}{r} 130 \\ \times\ 10 \\ \hline 1{,}300 \end{array}$$ ← 6 > 5, so round up.
← 2 < 5, so round down.

The school needs to order about 1,300 pounds of clay.

More Examples

A. $1\underline{4}7 \times 3\underline{5}3 = n$ Round each factor to the nearest hundred.
$\quad\downarrow\qquad\ \downarrow$
$100 \times 400 = 40{,}000$

B. $\underline{2}{,}168 \times \underline{5}23 = n$ Round each factor to its greatest place.
$\quad\ \downarrow\qquad\quad \downarrow$
$2{,}000 \times 500 = 1{,}000{,}000$

Think and Discuss Sometimes it makes sense when estimating with money to round both factors up. Explain why.

Try It Out

Estimate each product. Round to the greatest place.

1.	2.	3.	4.
77	87	566	128
× 29	× 23	× 23	× 3

Practice

Estimate each product. Round to the nearest 10.

5.	6.	7.	8.
54	69	88	297
× 19	× 32	× 42	× 4

◄ **Math Note**

Remember that you do not need to round one-digit factors.

Estimate. Round to the greatest place.

9. 66 × 59   **10.** 92 × 86   **11.** 276 × 88   **12.** 412 × 83

13. 159 × 25   **14.** 146 × 13   **15.** 208 × 263   **16.** 721 × 562

Problem Solving

17. If you used 17 pounds of clay to make a model, about how much clay would you need to make 32 models?

18. A sculptor uses $13 of supplies for each small bird she makes and $17 for each large one. If she has $120 and wants to make the same number of large and small birds, how many can she make?

19. What If? Mark Slatcoff spent about 258 hours carving one bird. If every bird took the same amount of time, about how long would it take him to carve 12 birds?

Kid Connection Mark A. Slatcoff, PA, won first place in the age-15-and-under category at the 1996 Ward World Championship Wildfowl Carving Competition for his blackthroated blue warbler carving. ▼

Review and Remember

Using Mental Math Find each answer.

20. 56 ÷ 8   **21.** 7 × 6   **22.** 28 ÷ 4   **23.** 8 × 8   **24.** 19 + 73

25. 51 − 25   **26.** 18 ÷ 9   **27.** 12 × 2   **28.** 99 + 21   **29.** 5 × 11

Critical Thinking Corner

Number Sense

Finding a Range

Another way to estimate products is to find a range.

Example

120	round down	**125**	round up	130
× 10		**× 12**		× 20
1,200				2,600

The range is from 1,200 to 2,600. The product of 125 × 12 is between 1,200 and 2,600.

Estimate by finding the range.

1. 29 × 8   **2.** 7 × 96

3. 89 × 73   **4.** 68 × 82

5. 138 × 26   **6.** 92 × 456

7. Describe This method is sometimes called the "floors and ceilings method." Why?

For Extra Practice, see Set C, page 160.

Shear Delight

You can use basic facts to multiply by one-digit numbers.

Learning About It

Did you know that sheep are usually sheared only once a year? If a sheep-shearer clips 176 sheep a day, how many sheep can he clip in 5 days?

$$176 \times 5 = n$$

Estimate first: **$200 \times 5 = 1,000$**

Then find the exact product.

May

S	M	T	W	T	F	S
	1 176	2 176	3 176	4 176	5 176	6
7	8	9	10	11	12	13
14	15	16	17	18	19	20
21	22	23	24	25	26	
28	29	30	31			

An expert sheep-shearer can clip up to 200 sheep in a day. ➤

THERE'S ALWAYS A WAY!

● **One way** is to use paper and pencil.

Step 1 Multiply the ones. Regroup if you can.	**Step 2** Multiply the tens. Add the regrouped tens. Regroup if you can.	**Step 3** Multiply the hundreds. Add the regrouped hundreds.
3 176 × 5 —— 0	3 3 176 × 5 —— 80	3 3 176 × 5 —— 880

● **Another way** is to use the Distributive Property and mental math.

Think of 176 as $100 + 70 + 6$. Multiply each part by 5.

(100×5) (70×5) (6×5)

$$500 \quad + \quad 350 \quad + \quad 30 \quad = \quad 880$$

The sheepshearer can clip 880 sheep in 5 days. The answer 880 is reasonable, since it is close to the estimate.

Think and Discuss Explain how the two ways shown are alike.

Try It Out

Estimate each product. Then find the exact answer.

1. 27×9 **2.** 92×3 **3.** 70×2 **4.** 914×5 **5.** 451×7

Practice

Find each product. Estimate to be sure your answer is reasonable.

6.	**7.**	**8.**	**9.**	**10.**
57	19	350	278	522
$\times\ 8$	$\times\ 7$	$\times\ 4$	$\times\ 4$	$\times\ 3$

11. 72×5 **12.** 93×4 **13.** 232×6 **14.** 766×6 **15.** 845×9

16. 589×5 **17.** 157×3 **18.** $3 \times 1,086$ **19.** $\$8.77 \times 7$ **20.** $\$1.63 \times 4$

21. 463×9 **22.** 621×6 **23.** 418×2 **24.** 259×7 **25.** $1,325 \times 3$

Problem Solving

26. If a shearer gets 5 pounds of fleece from each sheep, how many pounds of fleece will he get from 87 sheep?

27. Using Estimation Three shearers worked for 4 days. One shearer clipped 200 sheep a day, another clipped 198 sheep a day, and a third shearer clipped 187 sheep a day. About how many sheep were sheared by the end of the fourth day?

28. Journal Idea Write a paragraph describing a situation outside of school when you would multiply by a one-digit number.

▲**Social Studies Connection**
Today many Navajo weavers continue a long tradition of using wool to make colorful rugs and blankets with striking designs.

Review and Remember

Find each answer.

29. $5.25 + 0.75$ **30.** $\$0.35 - \$0.12$ **31.** 22×4 **32.** $25.15 - 5.15$

33. $\$6.33 + \$5.96$ **34.** $12.99 - 1.01$ **35.** $82 \div 2$ **36.** $\$16.16 + \$12.12$

37. $0.35 + 0.65$ **38.** $\$16.40 \div 4$ **39.** 44×2 **40.** $\$18.50 - \$17.25$

For Extra Practice, see Set D, page 161.

Checkpoint

Multiplying by One-Digit Numbers

Write the name of each multiplication property described. (pages 130–131)

1. The order of the factors does not change the product.

2. When 0 is a factor, the product is 0.

3. The way in which the factors are grouped does not change the product.

4. When 1 is one of two factors, the product is the other factor.

5. One factor is expressed as a sum of two addends. Then each of the addends is multiplied by the other factor, and the partial products are added.

What do you think?

Is it easier to multiply numbers with zeros or numbers without zeros? Use examples to explain.

Using Mental Math Find each product. Use patterns to help you. (pages 134–137)

6. 580×10

7. 100×400

8. $9,000 \times 6$

9. 70×300

10. 30×80

11. $76 \times 1,000$

12. 25×200

13. 80×600

Estimate each product. (pages 138–139)

14.
$$\begin{array}{r} 55 \\ \times\ 7 \\ \hline \end{array}$$

15.
$$\begin{array}{r} 38 \\ \times\ 6 \\ \hline \end{array}$$

16.
$$\begin{array}{r} 68 \\ \times\ 7 \\ \hline \end{array}$$

17.
$$\begin{array}{r} 99 \\ \times\ 9 \\ \hline \end{array}$$

18.
$$\begin{array}{r} 79 \\ \times\ 68 \\ \hline \end{array}$$

19.
$$\begin{array}{r} 14 \\ \times\ 48 \\ \hline \end{array}$$

20.
$$\begin{array}{r} 149 \\ \times\ 36 \\ \hline \end{array}$$

21.
$$\begin{array}{r} 472 \\ \times\ 21 \\ \hline \end{array}$$

22.
$$\begin{array}{r} 298 \\ \times\ 165 \\ \hline \end{array}$$

23.
$$\begin{array}{r} 378 \\ \times\ 456 \\ \hline \end{array}$$

Multiply. (pages 140–141)

24. 58×4

25. 23×8

26. 18×7

27. 5×72

28. 8×92

29. 3×927

30. 890×7

31. 609×5

32. 129×5

33. $\$4.85 \times 3$

34. 857×6

35. 4×685

36. 417×8

37. $54 \times 1,000$

38. $\$9.99 \times 11$

39. $10 \times \$5.37$

Mixed Practice

Use mental math or paper and pencil to find each product.

40. 500×6 **41.** 7×81 **42.** 530×8 **43.** $2,000 \times 9$

44. 740×5 **45.** 39×6 **46.** 926×2 **47.** 5×478

48. $3 \times 9,000$ **49.** $100 \times \$55$ **50.** $4 \times \$4.92$ **51.** $7,000 \times 70$

Problem Solving

52. The camel and elephant handlers at a zoo make $10.75 an hour. They work for 7 hours each day. How much will they each earn in a 5-day work week?

53. **Using Estimation** Scientists may collect crocodile eggs to protect them until they hatch. A crocodile can lay about 50 eggs. About how many eggs would 7 crocodiles lay?

54. In order to take pets on a train or plane, you need to have a pet carrier. If a carrier for a medium-sized dog costs $44.95, how much would it cost to buy carriers for three medium-sized dogs?

55. **Analyze** Ken's family is building a dog run. They will put a post at each corner of the square run. There will be a total of four posts on each side of the run. How many posts does Ken's family need to buy?

Journal Idea

Make a drawing to show why 3×12 is the same as $(3 \times 10) + (3 \times 2)$. Then tell how your drawing illustrates this.

Critical Thinking Corner

Logical Thinking

Number Puzzler

Place the numbers 1 through 7 in the boxes so that the sum of any three boxes in a straight line is 12. Use each number only once.

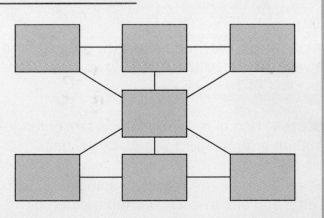

Going Bananas!

An array can help you understand partial products.

Learning About It

Chimpanzees like to eat fruit, especially bananas. Some chimps eat six bananas each day. You can use an array to find out how many bananas are needed to feed a chimp for two weeks.

You need to find **6 × 14**.

What You Need

For each pair:
grid paper
straightedge
colored pencils

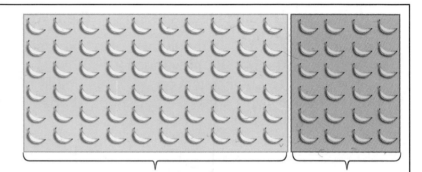

Since 14 = 10 + 4, this array shows that 6 × 14 = 6 × (10 + 4).

The Distributive Property allows you to express the product like this.	(6 × 10) +	(6 × 4)
These are partial products.	60 +	24
The sum of the partial products is the product of 6 × 14.	84	

The number of bananas needed is 84.

Work with a partner. Follow the steps to see how partial products can help you find the product of 14 × 16.

Step 1 Use grid paper. With a straightedge, outline a rectangle 14 units by 16 units.

Step 2 Break the rectangle into sections. Label and shade each section a different color as shown.

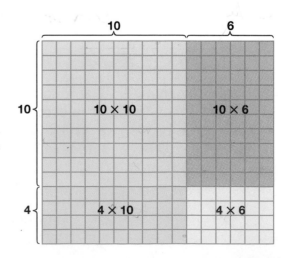

Step 3 Write a multiplication sentence for each shaded section. Record each sentence in a chart like the one at the right.

Step 4 Look at your chart. Find the sum of the partial products. What is the product of 14 × 16?

Step 5 Repeat Steps 1–4 to find the product of 17 × 28. Make a new chart to record your multiplication sentences.

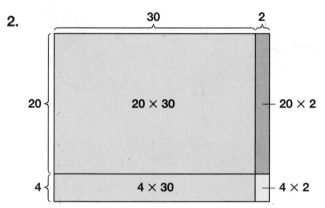

Finding Partial Products

Section Color	Multiplication Sentence
Blue	10 × 10 = 100

Think and Discuss How can drawing an array help you find the product of two numbers?

Practice

Write the partial products for each model. Then write a multiplication sentence.

1.

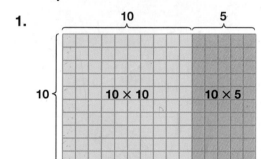

10   5

10 | 10 × 10 | 10 × 5 |

3 | 3 × 10 | 3 × 5 |

2.

30   2

20 | 20 × 30 | 20 × 2 |

4 | 4 × 30 | 4 × 2 |

Draw an array to find each product.

3. 19 × 24   **4.** 21 × 35   **5.** 22 × 18   **6.** 17 × 23

Use the model shown below for Exercise 7.

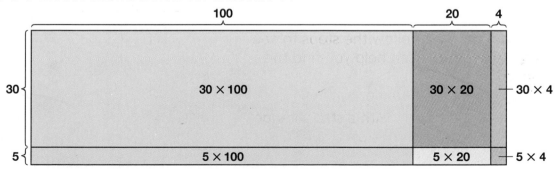

100   20   4

30 | 30 × 100 | 30 × 20 | 30 × 4 |

5 | 5 × 100 | 5 × 20 | 5 × 4 |

7. Analyze List the partial products and find their sum. Then write a multiplication sentence.

Who Would Think?

Use multiples of 10 and partial products to multiply two-digit numbers.

Learning About It

The heartbeats of a horse and an octopus are about 40 beats per minute. At that rate, how many times would a horse's heart beat in 18 minutes?

$$40 \times 18 = n$$

Estimate first: $40 \times 20 = 800$

Then find the exact product.

▼ **Science Connection** It might sound strange, but a horse and an octopus can each have the same number of heartbeats per minute!

THERE'S ALWAYS A WAY!

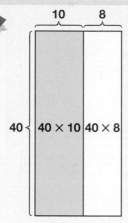

• **One way** is to use an array and find the sum of the partial products.

$$400 + 320 = 720$$

• **Another way** is to use paper and pencil.

Step 1 Multiply by the ones.	**Step 2** Multiply by the tens. Regroup if you can. Use 0 as a placeholder for the ones. Add the partial products.
$\begin{array}{r} 18 \\ \times\ 40 \\ \hline 00 \end{array}$ $0 \times 18 = 0$	$\begin{array}{r} \overset{3}{}18 \\ \times\ 40 \\ \hline 00 \\ +\ 720 \\ \hline 720 \end{array}$ 4 tens $\times$ 18 = 720

A horse's heart beats about 720 times in 18 minutes.
The answer is close to the estimate of 800.

Connecting Ideas

What you have learned about multiplying by multiples of
10 can help you multiply by any two-digit number.

$$23 \times 34 = n$$

Estimate first: $20 \times 30 = 600$

Then find the exact product.

THERE'S ALWAYS A WAY!

- **One way** is to use an array and find the sum of the partial products.

$$600 + 80 + 90 + 12 = 782$$

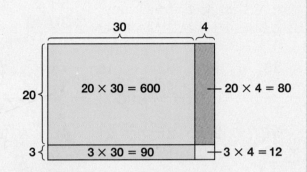

- **Another way** is to use paper and pencil.

Step 1 Multiply by the ones. Regroup if you can.	**Step 2** Multiply by the tens. Use 0 as a placeholder for the ones. Regroup if you can.	**Step 3** Add the partial products.
$\begin{array}{r} 1 \\ 34 \\ \times\ 23 \\ \hline 102 \end{array}$ 3 ones × 34 = 102	$\begin{array}{r} 1 \\ 34 \\ \times\ 23 \\ \hline 102 \\ 680 \end{array}$ 2 tens × 34 = 680	$\begin{array}{r} 1 \\ 34 \\ \times\ 23 \\ \hline 102 \\ +\ 680 \\ \hline 782 \end{array}$

The product of 23 × 34 is 782.

More Examples

A.
$$\begin{array}{r} 20 \\ \times\ 48 \\ \hline 160 \\ +\ 800 \\ \hline 960 \end{array}$$
160 8 ones × 20
+ 800 4 tens × 20

B.
$$\begin{array}{r} 56 \\ \times\ 79 \\ \hline 504 \\ +\ 3\,920 \\ \hline 4{,}424 \end{array}$$
504 9 ones × 56
+ 3 920 7 tens × 56

C.
$$\begin{array}{r} \$86 \\ \times\ 67 \\ \hline 602 \\ +\ 5\,160 \\ \hline \$5{,}762 \end{array}$$
602 7 ones × 86
+ 5 160 6 tens × 86

Think and Discuss In Examples A, B, and C above,
name the partial products and tell how they were found.

Try It Out

Estimate each product. Then find the exact answer.

1. 26
   × 50

2. 42
   × 39

3. 28
   × 70

4. 64
   × 14

5. 57
   × 30

6. 91
   × 36

Practice

Multiply. Use an array, if you wish.

7. 27
   × 13

8. 72
   × 40

9. 53
   × 30

10. 65
    × 38

11. 21
    × 17

12. 16
    × 15

13. 38
    × 77

14. 82
    × 46

15. 74
    × 34

16. 63
    × 43

17. 96
    × 54

18. 59
    × 66

19. 61
    × 40

20. 25
    × 19

21. 46
    × 78

22. 35
    × 44

23. 37
    × 41

24. 87
    × 51

25. 45
    × 70

26. 21
    × 13

27. 39
    × 23

28. 18
    × 27

29. 92
    × 45

30. 76
    × 81

Using Algebra Use mental math or paper and pencil to compare. Write >, <, or = for each ⬤.

31. 52×8 ⬤ 63×6

32. 18×3 ⬤ 29×2

33. 5×28 ⬤ 4×32

34. 25×20 ⬤ 500

35. 72×40 ⬤ $2{,}800$

36. 12×36 ⬤ 9×47

Problem Solving

Complete the chart. Then use it to answer Problem 41.

Heart Rates		
Animal	Beats per Minute	Beats per Hour
37. Elephant	30	▪
38. Mouse	600	▪
39. Bird	500	▪
40. Large dog	80	▪

41. What is the difference between the heart rate per hour of the elephant and the mouse?

42. **Analyze** Without multiplying, tell how you know that 45×32 is greater than 35×20.

43. Using Algebra An elephant has a heart rate of about 30 beats per minute.

a. Make a chart that shows an elephant's heart rate for 0, 5, 10, 15, 20, 25, and 30 min.

b. Write a rule that tells how many times an elephant's heart beats in any number of minutes.

c. Use your rule to find the number of times an elephant's heart would beat in 45 minutes.

44. Create Your Own Draw an array to represent the product of 2 two-digit numbers. Have a classmate list the partial products and find the answer.

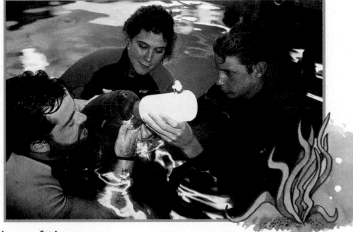

▲ **Science Connection**
Two marine biologists assist Dakota Blair, age 13, as he feeds an orphaned manatee at the National Aquarium in Santo Domingo.

Review and Remember

Using Algebra Find each *n*. Name the property used.

45. $426 + 275 = 275 + n$

46. $(93 + n) + 158 = 93 + (28 + 158)$

47. $0 + 5,629 = n$

48. $150 + (38 + 49) = (150 + 38) + n$

Time for Technology

Using a Calculator

Patterns in Multiplication

Using Algebra You can find some interesting patterns in multiplication.

1. Use your calculator to find the products.

    a. 15×15 **b.** 25×25

    c. 35×35 **d.** 45×45

Describe any pattern you see.

2. Predict Use the pattern you found to predict each product.

    a. 55×55 **b.** 65×65

    c. 75×75 **d.** 85×85

Use your calculator to verify your predictions.

A Zoo Redo

You have learned to multiply with 2 two-digit numbers. Now you will use the same process to multiply with a three-digit number.

Learning About It

The animal nursery at a zoo is getting a new floor. Each floor tile covers one square foot of space. How many tiles are needed to cover the floor?

$$48 \times 134 = t$$
Estimate first: $50 \times 130 = 6,500$

Then find the exact product.

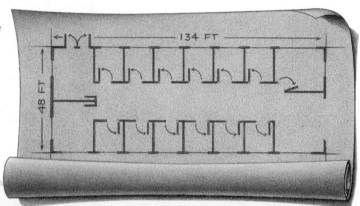

THERE'S ALWAYS A WAY!

● **One way** is to use paper and pencil.

Step 1 Multiply by the ones. Regroup if you can.	**Step 2** Multiply by the tens. Use 0 as a placeholder. Regroup if you can.	**Step 3** Add the partial products.
$\begin{array}{r} {\scriptstyle 2\,3} \\ 134 \\ \times\ \ 48 \\ \hline 1072 \end{array}$ 8 ones × 134 = 1,072	$\begin{array}{r} {\scriptstyle 1\,1} \\ {\scriptstyle 2\,3} \\ 134 \\ \times\ \ 48 \\ \hline 1072 \\ 5360 \end{array}$ 4 tens × 134 = 5,360	$\begin{array}{r} {\scriptstyle 1\,1} \\ {\scriptstyle 2\,3} \\ 134 \\ \times\ \ 48 \\ \hline 1\ 072 \\ +\ 5\ 360 \\ \hline 6,432 \end{array}$

● **Another way** is to use a calculator.

Press: ④ ⑧ ✕ ① ③ ④ =

Display: *6432*

Place a comma in your answer: 6,432.

To cover the floor, 6,432 tiles are needed.

Think and Discuss When using a calculator to multiply, why would it be a good idea to determine the value of the ones digit in the product?

Try It Out

Estimate each product first. Then use paper and pencil or a calculator to find the exact answer.

1. $\begin{array}{r} 45 \\ \times\ 15 \\ \hline \end{array}$

2. $\begin{array}{r} 786 \\ \times\ 13 \\ \hline \end{array}$

3. $\begin{array}{r} 654 \\ \times\ 23 \\ \hline \end{array}$

4. $3,111 \times 87$ 5. $\$4.50 \times 20$ 6. $97 \times \$1.02$

◀ **Math Note**

When multiplying money, remember to place a dollar sign and decimal point in your answer.

Practice

Choose a Method Use paper and pencil or a calculator to find each product. Tell which method you chose.

7. 122×53 8. 104×29 9. 718×36 10. 998×15

11. 342×52 12. 28×379 13. $6,293 \times 67$ 14. $1,024 \times 92$

15. 67×896 16. $\$14.06 \times 23$ 17. $\$1,302 \times 82$ 18. $\$253.98 \times 26$

Problem Solving

19. Tiles are sold for $0.88 each or in boxes of 500 tiles for $415. A new floor at the zoo will need 6,432 tiles. How much will the floor cost if the tiles are bought separately? by the box?

20. A young tiger had to be cared for by humans after its mother abandoned it. At seven months of age, it weighed 129 pounds. When fully grown, it weighed 785 pounds. How much weight did it gain?

Review and Remember

Round to the underlined place.

21. 2̲3   22. 5̲9̲8   23. 1,7̲89   24. 6.8̲5   25. 1̲2.78   26. 3̲.099

Money $ense

Think Before You Leap!

Pete's uncle asked him to walk his dog for an hour each day for 10 days. Pete was told to choose how he would like to be paid. He could choose to earn $5.00 an hour <u>or</u> he could choose to get $0.05 for the first hour and have the pay double every hour after that.

What would you choose? Explain why.

$.05 or $5

On the Job

Multiplying by a three-digit number is like multiplying by a two-digit number, except there is one more partial product.

Learning About It

Manatees are large, gentle creatures sometimes called sea cows. If a manatee eats 112 pounds of water plants each day, how many pounds does it eat in a year?

$$112 \times 365 = n$$
Estimate first: $100 \times 400 = 40,000$

Then find the exact product.

▲ **Science Connection**
Because manatees eat so many water plants, they are used to keep waterways in Guyana clear of weeds.

INTERNET ACTIVITY
www.sbgmath.com

THERE'S ALWAYS A WAY!

● **One way** is to use paper and pencil.

Step 1 Multiply by the ones.	**Step 2** Multiply by the tens. Use one zero as a placeholder.	**Step 3** Multiply by the hundreds. Use two zeros as placeholders.	**Step 4** Add the partial products.
$\begin{array}{r} 1\,1 \\ 365 \\ \times 112 \\ \hline 730 \end{array}$	$\begin{array}{r} 1\,1 \\ 365 \\ \times 112 \\ \hline 730 \\ 3650 \end{array}$	$\begin{array}{r} 1\,1 \\ 365 \\ \times 112 \\ \hline 730 \\ 3650 \\ 36500 \end{array}$	$\begin{array}{r} 1\,1 \\ 365 \\ \times 112 \\ \hline 730 \\ 3\,650 \\ +36\,500 \\ \hline 40,880 \end{array}$

● **Another way** is to use a calculator.

Press: (1)(1)(2)(×)(3)(6)(5)(=)

Display: *40880*

Place a comma in your answer: 40,800

A manatee eats 40,880 pounds of water plants in a year. The estimate shows that the answer makes sense.

More Examples

A.
$$\begin{array}{r} 287 \\ \times\,104 \\ \hline 1\,148 \\ 0\,000 \\ +\,28\,700 \\ \hline 29{,}848 \end{array}$$

To multiply by a factor with a zero, you can use a row of zeros as placeholders or just use extra zeros as placeholders.

B.
$$\begin{array}{r} 287 \\ \times\,104 \\ \hline 1\,148 \\ +\,28\,700 \\ \hline 29{,}848 \end{array}$$

Think and Discuss Compare Examples A and B above. Why could you leave out the row of zeros in Example A?

Try It Out

Estimate each product. Then find the exact answer.

1. $\begin{array}{r} 501 \\ \times\,143 \end{array}$
2. $\begin{array}{r} 558 \\ \times\,295 \end{array}$
3. $\begin{array}{r} 227 \\ \times\,161 \end{array}$
4. $\begin{array}{r} 413 \\ \times\,287 \end{array}$
5. $\begin{array}{r} 303 \\ \times\,709 \end{array}$

Practice

Choose a Method Use paper and pencil or a calculator to find each product. Estimate to be sure your answer is reasonable.

6. 89×32
7. 147×78
8. 370×496
9. 896×111

10. 651×782
11. 306×451
12. 210×402
13. $202 \times \$5.72$

14. $\$4.09 \times 786$
15. $\$4.88 \times 523$
16. $412 \times \$8.90$
17. $1{,}437 \times 180$

Problem Solving

18. If each manatee in a family of 15 ate 108 pounds of food daily, how many pounds of food would the family of manatees eat daily? weekly? yearly?

19. **Using Estimation** If a colony of bees collected about 105 pounds of nectar in a week, about how many pounds of nectar would they collect in four months?

20. **Journal Idea** Explain why you used an estimate rather than an exact amount in Exercise 19.

Review and Remember

Using Algebra Find each n.

21. $n + 3 = 9$
22. $2 \times 8 = n$
23. $5 \times n = 35$
24. $7 - n = 5$

25. $49 \div n = 7$
26. $9 \times n = 72$
27. $65 - 23 = n$
28. $39 \div n = 3$

For Extra Practice, see Set G, page 162.

Problem Solving
Using Money

You need to know how to add, subtract, and multiply money to solve problems.

The Anderson family and some friends spent a day at the zoo. The group included one senior citizen, two adults, four students, and a baby. How much did admission to the zoo cost this group?

 ### UNDERSTAND

What do you need to find?

You need to find the total cost for the group.

 ### PLAN

How can you solve the problem?

Use a multistep approach. First, multiply the number of people in each group by the admission cost. Then add to find the total cost.

Zoo Admission

Children under 4	Free
Students	
4–18 years	$4.25
Adults	$7.50
Senior Citizens	$5.75
(65 and over)	

 ### SOLVE

Step 1	Step 2	Step 3	
Students 4–18 years	Adults	Everyone	
		Students	$17.00
$4.25	$7.50	Adults	$15.00
× 4	× 2	Senior Citizen	$ 5.75
$17.00	$15.00	Baby	0.00
			$37.75

The cost of admission to the zoo is $37.75 for this group.

 ### LOOK BACK

What if the cost of an adult ticket were only $6.50? What would be the total cost then? Tell how you found your answer.

Show What You Learned

Use the zoo admission prices on page 156 for Problems 1–4. When appropriate, use a multistep approach to solve.

1 **What If?** What would the admission cost be for six students, four adults, and two senior citizens? What if there was also a baby in a stroller? What would the cost be then?

2 Coupons for $1.00 off each ticket to the zoo were printed in a newspaper. What would be the admission cost for one adult, one student, and one senior citizen if coupons were used for all three tickets?

3 Grandma and Grandpa, aged 65 and 66, took their grandchildren, aged 4 and 1, to the zoo. What was the admission cost?

4 What would the admission be for five adults and four children under age 4?

Use the signs at the right for Problems 5–9.

5 **Describe** Three large wooden elephants are being sold for $40. If sold separately, they cost $14.95 each. How much can be saved by buying three at a time? Tell how you found your answer.

6 **Explain** At the souvenir shop, Gary wants to buy two mid-size animals and five small animals. He has $30.00. Does he have enough money to buy the items? How do you know?

7 The souvenir shop sells mid-size figurines of tigers at $6.95 each, or five for $30.00. The science teacher wants to buy 12 tigers. How could she save money on the purchase? How much will be saved?

8 Alberto has $15.06 to buy one mid-size animal and two small animals. If the tax is $0.65, how much change should he receive?

9 **Create Your Own** Use the zoo admission prices or the cost of souvenirs to write a problem. Explain how you would solve the problem you wrote.

Small Animals
$1.98 each

Mid-size Animals
$6.95 each

Large Animals
$14.95 each

Practice What You Learned

Choose the correct letter for each answer.

1 Bob is older than Joe, but younger than Susan. Susan is older than Al. Which is a reasonable conclusion?

A. Bob is older than Al.
B. Joe is older than Al.
C. Bob is the oldest.
D. Susan is older than Joe.

Tip

Using the *Make a List* strategy can help you solve this problem.

2 Leon has 20 coins. Some are dimes and some are quarters. The total amount is $3.05. How many dimes and how many quarters does Leon have?

A. 11 dimes, 9 quarters
B. 12 dimes, 8 quarters
C. 13 dimes, 7 quarters
D. 14 dimes, 6 quarters

Tip

Use one of the strategies to solve this problem.
• *Guess and Check*
• *Draw a Diagram*

3 Rosa is having a fence built around an 18 ft by 24 ft yard. The 24-ft side of the yard against the house doesn't need fencing. How much fencing does Rosa need?

A. 42 feet
B. 60 feet
C. 66 feet
D. 84 feet
E. Not Here

Tip

Make a Diagram to help you solve this problem. Sketch the lawn and mark the sides that need fencing.

4 Harry bought 2 sweaters at $38.89 each and a pair of shoes for $43.90. Which is the best estimate of how much he spent before taxes?

A. About $70
B. About $80
C. About $115
D. About $120

5 The regular ticket price for a concert is $8.50. Senior citizens pay $5.00, and children under 6 are free. A senior citizen takes four children, ages 4, 6, 8, and 9, to the concert. Which is the best estimate for the cost of their tickets?

A. Less than $20.00
B. About $25.00
C. About $30.00
D. More than $35.00
E. Not Here

6 Eve is twice as tall as her little sister Sue (s). Eve's Dad is 3 times as tall as Sue. Which number sentence shows that the difference between Eve's height and her Dad's height is 18 inches?

A. $2 \times 3 \times s = 18$
B. $3 \times s - 2 = 18$
C. $(3 \times s) - (2 \times s) = 18$
D. $(3 + s) + (2 + s) = 18$

7 Boxes of light bulbs are on sale at 3 boxes for $8.97. Which of these is reasonable for the cost of 2 boxes?

A. About $2.00
B. About $3.00
C. About $4.50
D. About $6.00

8 This graph shows how many students prefer seeing a movie at home or in a theater.

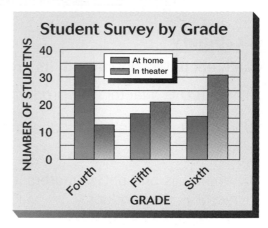

Student Survey by Grade

NUMBER OF STUDETNS

At home
In theater

GRADE

Fourth Fifth Sixth

About how many students would rather watch movies at home?

A. 55
B. 60
C. 65
D. 70

9 Zelda and 3 friends went out to lunch. The bill was $46.85, and they decided to share the cost equally. How could you find each person's share of the bill?

A. Multiply $46.85 by 3.
B. Multiply $46.85 by 4.
C. Divide $46.85 by 3.
D. Divide $46.85 by 4.
E. Not Here

10 For the recycling drive, each of 27 students is trying to collect 85 pounds of paper. Which of the following is needed to find about how many pounds the students hope to collect in all?

A. An estimate of the sum
B. The exact sum
C. An estimate of the product
D. The exact product

✔ Checkpoint

Multiplying by Two- and Three-Digit Numbers

Vocabulary

Match each description with its property.

1. When 0 is a factor, the product is 0.

2. The order of the factors does not change the product.

3. When 1 is one of two factors, the other factor is the product.

Word Bank

Associative Property
Commutative Property
Distributive Property
Identity Property
Zero Property

Concepts and Skills

Draw a model to find each product. (pages 146–147)

4. 11×12
5. 19×27
6. 22×14
7. 25×29

Estimate first. Then find the exact answer. (pages 148–151)

8. $\begin{array}{r} 49 \\ \times\, 40 \\ \hline \end{array}$

9. $\begin{array}{r} 68 \\ \times\, 27 \\ \hline \end{array}$

10. $\begin{array}{r} 94 \\ \times\, 15 \\ \hline \end{array}$

11. $\begin{array}{r} 83 \\ \times\, 60 \\ \hline \end{array}$

12. $\begin{array}{r} 62 \\ \times\, 47 \\ \hline \end{array}$

Choose a Method Use paper and pencil or a calculator to find each product. (pages 152–153)

13. $\begin{array}{r} 112 \\ \times\, 70 \\ \hline \end{array}$

14. $\begin{array}{r} 223 \\ \times\, 18 \\ \hline \end{array}$

15. $\begin{array}{r} 104 \\ \times\, 25 \\ \hline \end{array}$

16. $\begin{array}{r} 247 \\ \times\, 48 \\ \hline \end{array}$

17. 108×28
18. 216×36
19. 441×59
20. 67×584

Choose a Method Use paper and pencil or a calculator. (pages 154–155)

21. $\begin{array}{r} 123 \\ \times\, 114 \\ \hline \end{array}$

22. $\begin{array}{r} 225 \\ \times\, 104 \\ \hline \end{array}$

23. $\begin{array}{r} 431 \\ \times\, 212 \\ \hline \end{array}$

24. $\begin{array}{r} 353 \\ \times\, 310 \\ \hline \end{array}$

25. 643×188
26. 591×109
27. 178×774
28. 421×603

Mixed Practice

Using Algebra Compare. Write >, <, or = for each ●.

29. 40×80 ● 8×400
30. 15×30 ● 14×31
31. $70 \times 1,000$ ● $35 \times 2,000$
32. 18×200 ● 22×165

Problem Solving

33. Analyze The floor in a zoo cafeteria needs new tiles. The floor measures 36 by 42 feet. Tiles that are 1 foot by 1 foot cost $0.92 each. A box of 500 tiles is $450. What combination of boxes and single tiles should the zoo buy to get the lowest cost?

34. Jan's heart rate is 70 beats per minute. Her dog Corky has a heart rate of 100 beats per minute. What is the difference between the number of times Jan's heart beats in a day and the number of times Corky's heart beats in that time?

35. Some tropical fish are on sale this week. Black tetra are $1.29, barbs are $2.19, and angelfish are $3.15. How much would it cost to buy 12 of each?

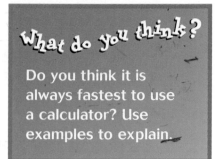

What do you think?

Do you think it is always fastest to use a calculator? Use examples to explain.

Journal Idea

Tell how you would use two-digit multiplication to show how much money you could save in a year. Or think of something else in your own life and tell how multiplication relates to it.

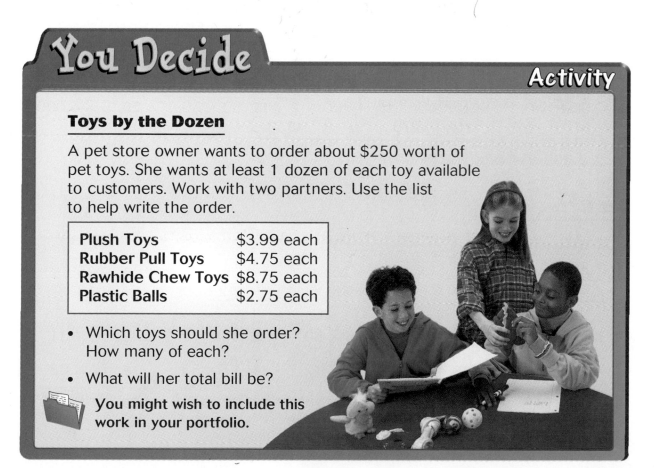

You Decide

Activity

Toys by the Dozen

A pet store owner wants to order about $250 worth of pet toys. She wants at least 1 dozen of each toy available to customers. Work with two partners. Use the list to help write the order.

Plush Toys	$3.99 each
Rubber Pull Toys	$4.75 each
Rawhide Chew Toys	$8.75 each
Plastic Balls	$2.75 each

• Which toys should she order? How many of each?

• What will her total bill be?

You might wish to include this work in your portfolio.

Extra Practice

Set A   (pages 130–131)

Using Algebra   Find each *n*. Use multiplication properties.

1. $3 \times n = 3$

2. $4 \times 3 = 3 \times n$

3. $(2 \times 5) \times 4 = 2 \times (5 \times n)$

4. $4 \times (n \times 5) = 0$

5. $(3 + 1) \times 12 = n$

6. $(6 \times 1) \times n = 5 \times (6 \times 1)$

7. $17 \times 1 = n$

8. $142 \times 36 \times 0 = n$

9. $(8 \times 4) \times 3 = 3 \times (n \times 4)$

10. A dog trainer has 36 show ribbons to display. What are five ways she could arrange the ribbons to have the same number of ribbons in each row?

Set B   (pages 134–137)

Find each product. Use patterns to help you.

1. $\begin{array}{r} 70 \\ \times\ 4 \\ \hline \end{array}$

2. $\begin{array}{r} 80 \\ \times\ 3 \\ \hline \end{array}$

3. $\begin{array}{r} 300 \\ \times\ 2 \\ \hline \end{array}$

4. $\begin{array}{r} 400 \\ \times\ 8 \\ \hline \end{array}$

5. $\begin{array}{r} 80 \\ \times\ 6 \\ \hline \end{array}$

6. 40×60

7. 30×70

8. 35×100

9. 90×200

10. 170×10

11. 200×5

12. 80×20

13. $54 \times 1{,}000$

14. 400×60

15. 300×20

16. $2{,}000 \times 4$

17. 900×40

18. $1{,}200 \times 2$

19. 80×50

20. $5 \times 6{,}000$

21. Find a pair of factors whose product is equal to 2×400. Tell how you found the factors.

Set C   (pages 138–139)

Estimate each product.

1. $\begin{array}{r} 62 \\ \times\ 41 \\ \hline \end{array}$

2. $\begin{array}{r} 37 \\ \times\ 19 \\ \hline \end{array}$

3. $\begin{array}{r} 25 \\ \times\ 36 \\ \hline \end{array}$

4. $\begin{array}{r} 81 \\ \times\ 22 \\ \hline \end{array}$

5. $\begin{array}{r} 95 \\ \times\ 13 \\ \hline \end{array}$

6. 28×84

7. 55×15

8. 16×89

9. 31×77

10. 56×31

11. 41×75

12. 26×43

13. 99×12

14. 17×53

15. 72×68

16. 136×21

17. 118×42

18. 13×241

19. 207×16

20. 67×689

21. A purple martin can eat 123 mosquitoes in a day. About how many mosquitoes can it eat in a week?

Extra Practice

Set D (pages 140–141)

Find each product.

1. 21 × 3	**2.** 48 × 8	**3.** 16 × 7	**4.** 57 × 3	**5.** 92 × 5
6. 86 × 7	**7.** 35 × 9	**8.** 72 × 5	**9.** 84 × 4	**10.** 12 × 3

11. 66 × 8   **12.** 6 × 29   **13.** 51 × 4   **14.** 5 × 81   **15.** 121 × 9

16. 765 × 2   **17.** 43 × 6   **18.** $1.05 × 9   **19.** 62 × 7   **20.** $1.21 × 8

21. A sled dog runs 65 miles a day. How many miles will the sled dog run in a two-day dog-sled race?

Set E (pages 148–151)

Multiply.

1. 62 × 21	**2.** 54 × 14	**3.** 13 × 82	**4.** 34 × 24	**5.** 73 × 42
6. 75 × 36	**7.** 15 × 47	**8.** 28 × 19	**9.** 63 × 18	**10.** 92 × 35

11. 38 × 25   **12.** 72 × 26   **13.** 16 × 31   **14.** 55 × 22   **15.** 91 × 12

16. 40 × 37   **17.** 68 × 32   **18.** 98 × 50   **19.** 46 × 17   **20.** 23 × 71

21. 51 × 81   **22.** 85 × 27   **23.** 49 × 58   **24.** 99 × 56   **25.** 77 × 84

26. Companies often sell their goods to distributors who see that the products get to stores near you. If a company sells a bird cage to a distributor for $14.99, and each distributor adds $1.29 to the cost, how much will the customer pay if there are three distributors?

27. You have a chance to adopt a cat. A collar costs $4.59. Registration costs $15.00. The cat eats a can of food a day. You can buy four cans for $1.00. How much will it cost to feed the cat for a month with 31 days?

Extra Practice

Set F   (pages 152–153)

Multiply.

1. $1.75
   × 40

2. 293
   × 21

3. 438
   × 18

4. 786
   × 14

5. 295 × 36

6. 482 × 31

7. 217 × 53

8. 244 × 24

9. 681 × 39

10. 770 × 52

11. 408 × 62

12. 528 × 95

13. 391 × 72

14. 502 × 36

15. 867 × 23

16. 994 × 16

17. At the local pet store, a medium-sized angelfish costs $2.98. How much would a dozen cost?

18. After a class trip to a natural animal habitat, class members can order photographs of the day. Fifteen students out of a class of 26 order two prints each. The rest of the class orders three prints each. If the prints cost $0.43 each, how much does the class owe?

Set G   (pages 154–155)

Find each product.

1. 296
   × 321

2. 784
   × 916

3. 401
   × 123

4. 406
   × 398

5. 592
   × 174

6. 332
   × 135

7. 721
   × 309

8. 651
   × 149

Choose a Method Use paper and pencil or a calculator to find each product.

9. $1.75 × 321

10. $2.06 × 786

11. 566 × 328

12. 325 × 681

13. 942 × 370

14. 688 × 757

15. 451 × 117

16. $4.10 × 381

17. $3.85 × 385

18. 298 × 721

19. 623 × 219

20. 689 × 992

21. Sheila's horse Champion exercises from 1 to 2 hours a day. Champion eats 105 pounds of hay each week. How much hay will Champion eat in a year?

Chapter Test

Find each _n_. Write the multiplication property that helped you.

1. $23 \times n = 23$

2. $n = 5 \times (10 + 3)$

3. $(2 \times 3) \times 4 = 2 \times (3 \times n)$

4. $4 \times 9 = n \times 4$

Compare. Write >, <, or = for each ⬤.

5. 700×40 ⬤ 70×400

6. $6,000 \times 20$ ⬤ $1,000 \times 60$

7. 25×300 ⬤ 250×300

8. 90×80 ⬤ 720×10

Estimate each product.

9. 89×24

10. $\$78 \times \$39$

11. 413×88

12. 209×69

Multiply.

13. $\begin{array}{r} 56 \\ \times\ 8 \\ \hline \end{array}$

14. $\begin{array}{r} 24 \\ \times\ 25 \\ \hline \end{array}$

15. $\begin{array}{r} 462 \\ \times\ 37 \\ \hline \end{array}$

16. $\begin{array}{r} 158 \\ \times\ 53 \\ \hline \end{array}$

17. $\begin{array}{r} 116 \\ \times\ 213 \\ \hline \end{array}$

18. $\begin{array}{r} 67 \\ \times\ 89 \\ \hline \end{array}$

19. $\begin{array}{r} \$35 \\ \times\ 21 \\ \hline \end{array}$

20. $\begin{array}{r} \$1.25 \\ \times\ 22 \\ \hline \end{array}$

21. $\begin{array}{r} \$3.97 \\ \times\ 166 \\ \hline \end{array}$

22. $\begin{array}{r} \$1.89 \\ \times\ 45 \\ \hline \end{array}$

Solve.

23. It takes Adam's grandfather 27 hours to carve one wooden bird. How many hours would it take him to carve 112 birds?

24. Each side of a rabbit hutch requires 124 centimeters of wire. How many centimeters of wire will be needed for the four sides of the hutch?

25. A wildlife park needs 34 pounds of fruit a day to feed its monkeys. At this rate, how many pounds of fruit will the park need to buy in a year? (On average, there are 365 days in a year.)

 Self-Check

Did you place each dollar sign and decimal point correctly in Questions 19–22?

Performance Assessment

Show What You Know About Multiplication

1 Use three spinners as shown and a number cube with numbers 1–6 on it.

What You Need

number cube
3 five-part spinners

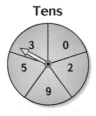 

Hundreds   Tens   Ones

a. Spin all three spinners. Write a three-digit number using one number from each spinner.

b. Roll the number cube. Multiply your three-digit number by the number that comes up on the number cube.

c. Is it possible to get an even product? Explain why or why not.

Self-Check Did you remember to write a three-digit number by spinning each spinner once?

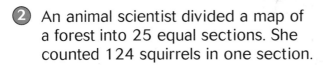

2 An animal scientist divided a map of a forest into 25 equal sections. She counted 124 squirrels in one section.

a. If the same number of squirrels are in each section, how many squirrels might she expect to find in the entire forest?

b. If she estimates that each squirrel stores 50 nuts before winter, how many nuts might be stored in the forest?

Self-Check Did you remember to label each of your answers?

For Your Portfolio

You might wish to include this work in your portfolio.

Extension

Lattice Multiplication

People long ago did not have calculators to help them multiply greater numbers, so creative ways were invented to solve problems. One such method is called lattice, or cell, multiplication. It was one of the devices used by mathematicians in India.

Find the product of 114 × 36.

① Use grid paper to draw 2 rows of 3 squares.

② Draw a diagonal line through each square.

③ Write the digits of the three-digit factor across the top. Write the digits of the two-digit factor down the right side.

④ Multiply the digits and record the products in the lattices. If you do not need both lattices of a square, write a zero in the top lattice as a placeholder.

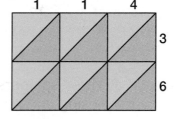

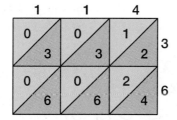

$4 \times 3 =$

$4 \times 6 =$

Did You Know?

Social Studies Connection Arabs used this method hundreds of years ago. They called it the method of the sieve or the method of the net.

⑤ Start with the lower right lattice. Add along the diagonals from right to left. Regroup and add to the next diagonal when necessary.

⑥ To form the product, write the digits in order from the outside top left to the outside bottom right.

0 4 1 0 4

114 × 36 = 4,104

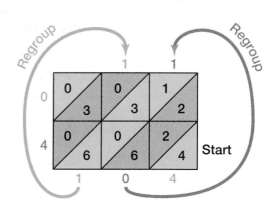

Make lattices and find the products.

1. 36 × 88   **2.** 92 × 13   **3.** 932 × 64   **4.** 602 × 73   **5.** 412 × 50

165

Cumulative Review

★ ★ ★ ★ ★ **Preparing for Tests**

Choose the correct letter for each answer.

Number Concepts	Operations

1. Which of these numbers is 6.5 when rounded to the nearest tenth and 6 when rounded to the nearest one?

- **A.** 6.28
- **B.** 6.48
- **C.** 6.52
- **D.** 6.54

2. Three young gymnasts had very close scores. Which set of numbers could represent their scores ordered from *least* to *greatest*?

- **A.** 4.033, 4.03, 4.066
- **B.** 4.03, 4.033, 4.066
- **C.** 4.03, 4.066, 4.033
- **D.** 4.033, 4.066, 4.03

3. Which number sentence is true?

- **A.** $\frac{1}{9} < \frac{1}{10}$
- **B.** $\frac{1}{8} > \frac{1}{6}$
- **C.** $\frac{1}{4} < \frac{1}{6}$
- **D.** $\frac{1}{2} > \frac{1}{3}$

4. Which of these fractions is **NOT** equivalent to $\frac{1}{4}$?

- **A.** $\frac{2}{8}$
- **B.** $\frac{3}{12}$
- **C.** $\frac{6}{8}$
- **D.** $\frac{4}{16}$

5. It takes Mrs. Cortez 120 hours to make a small quilt. It takes her 14 hours longer to make a large quilt. She has orders for 13 large quilts. If each large quilt takes her the same amount of time to make, how long will it take her to complete the orders?

- **A.** 147 h
- **B.** 402 h
- **C.** 536 h
- **D.** 1,742 h

6. An airline charges $120 round trip to transport dogs in medium carriers and $180 to transport dogs in large carriers. How much will it cost to transport 3 dogs in medium carriers and 5 in large carriers?

- **A.** $360
- **B.** $900
- **C.** $1,260
- **D.** $2,400

7. What is the product of 515 and 55?

- **A.** 27,225
- **B.** 27,325
- **C.** 28,225
- **D.** 28,325

8. Two cats eat about 4 pounds of dry cat food every 14 days. About how many pounds of cat food would they eat in 12 *weeks*?

- **A.** 4 lb
- **B.** 8 lb
- **C.** 24 lb
- **D.** 48 lb

Probability and Statistics	Geometry and Spatial Reasoning

Use the bar graph for Questions 9–11.

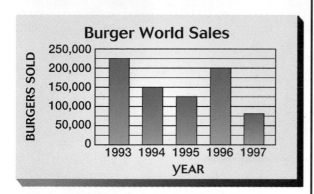

Burger World Sales

9. In which year were fewer than 100,000 burgers sold?

- **A.** 1994
- **B.** 1995
- **C.** 1996
- **D.** 1997

10. Which of the following best describes the difference between the greatest and the least number of sales in 1 year?

- **A.** About 75,000 burgers
- **B.** About 95,000 burgers
- **C.** About 100,000 burgers
- **D.** About 150,000 burgers

11. Which is the best estimate of the average number of burgers sold per year?

- **A.** 155,000
- **B.** 200,000
- **C.** 275,000
- **D.** 875,000

12. Hank, Fred, Sara, and Jill are lining up in a row. Two boys cannot stand next to each other. In how many different ways can the four of them line up?

- **A.** 6
- **B.** 9
- **C.** 12
- **D.** 16

13. Which figure is **NOT** a polygon?

- **A.**
- **B.**
- **C.**
- **D.**

14. Which pair of lines always forms right angles?

- **A.** Parallel
- **B.** Perpendicular
- **C.** Intersecting
- **D.** Congruent

15. Which dotted line is a line of symmetry?

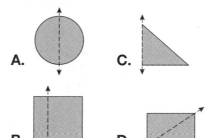

- **A.**
- **B.**
- **C.**
- **D.**

16. Which picture shows the *reflection* of Figure X?

Figure X

- **A.**
- **B.**
- **C.**
- **D.**

Chapter 5

Dividing by One-Digit Divisors

Chapter Theme: TRANSPORTATION

REAL-WORLD Math

·············Real Facts·················

Pedal power is more popular than ever with people of all ages! Across the country, more and more people are riding bicycles. Today, there are many different styles of bicycles. The graph below shows the styles and the average number of bicycles a bicycle dealer might sell in one year.

Average Yearly Bicycle Sales

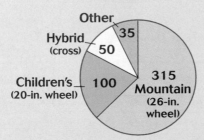

Other 35
Hybrid (cross) 50
Children's (20-in. wheel) 100
315 Mountain (26-in. wheel)

• Suppose all the hybrid (cross) bicycles were bought by 5 different bicycle clubs. If each club bought the same number, how many bicycles did each club buy?

• About how many times as many mountain bicycles were sold than were children's bicycles?

···········Real People···················

Meet Marty Epstein, bicycle-shop owner. In his shop, Marty sells and fixes bicycles, including his own. Like the children pictured on the right, Marty feels free and independent while riding his bicycle.

Up, Up, and Away!

Using Algebra

Knowing that multiplication and division are inverse operations can help you complete number sentences.

Learning About It

On the Masai Mara in Africa, hot-air balloons cruise at a height just above the trees to get a bird's-eye view of the wildlife below.

Suppose a hot-air balloon rises 9 feet per minute. How many minutes will it take the hot-air balloon to reach a height of 72 feet?

height of balloon		feet per minute		minutes
72	÷	**9**	=	*n*

Since multiplication and division are inverse operations, you can use a related multiplication fact to find *n*.

Fact family for 8, 9, and 72	$8 \times 9 = 72$ $72 \div 9 = 8$	$9 \times 8 = 72$ $72 \div 8 = 9$

It will take the hot-air balloon 8 minutes to rise to 72 feet.

Connecting Ideas

Knowing how multiplication and division are related helps you find the input or output of a function table.

Find each *n*. Use the rule: Multiply by 6.

Input	Output
3	*n*
n	30

← Use the rule: $3 \times 6 = 18$

← Use the inverse operation: $30 \div 6 = 5$
  Or use a related fact: $5 \times 6 = 30$

72 ft

9 ft

AFRICA
KENYA

Think and Discuss What values for n make $n \div 1 = n$ a true statement? Tell why.

Try It Out

Write a related multiplication or division sentence. Then find each n.

1. $54 \div 6 = n$ **2.** $5 \times n = 40$ **3.** $n \times 6 = 12$ **4.** $n \div 2 = 9$

Practice

Complete each input/output table.

Rule: Multiply by 8

	Input	Output
5.	4	▧
6.	5	▧
7.	▧	64

Rule: Divide by 4

	Input	Output
8.	16	▧
9.	32	▧
10.	▧	5

11. Rule: _____?_____

Input	Output
2	14
7	49
5	35

Find each n.

12. $n \times 3 = 27$ **13.** $0 \div 9 = n$ **14.** $6 \times n = 48$ **15.** $n \times 4 = 0$

16. $80 \div n = 10$ **17.** $n \div 9 = 4$ **18.** $15 \div n = 3$ **19.** $63 \div n = 7$

20. $64 \div 8 = n$ **21.** $7 \times n = 42$ **22.** $n \div 6 = 9$ **23.** $48 \div n = 6$

Problem Solving

24. Analyze A balloon rises to a height of 500 feet in four minutes. If the distance it rises each minute is the same, how far does it rise in the first minute?

25. Explain It takes you at least five minutes to blow up six small balloons. What is the least amount of time it will take you to blow up 42 small balloons?

26. Journal Idea Use the rule below. Choose any three inputs. What are the outputs? Tell what happens when you multiply and divide by the same number.

Rule: Input $\times 6 \div 6$ = output

Review and Remember

Find each answer.

27. $1.234 + 6.78$ **28.** $17.06 - 8$ **29.** $9 \times 1,987$ **30.** $11,376 + 9,056$

31. $42.385 - 9.644$ **32.** $8.36 + 11.94$ **33.** $8 \times 6,021$ **34.** $76 \times 10,325$

For Extra Practice, see Set A, page 202.

Using Algebra

Order Counts!

You can find the value of a number sentence by using the order of operations.

Learning About It

Jed, Amy, and Sue are trying to find *n* in the number sentence below. Each has found a different answer. Who do you think followed the correct order—Jed, Amy, or Sue?

$$6 + 12 \div (2 \times 3) - 6 \times 1 = n$$

Jed thinks *n* = 21

Amy thinks *n* = 18

Sue thinks *n* = 2

When a number sentence contains more than one operation, people need to follow a certain order to get the same answer.

Word Bank

order of operations

To find out, follow the **order of operations**.

- **First**, do operations inside parentheses.

$$6 + 12 \div (2 \times 3) - 6 \times 1 = n$$

- **Next**, do all **multiplication** and **division** from left to right.

$$6 + \underline{12 \div 6} - \underline{6 \times 1} = n$$

- **Last**, do all addition and subtraction from left to right.

$$6 + 2 - 6 = n$$
$$2 = n$$

Sue followed the correct order.

Think and Discuss How did Jed and Amy find their values for *n*?

Try It Out

Tell which operation should be done first. Then find each *n*.

1. $3 \times 5 + 12 = n$ **2.** $27 \div (18 - 9) = n$ **3.** $14 - 8 \div 4 + 6 = n$

4. Describe Explain how the number sentence shown below represents this problem: Find the total cost of twelve $8 train tickets and ten $3 subway tokens.

$$(12 \times \$8) + (10 \times \$3) = n$$

Practice

Choose a value from the box at the right to make each sentence true.

5. $8 - 6 \div 3 + 4 = n$ **6.** $10 \div 5 \times 4 - 8 = n$

7. $6 \times (8 + 4) - 2 \times 2 = n$ **8.** $(9 + 1) \div 2 \times 3 \times 3 = n$

9. $8 + 2 \div 2 - 1 = n$ **10.** $16 + 3 - 2 \times 3 = n$

11. $6 \times 6 + (5 - 3) = n$ **12.** $(7 + 7) \div 7 \times 7 = n$

13. $16 \div 8 + 5 \times 2 = n$ **14.** $n \times (3 + 4) = 63$

10	4	21
8	12	0
14	38	45
68	44	18
16	13	9

Problem Solving

15. There are four cars with five people in each car and two vans with eight people in each van. Write a number sentence that tells the total number of travelers. Then find the answer.

16. **Create Your Own** Use the picture at the right to write a problem. Have a classmate solve it.

Review and Remember

Find each answer.

17. $999 \div 9$ **18.** 48×6 **19.** $328 + 62$ **20.** $567 \div 7$ **21.** $8.5 - 7$

Time for Technology

Surf the Net

Bookmarks

Bookmarks help you get back quickly to your favorite places on the Internet. Bookmarks have different names in different browsers with different Internet service providers. They are sometimes called favorite places or hot lists or hot spots.

- Find out how you mark bookmarks or favorite places when you use your browser with your Internet service provider.
- Go to this site: www.sbgschool.com
- Follow the links to Kids Central.
- Make a bookmark to mark this site.
- Share your findings with the class.

For Extra Practice, see Set B, page 202.

Cycling Across a State

Using Algebra

You can use mental math, basic facts, and patterns to find quotients.

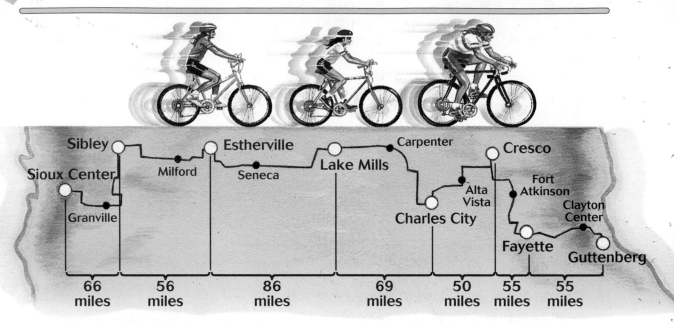

Learning About It

RAGBRAI®—Register's Annual Great Bicycle Ride Across Iowa—is a seven-day event. RAGBRAI® is the longest, largest, and oldest bicycle tour in the world. If a cyclist traveled 8 miles an hour, how many hours would it take to ride 160 miles from Charles City to Guttenberg?

$$160 \div 8 = n$$

Use what you already know about basic facts and patterns of zeros to help you.

$$16 \div 8 = 2$$
$$160 \div 8 = 20$$

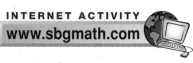
16 tens ÷ 8 = 2 tens or 20

It would take a cyclist 20 hours.

INTERNET ACTIVITY
www.sbgmath.com

Did You Know?

In 1997, RAGBRAI® had 7,500 cyclists. They were chosen by a computer drawing from about 10,000 applicants.

More Examples

A.
$$30 \div 5 = 6$$
$$300 \div 5 = 60$$
$$3,000 \div 5 = 600$$
$$30,000 \div 5 = 6,000$$

B.
$$42 \div 6 = 7$$
$$420 \div 6 = 70$$
$$4,200 \div 6 = 700$$
$$42,000 \div 6 = 7,000$$

Think and Discuss Tell how basic facts and patterns are used in Examples A and B above.

Try It Out

Use a basic fact and patterns to find each n.

1.
$$32 \div 4 = n$$
$$320 \div 4 = n$$
$$3{,}200 \div 4 = n$$
$$32{,}000 \div 4 = n$$

2.
$$40 \div 8 = n$$
$$400 \div 8 = n$$
$$4{,}000 \div 8 = n$$
$$40{,}000 \div 8 = n$$

3.
$$48 \div 6 = n$$
$$480 \div n = 80$$
$$n \div 6 = 800$$
$$48{,}000 \div 6 = n$$

4. Analyze In Exercises 1–3, how is the number of zeros in the quotients related to the number of zeros in the dividends?

Practice

Use a basic fact and patterns to find each quotient.

5. $2\overline{)140}$ **6.** $6\overline{)2{,}400}$ **7.** $3\overline{)270}$ **8.** $4\overline{)3{,}600}$

9. $8\overline{)7{,}200}$ **10.** $2\overline{)10{,}000}$ **11.** $3\overline{)2{,}400}$ **12.** $9\overline{)63{,}000}$

13. $6\overline{)4{,}200}$ **14.** $4\overline{)2{,}400}$ **15.** $5\overline{)500}$ **16.** $7\overline{)5{,}600}$

17. $5\overline{)4{,}500}$ **18.** $8\overline{)32{,}000}$ **19.** $2\overline{)160}$ **20.** $4\overline{)1{,}600}$

21. $450 \div 9$ **22.** $5{,}600 \div 7$ **23.** $1{,}000 \div 10$ **24.** $40{,}000 \div 5$

Problem Solving

25. Social Studies Connection The Tour de France is a team bike race that takes place every year in Europe. Suppose there are 180 cyclists. If there are nine riders on a team, how many teams are there?

26. If cyclists made a 300-mile trip in 6 days and pedaled the same number of miles each day, how many miles a day did they ride?

27. Use the map on page 172. What is the total number of miles in the RAGBRAI?[®]

▲ Annual Tour de France

Review and Remember

Round each number to the underlined place.

28. 7,9<u>3</u>2 **29.** 5.<u>6</u>78 **30.** 1.<u>7</u>02 **31.** <u>9</u>.79 **32.** 4.5<u>2</u>1

33. 6,<u>9</u>96 **34.** 4<u>5</u>,789 **35.** <u>2</u>9.799 **36.** 99.9<u>9</u>9 **37.** 1.0<u>2</u>3

Walking the Wall

You can estimate quotients by using compatible numbers.

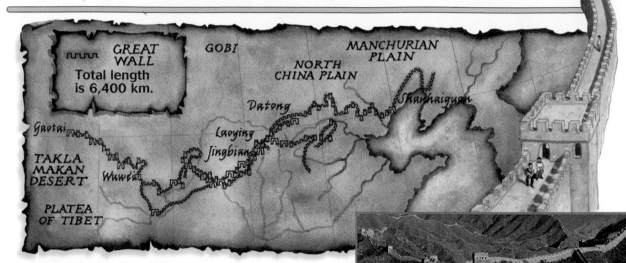

GREAT WALL
Total length is 6,400 km.

GOBI

MANCHURIAN PLAIN

NORTH CHINA PLAIN

Datong

Shanhaiquan

Gaotai

Laoying

Jingbian

TAKLA MAKAN DESERT

Wuwei

PLATEA OF TIBET

Learning About It

Suppose you could walk from one end of the Great Wall to the other. If you walked 7 km an hour, how many hours would it take to walk the entire length of the wall? Use the map above to help you solve the problem.

$$6{,}400 \div 7 = n$$

To estimate the quotient, you can use **compatible numbers**. These are numbers that are easy to compute mentally. Change the dividend to a number that is compatible with the divisor.

$$6{,}400 \div 7 \longrightarrow 6{,}300 \div 7 = 900$$

It would take about 900 hours to walk the Great Wall if you walked 7 km an hour.

▲ **Social Studies Connection** Parts of the Great Wall, located in China, have crumbled and are no longer passable.

Word Bank

compatible numbers

More Examples

A. $501 \div 6 \longrightarrow 480 \div 6 = 80$

48 tens ÷ 6 = 8 tens or 80

B. $4{,}128 \div 8 \longrightarrow 4{,}000 \div 8 = 500$

40 hundreds ÷ 8 = 5 hundreds or 500

Think and Discuss In the division sentence $230 \div 5$, tell what compatible numbers you would use to estimate the quotient. Explain your choice.

Try It Out

Estimate each quotient. Tell what compatible numbers you used.

1. 9)4,300   **2.** 5)293   **3.** 6)3,712   **4.** 3)912

5. Suppose you were estimating 189 ÷ 5. Which will give the closer estimate, 200 ÷ 5 or 150 ÷ 5? Explain how you know.

Practice

Estimate each quotient. Tell what compatible numbers you used.

6. 8)6,188   **7.** 4)3,401   **8.** 3)271   **9.** 7)1,398

10. 2)170   **11.** 6)2,500   **12.** 8)4,109   **13.** 5)246

14. 1,521 ÷ 3   **15.** 501 ÷ 8   **16.** 1,196 ÷ 2   **17.** 4,500 ÷ 4

18. 820 ÷ 9   **19.** 300 ÷ 8   **20.** 5,321 ÷ 6   **21.** 7,395 ÷ 9

22. 434 ÷ 5   **23.** 2,095 ÷ 3   **24.** 1,694 ÷ 7   **25.** 36,211 ÷ 5

Problem Solving

26. Suppose you wanted to walk 215 km of the Great Wall at a pace of 9 km each day. About how many days would it take you?

27. Watchtowers on the Great Wall were built about the same distance apart. You start at one watchtower and walk 900 m, passing four other watchtowers and stopping at a sixth tower. About how far apart are any two of the watchtowers?

28. The heights of different sections of the Great Wall range from 6.1 m to 15.2 m. What is the greatest possible difference in height?

▲ Watchtowers along the Great Wall

Review and Remember

Using Algebra Name the multiplication property that makes each of the following true.

29. 3 × 4 = 4 × 3   **30.** 8 × 1 = 8   **31.** 7 × 12 = (7 × 10) + (7 × 2)

32. 10 × 1 = 1 × 10   **33.** 4 × 0 = 0   **34.** (9 × 3) × 6 = 9 × (3 × 6)

Test It Out

*Learning divisibility rules can help you
tell if there will be a remainder when dividing.*

Learning About It

A number is **divisible** by another number when the quotient is a whole number and the remainder is 0.

You can test numbers to check for divisibility.

Follow these steps to find the numbers from 1 to 50 that are divisible by 2, 5, and 10.

> **Word Bank**
>
> **divisible**

Step 1 Write the numbers from 1 to 50 in rows, as shown.

Step 2 Circle the number 2. Counting by twos, continue to circle every other number. These numbers are divisible by 2.

Step 3 Draw a square around the number 5. Counting by fives, draw a square around every fifth number. These numbers are divisible by 5.

Step 4 Mark an *X* on the number 10. Counting by tens, mark an *X* on every tenth number. These numbers are divisible by 10.

1	②	3	4	⑤	6	7	8	9	⊠⑩
11	12	13	14	15	16	17	18	19	20
21	22	23	24	25	26	27	28	29	30
31	32	33	34	35	36	37	38	39	40
41	42	43	44	45	46	47	48	49	50

Step 5 Look for patterns in your chart. What do you notice about the numbers that are divisible by 2? by 5? by 10? Write rules that tell if a number is divisible by 2, by 5, or by 10.

Step 6 Make a chart like the one at the top of page 177 that states the rules for divisibility by 2, 5, and 10. Include an example of each rule.

Step 7 Continue your chart from Step 6 to include these divisibility rules for 3, 4, 6, and 9.

Divisibility Rules for 3, 4, 6, and 9

Divisible by	Rule	Example
3	The sum of the digits is divisible by 3.	138 $1 + 3 + 8 = 12$ $12 \div 3 = 4$
4	The last two digits form a number that is divisible by 4.	2,324 $24 \div 4 = 6$
6	The number is divisible by both 2 and 3.	2,622 2,622 is even, so it is divisible by 2. $2 + 6 + 2 + 2 = 12$ and $12 \div 3 = 4$, so 2,622 is also divisible by 3.
9	The sum of the digits is divisible by 9.	567 $5 + 6 + 7 = 18$ $18 \div 9 = 2$

Connecting Ideas

You have learned to tell if a division example will have a remainder. You can also tell what remainders are possible.

Follow the steps below to explore which remainders can occur when dividing by 4. Use counters if you wish.

Step 1 Copy and complete the chart. Record the number of groups of 4 and the remainder.

Step 2 Look for patterns in the remainder column. What are the possible remainders when dividing by 4?

Step 3 Predict the possible remainders when dividing by 5. Check your prediction by testing the numbers from 5–15.

Think and Discuss Which numbers below are divisible by 2, 5, and 10? How do you know? What are the possible remainders when dividing by 2? by 5? by 10?

124   230   455

Example	Drawing	Number of Groups	Remainder
4 ÷ 4	XXXX	1	0
5 ÷ 4	XXXX X	1	1
6 ÷ 4	XXXX XX	1	2
7 ÷ 4			
8 ÷ 4			
9 ÷ 4			
10 ÷ 4			
11 ÷ 4			
12 ÷ 4			

Try It Out

Copy the chart. Use the divisibility rules to decide if each number is divisible by 2, 3, 4, 5, 6, 9, and 10. Write *yes* or *no*.

		2	3	4	5	6	9	10
1.	250							
2.	963							
3.	1,248							

4. Analyze Can 7 be a remainder when dividing by 5? Explain your answer.

5. Write a four-digit number that is divisible by 2 and by 3, but not by 4.

6. Explain Change one digit in 56,620 so that the number gives a remainder of 0 when divided by 6. Explain your thinking.

Practice

Using Mental Math Tell if each number is divisible by 2, 3, 4, 5, 6, 9, or 10.

7. 84   **8.** 31   **9.** 555   **10.** 138   **11.** 800

12. 324   **13.** 720   **14.** 815   **15.** 910   **16.** 1,902

17. 1,000   **18.** 4,935   **19.** 9,168   **20.** 6,357   **21.** 52,430

22. 73,610   **23.** 11,111   **24.** 18,474   **25.** 78,983   **26.** 965,476

27. Describe What are the possible remainders when dividing by 8? Give examples to explain.

Problem Solving

28. You Decide There are 222 students on a rafting trip. Students can raft in groups of 2, 3, 4, or 10. How could the students be grouped so that there are no students left over?

29. Analyze A raft can fit five students and one adult. If there are enough rafts to transport 128 students, will there be any empty seats? Explain your answer.

30. Twelve vans transport a group of rafters 76 miles from a camp to the river. If the vans then return to the camp, how many miles do the vans travel?

31. Use the divisibility rules for 3 and 9.

    a. Do you think that all numbers divisible by 9 are also divisible by 3? Test 9, 18, 27, and 36 to help you decide.

    b. Do you think that all numbers divisible by 3 are also divisible by 9? Test 3, 6, 9, 12, 15, and 18 to help you decide.

    c. Generalize Write a statement about numbers divisible by 3 and 9.

Review and Remember

Using Algebra Compare. Write > or < for each ●.

32. $2.34 - 0.012$ ● $1.2 + 0.98$ **33.** $9.13 + 3.45$ ● $8.32 + 1.9$

34. $7.21 - 4.7$ ● $6.9 - 3.1$ **35.** $5.9 + 2.34$ ● $9.41 - 2.011$

Find each answer.

36.	**37.**	**38.**	**39.**	**40.**
129 $\times$ 12	14,998 $-$ 2,099	249 $\times$ 8	4.56 $+$ 1.09	5.43 $-$ 3.21

Money $ense

Interested in Interest?

Banks earn money by lending money. Tom's family took out a bank loan to pay for their new computer. The form below shows the terms of the loan.

Bank Loan	
Principal	$1,500
8% Interest	$120
Period	6 months

They agreed to repay the loan and interest in 6 equal monthly payments. How much will they pay each month?

For Extra Practice, see Set E, page 203.

Checkpoint

Division Patterns, Estimation, and Divisibility

Write the missing words that complete each sentence.

1. A number is __?__ by another number when the quotient is a whole number and the remainder is 0.

2. When solving $3 + (8 \times 2) \div 4 = n$, it is important to follow the __?__.

3. When you change one number to another to make it easier to estimate a quotient, you use a __?__.

Word Bank

compatible number
divisible
order of operations

Using Algebra Write a related multiplication or division sentence. Then find each *n*. (pages 168–169)

4. $21 \div 7 = n$ 5. $4 \times n = 12$ 6. $n \times 7 = 14$ 7. $45 \div n = 9$

8. $10 \times n = 10$ 9. $50 \div n = 5$ 10. $n \div 8 = 5$ 11. $6 \times 6 = n$

Using Algebra Find each *n*. (pages 170–171)

12. $5 \times 6 \div 3 + 2 = n$ 13. $4 + 2 - 3 - 1 + 5 = n$

14. $(3 + 2) \div 5 + 6 = n$ 15. $(10 - 2) + 1 \times 3 = n$

16. $(8 + 2) \div (3 + 2) = n$ 17. $13 - 4 \times 2 + 5 \times 6 = n$

Using Mental Math Find each quotient. (pages 172–173)

18. $4,500 \div 9$ 19. $4,000 \div 8$ 20. $21,000 \div 3$ 21. $81,000 \div 9$

22. $72,000 \div 8$ 23. $28,000 \div 7$ 24. $5,400 \div 6$ 25. $160 \div 4$

26. $5,000 \div 5$ 27. $6,400 \div 8$ 28. $63,000 \div 9$ 29. $120,000 \div 3$

Use compatible numbers to estimate each quotient.
(pages 174–175)

30. $756 \div 8$ 31. $273 \div 5$ 32. $310 \div 9$

33. $134 \div 3$ 34. $500 \div 6$ 35. $299 \div 7$

Tell if each number is divisible by 2, 3, 4, 5, 6, 9, or 10.
(pages 176–179)

36. 200 37. 102 38. 148 39. 250 40. $3,000$

Problem Solving

41. A group of 500 students is taking a trip to the Henry Ford Museum. If 50 students can fit on a bus, how many buses will they need?

42. Marcy, Kayla, Dominic, and Trish split the cost of a $10 taxi ride equally. How much did each person pay?

43. Annie is getting ready for a picnic. She buys three cookies for $0.15 each, a brownie for $0.20, and two cupcakes. She spends $1.25 altogether. How much did each cupcake cost? Tell which strategy you used.

44. In seven days 2,675 people visit a library. About how many people visit the library each day?

45. You travel 200 miles each day. How many days will it take you to travel 700 miles? Explain your answer.

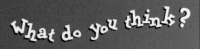

When estimating quotients, why is it sometimes easier to use compatible numbers than to round? Use the division sentence $6,725 \div 8 = n$ to explain.

Journal Idea

Why are multiplication and division called inverse operations? Use examples to explain your answer.

Critical Thinking Corner

Number Sense

Mystery Numbers

Using Algebra In each riddle the answer is one or more different whole numbers. Use the clues to find each mystery number.

1. **Clue:** I am less than 100.

   Clue: The sum of my digits is 4.

   Clue: If you divide me by 2, you get an odd number.

   I am the number ___?___ .

2. **Clue:** If multiplied by 2, I become a number greater than 20 and less than 40.

   Clue: If multiplied by 6, I end in 8.

   Clue: If multiplied by 4, I end in 2.

   I am the number ___?___ .

Developing Skills for
Problem Solving

*First read for understanding and then
focus on interpreting remainders.*

READ FOR UNDERSTANDING

A campground rents motorboats, sailboats, and canoes. Thirty-seven campers have signed up for a Friday sailing trip, and 26 campers have signed up for a Saturday sailing trip. A sailboat can hold up to four people. No sailboat can go out with fewer than two people.

1 How many campers have signed up for the Friday trip?

2 What is the greatest number of campers that can go out in a sailboat? the least number?

THINK AND DISCUSS

Interpreting Remainders When you divide, sometimes you need to interpret a remainder to find the solution. You may need to include the remainder, to drop it, or to increase the quotient to the next whole number.

Weekend Sign up	
Friday Trip	37
Saturday Trip	26

Reread the paragraph at the top of the page.

3 What is the least number of boats that must be rented for the Friday trip so that everyone can go? How does the remainder affect your answer?

4 At least how many boats should be rented for the Saturday trip? How does the remainder affect your answer?

5 Name a situation in everyday life where interpreting the remainder correctly is important.

Show What You Learned

Answer each question. Give a reason for your choice.

The campground follows strict safety regulations. The rowboats must have exactly three people on board at all times. Boats are sent out every hour, and campers must wait at the dock for the next available boat. At 2:00 P.M., 19 people want to go out in rowboats.

1 How many people can go out in 1 rowboat?

  a. less than 3

  b. exactly 3

  c. more than 3

2 How many people are waiting to go out in a rowboat?

  a. 2 people

  b. 3 people

  c. 19 people

3 Which statement best describes the number of rowboats that will go out at 2:00 P.M.?

  a. 7 boats will go out. 6 boats will have 3 people in them, and 1 boat will have 1 person in it.

  b. 6 boats will go out. Only 6 boats can be completely filled with 3 people.

  c. 8 boats will go out. Only 8 boats can be completely filled with 2 people.

4 Which number sentence could be used to find the number of rowboats that will go out at 2:00 P.M.?

  a. $19 \div 6 = 3 \text{ R}1$

  b. $3 \times 19 = 57$

  c. $19 \div 3 = 6 \text{ R}1$

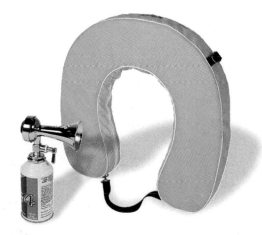

5 How many people have to wait until 3:00 P.M. for a rowboat?

  a. 1 person

  b. 6 people

  c. 18 people

When boaters are in trouble, such as during a storm, emergency crews go out in motorboats. Such emergency boats must have four crew members. Today, 23 staff members are on duty when a storm warning comes in.

6 **Explain** Write the division sentence you could use to find out how many motorboats can go out during the storm. What would you do with the remainder? Why?

Riding the Rails

Basic facts can help you divide any number by a one-digit number.

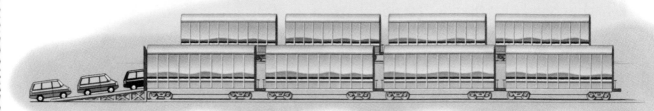

Learning About It

An auto train consists of passenger cars, automobile carriers, and van carriers. An auto train traveling from Virginia to Florida needs eight van carriers to transport 96 vans. If each carrier transports the same number of vans, how many vans are transported in each van carrier?

$$96 \div 8 = n$$

Estimate first: $80 \div 8 = 10$

Then find the exact quotient.

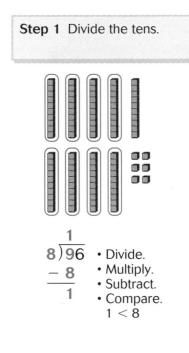

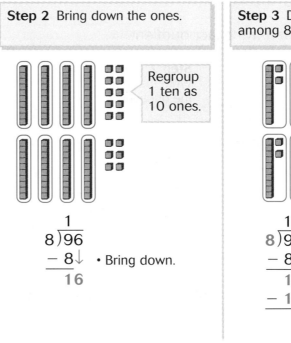

Step 1 Divide the tens.	**Step 2** Bring down the ones.	**Step 3** Divide the ones among 8 groups.

Step 1:
$$\begin{array}{r} 1 \\ 8\overline{)96} \\ -8 \\ \hline 1 \end{array}$$
• Divide.
• Multiply.
• Subtract.
• Compare.
  $1 < 8$

Step 2:
$$\begin{array}{r} 1 \\ 8\overline{)96} \\ -8\downarrow \\ \hline 16 \end{array}$$
• Bring down.

Regroup 1 ten as 10 ones.

Step 3:
$$\begin{array}{r} 12 \\ 8\overline{)96} \\ -8\downarrow \\ \hline 16 \\ -16 \\ \hline 0 \end{array}$$
• Divide.
• Multiply.
• Subtract.
• Compare.
  $0 < 8$

There are 12 vans transported in each van carrier. Since the answer is close to the estimate, the answer is reasonable.

Proble

31. Usi...
bus...
Orl...
pas...

33. Exp...
to t...
car...
you...

35. A fa...
trai...
you...

36. Jou...
in y...
sent...

Review

Find ea

37. 123

41. 6,42

45.   2
    − 1

Connecting Ideas

You divide three-digit numbers the same way that you divide two-digit numbers. It is just one more step.

◄ **Social Studies Connection** The journey from Singapore to Bangkok is almost 2,000 km through Thailand and Malaysia. One of the stops along the Thailand coast is at Hua Hin, which offers local wares to shoppers.

The Eastern & Oriental Express train travels in Southeast Asia. If each sleeper car can accommodate eight passengers, how many sleeper cars are needed for 230 passengers?

$$230 \div 8 = n$$

Estimate first: **240 ÷ 8 = 30**

Then divide to find the exact quotient.

Step 1 Use the estimate to place the first digit. Divide the tens.

Since 2 < 8, you cannot divide hundreds.

$$\begin{array}{r} 2 \\ 8)\overline{230} \\ -16 \\ \hline 7 \end{array}$$

• Divide.
• Multiply.
• Subtract.
• Compare.
  7 < 8

Step 2 Divide the ones. Write the remainder in the quotient.

$$\begin{array}{r} 28 \text{ R6} \\ 8)\overline{230} \\ -16\downarrow \\ \hline 70 \\ -64 \\ \hline 6 \end{array}$$

• Bring down.
• Divide.
• Multiply.
• Subtract.
• Compare.
  6 < 8

Step 3 Multiply to check.

$$\begin{array}{r} 28 \\ \times\ 8 \\ \hline 224 \\ +\ 6 \\ \hline 230 \end{array}$$

• Multiply the quotient by the divisor.
• Add the remainder.
• The sum is the dividend.

Twenty-nine sleeper cars are needed. The answer 29 is close to the estimate of 30, so the answer is reasonable.

Think and Discuss When dividing a three-digit number by a one-digit number, how can you tell how many digits will be in the quotient?

Wha

Mar...
shelv...
a 9-f...
three...
yard...
the b...
Marc...
upse...
too n...

Short on Time?

You can use a shortcut when dividing by one digit.

Learning About It

The Concorde, which began flying in 1969, is the only supersonic commercial aircraft.

Because the Concorde can travel at high speeds, it is able to fly the 3,529 miles from New York to Paris, France, in about three hours. At this speed, how many miles can the Concorde fly in one hour?

$$3,529 \div 3 = n$$

Estimate first: $3,000 \div 3 = 1,000$

You can use a short form of division to find the exact quotient.

3,529 miles

New York

Step 1 Divide the thousands. Write the remainder in the dividend.	**Step 2** Divide the hundreds. Write the remainder in the dividend.	**Step 3** Divide the tens. Write the remainder in the dividend.	**Step 4** Divide the ones. Write the last remainder as part of the quotient.
$\dfrac{1}{3\overline{)3,^{0}529}}$	$\dfrac{1,1}{3\overline{)3,5^{2}29}}$	$\dfrac{1,1\ 7}{3\overline{)3,5^{2}2^{1}9}}$	$\dfrac{1,1\ 7\ 6\ \text{R}1}{3\overline{)3,5^{2}2^{1}9}}$
$1 \times 3 = 3$ $3 - 3 = 0$	$1 \times 3 = 3$ $5 - 3 = 2$	$7 \times 3 = 21$ $22 - 21 = 1$	$6 \times 3 = 18$ $19 - 18 = 1$

The Concorde can fly 1,176 miles in an hour! The answer is close to the estimate.

You can multiply to check. $1,176 \times 3 = 3,528$
$3,528 + 1 = 3,529$

Remember to add the remainder.

(Partial content from adjacent page 186)

Try It

Estimat
by mult

1. 4⟌6

5. Exp
888

Pract

Divide.

6. 6⟌1

10. 3⟌9

14. 98

18. 1,99

22. 1,31

26. Ana
quot

Copy ea

27.
5⟌1
− 15

Social S
Japan's "
of 130 mil
the main i

More Examples

$$\begin{array}{r} 7\ 2\ 9\ \text{R3} \\ \textbf{A. } 7)\overline{5,1^2 0^6 6} \end{array}$$

$$\begin{array}{r} \$\ \ 4\ 2\ 7 \\ \textbf{B. } 5)\overline{\$2,1^1 3^3 5} \end{array}$$

Think and Discuss What part does mental math play in short division?

Try It Out

Use short division to divide. Then check by multiplying.

1. $4)\overline{729}$ 2. $9)\overline{981}$ 3. $2)\overline{1,946}$ 4. $3)\overline{8,120}$

INTERNET ACTIVITY
www.sbgmath.com

Practice

Use short division to find each quotient.

5. $3)\overline{56}$ 6. $5)\overline{705}$ 7. $2)\overline{192}$ 8. $7)\overline{325}$

9. $6)\overline{684}$ 10. $4)\overline{967}$ 11. $8)\overline{500}$ 12. $3)\overline{6,375}$

13. $7)\overline{3,195}$ 14. $2)\overline{4,850}$ 15. $5)\overline{1,235}$ 16. $7)\overline{7,721}$

17. $39,480 \div 8$ 18. $20,880 \div 7$ 19. $84,980 \div 9$

Problem Solving

20. **Using Estimation** The Concorde is just about 62 meters in length. If a luggage carrier is 9 meters long, about how many luggage carriers would have to line up end to end to match the length of the jet?

21. **What If?** Ms. Deal traveled 5,778 miles in 3 months. If she made the same trips each month, how many miles did she travel each month? If she arranged to make the same trips in 2 months instead of 3 months, how far would she travel each month?

Review and Remember

Using Algebra Find each n. Write the property you used.

22. $3 + 4 = 4 + n$
23. $(6 + n) + 2 = 6 + 20$
24. $n + 0 = 12$
25. $10 + (4 + n) = 14 + 7$
26. $31 + n = 9 + 31$
27. $n + 14 = 1 + (3 + 14)$
28. $5 + n = 5 + 7$
29. $27 = n + 0$
30. $8 + (n + 12) = 8 + 16$

For Extra Practice, see Set G, page 204.

Paris

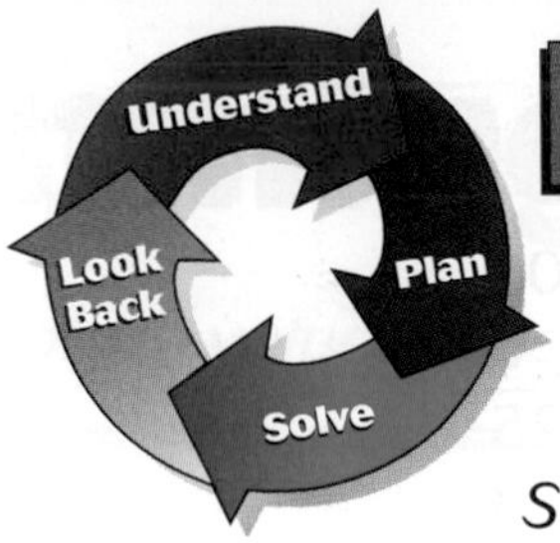
Understand
Plan
Solve
Look Back

Problem Solving
Work Backwards

Sometimes you need to work backwards to solve problems.

The McMullens are renting a car for a family vacation. The total cost for a 7-day rental is $291.30, including $11.30 in taxes and $70.00 for insurance. How much is the daily car rental fee alone, without taxes and insurance?

FAMILY
RENT-A-CAR
SPECIAL
MINIVAN
7 DAYS
UNLIMITED MILEAGE
$ 291.30
See our friendly service representative for details.

UNDERSTAND

What are you asked to find?

You are asked to find the daily car rental fee, without taxes and insurance.

PLAN

How can you solve the problem?

You can **work backwards**. Use the information you have on the rental fees, taxes, and insurance.

SOLVE

To work backwards, subtract the taxes and insurance from the total cost. Then divide by 7.

Total rental cost	$291.30
Taxes	− 11.30
Cost without taxes	$280.00
Insurance	− 70.00
Cost without taxes and insurance	$210.00
Cost per day	$210 ÷ 7 = $30

The daily car rental fee is $30.

LOOK BACK

Now that you have worked backwards to find the daily car rental fee, how can you check your answer? Explain.

Using the Strategy

Work backwards to solve Problems 1–6.

1 It took the McMullens 20 minutes to drive from the hotel to the museum. They toured the museum for 2 hours. They spent another 20 minutes driving back to the hotel. They arrived back at 4:40 P.M. What time did they leave for the museum?

2 Mrs. McMullen sent 8 postcards. The 3 children sent 2 postcards each. If they have 4 postcards left, how many postcards did they start with?

3 Mr. and Mrs. McMullen and their three children visited a museum. They spent $15.00 on souvenirs, $25.75 for lunch, and $8.00 on the adult tickets. If they spent a total of $56.25 at the museum, what did they spend on the children's tickets?

4 The McMullens joined a group going to a concert. The group spent $273 for the tickets to the concert. They bought seven balcony tickets at $17 each. If orchestra tickets cost $22, how many orchestra tickets did they buy?

5 **Explain** Cindy collected stickers on her vacation. She gave 5 to her brother and twice as many to her sister. If she has 18 stickers now, how many stickers did Cindy collect? Tell how you found your answer.

6 **Using Mental Math** Brian was playing number games with his sisters. He told them to pick a number, multiply it by 3, and add 8. Cindy ended up with 44. What number did she start with?

Mixed Strategy Review

Try these or other strategies to solve each problem. Tell which strategy you used.

THERE'S ALWAYS A WAY!

Problem Solving Strategies

- *Draw a Diagram*
- *Guess and Check*
- *Use Logical Reasoning*
- *Write an Equation*

7 The McMullens left their hotel and drove 15 miles east and 25 miles north. Next, they drove 10 miles west and 25 miles south to an inn. How far are they from their hotel?

8 Mr. McMullen filled his empty gas tank with 20 gallons of gas. He drove 250 miles and then bought 10 gallons to fill his tank. How many miles per gallon did he get?

9 The McMullens traveled 320 miles in one day. If they drove 178 miles before lunch, how many miles did they drive after lunch?

Step by Step

You can use division to find the average of a set of data.

Learning About It

What is the average number of steps it takes the students in your class to walk the length of the classroom?

Work with a group. Follow these steps to find out.

Step 1 Use a chart like the one shown. Record the number of steps it takes each student in your group to walk the length of the classroom.

Name of Student	Number of Steps
Jill	30
Anthony	33
Suzanne	36

Step 2 Find the average number of steps it took your group to walk this distance by finding the **mean**. To find the mean, add together each student's total number of steps and then divide the sum by the number of students in your group.

Example: 30 + 33 + 36 = 99

$$
\begin{array}{r}
33 \leftarrow \text{mean} \\
3\overline{)99} \\
-\ 9 \\
\hline
09 \\
-\ 9 \\
\hline
0
\end{array}
$$

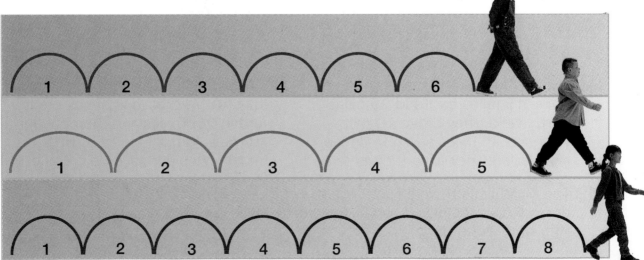

Step 3 Find the average number of steps for all the students in the class.

Make a new chart like the one on page 194. List the names of all the students in the class. Record the number of steps it took every student in the class to walk the length of the classroom.

Then find the mean of the total number of steps.

Think and Discuss Think back to the averages you found. How do you think the average number of steps would change if you counted first graders' steps? teachers' steps? Explain your answers.

Practice

Choose a Method Use mental math, paper and pencil, or a calculator to find the mean of each set of data.

1. 25, 16, 32, 39
2. 50, 30, 10, 40, 20
3. 1,284; 1,264

4. 21, 19, 17, 15, 13, 11, 9
5. $55, $27, $35, $31
6. $76, $84, $90, $102

7. 503, 922, 512, 361, 837
8. 183, 157, 170
9. 2,476; 2,295; 1,904

10. 562, 571, 538, 573
11. 425, 427, 425, 423
12. 158, 164, 185

13. 1,000; 2,000; 3,000
14. 328, 480, 550, 372, 422, 520, 492

15. Michael's times for the 100-yard dash are 13 seconds, 12 seconds, 16 seconds, and 11 seconds. What is his average time?

16. **Explain** Rolanda hiked trails that were 2 miles, 5 miles, and 6 miles long. She thinks that the length of her average hiking trail was 2 miles. Without finding the mean, tell if this makes sense. Explain.

 17. **Analyze** A fifth-grade class of 25 students collected bottles to turn in for a $0.05 deposit on each. If they got $17.50, what is the average number of bottles each student collected?

Off to Sea!

Dividing greater numbers is just like dividing other numbers.

Learning About It

The *Queen Elizabeth 2* is a famous ocean liner. There are nine galleys—or kitchens—on board. The chefs prepare meals for all 1,810 passengers. At least how many meals are prepared in each galley for any one mealtime, if the same number are prepared in each one?

$$1,810 \div 9 = n$$

Estimate first: $1,800 \div 9 = 200$

Then divide to find the exact quotient.

THERE'S ALWAYS A WAY!

● **One way** is to use paper and pencil.

Step 1 Use your estimate to place the first digit. Divide the hundreds.	Step 2 Divide the tens.	Step 3 Divide the ones.	Step 4 Check by multiplying.
$\begin{array}{r} 2 \\ 9\overline{)1,810} \\ -18 \\ \hline 0 \end{array}$	$\begin{array}{r} 20 \\ 9\overline{)1,810} \\ -18\downarrow \\ \hline 01 \\ -0 \\ \hline 1 \end{array}$	$\begin{array}{r} 201 \text{ R1} \\ 9\overline{)1,810} \\ -18 \\ \hline 01 \\ -0\downarrow \\ \hline 10 \\ -9 \\ \hline 1 \end{array}$	$\begin{array}{r} 201 \\ \times\ 9 \\ \hline 1\ 809 \\ +\ \ \ 1 \\ \hline 1,810 \end{array}$

● **Another way** is to use a calculator.

Press: (1)(8)(1)(0)(INT÷)(9)(=)

Display: [*201   1*]

Each of the galleys would prepare at least 202 meals.

Think and Discuss Why must each galley prepare at least 202 meals?

Try It Out

Estimate. Then divide. Use your estimate to check whether your quotient is reasonable.

1. $5\overline{)1,895}$ **2.** $3\overline{)2,439}$ **3.** $8\overline{)\$3,880}$ **4.** $4\overline{)36,802}$

5. Explain If eight people can be seated at a dining table, how many tables are needed to seat 1,810 passengers?

Practice

Choose a Method Use paper and pencil or a calculator to divide. Tell which method you chose.

6. $7,125 \div 5$ **7.** $4,287 \div 3$ **8.** $8,129 \div 8$ **9.** $5,926 \div 2$

10. $7,400 \div 6$ **11.** $2,324 \div 4$ **12.** $\$9,376 \div 4$ **13.** $\$1,500 \div 5$

14. $5,634 \div 2$ **15.** $6,917 \div 7$ **16.** $4,725 \div 9$ **17.** $\$5,776 \div 8$

Problem Solving

18. There is a 530-seat theater on the *Queen Elizabeth 2*. If only half the theater is used, how many people can be seated? What if only one fifth of the theater were used?

19. The *Queen Elizabeth 2* booked 900 people in deluxe cabins. Each cabin held 5 people. There were 50 empty cabins. How many cabins were there in all?

20. The *Queen Elizabeth 2* has a cruising speed of up to 33 knots per hour. At that speed, how many knots would it travel in one day?

◄ The *Queen Elizabeth 2* was first launched in 1969 and is still a popular transatlantic cruise ship. There are swimming pools, theaters, pet kennels, and even a hospital on board.

Review and Remember

Find each answer.

21. $42 - 0.4$ **22.** 901×8 **23.** 367×23 **24.** $759 + 69$ **25.** 314×97

26. $4.57 + 0.6$ **27.** $732 - 99$ **28.** 19×236 **29.** 86×686 **30.** $21 + 38 + 65$

Problem Solving
Mean, Median, and Mode

You can use the mean, median, or mode to describe a set of data and solve a problem.

A bus company collected data on the number of riders using Bus G. The company wanted to study the number of riders over the period of 1 week. What did the company find as the mode, median, and mean for its study?

 UNDERSTAND

What do you need to know?

You need to know the number of people riding Bus G each day.

 PLAN

How can you solve the problem?

You can use the numbers shown at the right to find the mean, median, and mode.

 SOLVE

To analyze a set of numbers, it is helpful to first order the numbers. This allows you to identify certain characteristics about the data.

Arrange the numbers from least to greatest.
15, 17, 44, 50, 50, 50, 54

- Mode = 50, the number that appears most often

- Median = 50, the middle number

- Mean is the average number.
  15 + 17 + 44 + 50 + 50 + 50 + 54 = 280
  Mean = 280 ÷ 7 = 40

Red Diamond
Bus Runs

Mon.	44
Tues.	50
Wed.	50
Thurs.	50
Fri.	54
Sat.	17
Sun.	15

 LOOK BACK

Which do you think best describes the usual number of riders—mean, median, or mode? Explain your answer.

Show What You Learned

Use the table at the right to solve Problems 1–5.

1 Find the mean for the number of riders on Tuesday. How does it compare with the median and mode for Tuesday?

2 Is the mean number of riders for Friday greater than or less than the median for Friday?

3 **Explain** The bus company used the mode to estimate the amount of money expected from Bus H on Saturday. Why do you think it did this?

Bus H					
Day	Week 1	Week 2	Week 3	Week 4	Week 5
Monday	45	47	50	17	46
Tuesday	55	68	36	63	68
Wednesday	45	58	41	65	51
Thursday	55	48	27	56	54
Friday	65	53	31	70	66
Saturday	44	55	55	60	55

4 What if 15 more people rode the bus on Monday of week 3? How would the mean, median, and mode for Monday change?

5 Find the mean number of riders for each day. Which day had the greatest average number of riders?

6 **Describe** On Sunday, Bus H had five runs. The passenger totals for Sunday runs were 31, 34, 24, 48, and 33. What is a useful way to describe the data?

7 The horse-drawn omnibus could carry up to 8 passengers. What would the mean, median, and mode be for the number of passengers on seven trips if the omnibus was completely filled each trip?

Social Studies Connection ➤
Today's bus began as the horse-drawn omnibus. In 1662, Blaise Pascal, the mathematician, helped introduce the first omnibus to Paris. It was designed to carry eight passengers and ran on a fixed route.

Problem Solving

Practice What You Learned

Choose the correct letter for each answer.

1 Lonnie spent two and one half times as long as John did studying for a test. If you knew how long John spent studying, how could you find Lonnie's study time?

   A. Add Lonnie's time to John's time.
   B. Subtract Lonnie's time from John's time.
   C. Multiply John's time by 2.5.
   D. Divide John's time by 2.5.

Tip

Decide which operation to use by thinking about the action in the problem situation.

---

2 On Monday a warehouse had 1,053 boxes to ship. On Tuesday, 351 boxes were left to be shipped. On Wednesday, 117 boxes were left. If this pattern continues, how many boxes will be left on Friday?

   A. 3
   B. 13
   C. 17
   D. 39

Tip

Use the *Find a Pattern* strategy. Think about divisibility rules to find the pattern.

---

3 The numbers of people who used the library monthly from December through March were 2,675; 4,482; 3,781; and 1,083. Which is the best estimate of the total number who used the library *after* New Year's Day?

   A. 9,000 people
   B. 12,000 people
   C. 14,000 people
   D. 16,000 people

Tip

Be sure you use only the numbers you need to solve the problem.

4 Charlie pays $2.45 for a piece of fabric that is 4.5 m long. Which number sentence could be used to find the number of 15-cm pieces, *n*, he can cut from the fabric?
(1m = 100 cm)

A. $4.5 \times 100 \div 15 = n$
B. $4.5 \div 100 \times 15 = n$
C. $4.5 \times 15 \div 100 = n$
D. $4.5 + 100 \times 15 = n$

5 Eight objects had these masses: 0.30 kg, 0.34 kg, 0.37 kg, 0.38 kg, 0.61 kg, 0.64 kg, 0.65 kg, 0.68 kg. Which two objects combine to equal exactly 1 kilogram?

A. 0.38 kg and 0.61 kg
B. 0.30 kg and 0.68 kg
C. 0.34 kg and 0.65 kg
D. 0.37 kg and 0.64 kg
E. Not Here

6 This graph shows how membership in the science club changed over a 7-month period.

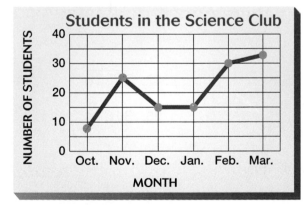

Students in the Science Club

When did the membership increase the most?

A. From Oct. to Nov.
B. From Nov. to Dec.
C. From Jan. to Feb.
D. From Feb. to Mar.

7 Phyllis estimates that the average length of each step she takes is 3 feet. Which is a reasonable number of steps for her to take in half a mile? (1 mi = 5,280 ft)

A. Fewer than 800 steps
B. Between 800 and 1,000 steps
C. Between 1,000 and 2,000 steps
D. More than 1,200 steps
E. Not Here

8 A vegetable garden is shaped like the letter **L**. The lengths of five of the sides are shown. What is the length of the sixth side?

A. 1 yard
B. 2 yards
C. 4 yards
D. 6 yards
E. Not Here

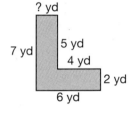

9 Alicia read 20 pages of a book in 60 minutes. Which is a reasonable amount of time for Alicia to take to read the rest of the 200-page book?

A. 3 hours
B. 9 hours
C. 10 hours
D. 20 hours

10 The number of minutes Rob spent driving to work during 1 week were 45, 38, 36, 44, and 39. Which is the best estimate for the average time he spent driving to work each day?

A. Less than 30 min
B. Between 30 and 35 min
C. Between 40 and 45 min
D. More than 45 min

✔ Checkpoint

Dividing by One-Digit Divisors

Vocabulary

Write the missing words that complete each sentence.

1. The ___?___ is the average of a set of data.

2. We say a number is not ___?___ by another number if there is a remainder in the quotient.

3. ___?___ are easy to compute mentally.

Word Bank

compatible numbers
divisible
mean
order of operations

Concepts and Skills

Estimate. Then find the exact quotient. (pages 184–187)

4. $5\overline{)63}$ 5. $7\overline{)85}$ 6. $3\overline{)19}$ 7. $4\overline{)86}$

8. $8\overline{)46}$ 9. $2\overline{)67}$ 10. $521 \div 8$ 11. $417 \div 9$

Use short division to find each quotient. (pages 188–189)

12. $5\overline{)632}$ 13. $9\overline{)254}$ 14. $6\overline{)982}$ 15. $3\overline{)754}$

16. $253 \div 6$ 17. $586 \div 7$ 18. $3{,}549 \div 2$ 19. $5{,}742 \div 4$

Divide. Check by multiplying. (pages 190–191)

20. $6\overline{)125}$ 21. $5\overline{)253}$ 22. $7\overline{)638}$

23. $2\overline{)803}$ 24. $7\overline{)761}$ 25. $3\overline{)614}$

Find the average of each set of data. (pages 194–195)

26. 46, 59, 80, 43 27. 110, 108, 98, 60, 139 28. $15, $18, $26, $21

Choose a Method Use paper and pencil or a calculator to divide. (pages 196–197)

29. $4\overline{)3{,}238}$ 30. $8\overline{)5{,}713}$ 31. $2\overline{)1{,}468}$ 32. $7\overline{)49{,}910}$

33. $23{,}549 \div 5$ 34. $56{,}701 \div 7$ 35. $21{,}486 \div 8$ 36. $1{,}200 \div 4$

Mixed Practice

Use long division or short division to find each quotient.

37. $3\overline{)124}$

38. $2\overline{)546}$

39. $5\overline{)6,219}$

40. $7\overline{)6,324}$

41. $3\overline{)2,881}$

42. $9\overline{)4,957}$

Problem Solving

43. A train has one conductor for every three cars. If the train is 26 cars long, how many conductors will there be? Explain your answer.

44. Jeremy spent $59, $129, $79, and $109 on plane tickets. What was the average amount that Jeremy spent on a plane ticket?

45. **Using Estimation** Justine and her family are traveling by car from Chicago to the Grand Canyon. If they use four tanks of gas and travel 1,235 miles, about how many miles do they travel on each tank of gas?

What do you think?

Suppose you need to divide to solve a word problem. Is the quotient always the solution to the problem? Explain. Include an example.

Journal Idea

Explain the differences between long division and short division.

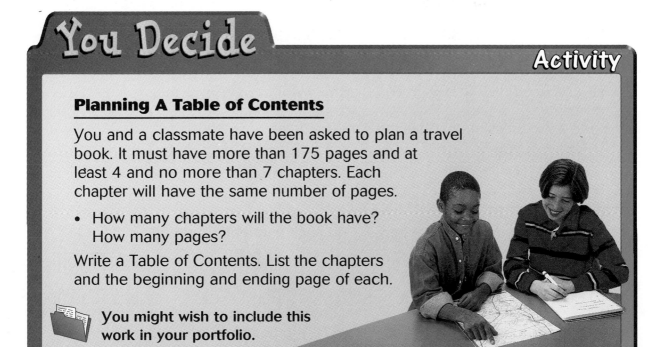

You Decide

Activity

Planning A Table of Contents

You and a classmate have been asked to plan a travel book. It must have more than 175 pages and at least 4 and no more than 7 chapters. Each chapter will have the same number of pages.

- How many chapters will the book have? How many pages?

Write a Table of Contents. List the chapters and the beginning and ending page of each.

You might wish to include this work in your portfolio.

Extra Practice

Set A (pages 168–169)

Using Algebra Complete each input/output table.

Rule: Multiply by 2

	Input	Output
1.	15	▓
2.	▓	24
3.	▓	10

Rule: Divide by 4

	Input	Output
4.	▓	8
5.	12	▓
6.	40	▓

7. Rule: ___?___

	Input	Output
	15	5
8.	▓	8
9.	30	▓

Using Algebra Find each n.

10. $12 \div 3 = n$ **11.** $n \times 4 = 20$ **12.** $36 \div n = 6$ **13.** $n \div 3 = 6$

14. $n \div 2 = 11$ **15.** $9 \times n = 72$ **16.** $0 \div 4 = n$ **17.** $27 \div n = 3$

18. Ellen is putting braid trim on the four equal sides of a drawing. She has a 64-inch piece of braid. How many cuts must she make to do this? How long will each piece be?

Set B (pages 170–171)

Using Algebra Find each n.

1. $12 \div 3 + 5 = n$ **2.** $7 + 10 \div 2 = n$ **3.** $15 - 10 \div 5 = n$

4. $10 \div (3 + 2) = n$ **5.** $16 - (5 + 5 \times 2) = n$ **6.** $5 \times (9 + 1) - 3 \times 3 = n$

7. $14 - 2 \times 6 \div 3 = n$ **8.** $7 \times (5 + 3) \div 2 = n$ **9.** $(10 \div 2) \times 3 + 4 \times 4 = n$

10. Write an expression that has the same value as $(0 \div 9) + 2 \times 3 - 12 \div 3$.

Set C (pages 172–173)

Use basic facts and patterns of zeros. Find each quotient.

1. $3\overline{)2{,}100}$ **2.** $7\overline{)3{,}500}$ **3.** $9\overline{)8{,}100}$ **4.** $8\overline{)4{,}800}$

5. $12{,}000 \div 6$ **6.** $30{,}000 \div 5$ **7.** $16{,}000 \div 4$ **8.** $7\overline{)630{,}000}$

9. A family of four people has set aside $160 to rent bicycles. If bikes rent for $8 per day, for how many days can the family rent bikes? Explain your answer.

Extra Practice

Set D (pages 174–175)

Estimate each quotient. Tell what compatible numbers you used.

1. $9\overline{)800}$
2. $4\overline{)250}$
3. $2\overline{)230}$
4. $8\overline{)750}$

5. $170 \div 8$
6. $30,000 \div 7$
7. $27,000 \div 5$
8. $41,968 \div 7$

9. **Using Estimation** Greenland is the largest island in the world. It is about 950 km wide. If you walked 8 km per day along a straight path, about how many days would it take you to walk across Greenland?

Set E (pages 176–179)

Tell if each number is divisible by 2, 3, 4, 5, 6, 9, or 10.

1. 354
2. 621
3. 6,125
4. 4,026
5. 5,840

6. 8,648
7. 15,310
8. 86,124
9. 22,198
10. 51,467

11. A tour guide has 3,582 travel booklets. She wants to place them in locations around the city. If she places the booklets in equal groups of 2, 3, 4, 5, 6, 9, or 10 in how many locations can she place them?

Set F (pages 184–187)

Estimate each quotient for Exercises 1–16. Then find the exact answer.

1. $6\overline{)93}$
2. $8\overline{)92}$
3. $7\overline{)95}$
4. $6\overline{)418}$

5. $204 \div 3$
6. $313 \div 7$
7. $271 \div 5$
8. $176 \div 8$

9. $912 \div 4$
10. $623 \div 7$
11. $817 \div 2$
12. $587 \div 5$

13. $1,622 \div 8$
14. $2,340 \div 4$
15. $3,876 \div 7$
16. $4,965 \div 6$

17. **Using Estimation** A train conductor takes 76 minutes to collect tickets from 4 cars. About how much time does it take him to collect tickets from one car?

Extra Practice

Set G (pages 188–189)

Use short division to find each quotient.

1. 4)29
2. 7)254
3. 9)486
4. 5)761

5. 3)985
6. 7)3,156
7. 6)5,421
8. 7)6,842

9. 2,488 ÷ 3
10. 4,866 ÷ 7
11. 3,360 ÷ 8
12. 72,946 ÷ 3

13. 96,987 ÷ 6
14. 456,789 ÷ 2
15. 5,126 ÷ 4
16. 556,941 ÷ 5

17. Chicago's O'Hare International Airport is the busiest airport in the world. Suppose 352 airplanes take off in 8 hours. How many airplanes take off each hour?

Set H (pages 190–191)

Divide. Check by multiplying.

1. 4)810
2. 4)1,606
3. 3)1,825
4. 7)1,458

5. 8)7,683
6. 4)2,819
7. 9)8,111
8. 6)609

9. 4,539 ÷ 5
10. 6,201 ÷ 3
11. 5,659 ÷ 8
12. 7,122 ÷ 4

13. 16,039 ÷ 5
14. 15,543 ÷ 5
15. 9,165 ÷ 9
16. 26,989 ÷ 6

17. A certain airboat traveled 357 miles in one week. How many miles did it travel per day?

Set I (pages 196–197)

Divide.

1. 6)2,124
2. 5)6,781
3. 8)7,954
4. 3)46,873

5. 6)24,125
6. 9)46,822
7. 2)65,125
8. 4)87,886

9. 7)81,044
10. 8)63,515
11. 9)73,421
12. 6)41,336

13. The staterooms of the *Queen Elizabeth 2* can hold 2,000 people. If four people stay in each stateroom, how many staterooms are on the ship?

Chapter Test

Write a related multiplication or division sentence.
Then find each *n*.

1. $25 \div 5 = n$

2. $6 \times n = 42$

3. $n \div 4 = 5$

Estimate each quotient. Tell what compatible numbers
you used. Then find the exact answer.

4. $7\overline{)495}$

5. $2\overline{)95}$

6. $8\overline{)645}$

7. $6\overline{)238}$

8. $9\overline{)548}$

9. $4\overline{)300}$

10. $5\overline{)2,700}$

11. $4\overline{)3,846}$

12. $9\overline{)9,146}$

Find each *n*.

13. $4 \times (6 + 4) \div 2 = n$

14. $12 - 8 \div 4 + 6 = n$

15. $18 + 4 \times 3 = n$

16. $84 - 28 \div (4 \times 7) = n$

Tell if each number is divisible by 2, 3, 5, or 10.

17. 96

18. 200

19. 510

20. 117

21. 350

Solve.

22. Eight friends paid $48 for a boat ride. How much did
each person pay?

23. Use the graph at the right. In which week did Carole
bike the farthest? What is the average number of
miles that she biked in a week?

24. Tasha sold 31 sketches at a flea market. She sold half
as many car sketches as van sketches. She sold 16
truck sketches. How many of each kind did she sell?

25. On a certain bus there are five seats per row. There
are 47 people on the bus, and people are seated in
each row. Without dividing, tell whether all the rows
will be full. Explain your reasoning.

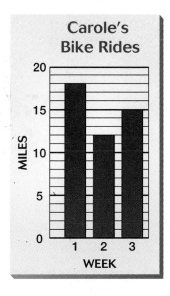

Carole's Bike Rides

Self-Check

Did you remember to write the remainder in the
quotient for Exercises 4–12?

Performance Assessment

Show What You Know About One-Digit Division

1 Use the numbers at the right to answer a, b, and c. Show your work.

> 252   4
>
> 9   3,864

    a. Divide the greatest number by the least number.

    b. Divide 252 by 9.

    c. Which quotient, a or b, is greater? By how much?

Self-Check Did you remember to find the greatest number and the least number?

Family Vacation Miles	
Day	Miles Driven
1	218
2	178
3	238
4	246

2 The number of miles driven by a family while vacationing are shown in the table.

    a. Find the average number of miles driven per day.

    b. If the family drove at an average speed of 55 miles per hour, how much time did they spend driving during the four days?

Self-Check Did you divide by the correct number of days to find the average number of miles driven?

For Your Portfolio
You might wish to include this work in your portfolio.

Extension

The Chinese Remainder Problem

In about A.D. 250, the Chinese mathematician Sun Zi wrote *Master Sun's Mathematical Manual*. Sun Zi's famous Chinese remainder problem appears in that book.

Here is the problem.

Find the smallest number in which

- when divided by 3, the remainder is 2

$$3\overline{)n} \quad R2$$

- and when divided by 5, the remainder is 3

$$5\overline{)n} \quad R3$$

- and when divided by 7, the remainder is 2

$$7\overline{)n} \quad R2$$

Test for 7	Make a list. Record numbers from 1 to 100 that when divided by 7 have a remainder of 2.
Test for 5	Check the list you made. Find the numbers that when divided by 5 have a remainder of 3. Circle those numbers.
Test for 3	Now find the circled number on the list that when divided by 3 has a remainder of 2.

The number 23 fits all of the tests.

Numbers that have a remainder of 2 when they are divided by 7

2	51
9	(58)
16	65
(23)	72
30	79
37	86
44	(93)

Make lists to help you solve each Chinese remainder problem. Find the smallest number possible.

1. When you divide the number by 2, the remainder is 1. When you divide it by 5, the remainder is 0. When you divide it by 4, the remainder is 3. What is the number?

2. When you divide the number by 3, the remainder is 2. When you divide it by 4, the remainder is 3. When you divide it by 5, the remainder is 1. What is the number?

3. When you divide the number by 10, the remainder is 3. When you divide it by 6, the remainder is 3. When you divide it by 4, the remainder is 3. What is the number?

4. **Create Your Own** Make up a Chinese remainder problem. Describe how you made up the problem.

Chapter 6

Dividing by Two-Digit Divisors

Chapter Theme: CELEBRATIONS

Real-World Math

.... **Real Facts** ....

Each New Year's Day, Pasadena, California, celebrates the start of the new year with its famous Tournament of Roses Parade. All the big floats in the parade are made from different kinds of flowers. The girls at right are working on one of the parade floats. The chart below shows the entries for the 1998 parade.

1998 Rose Parade Entries

Entry	Number of Entries
Bands	21
Floats	55
Equestrian Units	26
Special Cars	3

- If the average number of members in each band was 147, about how many band members in all were in the parade?

- Suppose every band was followed by either one or two equestrian units. How many bands were followed by two equestrian units?

.... **Real People** ....

Meet Raul Rodriguez, who designs floats for big celebrations like the Tournament of Roses Parade. In 1997, one of his floats featured giant dinosaurs. The float, completely covered with thousands of flowers and plants, won the Sweepstakes Award!

By the Book

You can estimate quotients by using compatible numbers.

Learning About It

Elena is reading a book for National Family Reading Week. If she reads 18 pages a day, about how long will it take her to finish *The Cricket in Times Square*? You can estimate to find out.

Book	Number of Pages
Not for a Billion Gazillion Dollars	121
The Secret Garden	298
Julie of the Wolves	170
The Cricket in Times Square	152

To estimate, find compatible numbers that are close to the actual numbers. Compatible numbers are ones that are easy to divide mentally.

$$152 \div 18 = n$$
$$160 \div 20 = 8$$

160 and 20 are compatible numbers, since 16 is divisible by 2.

It will take Elena about 8 days to read *The Cricket in Times Square*.

More Examples

A. $4,162 \div 55 = b$
$4,200 \div 60 = 70$
b is about 70.

B. $8,175 \div 23 = b$
$8,000 \div 20 = 400$
b is about 400.

Think and Discuss What other compatible numbers could you use to estimate the quotient in Example A?

National Family Reading Week

Try It Out

Estimate each quotient. Tell what compatible numbers you used.

1. $317 \div 78$　　**2.** $761 \div 42$　　**3.** $7,184 \div 89$

4. $938 \div 89$　　**5.** $6,124 \div 19$　　**6.** $572 \div 91$

Did you know that books are published in Braille? The Braille system allows blind people to read with their fingers. It uses raised dots in patterns to stand for letters and numbers. ➤

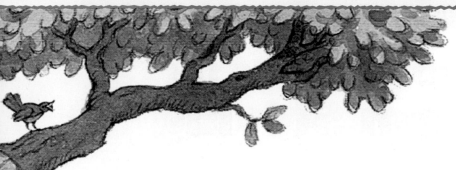

Practice

Use compatible numbers to estimate each quotient.

7. 52)438

8. 32)684

9. 83)391

10. 22)5,792

11. 35)2,850

12. 92)5,326

13. 57)5,623

14. 19)9,817

15. 77)2,249

16. 17)8,045

17. 17)3,594

18. 88)2,813

19. 59)4,911

20. 12)6,725

21. 58)5,360

22. 74)6,243

23. 62)1,860

24. 78)6,504

25. 72)20,963

26. 48)19,900

27. 275 ÷ 29

28. 1,392 ÷ 68

29. 421 ÷ 14

30. 312 ÷ 48

31. Analyze Give 3 different sets of compatible numbers you can use to estimate the quotient of 495 ÷ 25.

Problem Solving

Use the book table on page 212.

32. If Sam reads 25 pages a day, about how long will it take him to finish *Not for a Billion Gazillion Dollars*?

33. Analyze About how many days would it take you to read all the books if you read 16 pages a day?

34. Explain If Carla reads 20 pages a day, will she finish *The Secret Garden* in 2 weeks?

35. Create Your Own Use the book table to create a problem for your classmates to solve.

Review and Remember

Choose a Method Use paper and pencil or a calculator to find each answer. Tell which method you chose and why.

36. 214 × 6

37. 664 + 212

38. $474 ÷ 3

39. 572 ÷ 8

40. $111 × 79

41. 578 + 346

42.   9,089
       − 5,638

43.   98,737
       + 54,606

44.   146
       × 804

Developing Skills for
Problem Solving

*First read for understanding and then focus
on how to decide whether the answer to a problem is reasonable.*

READ FOR UNDERSTANDING

Smith School held a fund-raiser to buy new software for the computer center. The two fifth grade classes raised the most money, so they are celebrating by having a pizza party. Each class has 24 students. The students think that each person, including the two teachers, will eat two slices of pizza.

1 How many fifth grade classes are having a pizza party?

2 How many students are in each class?

3 How many slices of pizza do the students think each person will eat?

Pizza Party

THINK AND DISCUSS

MATH FOCUS

Reasonable Answers Whenever you solve a problem, always check to be sure that the answer is reasonable. Look back at the facts of the problem. Your answer should make sense when you compare it to the facts.

Reread the paragraph at the top of the page.

4 If each pizza has 8 slices, would it be reasonable to order 48 pizzas? Explain why or why not.

5 How many pizzas should they order for the party? Is 13 pizzas a reasonable answer? Explain why or why not.

6 How does looking back at the facts help you to decide whether your answer is reasonable?

Show What You Learned

Use the information below and on page 214 to answer each question. Give a reason for your choice.

The planning group decides to buy each fifth grader a fancy pencil and a number puzzle as a party favor. The pencils come in packs of 12. The number puzzles come in packs of 8.

1 How many people will receive party favors?

　a. less than 48 people

　b. exactly 48 people

　c. more than 48 people

2 How many packs of pencils do they need?

　a. 4 packs

　b. 3 packs

　c. 15 packs

3 How many packs of number puzzles do they need?

　a. 6 packs

　b. 10 packs

　c. 8 packs

4 Bob thinks that 10 packs of party favors should be bought. Is this reasonable?

　a. It is reasonable. Four packs of pencils and 6 packs of number puzzles should be bought.

　b. It is not reasonable. Bob did not add correctly.

　c. It is not reasonable. Bob only calculated the number of packs of pencils needed.

5 One number puzzle costs $0.89. A pack of 8 costs $6.00. Sara says buying a pack of 8 is a better buy than buying 8 puzzles separately. Which number sentence tells you that what Sara says is reasonable?

　a. $0.89 \times 12 = $10.68

　b. $0.89 \times 8 = $7.12

　c. $6.00 - 0.89 = $5.11

About $225 is needed for the party, so the classes decide to have a bake sale. The students sell 25 batches of cookies at $3.00 a batch and 25 cakes at $5.00 a cake.

6 Explain Is it reasonable to say that the class took in $200 from the bake sale? Tell why or why not.

7 Explain Is it reasonable to say that the class still needs to raise $100 more? Tell why or why not.

Save the Earth

Use estimation to help you divide by two-digit numbers.

Learning About It

Nineteen classes will plant tree seedlings as part of an Earth Day celebration. A local tree farm donated 144 tree seedlings. If each class plants the same number, how many seedlings will each class plant? How many seedlings will be left over?

$$144 \div 19 = s$$

Estimate first: $140 \div 20 = 7$

The estimate helps you place the first digit in the quotient.

Divide to find the exact answer.

Step 1 Divide using your estimate.	**Step 2** Check your answer. Remember to add the remainder.
$\begin{array}{r} 7 \text{ R11} \\ 19\overline{)144} \\ -133 \\ \hline 11 \end{array}$ • Divide. • Multiply. • Subtract. • Compare. 11 < 19	$\begin{array}{r} 19 \\ \times\ 7 \\ \hline 133 \\ +\ 11 \\ \hline 144 \end{array}$

Earth Day

Each class can plant 7 seedlings. There will be 11 seedlings left over. Seven is the same as the estimate.

More Examples

A. $339 \div 41 = n$

Estimate first: $320 \div 40 = 8$

$$\begin{array}{r} 8 \text{ R11} \\ 41\overline{)339} \\ -328 \\ \hline 11 \end{array}$$

B. $478 \div 79 = n$

Estimate first: $480 \div 80 = 6$

$$\begin{array}{r} 6 \text{ R4} \\ 79\overline{)478} \\ -474 \\ \hline 4 \end{array}$$

Connecting Ideas

Sometimes your estimate may be too high or too low. Then you need to adjust the quotient when you divide.

Mr. Song's class is recycling aluminum cans for Earth Day. It takes 32 cans to equal one pound of aluminum. If the class collects 268 cans, about how many pounds of aluminum will they collect?

$$268 \div 32 = p$$
Estimate first: $270 \div 30 = 9$

The estimate helps you place the first digit in the quotient.

INTERNET ACTIVITY
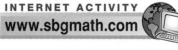
www.sbgmath.com

Divide to find the exact quotient.

Step 1 Divide, using your estimate.	**Step 2** Adjust the quotient.	**Step 3** Check your answer.
$$\begin{array}{r} 9 \\ 32\overline{)268} \\ -288 \end{array}$$ • Divide. • Multiply. 288 > 268 The estimate is too high.	$$\begin{array}{r} 8 \text{ R12} \\ 32\overline{)268} \\ -256 \\ \hline 12 \end{array}$$ • Divide. • Multiply. • Subtract. • Compare. 12 < 32	$$\begin{array}{r} 32 \\ \times\ 8 \\ \hline 256 \\ +\ 12 \\ \hline 268 \end{array}$$ Remember to add the remainder.

Mr. Song's class will collect more than 8 pounds of aluminum. Eight is close to the estimate of 9.

Another Example

Find $224 \div 37$.

Estimate.	Divide.	Adjust.	Check.
$200 \div 40 = 5$	$$\begin{array}{r} 5 \\ 37\overline{)224} \\ -185 \\ \hline 39 \end{array}$$	$$\begin{array}{r} 6 \text{ R2} \\ 37\overline{)224} \\ -222 \\ \hline 2 \end{array}$$	$$\begin{array}{r} 37 \\ \times\ 6 \\ \hline 222 \\ +\ 2 \\ \hline 224 \end{array}$$

39 > 37, so the estimate is too low.

Think and Discuss What is the greatest remainder you can have if you divide by 37? Explain.

Try It Out

Estimate. Then divide and check. Tell whether you needed to adjust your quotient.

1. 192 ÷ 56   **2.** 703 ÷ 82   **3.** 96 ÷ 43   **4.** 459 ÷ 75

5. 337 ÷ 81   **6.** 97 ÷ 23   **7.** 124 ÷ 59   **8.** 486 ÷ 97

Practice

Estimate the quotient. Then divide and check.

9. 26)84   **10.** 72)612   **11.** 33)$231   **12.** 62)432   **13.** 81)727

14. 94)500   **15.** 46)414   **16.** 31)85   **17.** 87)563   **18.** 75)306

19. 98)963   **20.** 72)561   **21.** 91)838   **22.** 42)384   **23.** 83)708

24. 29)210   **25.** 16)134   **26.** 39)244   **27.** 46)$375   **28.** 73)306

29. 274 ÷ 51   **30.** 88 ÷ 17   **31.** 117 ÷ 28   **32.** $342 ÷ 57   **33.** 365 ÷ 45

34. 96 ÷ 40   **35.** 328 ÷ 70   **36.** 299 ÷ 37   **37.** 56 ÷ 27   **38.** 483 ÷ 53

Problem Solving

39. During Earth Day activities at school, members of the photography club took 252 pictures. If they can take 36 pictures with one roll of film, how many rolls of film were used?

40. Explain For Earth Day a student council bought some saplings. They planted 15 saplings, gave each teacher two saplings for their classroom, and had one left over. If there were 32 teachers, how many saplings did the student council buy? Tell how you found your answer.

41. Using Algebra The energy saved by recycling one aluminum can could run a television for three hours. One aluminum can weighs half an ounce. How long could a television run on the energy saved by recycling a pound of aluminum cans?

▲ **Science Connection** As a teenager, Fiona Grant, from Canada, spent three years studying trees. She used math to measure and record their growth. Her goal was to find trees that would ensure a healthy future for forests.

Use the graph to solve Problems 42–47.

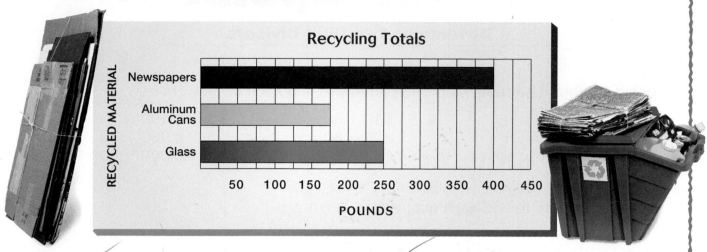

Recycling Totals

RECYCLED MATERIAL

| Newspapers | Aluminum Cans | Glass |

POUNDS: 50 100 150 200 250 300 350 400 450

42. Thirty-two aluminum cans weigh one pound. If the recycled aluminum cans were returned for a $0.05 deposit on each can, how much did the school get?

43. Using Estimation Twenty-seven classes participated in the school recycling drive. About what was the average number of pounds of glass each class collected?

44. A company will pay $0.12 per pound for newspapers tied in bundles and $0.09 per pound for loose newspapers. If 150 pounds of newspapers are in bundles, how much will they pay for all the newspapers that were collected?

45. After the glass is separated, there are 130 pounds of clear glass. There are twice as many pounds of brown glass as green glass. How many pounds of each color do you have? What strategy did you use to solve the problem?

46. You Decide If you were to make a pictograph of the information in the graph, what symbol would you use for the materials? What quantity would each symbol represent?

47. Create Your Own Use the information in the graph to write a problem for your classmates to solve. Be sure to write the solution to your problem.

Review and Remember

Find each answer.

48.
$$254 - 186$$

49.
$$613 + 585$$

50.
$$527 \times 56$$

51.
$$327 - 273$$

52.
$$391 - 358$$

53.
$$497 \times 32$$

54.
$$236 + 173$$

55.
$$783 + 395$$

56. $367 \div 68$

57. 408×77

58. $2\overline{)199}$

59. $3\overline{)\$590}$

For Extra Practice, see Set C, page 237.

✓ Checkpoint

Dividing by Two-Digit Divisors

Using Algebra Use basic facts and patterns to find each *n*. (pages 210–211)

1. $450 \div 50 = n$
   $4,500 \div 50 = n$
   $45,000 \div 50 = n$

2. $640 \div 80 = n$
   $6,400 \div 80 = n$
   $64,000 \div 80 = n$

3. $490 \div 70 = n$
   $4,900 \div 70 = n$
   $49,000 \div 70 = n$

Use mental math to find each quotient. (pages 210–211)

4. $5,400 \div 60$
5. $6,000 \div 30$
6. $270 \div 30$
7. $7,200 \div 90$

8. $15,000 \div 50$
9. $360 \div 60$
10. $12,000 \div 40$
11. $2,800 \div 70$

Estimate each quotient. (pages 212–213)

12. $62\overline{)5,860}$
13. $39\overline{)2,109}$
14. $23\overline{)4,365}$
15. $41\overline{)815}$

16. $37\overline{)7,631}$
17. $82\overline{)1,598}$
18. $53\overline{)63,601}$
19. $36\overline{)44,621}$

20. $92\overline{)51,152}$
21. $56\overline{)42,331}$
22. $72\overline{)36,104}$
23. $64\overline{)51,918}$

Estimate. Then divide. (pages 216–219)

24. $187 \div 62$
25. $369 \div 73$
26. $107 \div 51$
27. $\$563 \div 84$

Estimate. Then divide and check. (pages 216–219)

28. $26\overline{)128}$
29. $25\overline{)160}$
30. $41\overline{)376}$
31. $81\overline{)405}$

32. $37\overline{)280}$
33. $92\overline{)736}$
34. $68\overline{)544}$
35. $32\overline{)\$224}$

36. $55\overline{)387}$
37. $75\overline{)\$599}$
38. $61\overline{)438}$
39. $59\overline{)274}$

Mixed Practice

Choose a Method Use mental math or paper and pencil
to divide. Tell which method you chose and why.

40. $400 \div 50$
41. $1,600 \div 20$
42. $720 \div 80$
43. $4,200 \div 60$

44. $375 \div 50$
45. $248 \div 31$
46. $478 \div 73$
47. $273 \div 45$

48. $410 \div 82$
49. $\$144 \div 48$
50. $\$116 \div 29$
51. $\$312 \div 52$

Problem Solving

52. If each bus can carry 44 passengers, how many buses are needed to take 188 people to a festival? How do you know your answer is reasonable?

53. Describe The fifth grade has raised $1,500 for a class trip to a theater. It costs $30 per student. Do they have enough money for 48 students to go? Explain your thinking.

54. Using Estimation A concert hall can seat about 600 people. If there are 32 seats in each row, about how many rows does the hall have?

55. In 26 days, the fifth grade planted 234 saplings. If they planted an equal number each day, how many trees did they plant each day?

Journal Idea

When dividing, if the remainder is greater than the divisor, what must you do to correct the situation? Use an example to explain your answer.

What do you think?

Why does estimating the quotient first help you find the actual quotient?

Critical Thinking Corner

Number Sense

Missing Numbers

Copy the drawing. Fill in the missing numbers.

A point is scored each time one number matches a number next to it on the side of a different triangle. What score is shown with all the triangles complete?

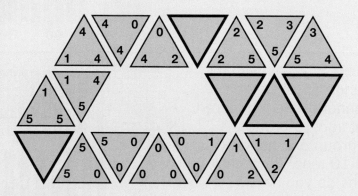

221

A Block Party!

Base-ten blocks can help you explore division with two-digit quotients.

Memorial Day Barbecue

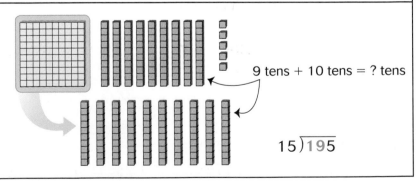

Learning About It

For a Memorial Day block party, 195 hamburgers were donated by 15 families. If each family gave the same number, how many hamburgers did each family donate?

Work with a group to find 195 ÷ 15.

Estimate first: **200 ÷ 20 = 10**

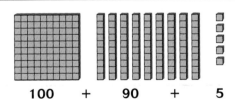

The quotient probably will have two digits.

What You Need

For each group:
base-ten blocks

Step 1 Use base-ten blocks to show 195.

100   +   90   +   5

Step 2 Begin with the hundreds. Since you cannot divide a hundred flat into 15 groups, regroup one hundred as 10 tens. How many tens do you have?

9 tens + 10 tens = ? tens

15⟌195

Step 3 Divide the tens into 15 equal groups. How many tens are in each group? How many tens are left?

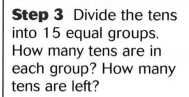

? ten in each of 15 groups $\longrightarrow$ 1

$$15\overline{)195}$$
$$-\ 15$$

4 left over $\longrightarrow$ 4

Step 4 You cannot divide 4 tens into 15 equal groups. Regroup 4 tens as 40 ones. How many ones are there in all?

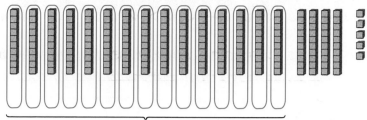

$$
\begin{array}{r}
1 \\
15\overline{)195} \\
-\ 15\downarrow \\
\hline
45
\end{array}
$$
$\longleftarrow$? ones in all

40 ones
+ 5 ones
= ? ones

Step 5 Divide the ones into 15 groups. How many ones are left? What is the quotient?

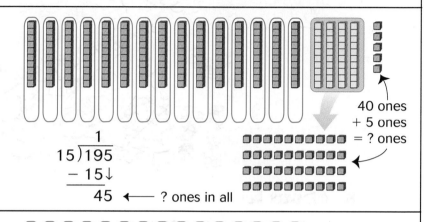

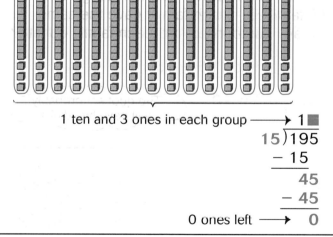

1 ten and 3 ones in each group $\longrightarrow$ 1■

$$
\begin{array}{r}
15\overline{)195} \\
-\ 15 \\
\hline
45 \\
-\ 45 \\
\hline
0
\end{array}
$$

0 ones left $\longrightarrow$ 0

Each family donated 13 hamburgers.

Think and Discuss How would the quotient be different if the example were 197 ÷ 15?

Practice

Use base-ten blocks to divide.

1. $18\overline{)216}$ **2.** $21\overline{)273}$ **3.** $28\overline{)420}$ **4.** $16\overline{)359}$ **5.** $17\overline{)189}$

Thanksgiving Vacation

Estimating first is still important when you have quotients with two or more digits.

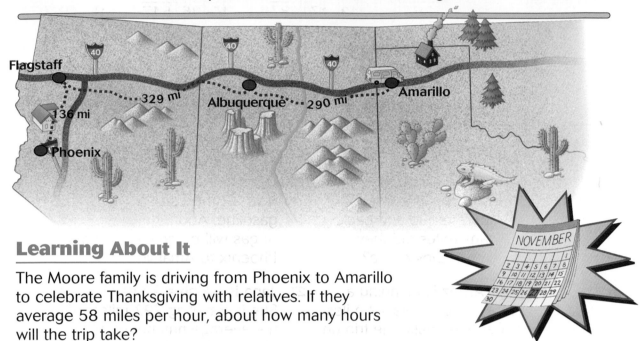

Flagstaff

329 mi   Albuquerque   290 mi   Amarillo

136 mi

Phoenix

Learning About It

The Moore family is driving from Phoenix to Amarillo to celebrate Thanksgiving with relatives. If they average 58 miles per hour, about how many hours will the trip take?

$$755 \div 58 = h$$

Estimate first: $600 \div 60 = 10$

The estimate tells you that the quotient is probably a two-digit number.

Step 1 Divide the tens.	**Step 2** Divide the ones.	**Step 3** Check.

$\begin{array}{r} 1 \\ 58)\overline{755} \\ -58 \\ \hline 17 \end{array}$ • Divide.
• Multiply.
• Subtract.
• Compare.
   $17 < 58$
	$\begin{array}{r} 13 \text{ R1} \\ 58)\overline{755} \\ -58\downarrow \\ \hline 175 \\ -174 \\ \hline 1 \end{array}$ • Bring down.
	• Divide: $175 \div 58$.
	• Multiply.
	• Subtract.
	• Compare.
	   $1 < 58$
		$\begin{array}{r} 13 \\ \times 58 \\ \hline 104 \\ +650 \\ \hline 754 \\ +\quad 1 \\ \hline 755 \end{array}$ Remember to add the remainder.

The trip will take more than 13 hours of driving time. Thirteen is close to the estimate, so 13 is reasonable.

Think and Discuss How would the time change if the Moores averaged 65 miles per hour? Explain.

Try It Out

Estimate. Then divide and check.

1. $21)\overline{483}$ **2.** $33)\overline{587}$ **3.** $71)\overline{891}$ **4.** $57)\overline{950}$ **5.** $14)\overline{439}$

Practice

Divide and check.

6. $30\overline{)840}$ 7. $17\overline{)586}$ 8. $23\overline{)957}$ 9. $75\overline{)900}$ 10. $63\overline{)895}$

11. $15\overline{)403}$ 12. $21\overline{)965}$ 13. $47\overline{)987}$ 14. $36\overline{)547}$ 15. $19\overline{)974}$

16. $864 \div 26$ 17. $767 \div 32$ 18. $924 \div 22$ 19. $673 \div 65$

20. $950 \div 19$ 21. $991 \div 27$ 22. $828 \div 59$ 23. $513 \div 57$

Problem Solving

Use the map on page 224 to solve Problems 24–25.

24. **What If?** Suppose it took the Moores 15 hours to drive from Phoenix to Albuquerque and back. About how many miles did they average each hour they drove?

25. **Using Estimation** The Moores' car gets 32 miles to a gallon of gasoline. About how many gallons of gas will be needed to go from Phoenix to Amarillo?

26. **Explain** Mrs. Arnez is planning a 500-mile trip. Her car gets 29 miles per gallon. Can she make the trip on 17 gallons of gas?

27. Jana is taking a 22-day bike tour. She is traveling 792 miles. What is the average number of miles she bikes each day?

INTERNET ACTIVITY
www.sbgmath.com

Review and Remember

Find each answer.

28. 31×18 29. $43 + 23$ 30. $50 - 17$ 31. $63 + 25$ 32. 59×72

33. $973 - 496$ 34. $486 + 512$ 35. 18×37 36. $674 - 585$ 37. 25×30

Time for Technology

Using a Calculator

Square Numbers

Using Algebra The divisor and quotient are the same for these examples. Use your calculator to find each number.

1. $\blacksquare\overline{)144}$ 2. $\blacksquare\overline{)529}$ 3. $\blacksquare\overline{)324}$ 4. $\blacksquare\overline{)961}$ 5. $\blacksquare\overline{)400}$

For Extra Practice, see Set D, page 237.

Problem Solving
Make a Table

Making a table to organize information can help you solve a problem.

The town council is planning a fireworks display for the Fourth of July. The council wants to buy 5 Wagon Wheels, 20 Ring Shells, and 40 Gold Spider fireworks. Wagon Wheels cost $35 each. Ring Shells cost $12 each. Gold Spiders cost $25 each. What will be the total cost of the display?

Health and Safety Connection
Fireworks displays should be set up only by trained professionals.▼

 UNDERSTAND

What do you need to find?

You need to find the total cost of the display.

Fourth of July

 PLAN

How can you solve the problem?

You can **make a table** to help you solve the problem. Then use the information in the table to find the total cost.

 SOLVE

Fireworks Displays			
Fireworks	**Number**	**Cost of One**	**Total Cost of Each**
Wagon Wheel	5	$35	$35 × 5 = $175
Ring Shell	20	$12	$12 × 20 = $240
Gold Spider	40	$25	$25 × 40 = $1,000

To find the total cost of the display, add.

$175 + $240 + $1,000 = $1,415

The fireworks will cost $1,415.

 LOOK BACK

How does making a table help solve the problem? Explain.

Using the Strategy

Make a table to solve Problems 1–4. Use the information from page 226 for Problem 1.

1 Each year the council has a different display. Suppose that the council wants 15 Wagon Wheels, 25 Ring Shells, and 16 Gold Spiders. How much will these fireworks cost?

2 A vendor sold 125 glow sticks for $3.00 each, 105 glow rings for $4.25 each, and 213 boxes of popcorn for $3.25 each. How much money did the vendor make?

3 **Predict** From 9:00 A.M. to 10:00 A.M., Tim sold 85 bottles of water. He had sold 170 bottles by 11:00 A.M. and 255 bottles by noon. If this pattern continues, how many bottles will Tim have sold by 4:00 P.M.? If he charges $0.95 a bottle, how much money will he take in between noon and 4 P.M.?

4 Wagon Wheels last 8 seconds, Ring Shells last 6 seconds, and Gold Spiders last 5 seconds. How long would a display of 12 Wagon Wheels, 13 Ring Shells, and 15 Gold Spiders last if the fireworks were set off one right after the other? How do you know if your answer is reasonable?

Mixed Strategy Review

Try these or other strategies you have learned. Tell which strategy you used.

Problem Solving Strategies

- *Guess and Check*
- *Draw a Diagram*
- *Work Backwards*
- *Make a Table*

5 Craig bought some crushed ice for $1.75. Then he spent twice as much on snacks. If Craig had $5.62 left, how much money did he have before buying the ice and snacks?

6 June leaves the playground and walks 120 yards west. Then she walks 40 yards north. After that, she walks 50 yards east and then 40 yards south. Where is she now?

7 Two vendors are selling the T-shirts advertised at the right. Vendor A sold 25 small shirts and 10 large shirts. Vendor B sold 12 medium shirts and 16 large shirts.

a. How much money did each vendor take in?

b. What is the difference in the total number of T-shirts sold by Vendor A and Vendor B?

T-SHIRT SALE

Large $10.00

Medium $9.00

Small $8.00

Music to My Ears

Understanding place value will help you divide greater numbers.

Learning About It

A music festival runs for 16 days. If a total of 4,288 posters of the orchestra are sold during the festival, what is the average number of posters sold each day?

Music Festival

$$4{,}288 \div 16 = p$$

Estimate first: $4{,}000 \div 20 = 200$

The estimate tells you that the quotient is probably a three-digit number.

Then divide to find the exact answer.

THERE'S ALWAYS A WAY!

● **One way** is to use paper and pencil.

Step 1 Divide the hundreds.	**Step 2** Divide the tens.	**Step 3** Divide the ones.
$\begin{array}{r}2\\16\overline{)4{,}288}\\-32\\\hline 1\,0\end{array}$ • Divide. • Multiply. • Subtract. • Compare. $\quad$ 10 < 16	$\begin{array}{r}26\\16\overline{)4{,}288}\\-32\downarrow\\\hline 1\,08\\-96\\\hline 12\end{array}$ • Bring down. • Divide: $\quad$ 108 ÷ 16. • Multiply. • Subtract. • Compare. $\quad$ 12 < 16	$\begin{array}{r}268\\16\overline{)4{,}288}\\-32\\\hline 1\,08\\-96\downarrow\\\hline 128\\-128\\\hline 0\end{array}$ • Bring down. • Divide: $\quad$ 128 ÷ 16. • Multiply. • Subtract. • Compare. $\quad$ 0 < 16

● **Another way** is to use a calculator.

Press: [4] [2] [8] [8] [INT÷] [1] [6] [=]

Display: 268

An average of 268 posters are sold each day. The answer is reasonable, since it is close to the estimate.

Connecting Ideas

Sometimes you need to put a zero in the quotient when you divide.

Tickets for a jazz concert cost $17. If the sales total $5,185, how many tickets have already been sold?

$$\$5,185 \div \$17 = t$$

Estimate first: $\$6,000 \div \$20 = 300$

The estimate tells you that the quotient is a three-digit number.

Divide to find the exact quotient.

Step 1 Divide the hundreds.	**Step 2** Divide the tens.	**Step 3** Divide the ones.
$$\begin{array}{r} 3 \\ 17\overline{)5,185} \\ -51 \\ \hline 0 \end{array}$$	$$\begin{array}{r} 30 \\ 17\overline{)5,185} \\ -51\downarrow \\ \hline 08 \\ -0 \\ \hline 8 \end{array}$$ 8 < 17, so place a 0 in the quotient.	$$\begin{array}{r} 305 \\ 17\overline{)5,185} \\ -51 \\ \hline 08 \\ -0\downarrow \\ \hline 85 \\ -85 \\ \hline 0 \end{array}$$

There were 305 tickets sold for the jazz concert.

More Examples

A.
$$\begin{array}{r} 470 \text{ R5} \\ 38\overline{)17,865} \\ -152 \\ \hline 266 \\ -266 \\ \hline 05 \\ -0 \\ \hline 5 \end{array}$$

B.
$$\begin{array}{r} 402 \text{ R4} \\ 14\overline{)5,632} \\ -56 \\ \hline 03 \\ -0 \\ \hline 32 \\ -28 \\ \hline 4 \end{array}$$

Think and Discuss Would 47 R5 be a reasonable answer for $17,865 \div 38$? Explain.

Try It Out

Estimate. Then divide.

1. $24\overline{)7,668}$ **2.** $43\overline{)4,653}$ **3.** $31\overline{)9,927}$ **4.** $54\overline{)11,670}$

5. $73\overline{)8,908}$ **6.** $59\overline{)36,654}$ **7.** $87\overline{)40,951}$ **8.** $47\overline{)26,548}$

Practice

Choose a Method Use mental math, paper and pencil, or a calculator to divide. Tell which method you chose and why.

9. 4,239 ÷ 38   **10.** 7,400 ÷ 10   **11.** 2,717 ÷ 13   **12.** 28,636 ÷ 91

13. 9,041 ÷ 86   **14.** 5,850 ÷ 25   **15.** 12,000 ÷ 40   **16.** 25,925 ÷ 62

17. 3,159 ÷ 15   **18.** 4,800 ÷ 24   **19.** 36,798 ÷ 73   **20.** 7,275 ÷ 58

21. 3,908 ÷ 37   **22.** 6,985 ÷ 75   **23.** 1,856 ÷ 83   **24.** 42,815 ÷ 91

25. 5,369 ÷ 45   **26.** 9,871 ÷ 64   **27.** 6,400 ÷ 80   **28.** 21,393 ÷ 56

Using Algebra Compare. Write >, <, or = for each ●.

29. 3,302 ÷ 26 ● 160

30. 41 x 21 ● 20,000 ÷ 40

31. 9,520 ÷ 85 ● 3,696 ÷ 33

32. 16,459 ÷ 83 ● 35,190 ÷ 94

33. 4,617 ÷ 19 ● 5,883 − 5,640

34. 6,058 ÷ 52 ● 3,943 ÷ 32

35. 1,118 ÷ 24 ● 4,144 ÷ 91

36. 7,813 ÷ 89 ● 2,352 ÷ 29

Problem Solving

37. Analyze Arrange the digits 1, 2, 3, 4, 5, 6, and 7 in the boxes to get the least quotient. Describe how you decided where to place the digits. Find the quotient.

■■)‾■■,■■■‾

38. An orchestra rents space for rehearsals before a concert. If the space costs $55 per hour, how much will it cost to rent the space for 15 three-hour rehearsals?

39. Journal Idea If you have a two-digit divisor and a four-digit dividend, will the quotient always have the same number of digits? Use examples to explain your answer.

40. Explain A concert is attended by 762 students and 30 adults. A local business provided the buses to take the students and adults to the concert. If a bus seats 52 people, how many buses were used? Explain your answer.

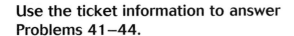

Use the ticket information to answer Problems 41–44.

41. Adult ticket sales for a jazz concert totaled $9,877. How many adult tickets were sold?

42. How many adult symphony tickets were sold for a Saturday concert if $6,100 was collected?

43. How much would you save by buying the Maestro Package instead of individual adult concert tickets?

44. **You Decide** The Jefferson family purchased $550 worth of symphony tickets for their family reunion. What combination of adult and youth tickets could they have purchased?

BELLINGHAM MUSIC FESTIVAL

Ticket Price Information

Ticket Price	Adult	Youth (15 and under)
Symphony Concerts	$20	$10
Jazz Concerts	$17	$ 8
Chamber Concerts	$17	$ 8

Maestro Ticket Package includes:
4 Symphony Concerts
6 Chamber Concerts
1 Jazz Concert
Total price: $150

Young People's Concert–free

Review and Remember

Find each answer.

45.   3.75
    + 8.53

46. $45.60
    − $13.95

47.   1,207
    ×   39

48.   87.9
    + 68.35

49. $56.98
    + $49.95

50.   263
    × 24

51.   4,987
    − 1,829

52.   7,372
    + 4,594

53.   5,170
    ×   13

54.   9,438
    − 5,651

 Money $ense

A Team Effort

Three teams of 6 students each collected cans and bottles to return for their deposit. The table shows how many cans and bottles were collected by each team. What was the total amount of money collected? If the money goes to charity, how much will each student donate?

- Cans are worth 5¢ each.
- Bottles are worth 10¢ each.

Team A	Team B	Team C
170 cans	157 cans	173 cans
92 bottles	111 bottles	96 bottles

For Extra Practice, see Set E, page 238.

Problem Solving
Using Operations

You can use addition, multiplication, subtraction, and division to solve problems.

Mr. Alvarado is in charge of ordering supplies and food for a 50th wedding anniversary party. He expects 172 people to attend. Round tables that can seat a maximum of 10 people will be used. How many tables should he order?

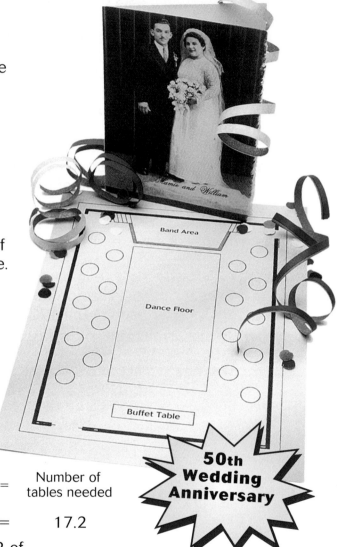

 UNDERSTAND

What do you need to know?

You need to know the number of people expected and the number of people that can be seated at a table.

 PLAN

How can you solve the problem?

You can **write an equation** using division to find out how many tables are needed.

 SOLVE

Number of people at party	÷	Number who can sit at a table	=	Number of tables needed
172	÷	10	=	17.2

Since Mr. Alvarado cannot order 0.2 of a table, he must order 18 tables to seat 172 people.

50th Wedding Anniversary

 LOOK BACK

What If? Suppose 185 people were expected to attend the party. How many tables should Mr. Alvarado order? Explain your answer.

Show What You Learned

Use the information on this page and on page 232 to solve each problem.

1 Mr. Alvarado is ordering a flower arrangement for each of the 18 tables. Each flower arrangement will cost $37.50. What is the total cost of flowers?

2 The caterer suggests ordering twice as many paper napkins as the number of guests expected. The napkins come in packs of 100, 50, and 25. Based on the suggestion, how many napkins will be needed for 172 guests? What combination of packs should be ordered?

3 Mr. Alvarado wants each party guest to have a 4-ounce serving of turkey. How many pounds of turkey should be prepared if Mr. Alvarado also wants enough for 8 extra guests?

4 **Explain** Balloons come in packages of one dozen. If Mr. Alvarado wants to order one for each of the 172 guests, how many packages must he order?

5 Mr. Alvarado wants each guest to have a noisemaker. How many packages must he order? What will be the total cost of noisemakers?

6 Mr. Alvarado needs 184 plates. Using the list of prices for plates, decide how he can get the best price.

7 The anniversary party will take place from 8:00 P.M. until 1:30 A.M. The band will play from 8:30 P.M. to 1:00 A.M. The band charges for a whole hour even if it plays for only part of an hour. If *The MusicMakers* are hired, how much will the band cost for the evening?

8 **Journal Idea** Use the party favors prices to write a problem that requires division to solve. Explain how you would solve your problem.

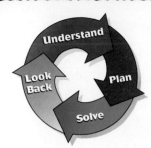

Problem Solving

★ ★ ★ ★ ★ **Preparing for Tests**

Practice What You Learned

Choose the correct letter for each answer.

1 Julio jogs 1.75 miles on Friday, 2.6 miles on Saturday, and 3.25 miles on Sunday. To the nearest whole number, which is the best estimate for how far he jogged on Saturday and Sunday?

A. 4 miles
B. 6 miles
C. 7 miles
D. 8 miles
E. Not Here

Tip

To estimate, first round the decimals you need to the nearest whole number.

---

2 Mark needs to have a board cut into 10 equal pieces. The lumber store charges $0.50 for the first cut it makes and $0.25 for each additional cut. How much will the store charge to cut Mark's board into the number of pieces he needs?

A. $2.50
B. $3.00
C. $3.25
D. $5.00
E. Not Here

Tip

You can *Make a Diagram* to solve this problem.

---

3 Mrs. Kelly gave Susie $10 to spend at the fair. Admission to the fair was $3.00. Susie bought a drink that cost $2.50. She went on 3 rides that each cost the same amount of money. If Susie spent all her money, how much did each of the rides cost?

A. $1.00
B. $1.50
C. $2.50
D. $4.50
E. Not Here

Rides:
Roller Coaster
Ferris Wheel
Carousel
Whip

Tip

Use one of these strategies to solve this problem.
• *Guess and Check*
• *Write an Equation*
• *Work Backwards*

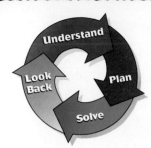

233

4 The first row of seats in a theater has 9 seats. The second row has 11 seats, the third row 14 seats, and the fourth row 18 seats. If the pattern continues, how many seats are in the *eighth* row?

A. 29
B. 36
C. 44
D. 49

5 The third-, fourth-, and fifth-grade classes collected 568 pounds of newspapers. The sixth-grade class collected 195 pounds. Together the third and fourth grades collected 365 pounds. Which number sentence could be used to find the number of pounds, n, collected by the fifth grade?

A. $568 - 365 = n$
B. $365 + 568 = n$
C. $568 - 195 = n$
D. $365 + 195 = n$

6 On an 18-day vacation, Eric and his family traveled a total of 3,955 mi. Which is the best estimate for the average distance they traveled each day?

A. Less than 150 miles
B. About 200 miles
C. About 300 miles
D. More than 400 miles

7 Carol and Meg have 2 dozen cookies. If Meg has 4 more cookies than Carol, how many cookies does each girl have?

A. Carol has 14. Meg has 10.
B. Carol has 10. Meg has 14.
C. Carol has 16. Meg has 20.
D. Carol has 14. Meg has 18.

8 This graph shows how many students signed up for recreational sports.

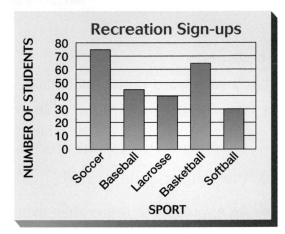

About how many more students signed up for the most popular sport than for the least popular sport?

A. 105
B. 60
C. 45
D. 30
E. 5

9 Jake arranges his model cars on 6 shelves. Each shelf can hold as many as 9 cars, and Jake always puts at least 5 cars on a shelf. Which is a reasonable total number of cars you might find on the shelves?

A. Less than 9
B. Between 5 and 14
C. Between 30 and 54
D. More than 54

10 Tricia's grades on 3 tests are 81, 93, and 89. Which number sentence could be used to find what grade, n, she needs to get on the next test to have a 90 average?

A. $90 - (81 + 93 + 89) = n$
B. $90 - n = 81 + 93 + 89$
C. $(81 + 93 + 89 + n) \div 3 = 90$
D. $(81 + 93 + 89 + n) \div 4 = 90$

✔ Checkpoint

More Two-Digit Division

Vocabulary

Match each word with its definition.

1. The number used to divide another number.

2. The answer in division.

3. The number to be divided.

4. An approximate rather than exact answer.

Word Bank

dividend
divisor
estimate
quotient

Concepts and Skills

Estimate first. Then divide and check. (pages 224–225)

5. $26\overline{)962}$

6. $19\overline{)855}$

7. $63\overline{)882}$

8. $33\overline{)924}$

9. $56\overline{)728}$

10. $48\overline{)643}$

11. $26\overline{)489}$

12. $39\overline{)586}$

13. $863 \div 21$

14. $977 \div 86$

15. $747 \div 22$

16. $553 \div 34$

17. $813 \div 42$

18. $289 \div 45$

19. $374 \div 18$

20. $525 \div 15$

Using Algebra Compare. Write >, <, or = for each ●. (pages 224–225)

21. $900 \div 45$ ● $665 \div 35$

22. $500 \div 25$ ● $600 \div 30$

23. $320 \div 16$ ● $420 \div 20$

24. $600 \div 12$ ● $760 \div 19$

25. $840 \div 30$ ● $520 \div 20$

26. $750 \div 15$ ● $8{,}190 \div 90$

Choose a Method Use mental math, paper and pencil, or a calculator to divide. Tell which method you chose and why. (pages 228–231)

27. $80\overline{)6{,}400}$

28. $53\overline{)7{,}208}$

29. $38\overline{)5{,}224}$

30. $18\overline{)1{,}928}$

31. $35\overline{)4{,}108}$

32. $65\overline{)8{,}971}$

33. $42\overline{)9{,}315}$

34. $59\overline{)4{,}511}$

35. $20\overline{)1{,}852}$

36. $611 \div 73$

37. $3{,}500 \div 50$

38. $903 \div 14$

Problem Solving

Use the table at the right for Problem 39.

39. A bus can carry 43 people. How many buses will be needed to take all of the Central School students to a parade if a driver and two teachers go on each bus? Explain how you found your answer.

40. Analyze When Mariko divided 1,954 by 19, she got an incorrect answer of 12 R16. Why is her answer not reasonable? What is the correct answer? What did Mariko do wrong?

Journal Idea

Interview an adult at your school to find three ways he or she uses division in everyday life. Then write a paragraph about your interview.

Central School	
Grade	Number of Students
K	34
1	42
2	47
3	53
4	44
5	45
6	51

What do you think?

People sometimes say that division "undoes" multiplication. Use an example to show why this is true.

You Decide

Activity

A Grandstand Play

Grandstands have been set up for 200 yards along both sides of the parade route. You and two friends have been asked to order decorations to be placed on poles located at 10-foot intervals along the front of each grandstand. You can use balloons, pennants, and streamers as decorations. Use two different items on each pole.

Use a drawing or diagram to help you decide how many of each type of decoration you need to order.

You might wish to include this work in your portfolio.

Extra Practice

Set A (pages 210–211)

Use mental math to find each quotient.

1. $30\overline{)180}$
2. $40\overline{)280}$
3. $20\overline{)800}$
4. $70\overline{)4,900}$

5. $90\overline{)5,400}$
6. $80\overline{)2,400}$
7. $80\overline{)40,000}$
8. $60\overline{)3,600}$

9. $30,000 \div 50$
10. $12,000 \div 30$
11. $4,200 \div 60$
12. $18,000 \div 90$

13. $36,000 \div 60$
14. $54,000 \div 90$
15. $45,000 \div 50$
16. $30,000 \div 30$

17. $64,000 \div 80$
18. $50,000 \div 10$
19. $20,000 \div 40$
20. $6,000 \div 20$

21. A school marching band spent $2,500 on costumes. How much did each costume cost if there were 50 people in the band and the costumes all cost the same amount?

22. An arena used for a Cinco de Mayo celebration can seat about 24,000 people. It has nearly 80 sections. About how many seats are in each section?

23. **Using Algebra** Explain how using patterns and basic facts can help you solve $49,000 \div 700$.

Set B (pages 212–213)

Use compatible numbers to estimate each quotient.

1. $64\overline{)32,000}$
2. $28\overline{)925}$
3. $21\overline{)433}$
4. $63\overline{)590}$

5. $47\overline{)41,065}$
6. $63\overline{)31,810}$
7. $75\overline{)48,472}$
8. $96\overline{)100,000}$

9. $3,908 \div 78$
10. $44,020 \div 4$
11. $60,357 \div 58$
12. $3,050 \div 48$

13. $4,815 \div 63$
14. $8,762 \div 27$
15. $1,533 \div 54$
16. $35,769 \div 88$

17. $23,599 \div 27$
18. $56,216 \div 73$
19. $27,908 \div 39$
20. $30,333 \div 22$

21. **Explain** Terrell's book has 312 pages. How many days will it take him to read the book if he reads 20 pages a day? Explain your answer.

22. Elaine can read about 135 words a minute. About how many words can she read in 30 minutes?

Extra Practice

Set C (pages 216–219)

Estimate. Then divide and check.

1. $13\overline{)27}$
2. $38\overline{)97}$
3. $26\overline{)84}$
4. $93\overline{)179}$

5. $59\overline{)466}$
6. $89\overline{)827}$
7. $71\overline{)395}$
8. $91\overline{)737}$

9. $546 \div 83$
10. $531 \div 64$
11. $423 \div 72$
12. $133 \div 24$

13. $183 \div 61$
14. $301 \div 45$
15. $115 \div 18$
16. $127 \div 13$

17. $245 \div 53$
18. $221 \div 33$
19. $648 \div 72$
20. $351 \div 55$

21. Forty-eight schools in Texas decided to plant trees for Earth Day. If a total of 240 trees were planted and each school planted the same number, how many trees did each school plant?

22. A fifth-grade class wants to plant 125 flowers for Earth Day. If they plan to put 15 flowers in each row, how many complete rows can they plant? How many flowers will be left over?

Set D (pages 224–225)

Estimate. Then divide and check.

1. $25\overline{)329}$
2. $16\overline{)425}$
3. $39\overline{)495}$
4. $25\overline{)900}$

5. $74\overline{)814}$
6. $34\overline{)816}$
7. $42\overline{)984}$
8. $61\overline{)753}$

9. $579 \div 38$
10. $568 \div 12$
11. $824 \div 46$
12. $998 \div 73$

13. $498 \div 45$
14. $759 \div 28$
15. $549 \div 41$
16. $955 \div 24$

17. The Ellenberg family plans to travel 458 miles to spend Thanksgiving with their family. If they average 55 miles per hour, about how long will it take them?

18. **Using Algebra** A community group plans to serve Thanksgiving dinner to 624 people who were evacuated from a flooded area. The chefs plan to have one pound of turkey for every 2 guests. If they purchase 24-pound turkeys, how many do they need?

Extra Practice

Set E (pages 228–231)

Choose a Method Use paper and pencil or a calculator to divide.

1. $12\overline{)3,215}$
2. $74\overline{)6,246}$
3. $81\overline{)5,223}$
4. $46\overline{)2,681}$

5. $46\overline{)3,469}$
6. $12\overline{)9,543}$
7. $32\overline{)16,992}$
8. $64\overline{)12,345}$

9. $42\overline{)25,487}$
10. $23\overline{)15,129}$
11. $45\overline{)30,712}$
12. $61\overline{)34,855}$

13. $16\overline{)13,184}$
14. $95\overline{)26,423}$
15. $26\overline{)16,205}$
16. $44\overline{)16,016}$

17. $52\overline{)25,334}$
18. $67\overline{)90,458}$
19. $83\overline{)10,643}$
20. $91\overline{)135,476}$

21. $443,018 \div 46$
22. $23,428 \div 26$
23. $5,887 \div 14$
24. $50,469 \div 63$

25. $3,528 \div 36$
26. $40,432 \div 76$
27. $21,944 \div 52$
28. $40,329 \div 98$

29. $17,286 \div 25$
30. $39,211 \div 55$
31. $78,521 \div 87$
32. $84,336 \div 93$

33. The town art show attracted 3,211 people during 14 days. What was the average number of people that visited the show each day?

Use the table for Problems 34–38.

34. About how many pretzels were sold each day?

35. What was the total amount of the snack bar's sales for the 14 days?

36. If the snack bar had sold $1,834.50 worth of juice, how many servings would have been sold?

37. The snack bar ordered 550 hot dogs. How much more money would they have collected if they had sold all of the hot dogs?

38. The snack bar buys ice pops in boxes of 24. How many boxes did they have to open?

Snack Bar Sales May 1–14			
Item	Price Each	Number Sold	Total
Chili	$1.50	162	$243.00
Hot dog	$1.25	490	$612.50
Hot pretzel	$0.75	630	$472.50
Ice pop	$1.00	536	$536.00
Juice	$1.50	1,079	$1,618.50

Chapter Test

Use basic facts and patterns to find each n.

1. $160 \div 40 = n$

2. $900 \div 30 = n$

3. $2,400 \div 80 = n$

4. $5,000 \div 50 = n$

5. $n \times 90 = 7,200$

6. $60 \times n = 36,000$

Use compatible numbers to estimate each quotient. Tell what compatible numbers you used.

7. $38\overline{)1,625}$

8. $83\overline{)4,250}$

9. $18\overline{)1,575}$

10. $2,521 \div 54$

11. $1,562 \div 83$

12. $4,275 \div 61$

Divide.

13. $19\overline{)113}$

14. $85\overline{)510}$

15. $41\overline{)861}$

16. $55\overline{)736}$

17. $28\overline{)341}$

18. $13\overline{)785}$

19. $631 \div 21$

20. $21,216 \div 52$

21. $24,124 \div 36$

Solve.

22. Using Estimation At the town Fourth of July picnic, there are 150 prizes. If 80 people come, about how many prizes are there for each person?

23. You are reading a 335-page book. If you read 38 pages a day, how long will it take you to finish the book?

24. The Rodriguez family was driving 270 miles from Miami to Tampa, Florida, to celebrate Cinco de Mayo with friends. After nearly 5 hours of driving, they stopped for lunch. Soon after they started again, they saw a sign that said Tampa—45 miles. What was the average miles per hour they drove for the first 5 hours?

25. Sherman has 36 magazines that he plans to share with his friends. He decides to give the same number to each friend. To how many friends can he give the magazines, and how many magazines will each friend get?

 Self-Check

For Exercises 13–21, did you check your division using multiplication and addition?

Performance Assessment

Show What You Know About Two-Digit Division

① Use the numbers at the right for a, b, and c. Always divide the greater number by the smaller number. Show your work.

a. Choose any two numbers and find their quotient.

b. Using any two numbers, is it possible to make a quotient with three digits? Explain.

c. Using any two numbers, is it possible to make a quotient with a remainder? Explain.

Self-Check Did you remember to show your work and explain your answers?

10   8,240

20

② A radio station is giving away a prize every 45 minutes.

a. How many prizes are given away in 24 hours?

b. If each prize had the same value and $1,600 in prizes was given away, what was the value of each prize?

c. If every other prize winner received an additional bonus prize, how many bonus prizes were given away?

d. In one contest, 168 prizes were given away. If one prize is given away every hour, 24 hours a day, how many days did the contest last?

Self-Check Did you remember that there are 60 minutes in 1 hour?

▲ Holly Haze is a disc jockey on a classic rock-and-roll radio station in Charlotte, North Carolina.

 For Your Portfolio

You might wish to include this work in your portfolio.

Extension

Exploring Sequences

A **sequence** is a set of numbers that follows a certain pattern. The numbers in a sequence are called **terms**.

$$\overset{+4}{\frown}\ \overset{+4}{\frown}\ \overset{+4}{\frown}\ \overset{+4}{\frown}\ \overset{+4}{\frown}$$
4, 8, 12, 16, 20, 24,…

In the sequence above, 4 is added to each term to get the next term. What are the next five terms in the sequence?

Study the pattern in the chart at the right. Then copy the chart and use the pattern to complete it.

The numbers representing the dots are called **triangular numbers** because they can be represented visually as a triangle. They form a sequence. Describe the pattern in the sequence.

Triangular Numbers			
Term	Number of Dots		Difference
First	•	1	
			⟩ + 2
Second	••	3	
			⟩ + 3
Third	•••	6	
			⟩ + 4
Fourth	••••		⟩
Fifth			⟩
Sixth			⟩
Seventh			⟩

Find the pattern for each sequence. Then write the next three terms.

1. 2, 4, 6, 8, ▪, ▪, ▪

2. 50, 45, 40, 35, ▪, ▪, ▪

3. 1, 3, 9, 27, ▪, ▪, ▪

4. 6, 5, 10, 9, 14, ▪, ▪, ▪

5. 8.9, 7.8, 6.7, 5.6, ▪, ▪, ▪

6. $\frac{2}{3}$, $\frac{4}{9}$, $\frac{8}{27}$, ▪, ▪, ▪

7. 1, 6, 9, 14, 17, 22, ▪, ▪, ▪

8. 2.1, 4.2, 8.4, ▪, ▪, ▪

9. 5; 20; 80; 320; 1,280; ▪; ▪; ▪

10. 15, 11, 14, 10, 13, ▪, ▪, ▪

11. Create Your Own Create a number sequence with five terms. Ask a classmate to write the next two terms.

Using Math in Science

*Use **measuring** and **graphing** to investigate some properties of different balls and their energy of motion.*

Follow the Bouncing Ball

You and your classmates have invented a new game. You need a small ball that bounces—but not too high. What type of ball will work best?

What You Need

For each pair:
3 different types of small balls
meterstick
graph paper

Explore

Step 1 Work with a partner. Make three charts, each like the one below.

Type of Ball:_____

Trial Number	Height of Bounce in Centimeters
1	
2	
3	
4	

Average Height of Bounce in Centimeters: _____

Step 2 Choose one of the three balls to test. Write the type of ball on one of your charts.

Step 3 Have your partner hold the meterstick perpendicular to the floor, as shown in the picture on page 243. The end of the meterstick with the zero mark should be against the floor.

Step 4 Stand next to the meterstick. Drop the ball from a height of 1 meter, as shown in the picture. Have your partner use the meterstick to estimate, in centimeters, how high the ball bounces. Record this height on your chart.

Step 5 Repeat Step 4 three more times.

Step 6 Find the average height of the four bounces. Record this average in your chart.

Step 7 Repeat Steps 3 through 6 for each of the remaining types of balls.

Step 8 Make a bar graph of the average heights of the bounces for all three balls. Compare the average heights. How does the graph reflect the data collected?

▲ Steps 3 and 4

Analyze

1. Why is it important to do several trials for each ball and then to find the average?

2. How could you use the data you collected to decide which type of ball is best for your game?

3. Suppose your game involved throwing the ball hard against a wall and catching it as it bounced back. Which ball would be the best choice? Explain your choice.

 For Your Portfolio

Write about what you discovered. Explain how graphing helped you organize and understand your data. Tell if the results of the activity surprised you. Why or why not?

Explore Further!

Hypothesize How does changing the height from which a ball is dropped affect the height of its bounce? Design an experiment to test your prediction.

Cumulative Review

★★★★★ **Preparing for Tests**

Choose the correct letter for each answer.

Number Concepts	Operations

1. Which of these numbers is 2,750 when rounded to the nearest ten and 2,700 when rounded to the nearest hundred?

    A. 2,766
    B. 2,746
    C. 2,744
    D. 2,656

2. Which number sentence is true?

    A. $0.098 > 0.19$
    B. $7.007 < 7.002$
    C. $23.177 < 23.018$
    D. $100.431 > 100.429$

3. What decimal is shown by the shaded part of the grid?

    A. 3.3
    B. 0.33
    C. 0.033
    D. 0.0033

4. Each student has some juice. Altogether, they have $2\frac{3}{8}$ quarts of juice. If Greg has $\frac{3}{4}$ qt, Frank has $\frac{1}{2}$ qt, Eve has $\frac{5}{8}$ qt, and Jill has $\frac{2}{4}$ qt, who has the *greatest* amount?

    A. Greg
    B. Eve
    C. Frank
    D. Jill

5. What is the product of 63 and 9?

    A. 562   **C.** 568
    B. 567   **D.** 657

6. Kayla is reading a book that has 210 pages. If she reads 30 pages a day, how many days will it take her to read the entire book?

    A. 5 days   **C.** 8 days
    B. 7 days   **D.** 10 days

Use the price list below to answer Questions 7–8.

Pizza Special		
Size	**Number of Slices**	**Price**
Large	10	$8.99
Medium	8	$6.99
Small	6	$5.99
Personal	4	$2.99

7. Jim has invited 15 friends for a pizza party. If each person will eat 3 slices, how many large pizzas should he buy?

    A. 3   **C.** 5
    B. 4   **D.** 6

8. Which pizza costs the *least* per slice?

    A. Large   **C.** Small
    B. Medium   **D.** Personal

Patterns, Relationships, and Algebraic Thinking	Measurement

9. Which is the rule for the number sequence below?

13.1, 10.9, 8.7, 6.5, 4.3, …

A. Add 2.
B. Subtract 2.1.
C. Subtract 2.2.
D. Multiply by 0.5.

10. The shops on the east side of the street have consecutive even numbers. The first shop is number 302. Which number sentence would you use to find the number of the **fifteenth** shop?

A. $302 + 14 = n$
B. $302 + 15 = n$
C. $302 + 28 = n$
D. $302 \times 2 = n$

11. Which is the correct rule?

Input	Output
0.05	0.5
0.50	5.0
5.0	50.0

A. Multiply by 1.
B. Multiply by 10.
C. Divide by 10.
D. Add 100.

12. What is $72,000 \div 8$? Use the pattern to help you.

$72 \div 8 = 9$
$720 \div 8 = 90$
$7,200 \div 8 = 900$
$72,000 \div 8 = \blacksquare$

A. 90   **C.** 9,000
B. 900   **D.** 90,000

13. What is the **volume** of the prism shown?

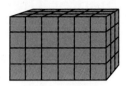

A. 12 cubic units
B. 18 cubic units
C. 24 cubic units
D. 72 cubic units

14. Gary went on a 4-day fishing trip with his family. He was proud of all the fish he caught, especially the one fish that was 5 feet long. How many **inches** long was this fish?

A. 60 inches
B. 30 inches
C. 20 inches
D. 12.5 inches

15. A jar holds 350 mL of water. How many liters is this?
(1 L = 1,000 mL)

A. 0.035 L
B. 0.35 L
C. 3.5 L
D. 35 L

16. The first thermometer shows the temperature at 6 A.M. and the second shows the temperature at noon. Which change took place in the last 6 hours?

A. ⁻23°F
B. ⁻13°F
C. ⁺13°F
D. ⁺23°F

6 A.M.   NOON

Chapter 7

Geometry

Chapter Theme: SHAPES AND FORMS

Real-World Math

Real Facts

How can a playground be mathematical? Every time you play on swings, a slide, a climbing rope, or a fort deck, you are playing on geometric shapes. Here is a materials list for building a wooden A-frame swing set.

Materials List for A-Frame Swing Set		
Description	Quantity Needed	Comments
4 in. × 8 in. wooden board, 14 ft in length	1	Used as main board across top
4 in. × 4 in. wooden board, 12 ft in length	4	Used as legs
bolts nuts washers	4 of each	Used to connect the pieces together
braces $11\frac{1}{4}$" 12" $63°$ $23\frac{1}{4}$"	2	Used to support the swing set

- What are the shapes of the nuts and washers?

- What shape are the braces? How many degrees should the base angles of the braces have?

Real People

Meet Rick Vaughn. He designs furniture. To make his furniture unique, he uses circles, triangles, prisms, and every other shape you can imagine in his designs!

The children in the photograph on the right are using many different shapes to build a playground. What shapes do you see?

Geometrically Speaking

*Learning the language of geometry will
help you see that geometry is all around you.*

Learning About It

The photograph on page 247 shows Mexico City as seen
from the air. The table below gives you some geometric terms
that you can use to describe the streets of Mexico City.

The Language of Geometry

Term and Description	Example	Symbol and How to Read It
point—an exact location in space	•B	•B point B
line—an endless collection of points along a straight path	←•—————•→ A B	$\overleftrightarrow{AB}$ line AB
line segment—part of a line that has two endpoints	•————————• X Y	$\overline{XY}$ line segment XY
ray—part of a line that has one endpoint and extends endlessly in the other direction	•————•→ S T	$\overrightarrow{ST}$ ray ST
plane—an endless, flat surface that is named by any three points not on the same line	L N •M	▱ LMN plane LMN

Connecting Ideas

The language of geometry helps to define three different ways that lines can relate to each other.

Social Studies Connection Streets of Mexico City are highlighted to show three different pairs of lines.

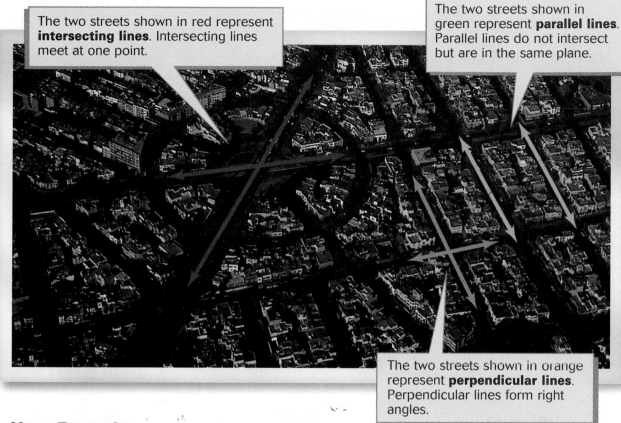

The two streets shown in red represent **intersecting lines**. Intersecting lines meet at one point.

The two streets shown in green represent **parallel lines**. Parallel lines do not intersect but are in the same plane.

The two streets shown in orange represent **perpendicular lines**. Perpendicular lines form right angles.

More Examples

A. $\overleftrightarrow{CD}$ is parallel to $\overleftrightarrow{AB}$.

B. $\overleftrightarrow{RS}$ intersects $\overleftrightarrow{TU}$ at point P.

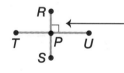

This symbol tells you that this is a square corner, which is also called a right angle. $\overleftrightarrow{RS}$ is perpendicular to $\overleftrightarrow{TU}$.

Think and Discuss Are intersecting lines always perpendicular? Explain your thinking.

Try It Out

Draw and label an example of each.

1. plane QRS **2.** line segment TH **3.** ray JK

Draw and label an example of each pair of lines described.

4. $\overleftrightarrow{AB}$ is perpendicular to $\overleftrightarrow{RS}$. **5.** $\overleftrightarrow{CD}$ is parallel to $\overleftrightarrow{UV}$. **6.** $\overleftrightarrow{EF}$ intersects $\overleftrightarrow{XY}$.

Practice

Draw an example of each of the following.

7. ray *GI*

8. plane *ABC*

9. two parallel lines

10. two perpendicular lines

11. a line with points *M* and *Z* on the line

12. a line segment with endpoints *Q* and *B*

Use the drawing at the right for Exercises 13–16.

13. Name four points.

14. Name three line segments.

15. Name two lines.

16. Name a ray.

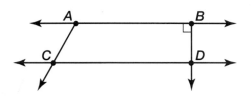

Look at the photograph of Albuquerque, New Mexico, below. Name an example of each of the following.

17. intersecting line segments

18. parallel line segments

19. perpendicular line segments

20. intersecting, but not perpendicular, line segments

Problem Solving

21. Describe something in your classroom that illustrates parallel lines. Explain your choice.

22. Analyze Plans for a park call for intersecting walks that are also perpendicular to each other. How might a landscaper tell that she has constructed the walks according to the plans?

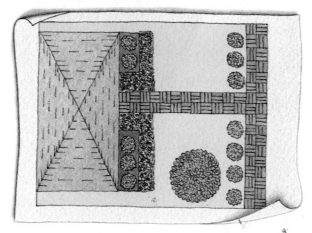

▲ As part of her work, an architect reads and interprets blueprints that have many intersecting lines.

 23. A landscaper built two separate walks with square patio blocks that were 12 in. on a side. Each walk used two rows of patio blocks. One walk was 17 patio blocks long. The other was 12 patio blocks long. How many blocks did the landscaper use for the two walks? How many inches long was each walk?

24. Create Your Own Use geometric terms to write directions for getting from your school to your home. Then have a classmate use the directions to draw a simple map.

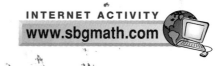

INTERNET ACTIVITY
www.sbgmath.com

Review and Remember

Find each answer.

25. $\begin{array}{r} 2.3 \\ + 0.54 \end{array}$

26. $\begin{array}{r} 12.8 \\ + 9.6 \end{array}$

27. $\begin{array}{r} 11.62 \\ - 2.11 \end{array}$

28. $\begin{array}{r} 9.8 \\ - 1.87 \end{array}$

29. 61×87

30. $1.126 + 0.95$

31. 22×38

32. $12.1 + 2.13$

33. $9.7 - 7.8$

34. $207 \div 9$

35. $36.1 - 1.8$

36. $864 \div 6$

37. 328×38

38. $1,270 \div 10$

39. 28×100

40. $6,528 \div 5$

It Takes Two

It takes two rays to make an angle. In this lesson you will learn how to identify angles.

Learning About It

An **angle** is formed when two rays have the same endpoint, called a **vertex**. The two rays that form the angle are called **sides**. The drawing shows angle *ABC*. It can also be named angle *CBA*.

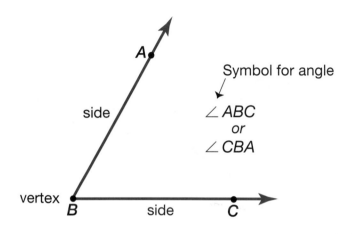

side

Symbol for angle

∠ *ABC*
or
∠ *CBA*

vertex
B   side   *C*

Word Bank

angle
vertex (*pl.*, vertices)
side
right angle
straight angle
acute angle
obtuse angle

What You Need

For each pair:
  2 paper plates (in two
    different colors)
  straightedge
  scissors
  index card

Work with a partner.

Use two paper plates to form different kinds of angles.

Step 1

- Mark the center of each plate.

- Use a straightedge to draw a line segment from the center to the edge of each plate.

- Use scissors to cut along the line segment of each plate.

Step 2 Slide the plates together as shown. As you turn the plates, you form angles of different sizes.

Step 3 Move the plates to form a **right angle**. A right angle forms a square corner. Use a corner of your index card to make sure you have a right angle.

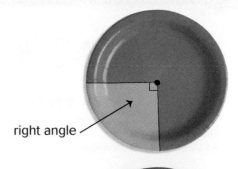

right angle

Step 4 Move the plates to form a **straight angle**. A straight angle forms a straight line. Use an edge of your index card to make sure you have a straight angle.

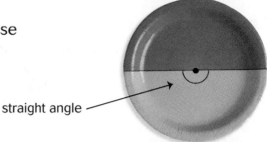

straight angle

Step 5 Move the plates to first form an **acute angle** and then an **obtuse angle**. An acute angle is less than a right angle. An obtuse angle is greater than a right angle and less than a straight angle.

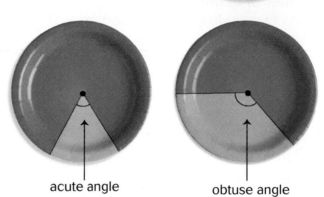

acute angle   obtuse angle

Think and Discuss Look back at Steps 3 and 4. How does using an index card help you know that you have a right angle? a straight angle?

Practice

Classify each angle as right, straight, acute, or obtuse.

1.
2.
3.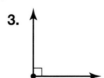
4.

Draw an example of each angle.

5. acute angle   6. obtuse angle

7. right angle   8. straight angle

9. Look back at Exercises 5–8. Tell how you know that you have drawn the angles correctly.

10. Make a drawing to show how two right angles can form a straight angle.

What's Your Angle?

You will use what you have learned about the sizes of angles to help you measure and draw them.

Learning About It

Draftspersons draw blueprints to design buildings. They need to measure and draw angles to make their blueprints accurate.

Angles are measured in **degrees** (°). To measure the number of degrees in an angle, you can use a **protractor**. It has two scales, each labeled from 0° to 180°.

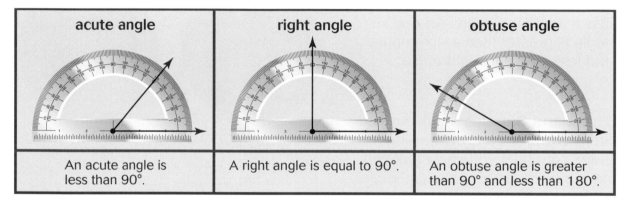

acute angle	right angle	obtuse angle
An acute angle is less than 90°.	A right angle is equal to 90°.	An obtuse angle is greater than 90° and less than 180°.

Before you measure an angle, first compare it to a right angle. Decide if the measure of the angle is less than or greater than 90°.

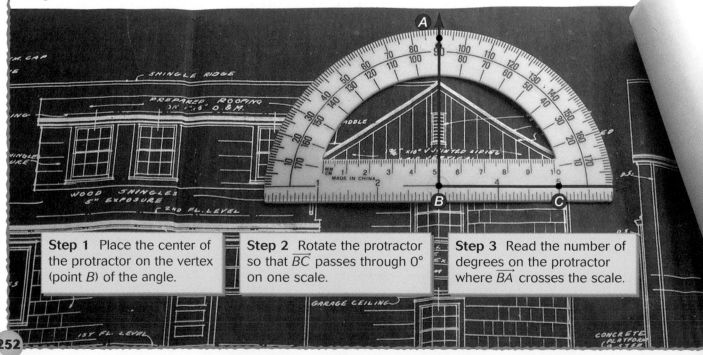

Step 1 Place the center of the protractor on the vertex (point *B*) of the angle.

Step 2 Rotate the protractor so that $\overrightarrow{BC}$ passes through 0° on one scale.

Step 3 Read the number of degrees on the protractor where $\overrightarrow{BA}$ crosses the scale.

Follow the steps below to draw an angle with a certain number of degrees.

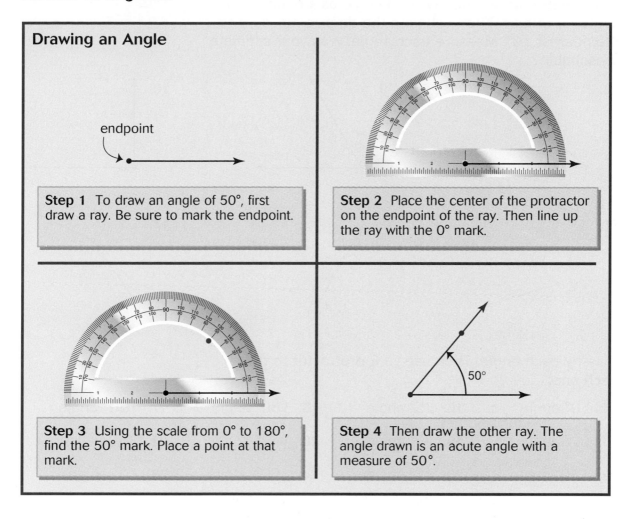

Drawing an Angle

endpoint

Step 1 To draw an angle of 50°, first draw a ray. Be sure to mark the endpoint.

Step 2 Place the center of the protractor on the endpoint of the ray. Then line up the ray with the 0° mark.

Step 3 Using the scale from 0° to 180°, find the 50° mark. Place a point at that mark.

Step 4 Then draw the other ray. The angle drawn is an acute angle with a measure of 50°.

50°

Think and Discuss How does deciding whether an angle is an acute, obtuse, or right angle help you estimate, measure, or draw it correctly?

Try It Out

Estimate the degree measure of each angle to the nearest 10°. Then measure each angle.

1.

2.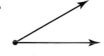

3.

Use your protractor to draw each angle.

4. 40° angle   **5.** 130° angle   **6.** 150° angle   **7.** 60° angle

Practice

Using Estimation Classify each angle as straight, right, acute, or obtuse. Then estimate the degree measure to the nearest 10°. Measure each angle. Was your estimate reasonable?

8.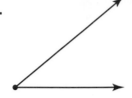

9.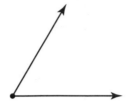

10.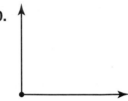

11.

12.

13.

Classify each angle. Then use your protractor to draw each one.

14. 50° angle   **15.** 75° angle   **16.** 180° angle   **17.** 130° angle

18. 62° angle   **19.** 90° angle   **20.** 142° angle   **21.** 38° angle

22. 150° angle   **23.** 25° angle   **24.** 160° angle   **25.** 10° angle

Problem Solving

26. A draftsperson uses two angles in his plans for a new building. The angles measure 45° and 35°. If he places these angles so that they have one side in common, will the resulting angle be acute, right, or obtuse? How do you know?

27. What If? Suppose the drafter in Problem 26 used angles measuring 55° and 35°. What kind of angle would result then?

28. Drafters use many types of tools. One of the tools they use is called a T Square. It is shaped like a letter T. What kinds of angles make a T?

▲ **Science Connection** A draftsperson reviews his plans for a new structure.

29. Analyze You measure an angle to be 60°. Your classmate uses the same protractor and thinks the angle is 120°. What's wrong with one of the measurements?

30. Fine Arts Connection The percussion section of a band includes rhythm instruments, such as the triangle shown at the right. In 1848, Franz Liszt wrote a solo for the triangle in his first piano concerto. Look at the triangle. Are the angles acute, obtuse, or right angles? Tell how you know.

31. You Decide Draw a triangle using any combination of acute angles. Tell which angles you used and their measures.

▲ Triangles probably originated in Turkey. They first appeared in Western European music in the 15th century.

Review and Remember

Choose a Method Use mental math, paper and pencil, or a calculator. Tell which method you used.

32. 28 × 24   **33.** 116 ÷ 25   **34.** 262 − 91   **35.** 32 ÷ 21

36. 819 + 99   **37.** 67)‾136   **38.** 25)‾100   **39.** 27)‾121

40. 1,792 + 9,998   **41.** 298 × 78   **42.** 1,050 − 937   **43.** 87 × 69

Critical Thinking Corner

Logical Thinking

Angle Measures

Use the drawings to find the measure of each of the following angles. Use a protractor to check. Explain how you found each angle measure.

1. ∠LHY   **2.** ∠EHY

3. ∠PCW   **4.** ∠XCW

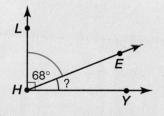

Plenty of Polygons

Polygons are common shapes that you see every day.
In geometry, a polygon is named by the number of its sides.

Learning About It

Many road signs around the world are in the shape of polygons. A **polygon** is a closed figure made up of three or more line segments. A **regular polygon** is one in which all sides have equal length and all angles have equal measure.

Polygons

Triangle	Quadrilateral	Pentagon	Hexagon	Octagon
3 sides 3 angles	4 sides 4 angles	5 sides 5 angles	6 sides 6 angles	8 sides 8 angles

Think and Discuss Look at these road signs. Which polygons do they represent? Which are regular polygons?

vertex

side

Try It Out

Name each polygon shown below.

1.

2.

3.

4.

Practice

Name the polygons in each photograph below.

5.

6.

7.

8.

9. Draw a pentagon. Identify the sides and the vertices.

Problem Solving

10. Using Algebra Look for patterns in the number of sides and angles of the polygons on page 256. A decagon has 10 sides. How many angles do you think it has? Explain.

11. Analyze Which of the following are hexagons? Which are regular hexagons? Explain how you decided.

a.

b.

c.

d.

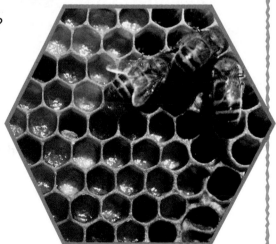

▲ **Science Connection** Did you know that each cell in a beehive is in the shape of a regular hexagon? Each cell contains a larva, which feeds on pollen and honey.

12. Create Your Own Write an "I am…" puzzle with clues to describe a polygon. Have a classmate solve your puzzle.

Review and Remember

Find each answer.

13. $16 + 23$ **14.** 12×58 **15.** $195 \div 46$ **16.** $117 - 12$ **17.** 175×75

18. 24×24 **19.** 45×79 **20.** $384 \div 96$ **21.** $635 \div 77$ **22.** $321 + 94$

For Extra Practice, see Set C, page 288.

Developing Skills for Problem Solving

First read for understanding and then focus on using spatial reasoning to solve problems.

READ FOR UNDERSTANDING

Four tiles like the one shown below are being used to cover a square tabletop for a craft project. Each of the tiles is decorated with 4 small squares.

1 How many tiles will be used?

2 How many small squares are on each tile?

3 How many small squares on each tile are beige?

THINK AND DISCUSS

MATH FOCUS

Spatial Reasoning Sometimes you can imagine changing the position or shape of objects. This process is called spatial reasoning.

▲ **Social Studies Connection**
Colorful tiles were used to decorate this building in Barcelona, Spain.

Reread the paragraph and look at the tile at the top of the page.

4 In how many different ways can the first tile be placed in the corner of the tabletop? Explain.

5 If the outside corners are patterned, what will the center of the table look like?

6 If the outside corners are beige, what will the center of the table look like?

7 How can the tiles be arranged to make a square checkerboard pattern? Explain how you used spatial reasoning to decide.

▲ Two tiles, side by side

Show What You Learned

Answer each question. Give a reason for your choice.

Pete's mother made a "Stars and Spots" patchwork quilt. Pete calls it "The Quilt of Many Squares." Each patchwork square is made up of four smaller squares, as shown below.

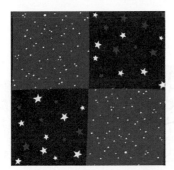

1 How many squares like the one above were used to make the quilt?

a. 8 **b.** 12 **c.** 24

2 How many small squares are in the quilt?

a. 24 **b.** 38 **c.** 48

3 The back of the quilt is one color. Pete folds the quilt in half from top to bottom so that the pattern is inside. What are the colors and positions of the two small squares in the top left corner of the folded quilt?

a. A blue square under a blue square

b. A red square under a blue square

c. A blue square under a red square

4 **Analyze** Pete's mother wants to add another row of patchwork squares around the quilt following the same pattern. How many squares does she need?

Jen is rolling the color cube below. Each face of the cube has a different color—orange, yellow, green, blue, red, and purple.

5 The pictures at the right show the same cube in different positions. Which color is opposite red?

Classify It!

You can classify triangles by the measures of their angles and by the lengths of their sides.

Learning About It

The triangle has been used for centuries in puzzles and on game boards. Part of a puzzle that contains 15 triangles is shown. Each triangle has equal sides and equal angles.

One way to classify a triangle is by the measures of its angles.

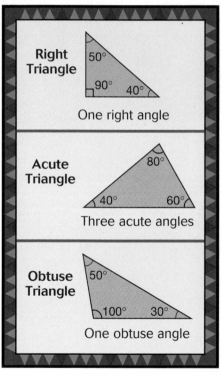

Right Triangle 50° 90° 40°
One right angle

Acute Triangle 80° 40° 60°
Three acute angles

Obtuse Triangle 50° 100° 30°
One obtuse angle

The triangle removed from the puzzle is an acute triangle because it has three acute angles.

More Examples

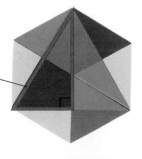

A. Right Triangle

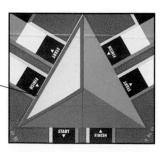

B. Obtuse Triangle

Connecting Ideas

You have classified a triangle by its angles. You can also classify a triangle by the lengths of its sides.

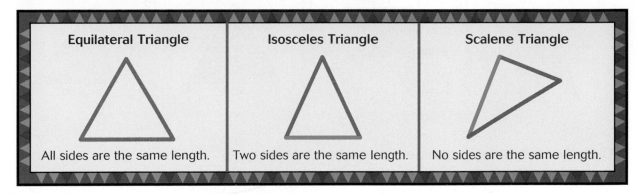

Equilateral Triangle	Isosceles Triangle	Scalene Triangle
All sides are the same length.	Two sides are the same length.	No sides are the same length.

Look again at the triangle removed from the puzzle on page 260. It is an equilateral triangle, since the lengths of its sides are the same.

More Examples

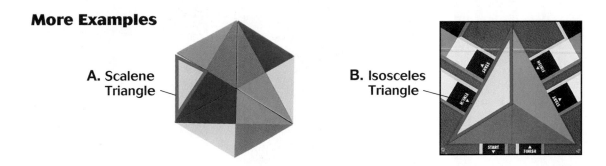

A. Scalene Triangle

B. Isosceles Triangle

Think and Discuss Can a triangle be an acute triangle and also a scalene triangle? a right triangle and also an isosceles triangle? Why or why not?

Try It Out

Classify each triangle by its angles.

1. 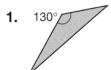 130°

2.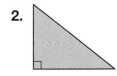

3. 50° 65° 65°

4. 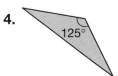 125°

Classify each triangle by its sides.

5. 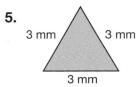 3 mm 3 mm 3 mm

6. 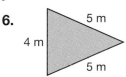 5 m 4 m 5 m

7. 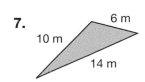 6 m 10 m 14 m

8. 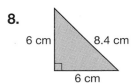 6 cm 8.4 cm 6 cm

Practice

Classify each triangle by its angles and sides.

9.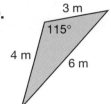
3 m
115°
4 m
6 m

10.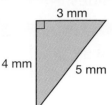
3 mm
4 mm
5 mm

11.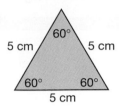
60°
5 cm   5 cm
60°   60°
5 cm

12.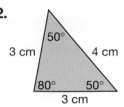
50°
3 cm   4 cm
80°   50°
3 cm

Classify each triangle outlined below by its angles and sides.

13. Backgammon

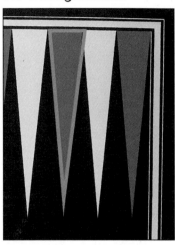

14. Chinese checkers

15. Triominos

Problem Solving

16. Meg designed a game board in the shape of an equilateral triangle. She plans to outline the triangle in yarn. If one side measures 12 cm, how much yarn is needed to outline the triangle?

17. **Analyze** A garden has a perimeter of 21 m. If the garden is in the shape of an equilateral triangle, what are the lengths of the sides?

18. A truck is loaded with 264 cases of games. Each case contains 12 boxes of games. Each box contains 6 dozen small travel games. How many small travel games are in the truck?

19. **Journal Idea** Can a triangle be both acute and obtuse? Explain why or why not.

> ◀ **Math Note**
>
> Remember that the perimeter is the distance around a polygon.

Review and Remember

Use the pictograph to answer Exercises 20–23.

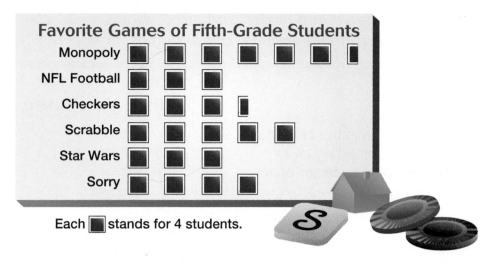

Favorite Games of Fifth-Grade Students

Each ■ stands for 4 students.

20. Which game was named by most students as their favorite game?

21. How many students selected Scrabble as their favorite?

22. How many students answered the survey? Check to be sure your answer is reasonable.

23. How many more students chose Monopoly than Sorry?

Time for Technology
Using the MathProcessor™ CD-ROM

Using the Geometry Tools

You can use the geometry tools to draw triangles and measure angles.

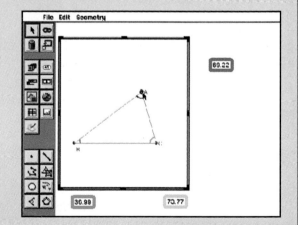

• Open a geometry workspace ⌂.

• Click ⊞. Click OK.

• Click ◁. Mark the three angles. Label each angle.

• Link each angle to a number space.

• Click-drag the vertex of any angle to reshape the triangle. Make a right triangle. Make an obtuse triangle. Make an acute triangle.

Sum It Up!

You know triangles have three sides and three angles.
Now you will learn about the sum of the angles.

Learning About It

Trim on barns and barn doors across the United States is sometimes painted a contrasting color. The trim on the red barn shown is made up of many triangles outlined in white.

Work with a group. Discover a property that all triangles share.

Step 1 Use a straightedge to trace the four triangles outlined on the photograph.

Step 2 Make a chart like the one shown.

Triangle	A	B	C	D
Angle 1				
Angle 2				
Angle 3				
Sum of angles				

What You Need

For each group:
  straightedge
  protractor

Step 3 Use a protractor to measure the angles in each triangle. Record your results in your chart. Then find the sum of the angles of each triangle.

Step 4 Compare your measurements with those of others in the class. Are the measurements the same or different? Explain.

Think and Discuss Compare your results with those of another group. Write a statement about the sum of the measures of the angles of a triangle.

Practice

1. **Predict** Draw a triangle and predict the sum of the measures of the angles. Then use a protractor to measure the angles and find the sum.

2. Look at the triangle you drew in Exercise 1. Why might your sum be different from your prediction?

3. Which of the following sets of angles could form a triangle? Tell how you know.

   a. 30°, 50°, 50°   **b.** 100°, 40°, 40°   **c.** 90°, 45°, 45°

4. Can a triangle have two right angles? Draw a diagram to help you explain why or why not.

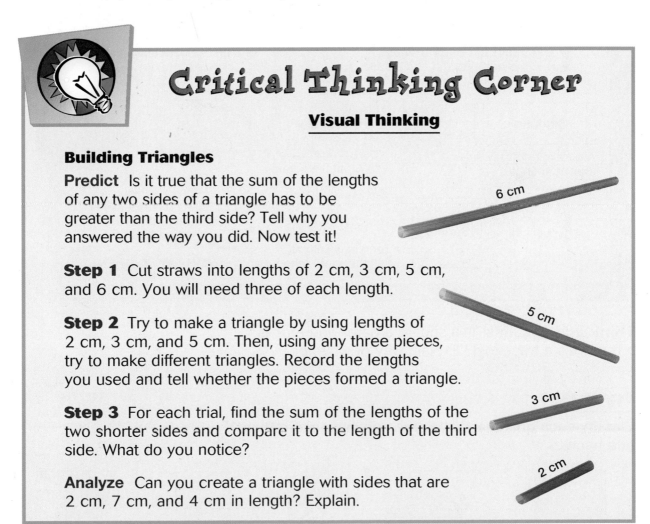

Critical Thinking Corner

Visual Thinking

Building Triangles

Predict Is it true that the sum of the lengths of any two sides of a triangle has to be greater than the third side? Tell why you answered the way you did. Now test it!

6 cm

Step 1 Cut straws into lengths of 2 cm, 3 cm, 5 cm, and 6 cm. You will need three of each length.

Step 2 Try to make a triangle by using lengths of 2 cm, 3 cm, and 5 cm. Then, using any three pieces, try to make different triangles. Record the lengths you used and tell whether the pieces formed a triangle.

5 cm

Step 3 For each trial, find the sum of the lengths of the two shorter sides and compare it to the length of the third side. What do you notice?

3 cm

Analyze Can you create a triangle with sides that are 2 cm, 7 cm, and 4 cm in length? Explain.

2 cm

Don't Be a Square!

You know that any four-sided figure is a quadrilateral.
Now you will identify quadrilaterals by their special properties.

Learning About It

Did you ever wonder what makes a square a square or why
a quadrilateral is called a quadrilateral? Four-sided polygons,
called quadrilaterals, have special names that identify them
by their angles or pairs of sides.

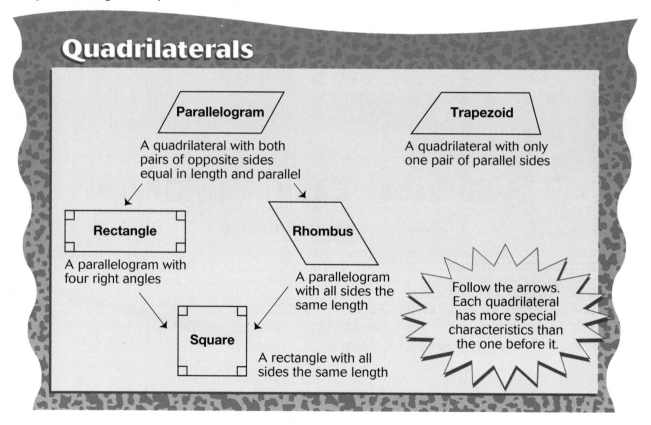

Quadrilaterals

Parallelogram
A quadrilateral with both pairs of opposite sides equal in length and parallel

Trapezoid
A quadrilateral with only one pair of parallel sides

Rectangle
A parallelogram with four right angles

Rhombus
A parallelogram with all sides the same length

Square
A rectangle with all sides the same length

Follow the arrows. Each quadrilateral has more special characteristics than the one before it.

Think and Discuss Is a square a parallelogram? Is
a rhombus a trapezoid? Explain why or why not.

Try It Out

**Classify each quadrilateral. Some may have more than
one name.**

1.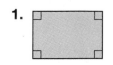

2.

3.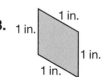
1 in.
1 in.
1 in.
1 in.

4.
2 ft
2 ft

5.

Practice

Classify each quadrilateral. Use as many names as possible.

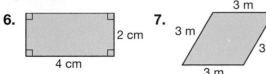

6. 4 cm, 2 cm

7. 3 m, 3 m, 3 m, 3 m

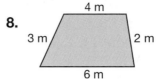

8. 4 m, 3 m, 2 m, 6 m

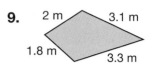

9. 2 m, 3.1 m, 1.8 m, 3.3 m

10. Social Studies Connection Use the photograph of Hong Kong below. Classify each quadrilateral that is outlined and labeled. Be as specific as possible.

Problem Solving

11. A square, a rectangle, a trapezoid, and a triangle were used in a sketch of a building. The square is above the rectangle and below the triangle. The trapezoid is below the triangle and above the square. What is the order of the figures from top to bottom?

12. What If? Suppose the trapezoid in Problem 11 was below the square and above the rectangle. Would the location of the triangle change? Explain why or why not.

13. Analyze Look at the drawing at the right. How many quadrilaterals can you find? How many triangles?

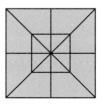

Review and Remember

Using Algebra Use mental math or paper and pencil to compare. Write >, <, or = for each ⬤.

14. 16×3 ⬤ 21×2

15. $101 \div 1$ ⬤ 25×4

16. $6 + 17$ ⬤ $19 - 5$

17. 16×12 ⬤ $576 \div 3$

18. 66×3 ⬤ 2×99

19. $45 \div 3$ ⬤ $35 - 21$

Use the drawing at the right for Exercises 1–8.
(pages 246–251)

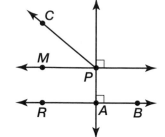

1. Name a segment.
2. Name a line.
3. Name a ray.
4. Name a point.
5. Name two lines that are parallel.
6. Name two lines that are perpendicular.
7. Name an acute angle.
8. Name a right angle.

Use a protractor. (pages 252–255)

9. Draw a 100° angle. Tell whether this angle is a right, an acute, or an obtuse angle.

Classify each angle. Then estimate each angle measure to the nearest 10°. Finally, measure each angle. (pages 252–255)

10.
11.
12.

Draw an example of each polygon. (pages 256–257)

13. pentagon
14. triangle
15. quadrilateral
16. octagon

Classify each triangle by side length and by angle measure. (pages 260–263)

17.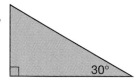
18.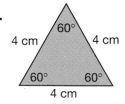
19.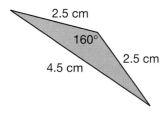

Classify each quadrilateral. Be as specific as possible.
(pages 266–267)

20.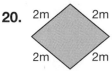
21.
22.
23.

Problem Solving

24. **Analyze** A tile floor has equilateral triangles arranged in the pattern shown at the right. What is the measure of ∠ADF? What is the sum of the measures of ∠ADF, ∠FDE, and ∠EDB? Tell how you know.

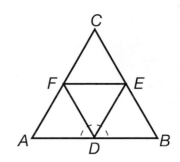

25. An architect's blueprint shows a window in the shape of a hexagon over a rectangular door. Draw a sketch of how the door and window might look.

Journal Idea

Choose a room in your home or in your school. Describe at least three items that are shaped like triangles or quadrilaterals. Then classify each shape described. Be as specific as possible.

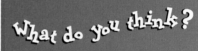

What do you think?

How can knowing the measures of the angles of a quadrilateral or a triangle help you classify it?

Critical Thinking Corner

Number Sense

Sums of Twenty

Using Algebra Copy the drawing on a sheet of paper. Place the numbers 1–9 in each of the nine sections so that the sum of the numbers in each pair of circles is 20. Use each number only once.

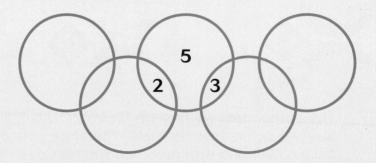

Explain Tell what strategy you used to find the answer.

Problem Solving
Find a Pattern

Sometimes you can solve a problem by finding and continuing a pattern.

Jen and Kate are painting a border on the walls in their bedroom. Kate painted the section of the border below and then went out to meet a friend. Jen wants to continue the border correctly. What shape and color should she paint next?

UNDERSTAND

What do you need to know?

You need to know the different shapes and colors in the border.

PLAN

How can you solve the problem?

You can **find a pattern** and use the pattern to decide what should be painted next.

SOLVE

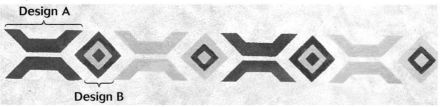

The border has two designs that alternate. It also has two colors that alternate. Therefore, Jen should paint a diamond with green on the outside.

LOOK BACK

What should be painted to the left of Kate's border?

Using the Strategy

Find the pattern. Then draw or describe the next three figures in each wallpaper border design.

1

2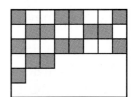

3

4 Stephen bought a house where the kitchen floor was only partly tiled. The builders left enough tiles to complete the floor, so Stephen is finishing the tiling. Based on the tile pattern shown at the right, draw a picture to show how he should finish tiling the floor.

5 **Analyze** Suppose you are making a picture frame like the one shown at the right. Continuing clockwise around the frame, what shape would come next? What shape would be placed last?

Mixed Strategy Review

Try these or other strategies to solve each problem. Tell which strategy you used.

Problem Solving Strategies

THERE'S ALWAYS A WAY!

- Solve a Simpler Problem
- Find a Pattern
- Work Backwards
- Write an Equation
- Draw a Diagram
- Make a Table

6 A wallpaper border consists of squares. Each square has one diagonal from the top left corner to the bottom right corner. How many triangles are in the first 4 squares?

7 James plans to put a wallpaper border along the top of each wall in a room that is 12 ft by 15 ft. How many yards of wallpaper border does he need?

8 Jo bought rolls of wallpaper border at $5.95 per roll, supplies for $12.95, and a "how-to" wallpaper book for $7.50. She gave the cashier $40 and received $1.70 in change. How many rolls did she buy?

9 If you fold a piece of paper in half 4 times, how many sections will you see when you unfold it? What if you fold it in half 6 times? Then how many sections will you see when you unfold it?

Double Take

In the first part of the chapter, you looked at individual figures.
Now you will look at pairs of figures.

Learning About It

Look around. You can see how shapes are used in patterns and designs you see every day. The figures outlined on the Navajo pottery pictured below are **congruent**. They have exactly the same size and shape.

You can tell if two figures are congruent by measuring the figures or by tracing one figure and placing the tracing on top of the other figure.

congruent figures

congruent figures

Connecting Ideas

You have looked at congruent figures. Now you will see that figures can change position and still be congruent.

Look at the triangles outlined on the sand painting in the photograph above. Notice that the triangles are in different positions but are still congruent.

▲ **Fine Arts Connection** Native American artists use many different geometric shapes to create beautiful patterns, such as those shown on the Navajo sand painting and pottery.

The change of position of a figure is called a **transformation**.

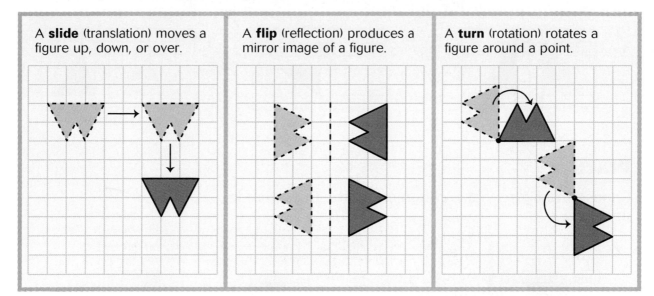

| A **slide** (translation) moves a figure up, down, or over. | A **flip** (reflection) produces a mirror image of a figure. | A **turn** (rotation) rotates a figure around a point. |

Compare each figure above with the tracing of it in its original position. Notice that the transformed figure is congruent to the tracing.

Think and Discuss In the design at the right, two congruent triangles have been outlined and labeled A and B. What are three ways in which Figure A could be moved to the position of Figure B?

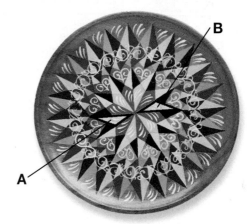

Try It Out

Choose the figure that is congruent to the first figure in each row.

▲ A plate from Costa Rica with a design often painted on a cart wheel

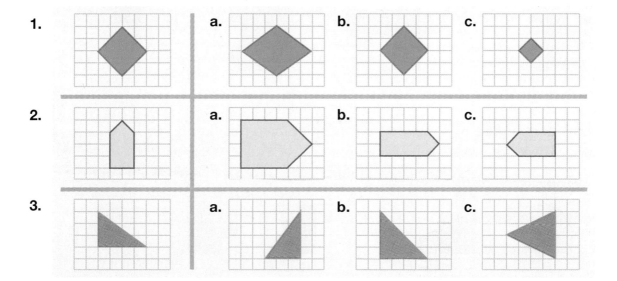

1.   a.   b.   c.

2.   a.   b.   c.

3.   a.   b.   c.

Tell how each triangle was moved from position A to position B. Write *slide, flip,* or *turn.*

4.

5.

6.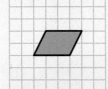

Practice

Choose the figure that is congruent to the first figure in each row.

7. 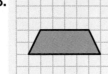   a.   b.   c.

8.   a.   b.   c.

9. 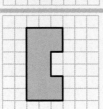   a. 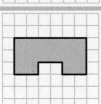   b. 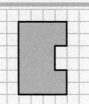   c.

10. 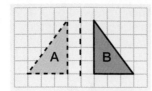   a. 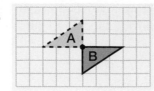   b. 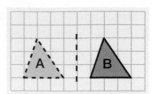   c.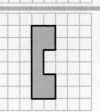

Tell how each figure was moved from position A to position B.

⭐ Hint ⭐ There are two steps.

11.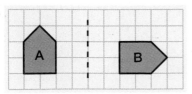

12.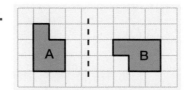

274

Problem Solving

13. **Using Algebra** The pattern at the right shows a pattern of transformations. Describe each step.

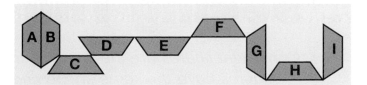

14. **Create Your Own** Study the pottery shown at the right. Identify two congruent figures. Have a classmate tell how one figure could be moved to the position of the other.

15. You buy four colors of sand to make a sand painting. The sand costs $0.79, $1.19, $0.99, and $2.25. The tax is $0.42. How much change should you receive if you pay with a $10 bill?

▲ Navajo pottery

Review and Remember

Using Algebra Evaluate. Follow the order of operations.

16. $3 + 2 \times 3$
17. $6 \times (2 + 8)$
18. $15 \times (1 + 2)$
19. $2 \times 6 \div 4$

20. $2 + 6 \times 3$
21. $8 \times 7 + 10$
22. $6 \times (5 - 1)$
23. $8 + 2 \div 2$

Critical Thinking Corner

Visual Thinking

Tessellations

Fine Arts Connection A **tessellation** is a pattern of congruent figures covering a plane. There are no gaps between the figures and no figures overlap. The mosaic tile pattern at the right is a tessellation.

Make a drawing to see if each figure will tessellate.

1. an equilateral triangle

2. a regular octagon

Create Your Own Use congruent shapes to create your own tessellation.

Mosaic tile pattern ➤

Seeing Things Alike

Congruent figures are the same shape and size, but sometimes figures have the same shape and are not the same size.

Learning About It

Flags have long been displayed many ways. You see them on flagpoles, on walls, in photographs, and in parades. The painting shown is of three **similar** flags.

Collection of Whitney Museum of Art, 50th Anniversary Gift of the Gilman Foundation, Inc., The Lauder Foundation, A. Alfred Taubman, an anonymous donor, and purchase 80.32. With permission of VAGA, New York.

Word Bank

similar

▲ **Fine Arts Connection** *Three Flags,* painted in 1958 by Jasper Johns, is an example of how geometry is often used in fine art. Johns, an American painter, used familiar objects such as American flags, numbers, and the alphabet for his paintings.

Similar figures have the same shape but may or may not be the same size. In the similar rectangles at the right, the length and the width of the blue figure are twice the length and width of the red figure.

Think and Discuss Look at the figures at the right. Would the figures be similar if the red figure were a square? Explain.

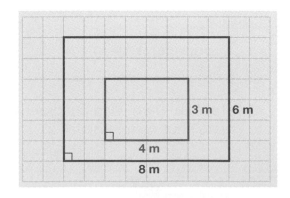

3 m   6 m

4 m

8 m

Try It Out

Tell if the shapes in each pair are similar. Write *yes* or *no*.

1.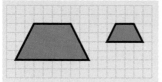

2.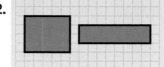

3.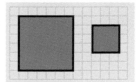

4. Discuss Explain why the figures at the right are similar. Include a comparison of the lengths of the sides in your explanation.

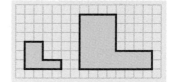

Practice

Tell if the shapes in each pair are similar. Write *yes* or *no*.

5.

6.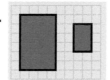

7.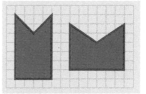

Problem Solving

8. Two flags are similar. One flag is three times as long as the other flag. The length of the smaller flag is 8 in. What is the length of the larger flag?

9. Material for flags is $1.69 a yard. What was the cost of three yards of blue material, two yards of red material, and two yards of white material?

Review and Remember

Find each answer.

10. 12×16　　　**11.** $76 + 23$　　　**12.** $112 \div 95$　　　**13.** $572 - 9$

Money $ense

Double Up

How could you switch three of the coins in the pentagon with two of the coins in the octagon and double the amount of money in the pentagon?

For Extra Practice, see Set G, page 290.

Problem Solving
Using Symmetry

You can sometimes use what you know about symmetry to solve problems.

Pam's Girl Scout troop is inviting parents to its gardening display. Pam is creating the design for the inside of the invitation. The invitations are to be folded and placed in envelopes, so Pam wants a design that will look the same on both halves of the folded paper. She has created the design shown at the right. Will it work?

 UNDERSTAND

What do you need to find?

You need to find out whether the design can be folded so one half of the design fits exactly on the other half. In other words, is the design **symmetrical**?

 PLAN

How can you solve the problem?

You can trace the design and cut it out. Then fold it to see if one half fits exactly on the other half.

 SOLVE

Trace the design. The design is symmetrical because it can be folded to form two congruent parts. A line that divides a figure into congruent parts is called a **line of symmetry**.

 LOOK BACK

Would Pam's design work if the paper were folded along the dashed lines, as shown? Explain.

line of symmetry

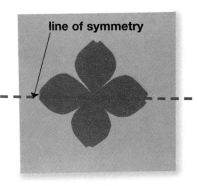

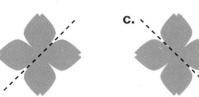

a.   b.   c.

Show What You Learned

Half of each design for a logo is missing. The dashed line is a line of symmetry. Solve Problems 1–6 by tracing the design and drawing the other half.

1

2

3

4

5

6

7 John wants to make a symmetrical design for a scout badge. Trace the figures that he could use. Show the lines of symmetry on each figure you choose.

a.

b.

c.

d.

8 Adam is about to stamp the design shown below on T-shirts for his club. How many lines of symmetry does it have?

9 **Explain** The logo below is used by a real estate agency. Is the design symmetrical? Tell why or why not.

10 **Analyze** The Gold Key Company uses capital letters as designs on the tags of their key chains. Which letters of the alphabet are symmetrical? Which letter has the most lines of symmetry?

 11 **Journal Idea** Draw your own symmetrical design. The design can represent a team, a club, a company, or just an interesting pattern. Write a short description of your design.

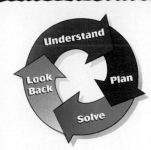

Problem Solving

★★★★★ **Preparing for Tests**

Practice What You Learned

Choose the correct letter for each answer.

1 Julie started with $78 in her savings account. During the next 3 months, she doubled her savings. Then she spent $23 on a magazine subscription. Which number sentence could be used to find the money she has left?

A. $(78 \times 2) - 23 = n$
B. $(78 \times 3) - 23 = n$
C. $(78 - 23) \times 2 = n$
D. $2 \times (78 - 23) = n$
E. Not Here

Subscription $23

Tip

When more than one step is needed to solve a problem, you must decide both what to do and in what order to do it.

2 Herman had an 18 in. by 24 in. sheet of paper. He folded it in thirds the long way so that each fold was 24 in. long. Then he folded the paper in half the short way. What was the length and width of each section of the folded paper?

A. 6 inches by 9 inches
B. 8 inches by 9 inches
C. 6 inches by 12 inches
D. 9 inches by 12 inches
E. Not Here

Tip

You can *Draw a Diagram* to help you solve this problem.

3 Fred has 10 pieces of scrap lumber. He paid $0.50 for the longest piece, which is 1.3 m. The shortest piece is 0.65 m. Which is reasonable for the total length of the scraps?

A. Between 0.65 m and 1.3 meters
B. Less than 6.5 meters
C. Between 6.5 m and 13 meters
D. Greater than 13 meters

Tip

Try using one of these strategies.
• *Draw a Diagram*
• *Solve a Simpler Problem*

4 One angle of a triangle measures 42°. The other two angles are congruent. What is the measure of the greatest angle in this triangle?

A. 42°
B. 48°
C. 96°
D. 138°
E. Not Here

5 Betty drove from her home to her uncle's house and back. This graph shows her trip.

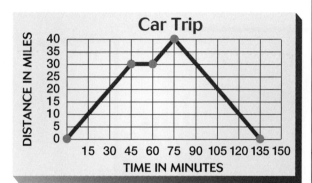

Car Trip

Which of these is **NOT** shown by the graph?

A. Betty traveled 40 miles to her uncle's house.
B. Betty stopped for 30 min on her way home.
C. It took Betty 75 min to reach her uncle's house.
D. Betty stopped to rest for 15 min after driving 45 min.

6 A shop sells picture frames in these sizes: 2 in. by 3 in., 4 in. by 6 in., 6 in. by 9 in., and 8 in. by 12 in. What would be the next largest frame if the pattern continues?

A. 8 inches by 14 inches
B. 9 inches by 12 inches
C. 9 inches by 15 inches
D. 10 inches by 15 inches

7 An airplane flight is scheduled to land at 3:30 P.M. Which information do you need to estimate how much time the flight should take?

A. The time the plane is scheduled to take off
B. How fast the plane will travel
C. The distance the plane will fly
D. The size and type of the plane

8 A fountain 6 meters high has sides with these lengths: 3.2 m, 5.6 m, 5.6 m, 2.08 m, and 2.08 m. Which is a reasonable measure of the distance around the fountain?

A. Less than 15 m
B. Between 15 m and 17 m
C. Between 17 m and 19 m
D. More than 20 m

9 How many right angles are there at the intersection of Pine and Third?

A. 0
B. 1
C. 2
D. 4
E. Not Here

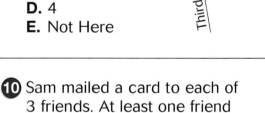

10 Sam mailed a card to each of 3 friends. At least one friend received the wrong card. Which of these **CANNOT** be true?

A. Only 1 person received the wrong card.
B. Exactly 2 people received the wrong cards.
C. All of them received the wrong cards.
D. Not enough information to decide.

Circling Around

Not all plane figures have line segments as sides.
Some have curves. One such curved plane figure is the circle.

Learning About It

You can see circular objects everywhere. A good example of such an object is a bicycle wheel. The tire is like a **circle**. The hub of the wheel is like the **center** of a circle.

Work with a partner to explore circles.

Word Bank

circle
center
diameter
radius (*pl.,* radii)
chord

center

Step 1 Construct a circle, using a compass.

Step 2 Cut out the circle. Fold it in half. The fold represents the **diameter**.

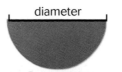
diameter

Step 3 Fold the circle in half again. Mark the point where the two diameters intersect. That point is the center of the circle. A fold line that passes from the center of the circle to the outer edge of the circle is a **radius**.

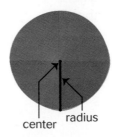
center radius

What You Need

For each group:
scissors
Triman compass
ruler

Step 4 Make and cut out several more circles of different diameters. Use a ruler to measure the radius and diameter of each circle you have made. Record the measures in a chart like the one shown.

Circle	Radius	Diameter
1		
2		

Think and Discuss Compare the lengths of the radius and diameter of each circle you made. Describe the relationship between the radius and the diameter of a circle.

Practice

1. Draw a circle. Label the center, a radius, and a diameter.

2. **Using Algebra** Write a number sentence that describes the relationship between the length of the radius (*r*) and the length of the diameter (*d*) of a circle.

3. A **chord** is any line segment with its endpoints on the circle. Describe the longest chord in a circle.

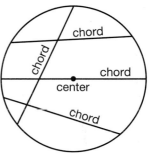

4. Find the length of the diameter of each circular object shown below.

It's Solid

Plane figures have many properties. In this lesson you will learn how plane figures form solid figures.

Learning About It

Look around you. Do you see an example of a solid, or space, figure? Cereal boxes, beach balls, books, computers, skateboards, and cars are all solid, or space, figures. Regardless of the shape, any object that takes up space is a solid figure.

One kind of space figure is a **prism**. A prism has two congruent **bases**. Prisms and pyramids are named by the shape of their bases.

Word Bank

prism
base
face
edge
vertex (*pl.*, vertices)
pyramid

Prisms

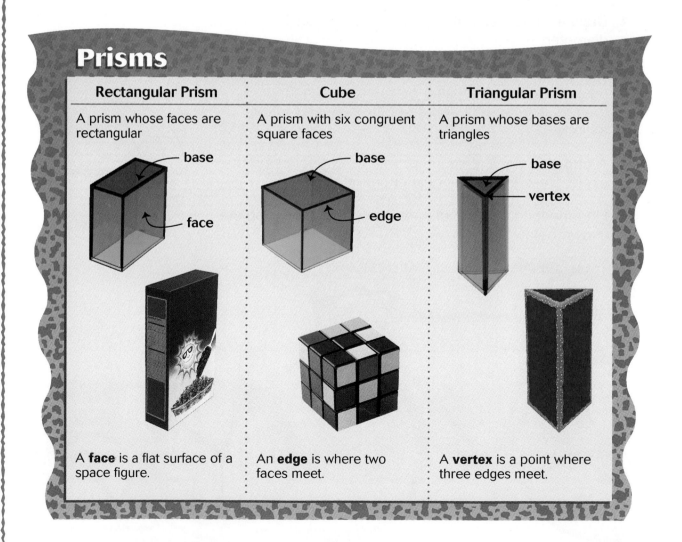

Rectangular Prism	Cube	Triangular Prism
A prism whose faces are rectangular	A prism with six congruent square faces	A prism whose bases are triangles
base, face	base, edge	base, vertex
A **face** is a flat surface of a space figure.	An **edge** is where two faces meet.	A **vertex** is a point where three edges meet.

Work with a group. Do the activity to help you understand more about prisms.

What You Need

For each group:
   dot paper
   scissors
   plastic tape

Step 1 Make a model of a prism.
- Copy the pattern on dot paper.
- Cut on the solid lines.
- Fold on the dotted lines.
- Tape the edges together.

What kind of prism have you formed?

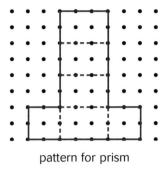

pattern for prism

Step 2 Count the number of faces, edges, and vertices of your prism. Record your findings in a chart like the one shown. Then complete the chart for a cube and a triangular prism. Compare the numbers of faces, edges, and vertices. Describe any patterns you see.

Space Figure	Number of Faces	Number of Edges	Number of Vertices
Rectangular prism			
Cube			
Triangular prism			

INTERNET ACTIVITY

www.sbgmath.com

Step 3 Some space figures have only one base. These figures are called **pyramids**. Extend your chart to include the pyramids shown. Describe any patterns you see.

Pyramids

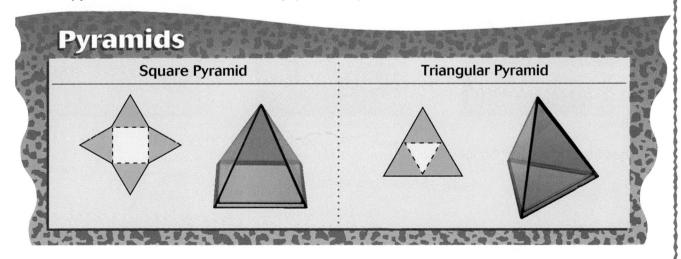

Square Pyramid   Triangular Pyramid

Not all space figures have all flat surfaces. Some space figures have curved surfaces.

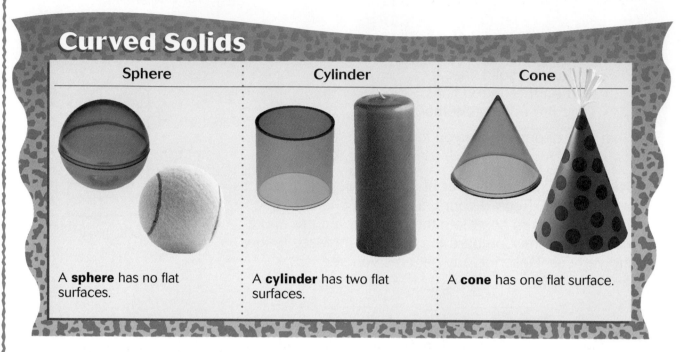

Curved Solids

Sphere	Cylinder	Cone
A **sphere** has no flat surfaces.	A **cylinder** has two flat surfaces.	A **cone** has one flat surface.

Think and Discuss Which of the figures above could be formed by this pattern? Why are there circles in this pattern?

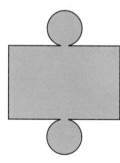

Try It Out

Name a space figure that you think of as you look at each photograph below.

1.

2.

3.

What kind of space figures can be made from each pattern?

4.

5.

6.

Practice

Name each solid figure shown below.

7.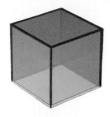

8.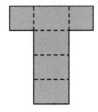

9.

10.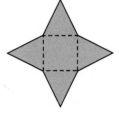

Name the solid figure that can be formed from each pattern.

11.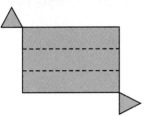

12.

13.

14. Describe What is the difference between a triangular pyramid and a triangular prism? Use real-life examples or drawings in your explanation.

15. Generalize Prisms are named by the shapes of their bases. Use what you know about a rectangular prism to describe a prism whose bases are pentagons.

Problem Solving

16. Tennis balls come in containers of three. A school orders 12 containers. Each week, two tennis balls are lost during gym class. After how many weeks will there be only two tennis balls left?

17. The first time the circus juggler appears, he juggles two balls; the second time, four balls; and the third time, six balls. If this pattern continues, how many balls will he juggle the fifth time?

 18. Square boxes 3 inches on each side are packed in a larger box 24 inches on each side. How many small boxes can be packed on the bottom layer of the box?

19. Analyze Carol wants to put a plate with a diameter of 10 inches into the box shown. Will the plate fit? Explain. What strategy did you use to solve the problem?

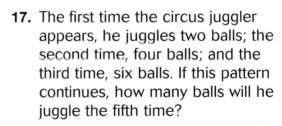

2 in.   6 in.   6 in.

Review and Remember

Choose a Method Use paper and pencil or a calculator to find each answer.

20. 63 ÷ 8

21. 113 × 6

22. 215 ÷ 5

23. 1,615 ÷ 3

24. 298 + 8

25. 6,804 + 199

26. 4,850 ÷ 7

27. 2,556 × 4

Checkpoint

Properties of Plane and Solid Figures

Vocabulary

Match each word with its definition.

1. A flat surface of a space figure.

2. A line segment with both endpoints on the circle.

3. Figures that have the same size and shape.

4. A face on which a figure rests.

Word Bank

base
chord
congruent figures
face
radius

Concepts and Skills

Are the figures congruent? Write *yes* or *no*. (pages 272–275)

5.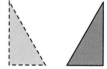

6.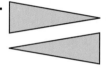

7.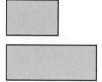

How was each figure moved? Write *slide*, *flip*, or *turn*. (pages 272–275)

8.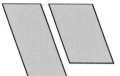

9.

10.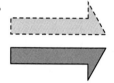

11.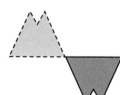

Are the figures similar? Write *yes* or *no*. (pages 276–277)

12.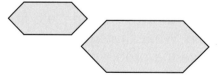

13.

14.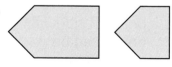

Use the circle for Exercises 15–17. (pages 280–281)

15. Name a radius.

16. Name a chord that is not a diameter.

17. What is the length of the diameter?

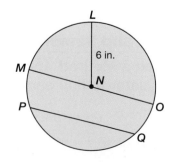

Trace each figure and then draw the lines of symmetry. (pages 278–279)

18.

19.

20.

Identify each solid figure. (pages 282–285)

21.

22.

23.

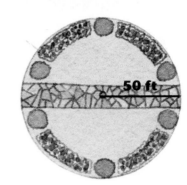
What do you think?
Tell how plane figures and solid figures are related.

Problem Solving

24. A solid figure has four faces. What is the figure?

25. A circular garden has a straight path that goes from the entrance to the exit and through the center. The distance from the entrance to the center is 50 feet. What is the distance from the center to the exit of the garden?

50 ft

Journal Idea

Think about a sphere and a cylinder. Tell where you might see similar solids when you are not in school.

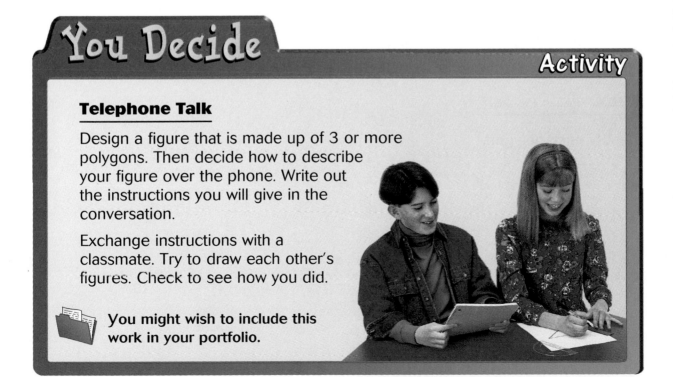

You Decide

Activity

Telephone Talk

Design a figure that is made up of 3 or more polygons. Then decide how to describe your figure over the phone. Write out the instructions you will give in the conversation.

Exchange instructions with a classmate. Try to draw each other's figures. Check to see how you did.

You might wish to include this work in your portfolio.

Extra Practice

Set A (pages 246–249)

Name or describe each figure.

1. A B

2. X Y

3. P Q

4.

5.

6.

Set B (pages 252–255)

Classify each angle as acute, obtuse, right, or straight.
Then use a protractor to measure each angle.

1.

2.

3.

4.

Use a protractor to draw each angle.

5. 75° angle

6. 130° angle

7. 35° angle

8. 90° angle

9. Can the sum of the measures of two acute angles be less than 90°? Give an example.

Set C (pages 256–257)

Identify each polygon.

1.

2.

3.

4.

5.

Decide if each polygon is regular. Write *yes* or *no*.

6.

7.

8.

9.

10.

11. Can a hexagon be classified as a pentagon? Explain.

Extra Practice

Set D (pages 260–263)

Classify each triangle by its sides and by its angles.

1.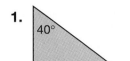

2.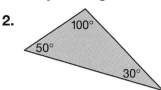

3.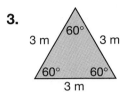

4.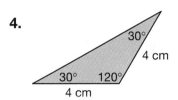

5.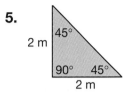

6.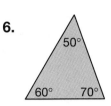

Set E (pages 266–267)

Identify each quadrilateral in the figure at the right.
Be as specific as possible.

1. A **2.** B **3.** C **4.** D **5.** E **6.** F

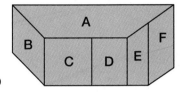

7. Classify the shape of a sheet of loose-leaf paper in two different ways.

Set F (pages 272–275)

Decide if each pair of figures is congruent. Write *yes* or
no. Explain how you know.

1.

2.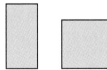

3.

4. Marcia likes to collect baseball cards. Are baseball cards usually congruent? Explain.

Tell how each figure was moved from position A to
position B. Write *slide*, *flip*, or *turn*.

5.

6.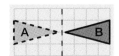

7.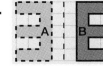

8.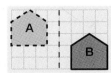

Extra Practice

Set G (pages 276–277)

Decide if each pair of figures is similar. Write *yes* or *no*.

1.
2.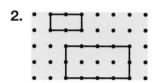
3.

4.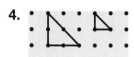
5.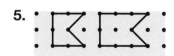
6.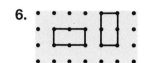

7. Two similar flags were flown on the flagpole outside of a town hall. The larger one was torn and needed to be replaced. To replace it, the mayor measured the smaller flag and found it to be 2 ft wide by 3.8 ft long. The larger flag was 6 ft wide. How long does the new flag need to be in order to be the same length as the old one?

Set H (pages 282–285)

Identify each space figure.

1.
2.
3.
4.

Tell which space figure each pattern will create.

5.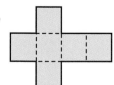
6.
7.
8.

9. Martha constructed a wooden block tower with a cylinder, a cone, a rectangular prism, and a cube.

- The rectangular prism was below the cube.
- The cube was above the cylinder and below the cone.
- The cube was not on the top.

Which block was used for the top of the tower?

 **Chapter Test**

Use the figure at the right for Exercises 1–2.

1. Name a line segment.

2. Name two pairs of intersecting lines—one that is perpendicular and one that is not.

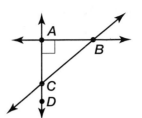

Classify each angle. Then estimate and measure each angle.

3.

4.

5.

Classify each figure. Be as specific as possible.

6.
3 in. 3 in.
2 in.

7.
4 in.
4 in.

8.

Draw each of the following.

9. Two congruent hexagons

10. A pentagon

11. A quadrilateral with four lines of symmetry

Decide if each pair of figures is similar. Write *yes* or *no*.

12.

13.

14.

Make a drawing to show each transformation.

15. a slide

16. a flip

17. a turn

Identify each space figure.

18.

19.

Solve.

20. A wheel has a radius of 10 inches. What is its diameter?

 Self-Check
For Question 11, did you draw all four lines of symmetry?

Performance Assessment

Show What You Know About Geometry

1 Describe this figure. Use as many geometry words as you can.

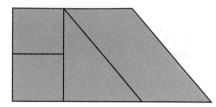

What You Need

ruler
protractor
grid paper

Self-Check Did you remember that the figure is made up of many smaller shapes, some of which may overlap?

2 Use the phrases below to make three different signs. Choose a different polygon for each sign that you make. Identify each polygon you use.

Keep Off the Grass
No Running
Have a Great Day!

Self-Check Did you remember to use a different polygon for each sign?

3 Use the drawing at the right. Measure ∠RPS, ∠SPY, ∠YPU, ∠UPV, ∠VPW, and ∠WPX.

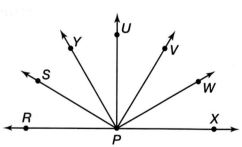

a. What can you conclude about the angle measurements? How would you classify these angles? Explain your reasoning.

b. Measure ∠RPU and ∠UPX. How would you classify these two angles?

Self-Check Did you position your protractor carefully when measuring the angles?

 For Your Portfolio

You might wish to include this work in your portfolio.

Extension

Exploring Equations

An **equation** is like a balance. The expression on the right side of the equal sign has the same value as the expression on the left side.

■ + 5 = 12

■ = 7, because 7 + 5 = 12

Each ▲ stands for the same number. What is the number?

(▲ + ▲) + 3 = 11
   8   + 3 = 11

Since (▲ + ▲) = 8, then ▲ = 4.

(4 + 4) + 3 = 11

Think of a number that when added to 3 equals 11.

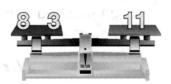

Each ● stands for the same number. What is the number?

(● + ● + ●) + 4 = 28
    24   + 4 = 28

Since (● + ● + ●) = 24, then ● = 8.

(8 + 8 + 8) + 4 = 28

Think of a number that when added to 4 equals 28.

In each exercise, the same shape stands for the same number. Find each number.

1. ✖ + 12 = 34

2. 4 × ☎ − 3 = 9

3. (★ + ★) + 6 = 16

4. (❤ + ❤ + ❤) + 5 = 26

Cumulative Review

★★★★★ **Preparing for Tests**

Choose the correct letter for each answer.

Operations	Geometry and Spatial Reasoning

1. What is the quotient of 105 divided by 30?

    A. 2 R13
    B. 3
    C. 3 R15
    D. 4

2. Gil sold stationery to help raise money for his school. He sold 2 boxes at $4.50 each, 3 boxes at $5.00 each, and 1 set of cards for $2.25. How much did he raise?

    A. $16.25
    B. $16.75
    C. $24.25
    D. $26.25
    E. Not Here

3. Rawhide dog bones are on sale at 4 for $5.00. How much would 20 bones cost?

    A. $20
    B. $25
    C. $40
    D. $100

4. What is the sum of 367 + 2,049 + 853 + 4,588?

    A. 7,857
    B. 7,587
    C. 6,857
    D. 6,557
    E. Not Here

5. A certain polygon has one more side than a pentagon. How many angles does that polygon have?

    A. 5   **C.** 7
    B. 6   **D.** 8

6. A polygon has three sides and three 60° angles. Which polygon is it?

    A. Pentagon
    B. Hexagon
    C. Equilateral triangle
    D. Isosceles triangle

7. Which transformation was used to move the figure from Position **A** to position **B**?

    A   B

    A. Reflection
    B. Translation
    C. Rotation
    D. Graph

8. Figure *ABCD* is a rhombus. Which line segment is parallel to line segment *AB*?

    A. $\overline{BC}$
    B. $\overline{DC}$
    C. $\overline{DA}$
    D. $\overline{BD}$

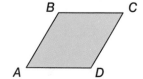

Measurement	Probability and Statistics

9. Andrew is putting a wallpaper border along the ceiling and the top of each wall in his room. The room is 12 ft wide and 18 ft long. How many feet of wallpaper border does he need?

A. 216 feet
B. 72 feet
C. 60 feet
D. 20 feet

10. Grant just built an addition with an area of 300 square feet onto his house. Last year he had a greenhouse with an area of 200 square feet built in the back yard. If the width of the new addition is 20 feet, what is the *length*? (Area = length × width)

A. 100 feet
B. 60 feet
C. 40 feet
D. 15 feet
E. Not Here

11. Lee's sister weighed 6 lb 13 oz when she was born. A year later she weighed 22 lb 10 oz. How much weight did she gain in one year? (1 lb = 16 oz)

A. 16 lb 13 oz
B. 16 lb 3 oz
C. 15 lb 13 oz
D. 15 lb 3 oz

12. A shoebox is 12 inches long by 5 inches wide by 4 inches deep. What is the *perimeter* of the bottom of the box?

A. 240 in.   **C.** 34 in.
B. 40 in.   **D.** 21 in.

13. Two sides of a cube are green, 1 is blue, 2 are red, and 1 is pink. If you toss the cube once, what is the probability that you will get green?

A. $\frac{1}{3}$

B. $\frac{1}{2}$

C. $\frac{2}{3}$

D. $\frac{3}{4}$

Use the graph below to answer Questions 14–16.

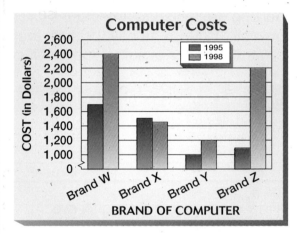

14. Which brand of computer had the lowest cost during both years?

A. Brand W   **C.** Brand Y
B. Brand X   **D.** Brand Z

15. Which brand doubled in cost between 1995 and 1998?

A. Brand W   **C.** Brand Y
B. Brand X   **D.** Brand Z

16. What is the difference between the cost of Brand Y in 1995 and the cost in 1998?

A. $50   **C.** $500
B. $200   **D.** $1000

Chapter 8

Multiplying and Dividing Decimals

Chapter Theme: USING MONEY

·············Real Facts·················

Let the fund-raising begin! Special Olympics and other sporting groups sometimes sell T-shirts and other souvenirs to raise money for their events. The list below shows the prices of some Special Olympics souvenirs.

Special Olympics Souvenir Price List	
Short-sleeve T-shirt	$10.00
Long-sleeve T-shirt	$15.00
Caps	$10.00
Pins	$2.00

- How much would 6 long-sleeve T-shirts cost?

- Suppose you and a friend equally shared the cost of 3 pins. How much money would each of you pay?

- If you buy a cap and 4 pins, what will be your change from $20?

- Your neighbor spends $27.00 on souvenirs but does not buy a cap. What did your neighbor buy?

·················Real People···················

Meet Shannon Oliver. She helps organize Special Olympics events, which are athletic competitions for children and adults with mental retardation. She volunteers her time to help young athletes, like those in the picture at the right, achieve their dreams. Shannon finds many ways to use mathematics in her work.

Using Algebra

Bagels for Dogs?

Using patterns can help you learn to multiply decimals.

Learning About It

Everyone deserves a special treat! Samantha and John are saving money to buy special treats for sheltered dogs. If one dog bagel costs $0.25, how much will 100 dog bagels cost?

Look for patterns in the table below. Notice what happens to the decimal point as a number is multiplied by 10, 100, and 1,000.

25¢

Multiply by	Example	Move the decimal point to the right.
10	$0.25 \times 10 = 2.5$	1 place
100	$0.25 \times 100 = 25.0$	2 places
1,000	$0.25 \times 1,000 = 250.0$	3 places

Since $0.25 \times 100 = 25$, 100 dog bagels cost $25.00.

More Examples

A. $2.38 \times 1 = 2.38$
$2.38 \times 10 = 23.8 = 23.8$
$2.38 \times 100 = 238. = 238$
$2.38 \times 1,000 = 2380. = 2,380$

B. $0.78 \times 1 = 0.78$
$0.78 \times 10 = 07.8 = 7.8$
$0.78 \times 100 = 078. = 78$
$0.78 \times 1,000 = 0780. = 780$

Think and Discuss Compare the process of multiplying by 10, 100, and 1,000 with the position of the decimal point in the product. Write a rule that relates the movement of the decimal point to the number of zeros in 10, 100, and 1,000.

Try It Out

Use patterns to find each product.

1. $5.13 \times 1 = $ ■
$5.13 \times 10 = $ ■
$5.13 \times 100 = $ ■
$5.13 \times 1,000 = $ ■

2. $0.0067 \times 10 = $ ■
$0.0067 \times 100 = $ ■
$0.0067 \times 1 = $ ■
$0.0067 \times 1,000 = $ ■

3. $14.38 \times 100 = $ ■
$14.38 \times 1 = $ ■
$14.38 \times 1,000 = $ ■
$14.38 \times 10 = $ ■

Practice

Using Mental Math Follow the rule to find each output.

Rule: Multiply by 100

	Input	Output
4.	0.83	▦
5.	4.7	▦
6.	39.5	▦

Rule: Multiply by 10

	Input	Output
7.	4.0	▦
8.	25.0	▦
9.	0.62	▦

Rule: Multiply by 1,000

	Input	Output
10.	2,600.0	▦
11.	15.0	▦
12.	426.5	▦

Find each _n_.

13. $6.59 \times n = 65.9$

14. $0.5 \times 1{,}000 = n$

15. $\$3.45 \times n = \$345.00$

16. $0.447 \times 10 = n$

17. $100 \times 0.0562 = n$

18. $\$16 \times 100 = n$

19. $1 \times 99.8 = n$

20. $n \times 0.216 = 21.6$

21. $0.00379 \times n = 3.79$

22. $75.8 \times 100 = n$

23. $n \times 0.17 = 17$

24. $9.8 \times n = 9{,}800$

25. $0.371 \times 10 = n$

26. $0.4589 \times 1 = n$

27. $0.008 \times 1{,}000 = n$

Problem Solving

28. Fine Arts Connection
In the filming of the movie _101 Dalmations_, 200 puppies were used. If it cost $0.75 for two rawhide chews, how much would it cost to give one rawhide chew to each of the puppies?

29. What If? Suppose you walked your dog 2.5 miles a day. How far would you walk in a week? How far would you walk in a 30-day month?

30. A puppy toy costs $1.25. At this price, how much will 100 puppy toys cost?

▲ **Kid Connection** Kennel Kids is an organization of kids who help out at local animal shelters. They walk, bathe, and feed cats and dogs. They also help bring food and supplies to pet owners who are homebound.

Review and Remember

Find each answer.

31. $0.682 + 3.37$

32. $6 - 1.19$

33. 325×38

34. $51{,}650 \div 96$

35. $2.197 + 0.65$

36. $10 - 2.85$

37. $36{,}899 \div 47$

38. $65 \times 4{,}879$

For Extra Practice, see Set A, page 326.

Seeds Plus

Multiplying decimals is like multiplying whole numbers, except that you have to keep track of the decimal point.

Learning About It

Dean, Kerri, Ashvi, and Nathan are planning a community garden that will be the size of one city block. They plan to plant five types of seeds. If each package of seeds covers 0.12 of a city block, how much of the block will five packages of seeds cover?

Multiply **5 × 0.12** to find out.

THERE'S ALWAYS A WAY!

- **One way** to find out is to draw a diagram.

- tomatoes
- corn
- carrots
- lettuce
- sunflowers

1 square = 0.01 of a city block.

12 squares are shaded for each seed package.

So, 60 out of 100, or 0.60, squares are shaded in all.

- **Another way** is to use paper and pencil.

  - Multiply as you do with whole numbers.
  - Decide where to place the decimal point in the product by finding the total number of decimal places in the factors.

$$
\begin{array}{r}
0.12 \leftarrow 2 \text{ decimal places} \\
\times \quad 5 \leftarrow 0 \text{ decimal places} \\
\hline
0.60 \leftarrow 2 \text{ decimal places}
\end{array}
$$

If five packages of seeds are planted, 0.60 of the city block will be covered.

More Examples

A.
$$
\begin{array}{r}
0.274 \leftarrow 3 \text{ decimal places} \\
\times \quad 13 \leftarrow 0 \text{ decimal places} \\
\hline
3.562 \leftarrow 3 \text{ decimal places}
\end{array}
$$

B.
$$
\begin{array}{r}
\$24.50 \\
\times \quad 7 \\
\hline
\$171.50
\end{array}
$$

C.
$$
\begin{array}{r}
0.95 \\
\times \quad 22 \\
\hline
20.90
\end{array}
$$

Think and Discuss How does the product of 5 × 12 compare with the product of 5 × 0.12?

Try It Out

Find each product.

1. 36.5
   × 8

2. $0.79
   × 2

3. 1.732
   × 24

4. 0.019
   × 12

Practice

Choose a Method Draw a diagram or use paper and pencil to multiply. Tell why you chose the method you did.

5. 0.12
   × 4

6. 1.365
   × 5

7. 0.37
   × 8

8. 7.9
   × 15

9. 2.907
   × 4

10. 0.004
    × 9

11. 3.025
    × 15

12. 6.324
    × 22

13. 0.014 × 5

14. 7.29 × 31

15. 0.824 × 3

16. 7.369 × 3

17. 6 × 6.8

18. 0.067 × 7

19. 36.25 × 9

20. 183 × 2.7

21. 12.6 × 35

22. 265.4 × 13

23. 6.325 × 7

24. 0.853 × 5

Problem Solving

25. Seed packages cost $1.29 each. How much do five packages cost? 50 packages?

26. Mrs. Smith spent $2.95, $3.50, $0.98, and $1.99 on a variety of vegetables. How much change did she receive from her $10 bill?

27. **Journal Idea** Describe a situation where it would be helpful to estimate when multiplying with decimals.

▲ **Social Studies Connection** Community gardens are beginning to take the place of run-down city lots. Volunteers get city-owned lots cleared and fenced. Then they plant beautiful gardens.

Review and Remember

Using Algebra Find each *n*. Name the property used.

28. $42 \times n = 13 \times 42$

29. $522 \times 1 = n$

30. $9 \times (6 \times n) = (9 \times 6) \times 3$

31. $(12 \times 8) \times 0 = n$

32. $0 \times 92 = n$

33. $(5 \times 4) \times 6 = 5 \times (n \times 6)$

Poster Power

Many times, finding an estimated product can give you the answer you need.

Learning About It

Ms. Sullivan's class is selling wildlife posters to help raise money for the protection of endangered species. All the money raised goes directly to saving the animals.

José has sold 12 large posters and 23 small posters. He wants to find out about how much money he has raised so far. Finding an estimate is the quickest way.

Estimate by rounding each number to the greatest place.

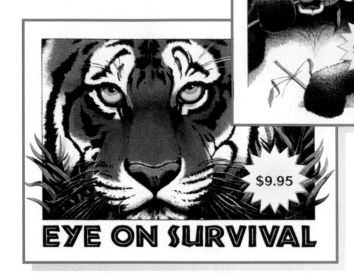

▲ **Science Connection** In 1973 the United States government passed the Endangered Species Act (ESA). Tigers and pandas are just two of the world's species that are protected.

$\underline{1}2 \times \$\underline{9}.95$ [rounds to] $10 \times \$10 = \$100$ large poster sales

$\underline{2}3 \times \$\underline{5}.75$ [rounds to] $20 \times \$6 = \$120$ small poster sales

So far, José has raised about $220 for endangered animals.

More Examples

A. Round to estimate.

938×0.17
↓   ↓
$900 \times 0.2 = 180.0$

Remember to place your decimal point correctly.

B. Round to estimate.

8.79×5
↓   ↓
$9 \ \times 5 = 45$

Remember that you do not have to round single-digit factors.

Think and Discuss Will the actual product for Example B be less than or greater than the estimated product? Explain your answer.

Try It Out

Round to the greatest place to estimate each product.

1. 5.9×8
2. 6×1.75
3. 3.2×20
4. 9×1.555

5. 3×7.6
6. 4.41×8
7. 60×8.6
8. 2.43×7

Practice

Round to the greatest place to estimate each product.

9. 8×3.28
10. 17.6×42
11. 45×3.9
12. 6×5.21

13. 4.291×8
14. 10.9×9
15. 6×43.2
16. 2.1×32

17. 75×1.87
18. 50.36×8
19. 10.1×99
20. 2.121×42

 Estimate each product first. Then decide if it will be greater than or less than the estimate. Use a calculator to check.

21. 12×0.6
22. 3.2×5
23. 20×3.9
24. 9.9×47
25. 2.5×4

26. 12×4.21
27. 19.7×36
28. 86×4.9
29. 2.36×53
30. 94×0.12

Problem Solving

31. Harriet wants animal posters on one wall of her room. Each poster is 16 in. high. How many can fit one above the other from the floor to the 8-ft ceiling?

32. **Explain** Mara needs 10.5 yards of ribbon to make 8 ties. Ribbon costs $1.00 a yard. If Mara has $10, does she have enough to buy her ribbon?

33. **Using Estimation** Caleb is using yarn to make the lion's mane on his art project. He needs 23 loops of yarn. Each loop takes 7.5 in. of yarn.

    a. About how much yarn will Caleb need?

    b. If he has 5 yards of yarn, about how much will be left over?

Review and Remember

Tell whether each number is divisible by 2, 3, 4, 5, 6, 9, or 10.

34. 94
35. 132
36. 515
37. 1,096
38. 1,725

39. 10,251
40. 41,292
41. 18,554
42. 40,001
43. 15,804

For Extra Practice, see Set C, page 327.

Developing Skills for
Problem Solving

*First read for understanding and then focus
on solving multistep problems.*

Betsy Ross House ▶

READ FOR UNDERSTANDING

Sandi and her two grandmothers are visiting
Philadelphia with two of Sandi's friends. They want to
visit the Betsy Ross House, Independence Hall, the
Liberty Bell, and other historic sites in the city. Sandi is
11 years old, and her friends are 10 and 14 years old.

1 How much do children's tickets cost?

2 How old are Sandi's two friends?

Tour of
Historic Philadelphia

Adults	$8.50
Children (under 12)	$6.25

THINK AND DISCUSS

MATH FOCUS

Multistep Problems To solve some
problems, you may need more than one
step. Each step gives you some of the
information you need.

Liberty Bell ▶

**Reread the paragraph at the top of the page.
Think about what you need to know to find out
how much it will cost the group to take the historic tour.**

3 How many adult tickets will the grandparents buy?
how many children's tickets?

4 How much will the adult tickets cost? the
children's tickets?

5 How does knowing the cost of the adult tickets
and the cost of the children's tickets help you find
how much it will cost for the whole group to take
the historic tour?

6 How much will it cost Sandi, her friends, and her
grandparents to take a tour of the city? List the
steps needed to find the answer.

▲ Independence Hall

Show What You Learned

Use the information below to answer each question. Give a reason for your choice.

Jim had $28.90. He bought 2 patches, 3 magnets, 1 cap, 2 flags, and 2 quill pens.

1 What information is not needed to find the amount Jim had left after his purchases?

a. The amount of money Jim had

b. The cost of a cap

c. The difference between the cost of a cap and the cost of a pen

2 How can you find the amount Jim had left after his purchases?

a. Add the cost of the items Jim bought and divide by 2.

b. Add the cost of the items Jim bought and subtract that total from the amount of money he started with.

c. Add the cost of the items Jim bought and add that total to the amount of money he started with.

3 Which number sentence tells you how much money Jim spent on flags and quill pens?

a. $9.75 + $1.50 = $11.25

b. (2 × $3.25) + (2 × $1.50) = $9.50

c. (2 × $3.25) − (2 × $1.50) + $1.50 = $5.00

4 Which number sentence tells you how much Jim spent for patches and magnets?

a. (2 × $3.25) + (3 × $2.00) = $12.50

b. (3 × $2.00) + (3 × $2.50) = $13.50

c. (2 × $2.50) + (3 × $2.00) = $11.00

5 How much did Jim have left after making his purchases? List the steps needed to find the answer.

6 **Create Your Own** Use the information in the picture above to write a problem that requires more than one step to solve. Then have a classmate solve the problem.

Multiplying in Color

You can use decimal grids to understand multiplying decimals.

Learning About It

You can use a 10 by 10 decimal grid to show the product of two decimals.

Work with a partner. Use grid paper to model 0.3 of 0.5.

$$0.3 \times 0.5 = n$$

Step 1 Shade 0.5 of a 10 by 10 grid with a colored pencil, as shown. Remember that each column represents 1 tenth.

Step 2 To find 0.3 of 0.5, mark 0.3 of the shaded area in a second color, as shown. The part of the entire square grid marked in both colors is the product of 0.3×0.5. Write the product. Remember that each small square represents 1 hundredth.

Step 3 Make a new grid to find the product 0.9×0.7. Then write the product.

Think and Discuss Suppose you multiply tenths by tenths. Is the product always hundredths? Use a grid to explain your answer.

What You Need

For each pair:
  grid paper
  crayons or colored
    pencils

Step 1

Step 2

Practice

Match each number sentence with the correct model.

1. $0.4 \times 0.7 = 0.28$ **2.** $0.4 \times 0.2 = 0.08$ **3.** $0.8 \times 0.5 = 0.40$

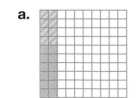   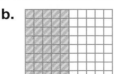   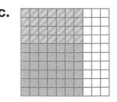

Match each number sentence with the correct model.

4. $0.2 \times 0.9 = 0.18$ **5.** $0.6 \times 0.7 = 0.42$ **6.** $0.1 \times 0.5 = 0.05$

a. 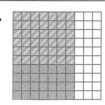   b. 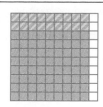   c.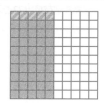

Draw a model to show each multiplication sentence. Then write the product.

7. 0.7×0.3 **8.** 0.3×0.4 **9.** 0.9×0.8 **10.** 0.1×0.7

11. Explain Tell how the model below represents this number sentence. $0.5 \times 0.6 = 0.30$

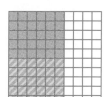

12. Analyze Write the number sentence that is represented by the grid below.

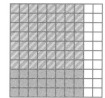

Critical Thinking Corner

Logical Thinking

What's Wrong?

Louise was given the following problem for homework.

In △ ABC, ∠A measures 50° and ∠B measures 60°. Find the number of degrees in ∠C.

Here is Louise's work:

$$\begin{array}{r} 50 \\ + 60 \\ \hline 110 \end{array} \qquad \begin{array}{r} 180 \\ - 110 \\ \hline 170 \end{array}$$

Louise's answer: The measure of ∠C is 170°.

What's wrong?

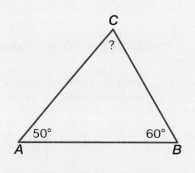

Pick a Snack

You can use a grid and what you know about multiplying whole numbers to multiply two decimals.

Learning About It

Ms. Pérez is buying snacks for an after-school group. Baked tortilla chips are a low-fat snack. There are 1.5 grams of fat in a 1-ounce serving. How many grams of fat are in a 2.3-ounce serving?

$$1.5 \times 2.3 = n$$
Estimate first: $2 \times 2 = 4$

Then find the exact answer.

THERE'S ALWAYS A WAY!

● **One way** to find out is to use a grid.

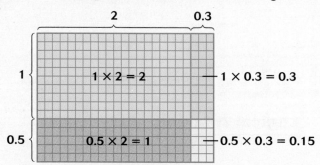

A 10 by 10 square is equal to 1.

Find the sum of the partial products.

$$2 + 0.3 + 1 + 0.15 = 3.45$$

● **Another way** is to use paper and pencil.

Step 1 Multiply as you would whole numbers.	Step 2 Use the estimate above to help you place the decimal point in the product.	
$\begin{array}{r} 2.3 \\ \times\ 1.5 \\ \hline 115 \\ +\ 230 \\ \hline 345 \end{array}$	$\begin{array}{r} 2.3 \leftarrow \text{1 decimal place} \\ \times\ 1.5 \leftarrow \text{1 decimal place} \\ \hline 115 \\ +\ 230 \\ \hline 3.45 \leftarrow \text{2 decimal places} \end{array}$	The number of decimal places in the product equals the total number of decimal places in the factors.

There are 3.45 grams of fat in a 2.3 ounce serving of tortilla chips. Since the estimate is 4, the answer is reasonable.

More Examples

A. $0.9 \times 0.76 = n$

Estimate: $0.9 \times 0.8 = 0.72$

$$
\begin{array}{r}
0.76 \leftarrow \text{2 decimal places} \\
\times \quad 0.9 \leftarrow \text{1 decimal place} \\
\hline
0.684 \leftarrow \text{3 decimal places}
\end{array}
$$

B. $3.4 \times 2.67 = n$

Estimate: $3 \times 3 = 9$

$$
\begin{array}{r}
2.67 \leftarrow \text{2 decimal places} \\
\times \quad 3.4 \leftarrow \text{1 decimal place} \\
\hline
106\,8 \\
+\,801\,0 \\
\hline
9.078 \leftarrow \text{3 decimal places}
\end{array}
$$

Think and Discuss How many decimal places would be in the product 3.24×3.38? Tell how you know.

Try It Out

Estimate first. Then find the exact product.

1.	5.8 $\times$ 2.9	2.	3.14 $\times$ 6.2	3.	0.62 $\times$ 1.7
4.	0.8 $\times$ 0.6	5.	7.36 $\times$ 0.4	6.	25.4 $\times$ 0.78
7.	0.73 $\times$ 2.1	8.	0.65 $\times$ 0.9	9.	4.7 $\times$ 6.3

10. 6×0.48　　**11.** 7.2×6.8

12. 2.5×0.6　　**13.** 23.5×0.4

Practice

Multiply. Estimate to check your answer for reasonableness.

14.	1.7 $\times$ 0.5	15.	9.34 $\times$ 1.6	16.	0.91 $\times$ 0.8	17.	15.4 $\times$ 0.23	18.	0.28 $\times$ 3.7
19.	18.6 $\times$ 4.3	20.	1.25 $\times$ 0.7	21.	6.43 $\times$ 8.1	22.	0.76 $\times$ 0.4	23.	12.39 $\times$ 3.5

24. 21.4×0.53　　**25.** 4.3×0.6　　**26.** 1.8×9.2　　**27.** 8.5×0.7

28. 0.54×0.9　　**29.** 38×0.27　　**30.** 0.32×4.6　　**31.** 54.1×0.5

Fats, oils, and sweets

Milk, yogurt, and cheese

Meat, poultry, fish, dry beans, eggs, and nuts

Vegetables

Fruits

Breads, cereals, rice, and pasta

▲ **Health and Fitness Connection**
The food pyramid shows the different kinds of foods you should eat each day.

INTERNET ACTIVITY
www.sbgmath.com

Using Algebra Compare. Write >, <, or = for each ●.

32. 5.2×3.6 ● 0.36×52

33. 0.9×2.6 ● 2.7×0.8

34. 1.6×5.5 ● 5.4×1.5

35. 0.72×0.42 ● 0.41×0.73

36. 33.3×1.5 ● 1.2×35.5

37. 22×0.65 ● 0.75×15

38. 47.6×25 ● 0.25×4.76

39. 0.45×100 ● 5.4×10

40. 62.5×6.4 ● 64×6.25

41. 2.7×30 ● 2.9×3.01

Using Estimation Decide if each product is greater than 10. If it is, find the product.

42. 4.7×3.8

43. 0.5×10.8

44. 12.1×1.6

45. 8.3×0.4

46. 6.5×0.6

47. 15.5×5

48. 0.9×9.9

49. 1.2×9

50. 3.7×3

51. 0.8×2.5

52. 6×3.2

53. 11.3×0.4

54. Describe How can you decide which products would be greater than 10 without multiplying?

55. Explain Will the product of 3.1×0.2 be greater than or less than 3.1? Explain.

Problem Solving

56. A bean burrito contains 3.5 ounces of refried beans. One ounce of refried beans has 0.56 gram of fat. How many grams of fat are in the beans of the burrito?

57. Using Estimation If there are 32.5 grams of fat in a fast-food cheeseburger, about how many grams of fat will there be in a fast-food double cheeseburger?

58. A bag of tortilla chips costs $2.19, and a jar of medium-hot salsa costs $1.59. How much will 3 bags of chips and 2 jars of salsa cost?

Use the information on the soup label to solve Problems 59–62.

59. Analyze How many grams of fat are there in one can of chicken noodle soup?

60. Using Mental Math How many calories are there in one can of chicken noodle soup?

61. What If? Suppose you ate three cans of chicken noodle soup in 1 week. How many calories would you consume?

62. You Decide For lunch, you can choose chicken noodle soup (90 calories), crackers (75 calories), peanut butter (150 calories), fruit (100 calories), or milk (72 calories). You want to eat between 300 and 400 calories. What should you have for lunch? Explain your reasoning.

Review and Remember

Find each answer.

63.	64.	65.	66.	67.
2.76	1,284	786	3,841	$49.88
2.85	3,146	3,642	− 1,218	+ 51.49
3.97	528	9,110		
+ 6.58	+ 8,009	+ 572		

68. 8)$832

69. 48)511

70. 27)$171.99

71. 15)$2,091.45

Time for Technology

Using a Calculator

Multiple Multiplying

When you want to do a multistep problem, the memory key on a calculator can help.

Suppose you buy three bags of pretzels that cost $1.89 each and two containers of dip that cost $2.29 each. What is the total cost?

Press: 3 × 1 . 8 9 = M+   This stores the product in the memory.

Press: 2 × 2 . 2 9 = M+   This adds the second product to the number stored in the memory.

Press: MR   Display: 10.25   Remember to place the dollar sign and decimal point in your answer.

The total cost for the pretzels and dip is $10.25.

Use your calculator to solve each problem.

1. What is the cost of two pounds of tomatoes at $1.29 a pound and two heads of lettuce at $1.59 a head?

2. At the bakery, cookies cost $0.59 each and brownies cost $0.99. What will be the total cost if you buy a half dozen of each?

For Extra Practice, see Set D, page 327.

Energize

When multiplying decimals, you may need to put zeros in the product.

Learning About It

Bailey uses her computer to do research on the Internet. Her computer uses 0.16 kilowatt of electricity per hour. You pay for electricity by the kilowatt hour (kWh). If the cost is $0.08 per kilowatt hour, how much does the electricity cost Bailey to use her computer for an hour?

$$\$0.08 \times 0.16 = n$$

Estimate first: $0.1 \times 0.2 = 0.02$

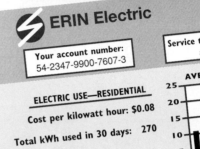

⚡ **ERIN Electric**

Your account number:
54-2347-9900-7607-3

Service to: John McDonald
at: 44 Pine Road

ELECTRIC USE—RESIDENTIAL

Cost per kilowatt hour: $0.08

Total kWh used in 30 days: 270

AVERAGE DAILY USE

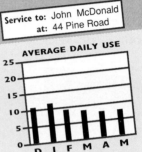

THERE'S ALWAYS A WAY!

● **One way** is to use paper and pencil.

Step 1 Multiply as you would whole numbers.	**Step 2** Place the decimal point in the product.
$$\begin{array}{r} 0.16 \\ \times\ 0.08 \\ \hline 128 \end{array}$$	$$\begin{array}{r} 0.16 \leftarrow \text{2 decimal places} \\ \times\ 0.08 \leftarrow \text{2 decimal places} \\ \hline \$0.0128 \leftarrow \text{4 decimal places} \end{array}$$

Write a zero in the product to place the decimal point correctly.

● **Another way** is to use a calculator.

Press: `.` `0` `8` `×` `.` `1` `6` `=`

Remember to press the decimal-point key when you enter a decimal number.

Display: `0.0128`

Round $0.0128 to the nearest hundredth (cent), and write the answer with a dollar sign.

Since $0.0128 rounds to $0.01, the electricity to run Bailey's computer for 1 hour costs about 1 cent.

Think and Discuss How does your estimate help you know that you need to place a zero in front of the digits 128?

Try It Out

Multiply.

1. 0.07×0.8 **2.** 1.3×0.06 **3.** 0.04×0.2 **4.** 0.4×0.15

5. 0.02×0.3 **6.** 6.1×0.09 **7.** 0.4×0.14 **8.** 7.2×0.09

9. Explain When you multiply 0.6×0.15 on the calculator, the display shows 0.09. Why?

Practice

Choose a Method Use mental math, paper and pencil, or a calculator for Exercises 10–17. Tell which method you chose and why.

10. 1.4×0.06 **11.** 0.05×0.9 **12.** 0.17×0.4 **13.** 0.013×7

14. 0.12×0.8 **15.** 5×0.008 **16.** 0.07×1.3 **17.** 3.2×0.03

Using Algebra Find each n.

18. $0.02 \times n = 0.006$ **19.** $n \times 0.1 = 0.07$ **20.** $2.2 \times 0.03 = n$

21. $0.3 \times n = 0.009$ **22.** $n \times 0.4 = 0.16$ **23.** $0.07 \times 0.2 = n$

24. $0.34 \times n = 3.4$ **25.** $0.06 \times 0.5 = n$ **26.** $4.8 \times 0.06 = n$

Problem Solving

27. Using Mental Math Computer Club members use the Internet after school. A computer uses 0.15 kilowatts of electricity per hour. If a member spends 10 hours on the Internet, how many kilowatt hours does she use?

28. Electricity costs $0.10 for 1 kWh, $0.15 for 2 kWh, and $0.20 for 3 kWh. What will 4 kWh cost? What strategy can you use to find out?

 29. To find the kilowatts used by an appliance, divide the number of watts by 1,000. Find the cost of using a 1,600-watt hair dryer per hour at a rate of $0.07 per kilowatt hour.

INTERNET ACTIVITY
www.sbgmath.com

Review and Remember

Find each answer.

30. $12.89 - 2.35$ **31.** 357×184 **32.** $\$4.95 + \$8.75$ **33.** $2,546 \div 8$

For Extra Practice, see Set E, page 328.

Problem Solving
Choose a Strategy

Read each problem carefully. Then decide which strategy you can use to solve it.

*E*ric bought two games, chess and checkers. He also bought some puzzles. He paid $46.48, including $2.00 tax. If the games together cost $12.48, how much did the puzzles cost?

Adventure $19.99	Mystery $12.99	Strategy $14.99
Checkers $4.99	Puzzle $8.00	Chess $7.49

UNDERSTAND

What do you need to find?

You need to find how much the puzzles cost.

PLAN

How can you solve the problem?

Sometimes you can **choose a strategy** to solve a problem.

SOLVE

Work Backwards		Write an Equation
Money paid	$46.48	Puzzle cost = total paid − (tax + cost of games)
Tax	− 2.00	$p = \$46.48 - (\$2 + \$12.48)$
	$44.48	$p = \$46.48 - \$14.48$
Cost of games	−12.48	$p = \$32$
Cost of puzzles	$32.00	

The puzzles cost $32.

LOOK BACK

How many puzzles did Eric buy?

Using Strategies

Try these or other strategies to solve each problem. Tell which strategy you used.

Problem Solving Strategies

- Draw a Diagram
- Make a Table
- Write an Equation
- Find a Pattern
- Guess and Check
- Work Backwards

1 Andrew gave Brent 8 marbles, and he gave Nick twice as many. Now Andrew has 48 marbles. How many marbles did he have before he gave away the marbles?

2 Ryan, Gary, Lauren, and Kayla want to play checkers with each other. If each person plays a game with every other person, how many games will they play?

3 Mr. Robinson made a window display of the games his store sells. The games were stacked so that the top row had one game, the next row had 3, the next row had 5, and so on. If there are 9 rows, how many games are in the bottom row?

4 **Analyze** The toy store is offering a special sale on puzzles. For every three puzzles you buy, you get one puzzle free. How much would six puzzles cost?

5 Stan works at the toy store 20 hours a week. He gets paid $5 per hour. When he works more than 20 hours, he earns $3 more for each hour of overtime. How much will he earn if he works 25 hours in one week?

6 Use the prices on page 312. Gregory bought a few adventure games and a few checkers games to give as gifts. Altogether the five games cost $69.95. How many of each game did he buy?

7 There are 35 mystery games and word games on a shelf. There are 15 more word games than mystery games. How many of each game are on the shelf?

8 Jill spent $37.95 at the game store. How much change did she receive from two $20 bills?

9 **Using Algebra** Bob and Jim played chess on Tuesday, Friday, Monday, and Thursday. If this pattern continues, when will they play next?

✔ Checkpoint

Multiplying Decimals

Using Algebra **Use patterns to find the products.** (pages 296–297)

1. $0.5 \times 10 =$ ■
$0.5 \times 100 =$ ■
$0.5 \times 1,000 =$ ■

2. $0.26 \times 100 =$ ■
$0.26 \times 1,000 =$ ■
$0.26 \times 10 =$ ■

3. $14.3 \times 1,000 =$ ■
$14.3 \times 10 =$ ■
$14.3 \times 100 =$ ■

Multiply. (pages 298–299)

4. 14.7×7

5. $\$4.05 \times 6$

6. 0.57×18

7. $\$49.90 \times 30$

8. 7.89×24

9. 2×13.5

10. 8.5×72

11. 0.69×3

12. 1.05×42

Estimate each product. (pages 300–301)

13. 6.8×5

14. 17.56×4

15. 10×4.4

16. 214×13.9

17. 21×6.5

18. $\$1.29 \times 32$

19. 69×21.9

20. 13×1.075

Estimate first. Then multiply. (pages 306–309)

21. $\begin{array}{r} 6.75 \\ \times\ 0.03 \\ \hline \end{array}$

22. $\begin{array}{r} \$42.60 \\ \times\ \ \ \ \ \ 5 \\ \hline \end{array}$

23. $\begin{array}{r} 0.65 \\ \times\ \ 2.6 \\ \hline \end{array}$

24. $\begin{array}{r} \$11.33 \\ \times\ \ \ \ \ 10 \\ \hline \end{array}$

25. $\begin{array}{r} 1.08 \\ \times\ 0.19 \\ \hline \end{array}$

26. $\begin{array}{r} \$21.90 \\ \times\ \ \ \ \ \ 3 \\ \hline \end{array}$

27. $\begin{array}{r} 12.5 \\ \times\ 0.38 \\ \hline \end{array}$

28. $\begin{array}{r} \$0.96 \\ \times\ \ 0.25 \\ \hline \end{array}$

29. $\begin{array}{r} \$15.50 \\ \times\ \ \ \ 3.5 \\ \hline \end{array}$

30. $\begin{array}{r} \$0.95 \\ \times\ \ \ \ 15 \\ \hline \end{array}$

Find each product. (pages 310–311)

31. $\begin{array}{r} 0.04 \\ \times\ \ 0.3 \\ \hline \end{array}$

32. $\begin{array}{r} \$0.03 \\ \times\ \ \ 0.3 \\ \hline \end{array}$

33. $\begin{array}{r} 0.14 \\ \times\ \ 0.6 \\ \hline \end{array}$

34. $\begin{array}{r} 0.009 \\ \times\ \ \ 0.4 \\ \hline \end{array}$

35. $\begin{array}{r} 0.097 \\ \times\ 0.124 \\ \hline \end{array}$

36. $\begin{array}{r} 0.06 \\ \times\ \ \ \ 5 \\ \hline \end{array}$

37. $\begin{array}{r} 0.08 \\ \times\ 0.04 \\ \hline \end{array}$

38. $\begin{array}{r} 0.007 \\ \times\ \ \ \ 0.3 \\ \hline \end{array}$

39. $\begin{array}{r} 0.005 \\ \times\ \ \ 0.2 \\ \hline \end{array}$

40. $\begin{array}{r} 0.648 \\ \times\ 0.25 \\ \hline \end{array}$

Problem Solving

41. Mary Ann ordered 3 pens and a box of writing paper from a catalog. Each pen cost $2.98. The writing paper cost $4.95. How much did she spend?

42. Using Estimation You ordered four paperback books that cost $6.95 each. Did you spend more or less than $25.00? About how much did you spend? Is your estimate reasonable?

Choose a Method Use mental math, paper and pencil, or a calculator to solve. Tell which method you chose and why.

43. Mr. Charles ordered a special deli lunch for friends. If he bought sliced turkey for $3.86, 5 rolls at $0.49 each, and 10 oranges at $0.25 each, how much did he spend on lunch?

44. Donald, Liz, and Jake each order new computer modems. If each modem weighs 2.2 pounds, what is the total weight of the modems?

45. Doug raised $1.25 per mile in a charity walkathon. If he walked 14 miles, how much money did he raise?

Journal Idea

Explain a real-life situation when knowing how to multiply decimals can be used.

What do you think?

How can you use mental math to multiply decimals by 10, 100, and 1,000?

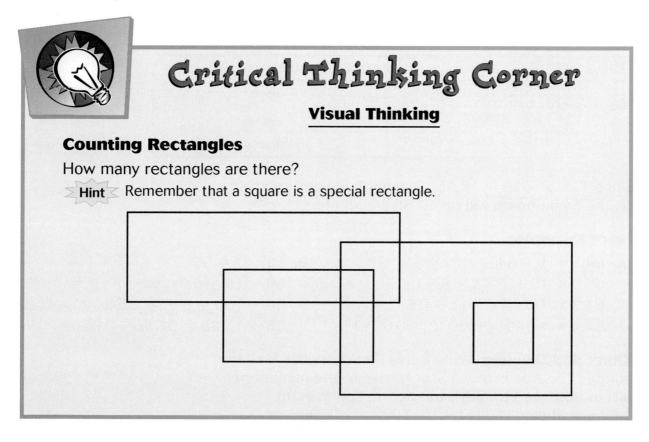

Critical Thinking Corner

Visual Thinking

Counting Rectangles

How many rectangles are there?

Hint Remember that a square is a special rectangle.

Using Algebra

Playing Games

Patterns can also help you divide by 10, 100, and 1,000.

|←————— 125.5 cm —————→|

Learning About It

Suppose you are designing a game to be sold by your school. Your game board is 125.5 centimeters long. If you have to divide the length of the board into 10 equal segments, how many centimeters long will each segment be?

125.5 ÷ 10 = *n*

Study the patterns in the table. What do you notice?

Divide by	Example	Move the decimal point to the left.
10	125.5 ÷ 10 = 12.55	1 place
100	125.5 ÷ 100 = 1.255	2 places
1,000	125.5 ÷ 1,000 = 0.1255	3 places

Since 125.5 ÷ 10 = 12.55, the length of each segment on the game board will be 12.55 centimeters.

More Examples

A. 64.3 ÷ 1 = 64.3
64.3 ÷ 10 = 6.43 = 6.43
64.3 ÷ 100 = 0.643 = 0.643
64.3 ÷ 1,000 = 0.0643 = 0.0643

B. 56 ÷ 1 = 56
56 ÷ 10 = 5.6 = 5.6
56 ÷ 100 = 0.56 = 0.56
56 ÷ 1,000 = 0.056 = 0.056

Think and Discuss Write a rule that describes how the number of zeros in the divisor relates to the number of places you need to move the decimal point in the quotient when dividing by 10, 100, or 1,000.

Try It Out

Use patterns to find each quotient.

1. 23.75 ÷ 1 = ■
   23.75 ÷ 10 = ■
   23.75 ÷ 100 = ■
   23.75 ÷ 1,000 = ■

2. 509.3 ÷ 10 = ■
   509.3 ÷ 100 = ■
   509.3 ÷ 1 = ■
   509.3 ÷ 1,000 = ■

3. 98.2 ÷ 100 = ■
   98.2 ÷ 1 = ■
   98.2 ÷ 1,000 = ■
   98.2 ÷ 10 = ■

Practice

Using Mental Math Use patterns to divide.

4. 21.9 ÷ 100

5. 0.45 ÷ 10

6. 6,394 ÷ 1,000

7. 0.04 ÷ 10

8. 5,050 ÷ 100

9. 2.75 ÷ 100

10. 398 ÷ 100

11. 10.9 ÷ 100

12. 46.7 ÷ 10

13. 51.6 ÷ 1,000

14. 0.282 ÷ 10

15. 73.06 ÷ 100

Find each *n*.

16. 908 ÷ *n* = 9.08

17. 1,298 ÷ 10 = *n*

18. 20.01 ÷ *n* = 0.2001

19. 19 ÷ 1,000 = *n*

20. 0.08 ÷ *n* = 0.0008

21. 3.11 ÷ 10 = *n*

Problem Solving

22. Cheryl and Carolyn created a game called Win It or Lose It. The game board is a grid 65 cm long and 40 cm wide. The length of the board has been divided into 10 segments. How many centimeters long is each segment?

23. Analyze A game company can buy in bulk from a manufacturer and save money. A set of 100 number cubes sells for $45.00, and a set of 1,000 number cubes sells for $380.00. What is the cost of one cube if you buy them in sets of 100? of 1,000?

24. Journal Idea Write a short story based on the problem $275 ÷ 10.

Review and Remember

Find each answer.

25. 234 × 352

26. 202.1 − 9.99

27. 123.1 + 234.67 + 12.234

28. 100.01 − 98.1

29. 19,987 ÷ 12

30. 12.09 + 235.2 + 2.789

For Extra Practice, see Set F, page 328.   **317**

Divide It Out

You used base-ten blocks to show whole-number division. You can also use them to show decimal division.

Learning About It

You have learned that base-ten blocks can be used to represent decimals. Work with a group.

Find 4.38 ÷ 3.

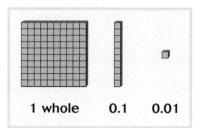

1 whole 0.1 0.01

What You Need

For each group:
  base-ten blocks

Step 1 Use base-ten blocks to show 4.38.

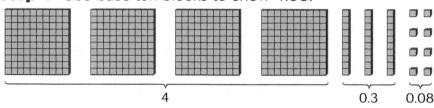

4   0.3   0.08

Step 2 Begin with the ones. Divide the ones into three equal groups. How many ones are in each group? How many ones are left over?

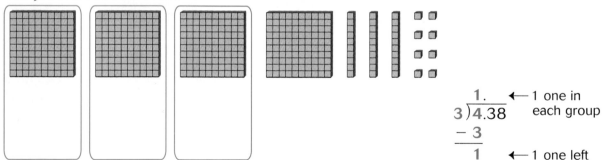

```
      1.      ← 1 one in
  3)4.38        each group
   - 3
   ___
     1        ← 1 one left
```

Step 3 Regroup 1 whole as 10 tenths. How many tenths do you have in all?

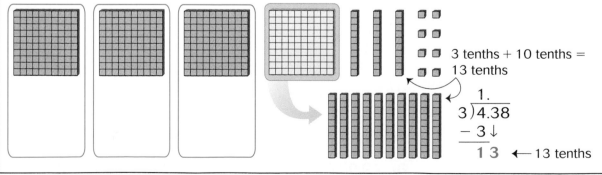

3 tenths + 10 tenths = 13 tenths

```
      1.
  3)4.38
   - 3↓
   ___
    1 3      ← 13 tenths
```

Step 4 Divide the tenths into the three groups. How many tenths are in each group? How many tenths are left over?

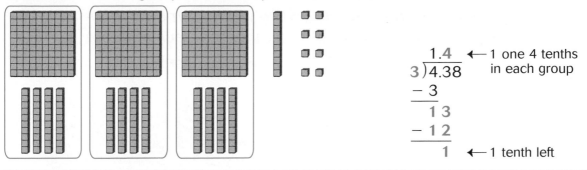

$$\begin{array}{r} 1.4 \\ 3\overline{)4.38} \\ -\ 3 \\ \hline 1\ 3 \\ -\ 1\ 2 \\ \hline 1 \end{array}$$

← 1 one 4 tenths in each group

← 1 tenth left

Step 5 Regroup 1 tenth as 10 hundredths. How many hundredths are there in all?

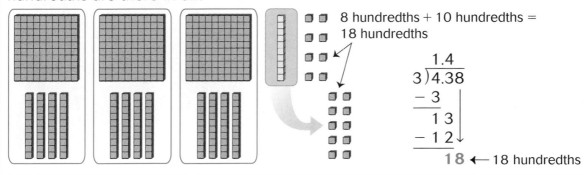

8 hundredths + 10 hundredths = 18 hundredths

$$\begin{array}{r} 1.4 \\ 3\overline{)4.38} \\ -\ 3 \\ \hline 1\ 3 \\ -\ 1\ 2 \\ \hline 18 \end{array}$$

← 18 hundredths

Step 6 Now divide the hundredths into the three groups. How many hundredths are in each group? What is the quotient?

Think and Discuss Explain how to use base-ten blocks to show that there is a zero in the quotient. Use 9.27 ÷ 9.

Practice

Use base-ten blocks to find each quotient.

1. 3.68 ÷ 2   **2.** 6.25 ÷ 5   **3.** 7.86 ÷ 3   **4.** 4.36 ÷ 4   **5.** 0.75 ÷ 3

Money $ense

Any Change?

You buy 3 notebooks, 2 pens, and a roll of tape. You give the clerk 4 one-dollar bills, 7 quarters, and 1 dime. How much change should you get back?

NOTEBOOK

59¢ each

$1.49

29¢

Calligraphy Connection

Use what you know about dividing whole numbers to divide decimals, but be sure to remember the decimal point.

Learning About It

The art teacher is teaching a calligraphy class after school. She ordered calligraphy sets from a catalog. She spent $79.60 on eight sets. How much did each set cost?

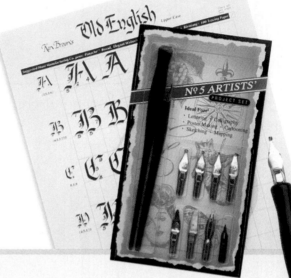

$$\$79.60 \div 8 = n$$

Estimate first: **$80.00 ÷ 8 = $10.00**

Then find the exact answer.

THERE'S ALWAYS A WAY!

- **One way** is to use paper and pencil.

Step 1 Place the decimal point in the quotient above the decimal point in the dividend.	Step 2 Divide as you would with whole numbers.	Step 3 Check by multiplying.
$$8\overline{)\$79.60}$$	$$\begin{array}{r} \$\ 9.95 \\ 8\overline{)\$79.60} \\ -72 \\ \hline 7\ 6 \\ -7\ 2 \\ \hline 40 \\ -40 \\ \hline 0 \end{array}$$	$$\begin{array}{r} \$9.95 \\ \times\ \ \ \ 8 \\ \hline \$79.60 \end{array}$$

- **Another way** is to use a calculator.

Press: ⑦ ⑨ ⦁ ⑥ ⓪ ÷ ⑧ =

Display: 9.95   Remember to place the dollar sign and decimal point in your answer.

The answer $9.95 is reasonable, since it is close to the estimate of $10.00. Each calligraphy set cost $9.95.

More Examples

A.
```
    0.06
21)1.26
  - 1 26
       0
```
When there are not enough ones to divide, write a zero in the ones place.

B.
```
    0.3046
5)1.5230
  -15
    023
    -20
      30
     -30
       0
```
Write this zero and continue dividing.

Think and Discuss Look at Example A. If the dividend were 2.26 you would not need a zero in the tenths place. Why?

Try It Out

Using Estimation Estimate. Then find the exact quotient.

1. $6.85 ÷ 5

2. 2.52 ÷ 12

3. 57.60 ÷ 45

4. 71.1 ÷ 5

Practice

Divide. Check by multiplying.

5. 8)24.8

6. 56)518.00

7. 34)2,723.4

8. 78)7.02

9. 6 ÷ 5

10. 174.08 ÷ 34

11. 1.136 ÷ 71

12. 153.6 ÷ 6

13. 48.30 ÷ 5

14. 1.15 ÷ 23

15. 0.12 ÷ 8

16. 103.53 ÷ 51

Problem Solving

17. A pack of calligraphy paper is $38.50. There are 55 sheets in a pack. What is the cost of each sheet?

18. Calligraphy markers sell in 8-packs for $4.16 and 12-packs for $5.76. In which size are the markers less expensive?

19. Analyze A sheet of paper is 17.5 in. long. Every line of calligraphy is 4 in. high. There is a 1-in. space above the first line, a 1-in. space after the last line, and an inch of space between each line. How many lines of calligraphy can be written on one sheet of paper?

Review and Remember

Name each figure.

20.

21. ←•——•→ A   B

22.

23.

24.

For Extra Practice, see Set G, page 328.

Problem Solving
Choose a
Computation Method

You can use paper and pencil, mental math, or a calculator to solve problems.

Sam hopes to join the cross-country track team at school. He plans to use the $48.00 he earned raking leaves to buy a sweat shirt, sweat pants, and a pair of sneakers at The Runner's Place. Does Sam have enough money to buy all of these items?

 ## UNDERSTAND

What do you know?

You know the price of each item Sam wants to buy.

 ## PLAN

How can you solve the problem?

You can add to find the total cost. First decide whether to use mental math, paper and pencil, or a calculator to find the sum. Sam thought the numbers were easy to add, so he chose paper and pencil.

 ## SOLVE

$$
\begin{array}{r}
\$\ 9.50 \\
9.50 \\
+\ 27.90 \\
\hline
\$46.90
\end{array}
$$

It will cost Sam $46.90 to buy the items he wants, so he has enough money.

 ## LOOK BACK

How can you use estimation to be sure your total is reasonable?

Show What You Learned

Solve each problem using mental math, paper and pencil, or a calculator. Tell which method you chose. Use the information at the right and on page 322 to solve Problems 1–5.

SALE
Jogging Suits
$42.50

T-SHIRTS
$8.00
or
3 for $20.00

1 Ben plans to buy nine T-shirts. How much will the T-shirts cost?

2 How much would it cost to buy a jogging suit and a pair of sneakers?

3 Heather and Rose want to buy their mother a jogging suit for $42.50 and a T-shirt for $8.00. They will share the cost equally. How much should each person pay?

4 Some states charge sales tax on purchases. If the sales tax is $0.05 on each dollar, what would be the tax on 4 pairs of sweat pants? What would be the total cost of buying 4 pairs of sweat pants with the tax?

5 **You Decide** Suppose you have $75 to spend at The Runner's Place. List the items that you would buy. Then, show the total cost and the amount of change that you would receive.

6 The Runner's Place total sales for 5 days was $19,369.65. What was the average total sales per day?

7 A shipment of 120 pairs of sneakers was sent to The Runner's Place. There are eight pairs of sneakers in each box. How many boxes were sent? If there were 10 pairs of sneakers in each box, how many boxes would be sent?

8 **Explain** Sara wants to buy a pair of track shoes that cost $49.95, a stopwatch that costs $24.99, and two packages of socks at $4.99 each. She has $70 and a $10-off coupon. Does she have enough money to buy the items?

9 **Analyze** On Monday Mr. David had a balance of $1,234.89 in his checking account. Then he wrote checks for $79.81, $215.46, and $654.20. On Tuesday he made a deposit of $150. How much was in his checking account after the deposit?

10 **Create Your Own** Use the display on page 322 or a newspaper ad to write a problem. Tell which method of computation you would use to solve the problem. Then have a classmate solve it.

Problem Solving

★★★★★ **Preparing for Tests**

Practice What You Learned

Choose the correct letter for each answer.

1 Eric was numbering the squares on a board for a game he had invented. The first four squares were numbered 1221, 2332, 3443, 4554. If he used the same pattern to number all the squares on the board, which two numbers might be included?

A. 5665 and 9889
B. 5665 and 8998
C. 6556 and 9889
D. 6556 and 8998

Tip

Use one of these strategies to solve this problem.
• *Find a Pattern*
• *Make a List*
• *Use Logical Reasoning*

2 Kate paid $7.98 for 5 pounds of chicken wings. Which is a reasonable estimate for the cost of 3 pounds of chicken wings?

A. About $2
B. About $3
C. About $5
D. About $7

Tip

When solving multiple-choice problems, you can sometimes eliminate one or more answer choices.

3 Mandy's computer uses 0.15 kilowatts of electricity per hour. On Sunday she used her computer for 3.2 hours in the morning and 1.85 hours in the afternoon. Which number sentence could be used to find the amount of electricity, n, she used on Sunday?

A. $3.2 \times 1.85 \times 0.15 = n$
B. $3.2 + (1.85 \times 0.15) = n$
C. $(3.2 \times 1.85) + 0.15 = n$
D. $(3.2 + 1.85) \times 0.15 = n$

Tip

When more than one step is needed to solve a problem, you must decide which step to do first.

4 If the 2 triangles shown below are congruent, which pair of sides must also be congruent?

A. Sides BC and AC
B. Sides BC and YZ
C. Sides BC and ZX
D. Sides BC and XY

---

5 Matt needs 560 cm of chain to make 8 key chains. It takes him 15 minutes to make one key chain. If 25 cm of chain costs 39¢, how much will Matt spend for the chain he needs?

A. $2.18
B. $8.58
C. $10.97
D. $17.47
E. Not Here

---

6 Diane and 3 friends bought a $48 sweater for Susan. They shared the cost equally. How could you find Diane's share of the cost?

A. Multiply $48 by 3.
B. Multiply $48 by 4.
C. Divide $48 by 3.
D. Divide $48 by 4.
E. Divide $48 by 5.

---

7 Kim lives 0.7 of the distance that Ari does from the school. Ari lives 3.14 kilometers from the school. Which is the best estimate of how far Kim lives from the school?

A. 21 km   **C.** 2 km
B. 4 km   **D.** 0.5 km

---

8 The graph shows the different animals who came to a clinic in May.

Animals Treated at the Clinic	
Cats	🐾 🐾 🐾 🐾
Dogs	🐾 🐾 🐾 🐾 🐾 🐾
Rabbits	🐾 🐾
Other	🐾 🐾 🐾 🐾

🐾 = 20 animals

If one third of all the animals needed medicine, how many animals did **NOT** need medicine?

A. 78   **C.** 200
B. 155   **D.** 310

---

9 Jim bicycled 8 miles in 20 minutes. If Suki rides at the same speed as Jim for 50 minutes, which is a reasonable distance for Suki to travel?

A. 10 miles
B. 20 miles
C. 30 miles
D. 50 miles

---

10 Pam has a dog-walking service. She walks dogs for several of her customers on Saturdays. She gives each dog a treat and then walks it for 45 minutes. What else do you need to know to find out the total time Pam spends walking dogs on Saturdays?

A. The distance Pam walks each dog
B. How much money Pam earns for walking each dog
C. How much time Pam spends between walks
D. The breeds of the dogs
E. The number of dogs Pam walks

✔ Checkpoint

Dividing Decimals

Vocabulary

Write the missing words that complete each sentence.

1. When multiplying two 2-digit numbers, you get a ___?___ after multiplying by ones.

2. The ___?___ is the answer in division.

3. A ___?___ number has one or more digits to the right of a decimal point.

4. An ___?___ is an approximate rather than exact number.

Concepts and Skills

Using Algebra Use patterns to find each quotient.
(pages 316–317)

5. $675 \div 1 = \blacksquare$
   $675 \div 10 = \blacksquare$
   $675 \div 100 = \blacksquare$
   $675 \div 1{,}000 = \blacksquare$

6. $7.05 \div 10 = \blacksquare$
   $7.05 \div 100 = \blacksquare$
   $7.05 \div 1 = \blacksquare$
   $7.05 \div 1{,}000 = \blacksquare$

7. $26.8 \div 100 = \blacksquare$
   $26.8 \div 1{,}000 = \blacksquare$
   $26.8 \div 1 = \blacksquare$
   $26.8 \div 10 = \blacksquare$

Using Algebra Find each *n*. (pages 316–317)

8. $0.1 \div 10 = n$

9. $23.4 \div 100 = n$

10. $68.1 \div n = 6.81$

11. $908 \div 100 = n$

12. $710 \div 1{,}000 = n$

13. $3.01 \div n = 0.0301$

14. $679.8 \div n = 6.798$

15. $8{,}000 \div n = 8$

16. $8.132 \div 10 = n$

17. $0.53 \div 1{,}000 = n$

18. $101 \div n = 1.01$

19. $571.1 \div n = 57.11$

Choose a Method Use paper and pencil or a calculator to find each quotient. (pages 320–321)

20. $41\overline{)1.435}$

21. $11\overline{)22.891}$

22. $21\overline{)42.84}$

23. $59\overline{)135.7}$

24. $99\overline{)152.46}$

25. $6\overline{)2.364}$

26. $4\overline{)217.4}$

27. $12\overline{)63.72}$

28. $1.24 \div 4$

29. $0.276 \div 23$

30. $0.336 \div 16$

31. $181.2 \div 8$

Mixed Practice

Divide. Use mental math or paper and pencil.

32. $31\overline{)0.372}$ **33.** $6\overline{)418.2}$ **34.** $75\overline{)2,350.5}$ **35.** $7\overline{)16.1}$

36. $59 \div 1,000$ **37.** $21.3 \div 10$ **38.** $729.8 \div 41$ **39.** $5.28 \div 10$

40. $103.5 \div 23$ **41.** $0.08 \div 100$ **42.** $9.8 \div 100$ **43.** $83.1 \div 10$

Problem Solving

44. From a catalog, Stephen ordered 3 lb of oranges at $3.25 per pound, 5 lb of grapefruit at $2.10 per pound, and 2 lb of clementines at $3.50 per pound. He had to pay $0.40 per pound for shipping. How much was his total order?

45. **Explain** Kimberly wants to buy eight dog posters. A set of three posters sells for $10.00, and a single poster sells for $4.25. What is the least amount of money Kimberly will have to pay for the eight posters? Explain.

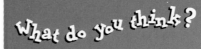

What do you think?

How can base-ten blocks help you understand division of decimals?

Journal Idea

Why is it important to place the decimal point correctly when working with money? Use an example to explain.

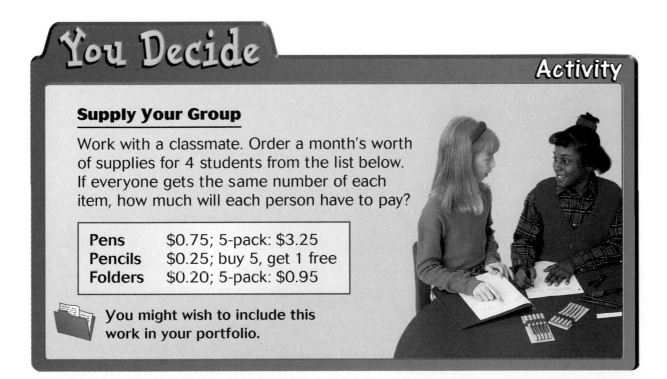

You Decide

Activity

Supply Your Group

Work with a classmate. Order a month's worth of supplies for 4 students from the list below. If everyone gets the same number of each item, how much will each person have to pay?

Pens	$0.75; 5-pack: $3.25
Pencils	$0.25; buy 5, get 1 free
Folders	$0.20; 5-pack: $0.95

You might wish to include this work in your portfolio.

Extra Practice

Set A (pages 296–297)

Using Algebra Find each *n*.

1. $3.21 \times n = 32.1$
2. $0.8 \times 1{,}000 = n$
3. $2.01 \times n = 201$

4. $0.31 \times 10 = n$
5. $n \times 2.16 = 216$
6. $3.75 \times 1 = n$

7. $\$1.25 \times n = \$12.50$
8. $100 \times n = 8.21$
9. $0.00245 \times n = 0.245$

10. $10 \times n = 4.5$
11. $n \times 100 = 2.75$
12. $0.109 \times 100 = n$

13. **Using Mental Math** A local animal shelter houses 100 dogs. If it costs $2.75 a day to feed each dog, how much money does the shelter spend on dog food each day?

14. Dave makes $5.50 a week for walking the neighbor's dog every day after school. How much will he have made after walking the dog for 10 weeks?

Set B (pages 298–299)

Multiply.

1. $\begin{array}{r} 13.3 \\ \times\ \ \ 4 \\ \hline \end{array}$
2. $\begin{array}{r} 64.5 \\ \times\ \ \ 8 \\ \hline \end{array}$
3. $\begin{array}{r} 88.8 \\ \times\ \ \ 3 \\ \hline \end{array}$
4. $\begin{array}{r} 0.37 \\ \times\ \ \ 9 \\ \hline \end{array}$
5. $\begin{array}{r} 2.09 \\ \times\ \ \ 7 \\ \hline \end{array}$

6. $\begin{array}{r} 28.9 \\ \times\ \ \ 5 \\ \hline \end{array}$
7. $\begin{array}{r} 77.8 \\ \times\ \ \ 9 \\ \hline \end{array}$
8. $\begin{array}{r} 2.09 \\ \times\ \ \ 8 \\ \hline \end{array}$
9. $\begin{array}{r} 9.99 \\ \times\ \ \ 8 \\ \hline \end{array}$
10. $\begin{array}{r} 34.6 \\ \times\ \ \ 7 \\ \hline \end{array}$

Using Algebra Find each *n*.

11. $21.2 \times 5 = n$
12. $17.3 \times 2 = n$
13. $19.2 \times 9 = n$

14. $\$2.41 \times 4 = n$
15. $6.11 \times 8 = n$
16. $12.6 \times 7 = n$

17. $16.4 \times 5 = n$
18. $13.7 \times 2 = n$
19. $16.9 \times 6 = n$

20. Kate decided to make a fruit salad for dessert for her friends. If she wants 9.5 ounces of fruit for each of her eight friends, how many ounces of fruit should she buy?

21. Marco spends $1.25 on a pretzel each day after school. How much will he spend on pretzels if he buys one every day for nine days?

Extra Practice

Set C (pages 300–301)

Find an estimated product for each.

1. 3.6 × 9	**2.** 8.4 × 3	**3.** 5.8 × 6	**4.** 9.4 × 2 2

5. 13.8 × 19   **6.** 47 × 8.5   **7.** 28.7 × 25   **8.** 0.15 × 27

9. 8.4 × 19   **10.** 78 × 6.8   **11.** $2.31 × 45   **12.** 22 × 9.9

13. 23 × 7.1   **14.** 3.8 × 29   **15.** 12.3 × 14   **16.** 76 × 0.5

17. Using Estimation Josh buys two posters for $9.95 each and three posters for $5.75 each. About how much change should Josh get back if he gives the salesperson two $20 bills?

Set D (pages 306–309)

Multiply.

1. 3.2 × 5.5	**2.** 7.3 × 2.1	**3.** 5.2 × 8.7	**4.** 0.07 × 1.5

5. 6.29 × 3.7   **6.** 4.7 × 9.02   **7.** 28.43 × 9.1   **8.** 31.6 × 2.5

9. 9.33 × 4.72   **10.** 6.38 × 4.59   **11.** 8.62 × 3.11   **12.** 17.1 × 2.4

13. 4.81 × 3.93   **14.** 7.29 × 6.38   **15.** 9.47 × 3.82   **16.** 0.8 × 28.75

17. 3.14 × 2.5   **18.** 45.83 × 12.1   **19.** 10.52 × 5.95   **20.** 32.65 × 0.15

21. Fernando practices the piano for 0.5 hour three times a week. How many hours does he practice in four weeks?

22. Explain Audrey works in the school bookstore. If she works 0.75 hour each day, how many minutes each day does she work?

23. To find the area of a rectangle, you multiply the length by the width. Area is measured in square units. Melissa's room is 13.2 feet long and 8.61 feet wide. What is the area of the floor of her room?

Extra Practice

Set E (pages 310–311)

Find each product.

1. 0.38
    × 0.2

2. 0.05
    × 0.5

3. 2.58
    × 0.01

4. 0.64
    × 0.05

5. 3.03
    × 0.5

6. 0.07×0.35 7. 0.6×0.05 8. 0.19×0.1 9. 0.26×0.09

10. 0.6×0.08 11. 0.3×0.04 12. 0.4×0.11 13. 0.05×0.07

14. 0.12×0.4 15. 0.48×0.2 16. 0.4×0.16 17. 0.91×0.1

18. Tyrone is participating in a walkathon for charity. Twelve people each pledge $1.25 for each mile he walks. How much will he earn for the charity if he walks 2.5 miles?

Set F (pages 316–317)

Using Algebra   Using Mental Math   Use patterns to divide.

1. $26.5 \div 10$ 2. $3.002 \div 100$ 3. $19.5 \div 10$ 4. $28.46 \div 100$

5. $396 \div 10$ 6. $369.5 \div 1,000$ 7. $198.15 \div 100$ 8. $3.56 \div 1,000$

9. $7,413 \div 100$ 10. $61.74 \div 100$ 11. $24.8 \div 1,000$ 12. $79.854 \div 10$

13. $4.8 \div 1,000$ 14. $1,313.8 \div 100$ 15. $149.03 \div 100$ 16. $5,729 \div 100$

Set G (pages 320–321)

Divide. Check by multiplying.

1. $25.92 \div 8$ 2. $61.2 \div 9$ 3. $80.4 \div 6$ 4. $0.56 \div 7$

5. $36.03 \div 3$ 6. $73.4 \div 5$ 7. $126.42 \div 7$ 8. $50.0 \div 4$

9. $28\overline{)303.24}$ 10. $15\overline{)637.65}$ 11. $12\overline{)3.72}$ 12. $32\overline{)601.6}$

13. $28\overline{)1.4}$ 14. $12\overline{)307.2}$ 15. $16\overline{)772.8}$ 16. $49\overline{)3,758.3}$

17. A package of six pens costs $2.94. Individual pens can also be bought for 60 cents each. Which is the better buy, a package of six pens or six individual pens? Explain.

 **Chapter Test**

Use patterns to multiply or divide.

1. 5.6×100 **2.** $0.079 \times 1{,}000$ **3.** $14.98 \div 10$ **4.** $6.23 \div 1{,}000$

Multiply.

5. $\begin{array}{r} 0.26 \\ \times\ \ \ 4 \\ \hline \end{array}$ **6.** $\begin{array}{r} 7.13 \\ \times\ \ \ 8 \\ \hline \end{array}$ **7.** $\begin{array}{r} 0.785 \\ \times\ \ \ \ \ 9 \\ \hline \end{array}$ **8.** $\begin{array}{r} 9.64 \\ \times\ \ 15 \\ \hline \end{array}$ **9.** $\begin{array}{r} 0.0038 \\ \times\ \ \ \ \ 27 \\ \hline \end{array}$

Estimate each product.

10. $\$0.35 \times 12$ **11.** 6.6×23 **12.** $\$1.63 \times 28$ **13.** 2.4×400

Find each product.

14. $\begin{array}{r} 1.9 \\ \times\ 0.7 \\ \hline \end{array}$ **15.** $\begin{array}{r} \$0.36 \\ \times\ \ 0.25 \\ \hline \end{array}$ **16.** $\begin{array}{r} 3.07 \\ \times\ \ 0.6 \\ \hline \end{array}$ **17.** $\begin{array}{r} 1.76 \\ \times\ 0.96 \\ \hline \end{array}$ **18.** $\begin{array}{r} 1.6 \\ \times\ 0.05 \\ \hline \end{array}$

Divide.

19. $6\overline{)17.4}$ **20.** $8\overline{)24.4}$ **21.** $25\overline{)\$53.50}$ **22.** $50\overline{)\$137.50}$

Solve.

23. The wilderness catalog is advertising corduroy shirts for $17.75. If Mr. Hayes wants to buy one for each of his four children, how much will he have to pay?

24. Matthew and his sister, Kate, ordered 32 sinkers for their fishing trip. The total bill is $14.40. If the sinkers each cost the same amount, how much did each sinker cost?

25. The shipping cost depends on the total cost of the order. Orders between $25.00 and $50.00 cost $5.00 for shipping. If the total is between $50.01 and $75.00, shipping is $6.00. If the order is $71.00, what is the total cost, including shipping?

 Self-Check

Look back at Exercises 21–22. Did you remember to place the dollar sign and decimal point correctly?

Performance Assessment

Show What You Know About
Multiplying and Dividing Decimals

1 Use two spinners with these numbers on them. Spin them each once.

Decimals

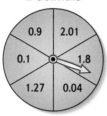

Whole Numbers

What You Need

2 spinners

a. Find the product of the two numbers. Then divide the decimal by the whole number.

b. Analyze Is it possible to spin the spinners and get a product greater than 50? Explain your thinking.

Self-Check Did you remember that a product is found by multiplying?

2 Hal decided to spend no more than $200 of his savings at a bike shop. He bought a bicycle. Then he spent the rest of his money on accessories and safety equipment. What accessories and safety equipment might he have purchased? Show your work. What change did he receive?

Self-Check Did you remember that Hal cannot spend more than $200 and that the first thing he bought was a bike?

Bicycles

Mountain $149.95
Racing $159.95
Road.....................$144.95

Accessories

Reflectors ....$3.15 each
Handle grips........... $5.89 pair
Lock.................... $8.00

Safety Equipment

Elbow pad .... $6.75 each
Helmet $24.50

For Your Portfolio

You might wish to include this work in your portfolio.

Extension

Mancala

Mancala, an African stone game, has been played in Africa and the Middle East for over 3,000 years. Today, people all over the world enjoy playing Mancala.

To begin playing, the game board is set up as shown, with the same number of stones in each pit. The game ends when one player's pits are empty. The player with the most stones in his or her Home Bin is the winner.

How to Play

On your turn, pick up all the stones from any one pit on your side of the board. Then, beginning with the next pit to the right and moving counterclockwise, put one stone in each pit, including the Home Bins and your opponent's pits, until you have no more stones.

Free Turn

You get a free turn if the last stone you place ends up in your Home Bin.

Capture

You can capture stones when the last stone you place ends up in an empty pit on your side of the board. You capture all of the stones in the pit opposite the pit that is empty. You place your opponent's stones in your Home Bin.

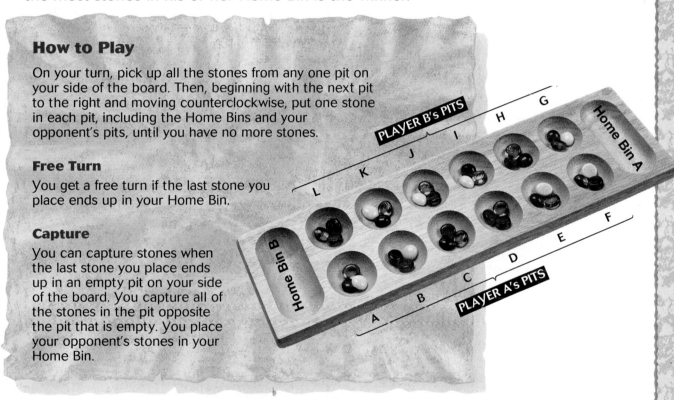

Use the Mancala boards shown for Questions 1–2.

1. Describe a move that will give Player A a free turn.

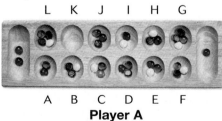

Player A

2. Describe a move that will give Player A a capture.

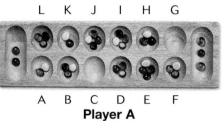

Player A

3. Draw your own Mancala board and play the game. Then write about what you think a best first move would be.

Cumulative Review

★ ★ ★ ★ ★ **Preparing for Tests**

Choose the correct letter for each answer.

Number Concepts	Operations

Number Concepts

1. What is 76.037 rounded to the nearest tenth?

   A. 80
   B. 76.4
   C. 76.04
   D. 76.0

2. Which of these numbers is 5,890 when rounded to the nearest ten and 5,900 when rounded to the nearest hundred?

   A. 5,809
   B. 5,879
   C. 5,887
   D. 5,896

3. Which number sentence is **NOT** true?

   A. $11.011 < 11.110$
   B. $9.011 < 9.101$
   C. $1.289 < 1.199$
   D. $0.0099 < 0.0988$

4. Which decimal is shown by the shaded part of the grid?

   A. 4.40
   B. 0.44
   C. 0.044
   D. 0.0044

Operations

5. What number is the product of 0.473×100?

   A. 0.0473
   B. 0.473
   C. 4.730
   D. 47.30
   E. Not Here

6. Jeff runs 14 laps a day in the gym for 20 days. Then he runs 16 laps a day for 10 days. How many laps does he run in the 30 days?

   A. 160
   B. 280
   C. 440
   D. 520

7. You can buy 10 replacement discs for the Dazer Disc toy for $13.50. How much does each disc cost?

   A. $135.00
   B. $1.35
   C. $0.35
   D. $0.14
   E. Not Here

8. Tia rode her bike 2.6 miles on Friday, 4.5 miles on Saturday, and 2.8 miles on Sunday. How many more miles did she ride on Saturday than on Sunday?

   A. 1.9 mi   C. 0.8 mi
   B. 1.7 mi   D. 0.7 mi

Patterns, Relationships, and Algebraic Thinking	Geometry and Spatial Reasoning

Patterns, Relationships, and Algebraic Thinking

9. Which is the rule for the number sequence below?

11, 1.1, 0.11, 0.011, ...

A. Add 0.1.
B. Subtract 10.1.
C. Divide by 10.
D. Multiply by 10.

10. Which letter best represents 6.75 on the number line?

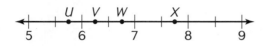

A. U **C.** W
B. V **D.** X

11. Study the input/output table shown below. Which of the following is the rule?

Input	Output
12.5	1.25
5.25	0.525
0.55	0.055

A. Multiply by 10.
B. Divide by 10.
C. Multiply by 100.
D. Divide by 100.

12. There are 3.4 grams of fat in a 1-ounce serving of frozen yogurt. Which number sentence shows how many grams of fat are in a 2.5-ounce serving?

A. $3.4 + 2.5 = n$
B. $3.4 \times 2.5 = n$
C. $3.4 - 2.5 = n$
D. $3.4 \div 3.5 = n$

Geometry and Spatial Reasoning

13. Which of these space figures has only one base?

A. Rectangular prism
B. Triangular prism
C. Cube
D. Pyramid

14. If you cut a sphere in half, what shape would you see on the cut surface?

A. Circle
B. Square
C. Rectangle
D. Triangle

15. Which one of the following line segments is perpendicular to $\overline{AG}$?

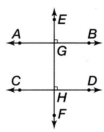

A. $\overline{GB}$
B. $\overline{HD}$
C. $\overline{GH}$
D. $\overline{CD}$

16. Which figure has only 1 line of symmetry?

A.   **C.**

B.    **D.**

Chapter 9

Fraction Concepts

Chapter Theme: PERFORMING ARTS

Real-World Math

····················**Real Facts**····················

Music is written in measures. In $\frac{4}{4}$ time, all the notes and rests in each measure must add up to 4 beats. Symbols, like those in the chart below, tell musicians when to play each note and how long to hold it. Dancers, like those from the National Dance Institute pictured on the right, use the rhythm pattern of the notes to plan their movements.

Musical Notation and Value in $\frac{4}{4}$ Time			
Name	Notation	Fraction of a Whole Note	Duration
Quarter note	♩	$\frac{1}{4}$	1 beat
Half note	♪	$\frac{1}{2}$	2 beats
Whole note	o	1	4 beats

• How many quarter notes equal the duration of a whole note?

• What combination of quarter notes and half notes equals one whole note?

·················**Real People**·················

Meet Steve McNicholas. Throughout his artistic career, he has been a writer, actor, street-band musician, director, and co-creator of a theater dance production. In the 1980s, Steve worked with a theater group called Cliff Hangers on a series of street comedy musicals that were presented at the Edinburgh Festival in Scotland.

Take a Bow

You can find common factors of two or more numbers and use them to solve problems.

Learning About It

Mrs. Barre is choreographing the curtain call for 18 dancers and 24 actors. As the performers take their bows, there must be the same number of people in each row. Dancers and actors cannot be in the same row.

To keep the curtain calls short, there must be the fewest number of rows possible. How many people will Mrs. Barre put in each row?

List all of the factors of each number. Remember to use divisibility rules.

18: 1, 2, 3, ⬚6, 9, 18 ◁ Equal groups of dancers

24: 1, 2, 3, 4, ⬚6, 8, 12, 24 ◁ Equal groups of actors

Word Bank

common factor
greatest common factor (GCF)

Then find the **common factors**. The common factors of 18 and 24 are 1, 2, 3, and 6. These are the equal rows into which both groups can be divided.

Since 6 is the **greatest common factor (GCF)** of 18 and 24, Mrs. Barre will put the performers in rows of 6.

More Examples

A. Find the GCF of 9 and 18.

Factors of 9: 1, 3, ⬚9
Factors of 18: 1, 2, 3, 6, ⬚9, 18

The GCF is ⬚9.

B. Find the GCF of 21 and 16.

Factors of 21: ⬚1, 3, 7, 21
Factors of 16: ⬚1, 2, 4, 8, 16

The GCF is ⬚1.

Think and Discuss What is the GCF of any two prime numbers? Explain.

Try It Out

List all the factors of each number. Then find the GCF of each pair.

1. 10, 12   **2.** 7, 15   **3.** 15, 20   **4.** 27, 36

5. Discuss Explain how this Venn diagram shows the GCF of 12 and 30.

Factors of 12: 4, 12
1, 3, 2, 6
Factors of 30: 5, 10, 30, 15

Practice

Find the GCF of each set of numbers.

6. 14, 26   **7.** 4, 12   **8.** 8, 12   **9.** 7, 21

10. 5, 9   **11.** 8, 16   **12.** 16, 18   **13.** 15, 24

14. 10, 20   **15.** 25, 40   **16.** 24, 32   **17.** 16, 32

18. 18, 24   **19.** 12, 15, 24   **20.** 18, 24, 36   **21.** 24, 36, 60

Problem Solving

22. There are three groups of performers—one with 24, one with 18, and one with 12. The groups will not be combined. If each row must have the same number of performers, how must they be grouped?

23. Using Algebra Every time the dancers rehearse, their practice time increases. The first rehearsal is 15 min, the second is 20 min, and the third is 25 min. If the pattern continues, how many minutes will the fifth practice be? the tenth? What strategy did you use to solve the problem?

24. The student council is raising money for new folders for the singers in the chorus. Each folder costs $11.98, and there are 38 students in the chorus. How much money should be raised? How do you know your answer is reasonable?

Dancers	
Rehearsal	**Time**
First day	
Second day	
Third day	

Review and Remember

Round each number to the underlined place.

25. 87,<u>6</u>94   **26.** 0.9<u>9</u>5   **27.** 67.<u>0</u>08   **28.** 1,<u>2</u>89,854

29. 34,2<u>9</u>7,005   **30.** 14.<u>4</u>51   **31.** 66,6<u>6</u>1   **32.** 19.8<u>6</u>5

For Extra Practice, see Set A, page 366.

In the Spotlight

Knowing about multiples can help you plan the lighting for a play.

Learning About It

A lighting crew has set the lights so that the red light goes on every 4 seconds, the blue light every 6 seconds, and the yellow light every 10 seconds. When the light panel is switched on, what is the first time that the red and blue lights will go on together?

List the first several **multiples** of each number.

4: 4, 8, 12 , 16, 20, **24**, . . . ◁ Seconds at which the red light goes on

6: 6, 12 , 18, **24**, 36, . . . ◁ Seconds at which the blue light goes on

Then find the **common multiples**. Two common multiples of 6 and 4 are 12 and 24. These are times that both lights will be on at the same time.

Since 12 is the **least common multiple (LCM)** of 6 and 4, the first time red and blue lights will go on together is at 12 seconds.

Think and Discuss What is the LCM of two prime numbers? Use 3 and 5 as an example.

Try It Out

List the first seven multiples of each number. Then find the LCM of each pair.

1. 12, 10	**2.** 5, 6	**3.** 10, 8
4. 9, 6	**5.** 2, 4	**6.** 20, 25
7. 3, 7	**8.** 5, 15	**9.** 6, 8

10. Discuss When is the LCM one of the numbers itself?

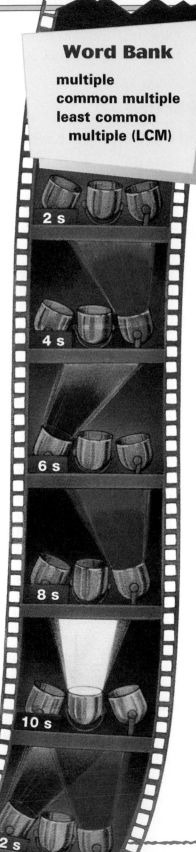

Word Bank

multiple
common multiple
least common
   multiple (LCM)

2 s

4 s

6 s

8 s

10 s

12 s

Practice

Find the LCM of each set of numbers.

11. 15, 18   **12.** 6, 4   **13.** 2, 3   **14.** 6, 2   **15.** 2, 7

16. 6, 8   **17.** 4, 9   **18.** 7, 5   **19.** 9, 6   **20.** 6, 10

21. 12, 8   **22.** 4, 8   **23.** 2, 3, 4   **24.** 6, 9, 12   **25.** 8, 10, 16

Problem Solving

26. Analyze A student can fold 20 programs in a half hour. If they all work at the same pace, how many programs can 15 students finish in 3 hours? 10 students in 5 hours?

27. Science Connection Red, blue, and yellow make white light. Look at the seconds listed for the three colors on page 338. When will there be white light for the first time?

28. The main performers in a play rehearse every 2 days, the other characters every 4 days, and the chorus every 5 days. If everyone rehearses on March 31, what is the next date when the entire cast will rehearse?

Review and Remember

Using Mental Math Multiply or divide.

29. $0.06 \div 10$ **30.** $5{,}700 \times 100$ **31.** 0.86×100 **32.** 0.0042×100

33. $1{,}538 \div 10$ **34.** $10 \times 4{,}950$ **35.** $9.8 \times 1{,}000$ **36.** $1{,}362.91 \times 100$

Critical Thinking Corner

Logical Thinking

Square Numbers

Using Algebra Study the pattern below. The numbers 1, 4, 9, 16, . . . are called square numbers. Explain why.

1. What are the next three figures in the pattern?

2. Write a rule to tell what any figure in the pattern would look like.

3. What does the tenth figure look like? How many small squares (square units) does it contain?

For Extra Practice, see Set B, page 366.

Developing Skills for
Problem Solving

First read for understanding and then focus on how to decide whether the answer to a problem is reasonable.

READ FOR UNDERSTANDING

The students hope that this year's play will raise at least $2,000 to help build a new playground.

The school theater seats 580 people. Student tickets are expected to account for one half of the total ticket sales. The rest will be sold as general admission tickets. There will be two performances, and it is expected that both will sell out.

① How many people can be seated in the school theater?

② What two types of tickets will bè sold?

③ What fractional part of the ticket sales are expected to be student tickets?

THINK AND DISCUSS

Reasonable Answers It is important to know whether an answer to a problem is reasonable. If you estimate first, you can check to see if the answer is close to the estimate. If it is, then the answer is reasonable.

Tickets

General
Admission.....$5.00

Students.......$3.00

Reread the paragraphs at the top of the page.

④ For each show, is it reasonable to print about 200 student tickets? How can an estimate help you decide?

⑤ For each show, is it reasonable to print 290 general admission tickets?

⑥ Explain how an estimate can be used to see if your answer is reasonable.

Show What You Learned

Use the information on page 340 and in the newspaper article at the right. Answer each question. Give a reason for your choice.

Following the school play, this story appeared in the local newspaper.

1 Which sentence tells how to estimate the total amount raised from student ticket sales?

   a. Multiply the approximate total number of student tickets sold by the cost of one ticket.

   b. Multiply the approximate total number of tickets sold by the number of performances.

   c. Neither of the above

2 Which expression would you use to estimate the total amount raised from student ticket sales?

   a. 2 x 500

   b. $3 x 500

   c. ($3 x 500) x 2

3 Is it reasonable to say that $1,584 was made on student ticket sales?

   a. No, about $1,500 x 2, or about $3,000, was made.

   b. Yes, about $3 x 500, or about $1,500, was made.

   c. Yes, about 1,000 tickets were sold.

The producer says the sale of general admission tickets brought in about $1,400 more than student ticket sales.

4 Which of the following should you do to decide if $1,400 is reasonable?

   a. Estimate the sum of the number of tickets sold at the two performances.

   b. Estimate the sum of the amount that each type of ticket made at the two performances.

   c. Estimate the amount made on general admission tickets and then subtract the amount made on student tickets.

5 How much more money did the sale of general admission tickets bring in than student ticket sales? Tell how you know that your answer is reasonable.

School Play Earns More Than $4,000!

This past weekend our local school staged a successful play! The school held two performances and sold a total of 596 general admission tickets and 528 student tickets! The school plans to donate the money to help build a new playground.

Setting the Stage

You can use fractions and decimals to express parts of regions and sets.

Learning About It

A **fraction** can be used to express part of a region.

Red section

$0.21 = \dfrac{21}{100}$ ← **numerator**—number of red parts
← **denominator**—number of equal parts in a region

twenty-one hundredths

Blue section $0.60 = \dfrac{60}{100}$ $0.6 = \dfrac{6}{10}$

sixty hundredths   or   six tenths

Green section $0.09 = \dfrac{9}{100}$

nine hundredths

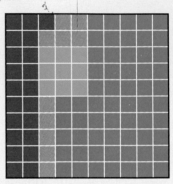

A fraction can also be used to express part of a set.

$\dfrac{3}{7}$ are open.

$\dfrac{4}{5}$ are used.

More Examples

A. $0.5 = \dfrac{5}{10}$

Five tenths
is shaded.

B. $0.4 = \dfrac{4}{10}$

Four tenths
are shaded.

C. $\dfrac{2}{8} = \dfrac{1}{4} = \dfrac{25}{100} = 0.25$

Two eighths
is shaded.

Think and Discuss Does 0.7 or $\dfrac{7}{10}$ represent the greater number? How do you know?

Try It Out

Write a fraction and decimal for each shaded part.

1.

2.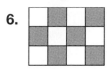

3.

4.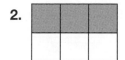

Practice

Write the fraction for each shaded part.

5.

6.

7.

8.

9. For exercises 6–8, write the decimal that names the shaded and unshaded sections of each.

Copy and complete the chart below.

	Word Form	Decimal Notation	Fraction Notation
10.	nine tenths	■	$\frac{9}{10}$
11.	■	1.0	$\frac{10}{10} = 1$
12.	one and one tenth	■	$1\frac{1}{10}$
13.	■	1.2	$1\frac{2}{10}$

Problem Solving

14. A piece of plywood is divided into four equal parts. Three fourths of the plywood is painted. What fraction of the plywood is not painted?

15. **Using Mental Math** Japanese theaters have a passageway called *hanamichi* for the actors to enter and exit. In a large Japanese theater, the hanamichi is 19.30 m long. In a small Japanese theater, the length of the hanamichi is 18.10 m. What is the difference in lengths of the two passageways?

▲ **Fine Arts Connection**
A Japanese theater

Review and Remember

Choose a Method Use paper and pencil or a calculator to find each answer. Tell which method you chose and why.

16. $5.44 \div 8$ 17. 22.01×31 18. $100.8 - 56$ 19. $8.24 \div 8$ 20. $29.5 + 693$

For Extra Practice, see Set C, page 366.

That's the Ticket!

You can understand fractions by comparing them to $\frac{1}{2}$ and 1.

Learning About It

Kate and Joshua share 46 tickets so that each has an equal share to sell. Exploring fair shares will help you understand how to find equal shares of 46 tickets.

What You Need

For each pair:
counters
fraction pieces

Step 1 Work with your partner. Share six counters so that you each have the same number.

- How many counters did you each get? What fraction of the 6 counters is this?

> What is $\frac{1}{2}$ of 6?

- Explain why $\frac{3}{6} = \frac{1}{2}$.

Step 2 Share the counters so that one person gets 1 counter and the other person gets 5 counters. Do you each have an equal share?

- Compare $\frac{1}{6}$ to $\frac{1}{2}$. > Is $\frac{1}{6}$ less than or greater than $\frac{1}{2}$?

- Compare $\frac{5}{6}$ to $\frac{1}{2}$. > Is $\frac{5}{6}$ less than or greater than $\frac{1}{2}$?

Step 3 Copy the chart at the right. Continue it for $\frac{4}{6}$, $\frac{5}{6}$, and $\frac{6}{6}$.

Step 4 Make a new chart, using eighths.

Step 5 Use your charts. Compare the numerators of the fractions less than $\frac{1}{2}$ with their denominators. Do the same for the fractions greater than $\frac{1}{2}$. Describe any relationships you see.

Fraction of Whole	Use >, <, or = to compare to $\frac{1}{2}$.
$\frac{0}{6}$	$\frac{0}{6} < \frac{1}{2}$
$\frac{1}{6}$	$\frac{1}{6} < \frac{1}{2}$
$\frac{2}{6}$	$\frac{2}{6} < \frac{1}{2}$
$\frac{3}{6}$	$\frac{3}{6} = \frac{1}{2}$

Step 6 Make a chart like the one shown below. Use what you know about equal shares to place each fraction from the Fraction List in the correct column.

Column 1 $< \frac{1}{2}$	Column 2 $= \frac{1}{2}$	Column 3 $> \frac{1}{2}$

Fraction List

$\frac{1}{5}$ $\frac{2}{3}$ $\frac{4}{5}$ $\frac{2}{8}$ $\frac{4}{6}$

$\frac{3}{7}$ $\frac{1}{8}$ $\frac{7}{8}$ $\frac{4}{8}$ $\frac{3}{6}$

$\frac{5}{10}$ $\frac{2}{4}$ $\frac{6}{12}$ $\frac{2}{5}$ $\frac{3}{4}$

Step 7 Use the chart in Step 6. Place fraction pieces that show two fractions from Column 2 side by side. Compare the result to one whole. Is it less than, equal to, or greater than 1? Repeat with other fractions from Column 2. Describe what you discover.

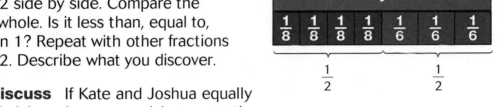

Think and Discuss If Kate and Joshua equally share their 46 tickets, how many tickets must they each sell? Why?

Practice

Compare. Write >, <, or = for each ⬤. Use fraction pieces if you wish.

1. $\frac{3}{4}$ ⬤ $\frac{1}{2}$ **2.** $\frac{5}{6}$ ⬤ $\frac{1}{2}$ **3.** $\frac{1}{3}$ ⬤ $\frac{1}{2}$ **4.** $\frac{1}{2}$ ⬤ $\frac{5}{10}$

5. $\frac{1}{2}$ ⬤ $\frac{3}{7}$ **6.** $\frac{2}{8}$ ⬤ $\frac{1}{2}$ **7.** $\frac{2}{9}$ ⬤ $\frac{1}{2}$ **8.** $\frac{1}{2}$ ⬤ $\frac{7}{14}$

9. $\frac{1}{2}$ ⬤ $\frac{5}{9}$ **10.** $\frac{3}{6}$ ⬤ $\frac{1}{2}$ **11.** $\frac{5}{12}$ ⬤ $\frac{1}{2}$ **12.** $\frac{3}{8}$ ⬤ $\frac{1}{2}$

Use your chart from Step 6 for Problems 13–14.

13. If you combine two fraction pieces showing fractions from Column 1 in Step 6, how will the result compare to one whole? Is your answer reasonable? Explain.

14. What If? Suppose you were to repeat Problem 13 using two fractions from Column 3. How would the result differ from the result achieved in Problem 13?

15. Create Your Own Using different fractions, make a fraction list similar to the one shown above. Challenge a classmate to use fraction pieces to complete a chart like the one shown at the top of the page.

INTERNET ACTIVITY
www.sbgmath.com

Take Your Seats

Knowing that a fraction such as $\frac{8}{8}$ is equal to 1 can help you understand fractions greater than 1.

Learning About It

On each side of the auditorium there are eight seats in a row. When 11 fifth graders were being seated to watch the dress rehearsal, they needed more than one row. How can a fraction represent the rows they needed?

$$\frac{11}{8} = \frac{8}{8} + \frac{3}{8} = 1\frac{3}{8}$$

A **mixed number** is a number written as a whole number and a fraction. → $1\frac{3}{8}$

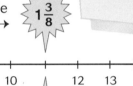

Word Bank

mixed number
improper fraction

Number line from 0 to past 1:
$\frac{1}{8}$ $\frac{2}{8}$ $\frac{3}{8}$ $\frac{4}{8}$ $\frac{5}{8}$ $\frac{6}{8}$ $\frac{7}{8}$ $\frac{8}{8}$ $\frac{9}{8}$ $\frac{10}{8}$ $\frac{12}{8}$ $\frac{13}{8}$

$\frac{11}{8}$

An **improper fraction** is a fraction in which → the numerator is greater than or equal to the denominator.

Write $\frac{13}{5}$ as a mixed number.

Since $\frac{13}{5}$ means $13 \div 5$, use division to change an improper fraction to a mixed number.

$$\frac{13}{5} \rightarrow 5\overline{)13} \atop \underline{-10} \atop 3 \begin{matrix}2\end{matrix} \rightarrow 5\overline{)13} \atop \underline{-10} \atop 3 \begin{matrix}2\frac{3}{5}\end{matrix}$$ ← Write the remainder as a fraction.

Write $2\frac{3}{5}$ as an improper fraction.

- Multiply the denominator by the whole number and add the numerator.

- Write the sum over the denominator.

$$10 + 3 = 13$$

$$2\frac{3}{5} \rightarrow 2\frac{3}{5} \rightarrow 2\frac{3}{5} \rightarrow \frac{13}{5}$$

$$5 \times 2 = 10$$

Think and Discuss Describe the relationship between the numerator and denominator when a fraction is less than 1, equal to 1, and greater than 1.

Try It Out

Write each mixed number as an improper fraction. Write each improper fraction as a mixed number.

1. $\frac{7}{3}$ **2.** $\frac{5}{2}$ **3.** $3\frac{2}{3}$ **4.** $6\frac{3}{8}$ **5.** $\frac{15}{14}$ **6.** $\frac{23}{5}$

Practice

Write each mixed number as an improper fraction. Write each improper fraction as a mixed number.

7. $1\frac{1}{2}$ **8.** $1\frac{2}{3}$ **9.** $2\frac{3}{8}$ **10.** $2\frac{1}{4}$ **11.** $3\frac{1}{3}$ **12.** $6\frac{2}{7}$

13. $\frac{12}{10}$ **14.** $\frac{25}{8}$ **15.** $\frac{74}{9}$ **16.** $\frac{48}{5}$ **17.** $\frac{29}{2}$ **18.** $\frac{13}{10}$

Compare. Write >, <, or = for each ⬤. Write each fraction greater than 1 as a mixed number.

19. $\frac{3}{8}$ ⬤ 1   **20.** $\frac{4}{4}$ ⬤ 1   **21.** $\frac{7}{2}$ ⬤ 1   **22.** $\frac{8}{6}$ ⬤ 1   **23.** $\frac{13}{5}$ ⬤ 1

24. $\frac{1}{8}$ ⬤ 1   **25.** $\frac{8}{1}$ ⬤ 1   **26.** $\frac{9}{9}$ ⬤ 1   **27.** $\frac{2}{5}$ ⬤ 1   **28.** $\frac{25}{25}$ ⬤ 1

Problem Solving

29. There are 27 fourth graders, and eight seats in each row. What mixed number represents the rows needed for fourth graders?

30. In 1865 there was one upper box and one lower box on each side of Ford's Theater. Each box held four people. In a week's time, how many people sat in a box seat if both performances each day were sold out?

Review and Remember

Using Algebra Find each *n*.

31. $8 \times 72 = n$ **32.** $434 \times 26 = n$

33. $371 \div 7 = n$ **34.** $234 - n = 188$

35. $n + 58 = 79$ **36.** $504 \div 8 = n$

▲ **Social Studies Connection**
As a tribute to Abraham Lincoln, productions at Ford's Theater feature Americans who have made significant contributions to our nation.

INTERNET ACTIVITY
www.sbgmath.com

✔ Checkpoint

Number Theory

Tell if each number is prime or composite. (pages 334–335)

1. 16   **2.** 37   **3.** 25   **4.** 99   **5.** 41

Write the factors for the numbers in each pair. Then find the GCF. (pages 336–337)

6. 12, 10   **7.** 7, 14   **8.** 21, 51   **9.** 16, 25   **10.** 36, 18

Write the first six multiples of each number. Then find the LCM for each pair of numbers. (pages 338–339)

11. 4, 6   **12.** 10, 5   **13.** 6, 8   **14.** 6, 9   **15.** 10, 12

Write the fraction that names each shaded part.
(pages 342–343)

16.    **17.**   **18.**

19.   **20.**   **21.**

> ### What do you think?
>
> Can a factor of a number be greater than the number itself? Can a multiple be less than the number itself? Explain.

22. For Exercises 18–21, write the decimals that name the shaded and unshaded parts.

Compare. Write >, <, or = for each ⬤. (pages 344–345)

23. $\frac{1}{2}$ ⬤ $\frac{5}{8}$ **24.** $\frac{3}{16}$ ⬤ $\frac{1}{2}$ **25.** $\frac{5}{10}$ ⬤ $\frac{1}{2}$ **26.** $\frac{12}{15}$ ⬤ $\frac{1}{2}$ **27.** $\frac{12}{10}$ ⬤ 1

Write each mixed number as an improper fraction and each improper fraction as a mixed number. (pages 346–347)

28. $3\frac{1}{2}$ **29.** $\frac{34}{8}$ **30.** $4\frac{6}{7}$ **31.** $7\frac{2}{3}$ **32.** $\frac{57}{8}$

33. $5\frac{4}{7}$ **34.** $\frac{24}{5}$ **35.** $\frac{30}{9}$ **36.** $5\frac{2}{5}$ **37.** $4\frac{3}{8}$

Problem Solving

38. Twenty-four chairs will be set up for the school orchestra. How many different ways can the chairs be arranged? Tell what strategy you used to solve the problem.

39. Some Japanese theaters are circular. The stages have center sections that revolve. These circular theaters have diameters of 20 m and 12.72 m. What is the difference in diameter size of the two circular theaters?

40. Using Estimation Twenty-nine yards of fabric and nine spools of thread are needed for costumes. The fabric is $2.15 per yard. The thread comes in packs of five spools at $1.75 each. About how much money is needed to make the purchases?

Journal Idea

When comparing fractions, why is it helpful to think about $\frac{1}{2}$?

Critical Thinking Corner

Number Sense

Missing Digits

Using Algebra Find each missing digit.

1.
```
       ■1 R■
  6)12■
  − 12
    0■
  −  6
     2
```

2.
```
      1■9
   × ■34
     67■
   5■70
  33 800
  ■■,54■
```

3.
```
      ■98
    × ■5
    14■■
   20 860
   2■,3■■
```

4.
```
      ■4■ R■
  8)2,■61
  − 24
    3■
  − 32
   ■■
  − ■■
    ■
```

5.
```
      ■■3 R■
  7)935
  − ■
    ■■
  − 21
    ■5
  − ■■
    ■
```

6.
```
      1■1
   × ■■2
     222
    ■■30
   2■200
   ■■,■■■
```

Ads Wanted

Now that you have worked with fractions greater than 1, you can build patterns of equivalent fractions and mixed numbers.

Learning About It

Buying a part of a page of a playbill is a great way to advertise a business. The price for a $\frac{1}{4}$-page ad is the same as the price for a $\frac{2}{8}$-page ad. Does a business have more space with the $\frac{1}{4}$- or $\frac{2}{8}$-page ad?

Try folding paper to find out. Work with your partner.

Word Bank

equivalent fractions

A playbill is a booklet for a performance. It has information about the members of the cast, a listing of the scenes, and pages of advertisements. ▼

Step 1 Fold a piece of paper in half and then fold in half again to form fourths.

Step 2 Color $\frac{1}{4}$ of the paper.

Step 3 Now fold your paper again on the same folds as before. Then fold it in half again. You now have eighths. Notice that $\frac{2}{8}$ of the page is shaded. Does a business have more space with the $\frac{1}{4}$-page or $\frac{2}{8}$-page ad? Tell how you know.

The fractions $\frac{1}{4}$ and $\frac{2}{8}$ are called **equivalent fractions**. Equivalent fractions name equal parts of a region or a set.

Step 4 Use your folded paper or the playbill at the right to name other equivalent fractions.

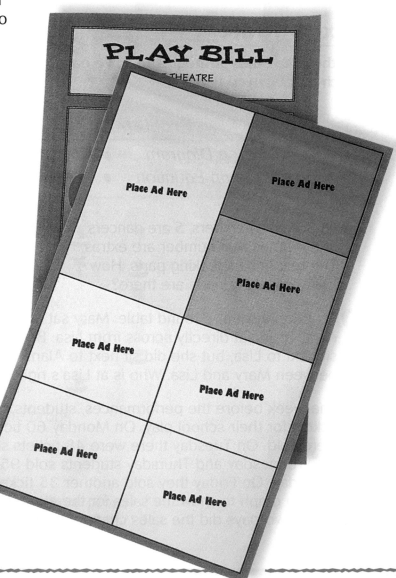

PLAY BILL
THEATRE

Place Ad Here
Place Ad Here
Place Ad Here
Place Ad Here
Place Ad Here
Place Ad Here
Place Ad Here

Find an equivalent fraction to see how many eighths are in $\frac{3}{4}$.

• **One way** is to use fraction pieces.

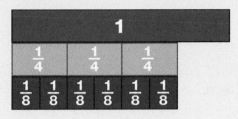

• **Another way** is to use paper and pencil.

$\frac{3}{4} = \frac{\blacksquare}{8}$

Multiply the numerator and denominator by the same number.

$\frac{3 \times \boxed{2}}{4 \times \boxed{2}} = \frac{6}{8}$

What factor, when multiplied by 4, will equal 8?

There are six eighths in $\frac{3}{4}$, so $\frac{3}{4}$ and $\frac{6}{8}$ are equivalent.

Connecting Ideas

You have used fraction pieces and multiplication to find an equivalent fraction. You can also use division.

Billboard ads can be put up in sections. One ad can have 24 sections. How many thirds of a billboard are covered if $\frac{16}{24}$ is finished? Find an equivalent fraction.

• **One way** is to draw a diagram.

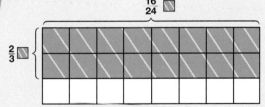

• **Another way** is to use paper and pencil.

$\frac{16}{24} = \frac{\blacksquare}{3}$

Divide the numerator and the denominator by the same number.

$\frac{16 \div \boxed{8}}{24 \div \boxed{8}} = \frac{2}{3}$

By what would you divide 24 to get 3?

There are two thirds in $\frac{16}{24}$, so $\frac{16}{24}$ and $\frac{2}{3}$ are equivalent.

More Examples

A. $\frac{3}{4} = \frac{\blacksquare}{12}$ Think: 4 times what number equals 12?

$\frac{3 \times \boxed{3}}{4 \times \boxed{3}} = \frac{9}{12}$, so $\frac{3}{4} = \frac{9}{12}$

B. $\frac{10}{15} = \frac{\blacksquare}{3}$ Think: 15 divided by what number is 3?

$\frac{10 \div \boxed{5}}{15 \div \boxed{5}} = \frac{2}{3}$, so $\frac{10}{15} = \frac{2}{3}$

Think and Discuss Look back at Example B. How might you use multiplication to find the equivalent fraction?

Try It Out

Using Algebra **Choose a Method** Use a model or paper and pencil to find each equivalent fraction.

1. $\frac{1}{2} = \frac{\blacksquare}{8}$

2. $\frac{1}{2} = \frac{\blacksquare}{6}$

3. $\frac{6}{10} = \frac{\blacksquare}{5}$

4. $\frac{\blacksquare}{4} = \frac{3}{12}$

5. $\frac{1}{3} = \frac{3}{\blacksquare}$

6. $\frac{2}{13} = \frac{\blacksquare}{26}$

7. $\frac{4}{7} = \frac{32}{\blacksquare}$

8. $\frac{7}{10} = \frac{70}{\blacksquare}$

9. $\frac{1}{12} = \frac{4}{\blacksquare}$

10. $\frac{11}{12} = \frac{\blacksquare}{60}$

Write the next three fractions in each pattern.

11. $\frac{1}{3}, \frac{2}{6}, \frac{3}{9}, \frac{4}{12}, \cdots$

12. $\frac{2}{5}, \frac{4}{10}, \frac{6}{15}, \frac{8}{20}, \cdots$

13. $\frac{1}{2}, \frac{2}{4}, \frac{4}{8}, \frac{8}{16}, \cdots$

14. Look back at Exercise 11. Write a rule to find any fraction in the pattern. Use your rule to find the 11th fraction.

Practice

Using Algebra Replace each ■ with a number that will make the fractions equivalent.

15. $\frac{5}{6} = \frac{\blacksquare}{18}$

16. $\frac{4}{24} = \frac{1}{\blacksquare}$

17. $\frac{6}{10} = \frac{3}{\blacksquare}$

18. $\frac{5}{8} = \frac{\blacksquare}{24}$

19. $\frac{5}{6} = \frac{10}{\blacksquare}$

20. $\frac{8}{18} = \frac{\blacksquare}{9}$

21. $\frac{1}{8} = \frac{3}{\blacksquare}$

22. $\frac{10}{12} = \frac{\blacksquare}{6}$

23. $\frac{11}{12} = \frac{\blacksquare}{48}$

24. $\frac{2}{9} = \frac{\blacksquare}{72}$

25. $\frac{2}{3} = \frac{\blacksquare}{21}$

26. $\frac{21}{56} = \frac{3}{\blacksquare}$

27. $\frac{1}{12} = \frac{\blacksquare}{60}$

28. $\frac{9}{27} = \frac{1}{\blacksquare}$

29. $\frac{5}{7} = \frac{40}{\blacksquare}$

30. $\frac{7}{8} = \frac{\blacksquare}{32}$

31. $\frac{3}{7} = \frac{21}{\blacksquare}$

32. $\frac{17}{51} = \frac{1}{\blacksquare}$

33. $\frac{54}{60} = \frac{9}{\blacksquare}$

34. $\frac{36}{72} = \frac{1}{\blacksquare}$

Write the next three fractions in each pattern.

35. $\frac{2}{3}, \frac{4}{6}, \frac{8}{12}, \frac{16}{24}, \cdots$

36. $\frac{10}{25}, \frac{20}{50}, \frac{30}{75}, \frac{40}{100}, \cdots$

37. $\frac{1}{6}, \frac{2}{12}, \frac{3}{18}, \frac{4}{24}, \cdots$

38. $\frac{3}{8}, \frac{6}{16}, \frac{9}{24}, \frac{12}{32}, \cdots$

39. $\frac{5}{100}, \frac{10}{200}, \frac{15}{300}, \frac{20}{400}, \cdots$

40. $\frac{64}{256}, \frac{32}{128}, \frac{16}{64}, \frac{8}{32}, \cdots$

41. Look back at Exercise 37. Write a rule to find any fraction in the pattern. Use your rule to find the 10th fraction.

Problem Solving

42. You Decide Advertisements for playbill pages are sold in eighths, sixths, fourths, halves, and whole pages. Your company wants its name on five different pages, but they can only pay for a total of $1\frac{1}{2}$ pages. What advertisement sizes would you order?

43. Analyze A billboard can be put up in 24 sections. If $\frac{3}{4}$ of the billboard is complete, how many sections still need to be added?

44. Create Your Own Write a problem about a billboard that has 24 sections. Then tell how you would solve it.

Review and Remember

Find each answer.

45. 38,023 + 9,129   **46.** 574 × 79   **47.** 8,120 ÷ 20

48. 196,422 + 18,367   **49.** 767,280 − 39,104   **50.** 6,016 ÷ 4

 Money $ense

Pay a Fraction of the Price!

Bargain prices are available on tickets to the play. The full price for a ticket is $1.00. (Special offers cannot be combined.)

- If you buy more than 5 tickets, the additional tickets are $0.75.

- If you buy 10 or more tickets, you can have 3 of the tickets for half the full price.

What is the least that you will spend for 12 tickets?

Opening Night!

For Extra Practice, see Set E, page 367.

Simply Makeup

*You learned in the last lesson that there are
many ways to name a fraction. One name is special.*

Learning About It

$$\frac{1}{2} = \frac{2}{4} = \frac{3}{6} = \frac{4}{8} = \frac{5}{10}$$

Word Bank

simplest form
lowest terms

All these fractions are equivalent to $\frac{1}{2}$. But only the
fraction $\frac{1}{2}$ is in **simplest form** or **lowest terms**. Follow
the steps to write $\frac{12}{18}$ in simplest form.

Step 1 Find the greatest common factor
(GCF) of the numerator and denominator.

Factors of 12: 1, 2, 3, 4, **6**, 12
Factors of 18: 1, 2, 3, **6**, 9, 18
GCF: **6**

Step 2 Divide both the numerator and
the denominator by the GCF.

$$\frac{12 \div \cancel{6}}{18 \div \cancel{6}} = \frac{2}{3}$$

A fraction is in simplest form when the GCF
of the numerator and the denominator is 1.

$\frac{2}{3}$ is the simplest form of $\frac{12}{18}$.

Think and Discuss Both the numerator and denominator
of the fraction $\frac{6}{24}$ are even, so Jim divides each by 2. Why
is the fraction not yet in simplest form? What should Jim do
now to find the simplest form?

Try It Out

Using Mental Math Write each fraction in simplest form.
Write *yes* if the fraction is already in simplest form.

1. $\frac{8}{20}$ **2.** $\frac{3}{63}$ **3.** $\frac{4}{7}$ **4.** $\frac{8}{19}$ **5.** $\frac{50}{90}$ **6.** $\frac{5}{11}$

7. $\frac{9}{12}$ **8.** $\frac{4}{8}$ **9.** $\frac{3}{14}$ **10.** $\frac{8}{18}$ **11.** $\frac{100}{101}$ **12.** $\frac{350}{700}$

Practice

Write the missing number to complete each fraction so that it is in simplest form.

13. $\frac{6}{12} = \frac{1}{\blacksquare}$ **14.** $\frac{4}{10} = \frac{\blacksquare}{5}$ **15.** $\frac{6}{24} = \frac{\blacksquare}{4}$ **16.** $\frac{9}{21} = \frac{3}{\blacksquare}$ **17.** $\frac{10}{55} = \frac{\blacksquare}{11}$

18. $\frac{50}{100} = \frac{1}{\blacksquare}$ **19.** $\frac{7}{56} = \frac{\blacksquare}{8}$ **20.** $\frac{75}{100} = \frac{3}{\blacksquare}$ **21.** $\frac{30}{90} = \frac{1}{\blacksquare}$ **22.** $\frac{35}{42} = \frac{\blacksquare}{6}$

Write each fraction in simplest form. Write *yes* if the fraction is already in simplest form.

23. $\frac{3}{9}$ **24.** $\frac{4}{5}$ **25.** $\frac{2}{3}$ **26.** $\frac{15}{25}$ **27.** $\frac{12}{36}$ **28.** $\frac{18}{20}$

29. $\frac{1}{7}$ **30.** $\frac{4}{12}$ **31.** $\frac{100}{100}$ **32.** $\frac{16}{24}$ **33.** $\frac{30}{50}$ **34.** $\frac{11}{13}$

Analyze Read each statement. Write *true* or *false*. Try different fractions to test each statement.

35. When the numerator is 1, the fraction is in simplest form.

36. When the numerator is not one, the fraction is not in simplest form.

37. When the denominator is a multiple of the numerator, the fraction is not in simplest form.

38. When the numerator and denominator are both prime, the fraction is in simplest form.

Problem Solving

39. For Scene II, all 18 performers need to wear makeup. If 6 already had their makeup done for Scene I, what fraction of the performers still need to be made up? Write the answer in simplest form.

40. **Using Estimation** Fifty dollars has been budgeted for makeup. When the artists were shopping, they needed items that cost $12.50, $22.75, and $14.00. Was enough money budgeted?

▲ **Fine Arts Connection** Since the earliest days in Hollywood, people have been amazed to see how makeup can change the way an actor looks.

Review and Remember

Find each answer.

41. 3,975 ÷ 75   **42.** 7,872 × 64   **43.** 732 − 98   **44.** 848 + 652

A Top-Notch Fit

Understanding equivalent fractions can help you decide which method to use to compare fractions.

Learning About It

Every production needs costumes, and every costume needs a hat! For the finale, the dancers are being measured for top hats. Would a hat size of $6\frac{3}{4}$ be greater than or less than a $6\frac{5}{8}$ hat size?

You can compare fractions and mixed numbers by finding the **least common denominator (LCD)** and using equivalent fractions.

Compare $6\frac{3}{4}$ and $6\frac{5}{8}$. Since the whole numbers are the same, compare the fractions.

Word Bank

least common denominator (LCD)

Head Size	Hat Size
About 20 inches	$6\frac{1}{2}$ to $6\frac{5}{8}$
About 21 inches	$6\frac{3}{4}$ to $6\frac{7}{8}$
About 22 inches	7 to $7\frac{1}{8}$

Step 1 Find the LCD of the fractions. The LCD is the least common multiple (LCM).

$\frac{3}{4}$ Multiples of 4: 4, 8, 12, 16

$\frac{5}{8}$ Multiples of 8: 8, 16, 24

The LCD is 8.

Step 2 Write an equivalent fraction for each fraction, using the LCD as the new denominator.

$\frac{3}{4} = \frac{3 \times 2}{4 \times 2} = \frac{6}{8}$

$\frac{5}{8} = \frac{5}{8}$

Step 3 Compare the numerators of the new fractions.

Since $6 > 5$, $\frac{6}{8} > \frac{5}{8}$.

Think back to the original form of the fractions.

$\frac{3}{4} > \frac{5}{8}$

So $6\frac{3}{4} > 6\frac{5}{8}$.

A hat size of $6\frac{3}{4}$ is greater than a hat size of $6\frac{5}{8}$.

Comparing Fractions

Ways to Compare	Example	It works because . . .
If the denominators are the same, compare the numerators.	$\frac{3}{4} > \frac{1}{4}$	The denominators are the same, so the fraction with more parts is greater.
If the numerators are the same, compare the denominators.	$\frac{1}{6} < \frac{1}{4}$	The greater the denominator, the smaller the piece. Think: The more people you share with, the smaller the share.
Relate the fractions to $\frac{1}{2}$. Think: Is the denominator 2 times the numerator?	$\frac{1}{3} < \frac{3}{4}$	All fractions less than $\frac{1}{2}$ are less than all fractions greater than $\frac{1}{2}$.
Relate the fractions to 1.	$\frac{3}{4} < \frac{4}{3}$	All fractions less than 1 are less than all fractions greater than 1.

Connecting Ideas

When ordering a set of fractions, first find a common denominator.

In what order should the hats be placed on the shelf, if they are ordered according to size from least to greatest?

Hat size $6\frac{5}{8}$ Hat size $6\frac{3}{4}$ Hat size $6\frac{1}{2}$

Step 1 Find the LCD of the fractions. Remember that the LCD is the LCM.

$\frac{1}{2} = \frac{\blacksquare}{8}$

$\frac{3}{4} = \frac{\blacksquare}{8}$ The LCM of 2, 4, and 8 is 8. So the LCD is 8.

$\frac{5}{8} = \frac{\blacksquare}{8}$

Step 2 Write equivalent fractions, using the LCD.

$\frac{1}{2} = \frac{4}{8}$

$\frac{3}{4} = \frac{6}{8}$

$\frac{5}{8} = \frac{5}{8}$

Step 3 Compare the numerators of the new fractions. Put them in order from least to greatest.

Since $4 < 5 < 6$,

$\frac{4}{8} < \frac{5}{8} < \frac{6}{8}$.

Think back to the original form of the fractions.

$\frac{1}{2} < \frac{5}{8} < \frac{3}{4}$

So $6\frac{1}{2} < 6\frac{5}{8} < 6\frac{3}{4}$.

The hats should be placed on the shelf in this order: $6\frac{1}{2}, 6\frac{5}{8}, 6\frac{3}{4}$.

Think and Discuss Without finding the LCD, how do you know that $6\frac{5}{8}$ and $6\frac{3}{4}$ are both greater than $6\frac{1}{2}$?

Try It Out

Compare. Write >, <, or = for each ⬤.

1. $\frac{1}{4}$ ⬤ $\frac{1}{2}$

2. $\frac{1}{3}$ ⬤ $\frac{1}{6}$

3. $\frac{1}{5}$ ⬤ $\frac{1}{9}$

4. $2\frac{3}{4}$ ⬤ $2\frac{5}{8}$

5. $\frac{2}{5}$ ⬤ $\frac{4}{5}$

6. $\frac{2}{4}$ ⬤ $\frac{3}{6}$

7. $\frac{10}{3}$ ⬤ $\frac{7}{9}$

8. $1\frac{11}{12}$ ⬤ $1\frac{14}{13}$

Order the following from least to greatest.

9. $\frac{9}{11}$, $\frac{2}{11}$, $\frac{7}{11}$

10. $\frac{1}{3}$, $\frac{1}{2}$, $\frac{2}{3}$

11. $\frac{5}{6}$, $\frac{2}{3}$, $\frac{1}{4}$

12. $1\frac{2}{3}$, $1\frac{3}{5}$, $2\frac{1}{8}$

13. $\frac{1}{8}$, $\frac{1}{2}$, $\frac{1}{4}$

14. $\frac{2}{5}$, $\frac{3}{4}$, $\frac{3}{10}$

15. $\frac{2}{3}$, $\frac{7}{8}$, $\frac{9}{12}$

16. $2\frac{5}{6}$, $2\frac{7}{8}$, $2\frac{3}{4}$

Practice

Compare. Write >, <, or = for each ⬤.

17. $\frac{2}{3}$ ⬤ $\frac{3}{7}$

18. $\frac{3}{8}$ ⬤ $\frac{3}{4}$

19. $\frac{7}{7}$ ⬤ $\frac{13}{13}$

20. $\frac{16}{15}$ ⬤ $\frac{17}{20}$

21. $\frac{1}{3}$ ⬤ $\frac{2}{5}$

22. $\frac{2}{5}$ ⬤ $\frac{1}{10}$

23. $\frac{6}{6}$ ⬤ $\frac{8}{8}$

24. $\frac{4}{7}$ ⬤ $\frac{3}{5}$

25. $\frac{3}{4}$ ⬤ $\frac{6}{8}$

26. $\frac{20}{12}$ ⬤ $\frac{3}{4}$

27. $\frac{40}{100}$ ⬤ $\frac{4}{100}$

28. $3\frac{2}{3}$ ⬤ $3\frac{1}{4}$

29. $6\frac{5}{12}$ ⬤ $6\frac{3}{4}$

30. $4\frac{1}{2}$ ⬤ $3\frac{7}{14}$

31. $5\frac{1}{5}$ ⬤ $5\frac{1}{7}$

32. $3\frac{3}{15}$ ⬤ $3\frac{1}{5}$

Order the following from least to greatest.

33. $\frac{2}{3}$, $\frac{1}{5}$, $\frac{6}{4}$, $\frac{3}{4}$

34. $\frac{4}{9}$, $\frac{4}{5}$, $\frac{1}{2}$, $\frac{5}{12}$

35. $2\frac{5}{6}$, $2\frac{1}{2}$, 3 , $2\frac{7}{8}$

36. 1.2 , 0.3 , $\frac{1}{2}$, $1\frac{1}{4}$

37. $8\frac{4}{5}$, $8\frac{1}{2}$, $8\frac{3}{4}$, $8\frac{7}{10}$

38. 0.3 , 0.9 , $\frac{2}{3}$, $\frac{1}{5}$

Analyze Decide if each statement is *always true*, *sometimes true*, or *never true*.

39. The fraction with the greater denominator is greater.

40. The fraction with the greater numerator is greater.

41. Fractions whose numerators and denominators are equal are greater than one.

42. Improper fractions are greater than proper fractions.

Problem Solving

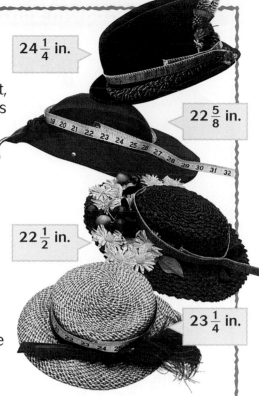

24 $\frac{1}{4}$ in.

22 $\frac{5}{8}$ in.

22 $\frac{1}{2}$ in.

23 $\frac{1}{4}$ in.

43. Using Estimation To decorate the hats at the right, Bob needs to buy enough ribbon. If he buys 3 yards of ribbon, will he have enough? Explain.

44. Barbara and Sara cut pieces of colored string to make braided bracelets. They measured them all in inches: $14\frac{1}{2}$, $13\frac{3}{4}$, $14\frac{3}{8}$, $13\frac{1}{4}$, $14\frac{9}{16}$, $13\frac{1}{2}$. They decided to order them from greatest to least so they could make the largest bracelet first. What should the order be?

45. Using Algebra The photographer arranged the dancers. She put 1 person in the first row, 2 in the second row, 3 in the third, and so on. There were 8 rows in all. How many dancers were there?

46. Journal Idea Explain how you would determine whether $\frac{15}{51}$ and $\frac{4}{12}$ are equivalent fractions.

▲ **Language Arts Connection**
A person who makes and sells men's hats is called a hatter. A person who makes and sells women's hats is called a milliner.

Review and Remember

Using Algebra Find the missing angle measurement for each triangle.

47. 90°, 50°   **48.** 40°, 45°   **49.** 100°, 35°   **50.** 120°, 20°   **51.** 15°, 55°

52. 19°, 78°   **53.** 116°, 26°   **54.** 32°, 59°   **55.** 66°, 76°   **56.** 123°, 19°

Time for Technology

Using the MathProcessor™ CD-ROM

Using Fraction Strips

Use fraction strips to compare mixed numbers like $7\frac{1}{2}$ and $7\frac{3}{8}$. Since the whole numbers are equal, compare the fractions.

- Open two fraction strips 🔲. Link each to a number space 🔲.

- Show $\frac{1}{2}$ in one strip and $\frac{3}{8}$ in the other.

- Compare the mixed numbers in a writing space.

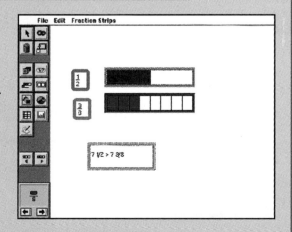

Problem Solving
Finding Fraction Patterns

*Sometimes you can solve a problem
by finding a pattern.*

$\mathcal{S}$et builders are making steps for the last scene in a play. The first step will be $\frac{1}{2}$ the width of the stage. The second step will be $\frac{1}{3}$ the width of the stage. The third step will be $\frac{1}{4}$ the width of the stage and so on. What fraction of the width of the stage will the ninth step be?

 ### UNDERSTAND

What do you need to find?

You need to find what fraction of the width of the stage the ninth step will be.

 ### PLAN

How can you solve the problem?

You can **look for a pattern** of how the fractions change with each step. Then you can continue the pattern for six more steps.

 ### SOLVE

Look for a pattern.

$\frac{1}{2}, \frac{1}{3}, \frac{1}{4} \cdots$

The numerators stay the same.

Continue the pattern.

$\cdots \frac{1}{5}, \frac{1}{6}, \frac{1}{7}, \frac{1}{8}, \frac{1}{9}, \frac{1}{10}$

The denominators increase by 1.

The ninth step will be $\frac{1}{10}$ the width of the stage.

 ### LOOK BACK

Check your work to be sure you have the correct number of steps.

Show What You Learned

Using Algebra Look for a pattern to solve these problems.

1 The set crew is hanging six banners across the stage. The first banner is $\frac{1}{2}$ the stage height. The second banner is $\frac{1}{4}$ the stage height. The third is $\frac{1}{8}$ the stage height, and so on. If this pattern continues, what fraction of the stage height is the sixth banner?

 2 **Predict** Use a calculator to write decimal equivalents for these fractions: $\frac{1}{9}$, $\frac{2}{9}$, $\frac{3}{9}$, and $\frac{4}{9}$.

a. What pattern do you notice?

b. Use the pattern to predict the next four decimal equivalents. Use a calculator to check.

c. Will the pattern continue for the decimal equivalent of $\frac{9}{9}$? Use a calculator to check.

3 Amy bought blocks that stack on top of each other. The first block is 80 cm wide; the second, 40 cm wide; the third, 20 cm wide; the fourth, 10 cm wide. What are the widths of the next two blocks? Describe how the widths are related.

4 The lighting crew will use a dial to dim the lights, making the stage grow darker. To dim the lights, a crew member turns the dial a fraction of a whole turn in this pattern: $\frac{1}{12}$, $\frac{1}{10}$, $\frac{1}{8}$, $\frac{1}{6}$. What is the next fraction in the pattern?

5 A set is being designed so that an actor appears to increase in height. As scenes change, the height of the room decreases from 16 ft to 15 ft to 13 ft and then to 10 ft. What is the next height in the pattern?

6 Tear a sheet of paper in half. Place the 2 pieces on top of each other, and tear them in half again. This gives you 4 pieces. How many pieces of paper would you have after 6 tears?

7 Find the next number in the pattern.

a. $\frac{2}{3}$, $\frac{4}{6}$, $\frac{8}{12}$, $\frac{16}{24}$ ...

b. $\frac{16}{32}$, $\frac{14}{28}$, $\frac{12}{24}$, $\frac{10}{20}$ ...

8 **Create Your Own** Write a problem involving a pattern. Give it to another student to solve.

Problem Solving
★★★★★ Preparing for Tests

Practice What You Learned

Choose the correct letter for each answer.

1 Cheryl's company shipped $\frac{5}{8}$ ton of lumber on Saturday and $\frac{3}{4}$ ton on Tuesday. Which number sentence could she use to compare the amounts shipped on the two days?

A. $\frac{5}{8} - \frac{3}{4} = n$

B. $\frac{3}{4} - \frac{5}{8} = n$

C. $\frac{5}{8} \times \frac{3}{4} = n$

D. $1 - (\frac{5}{8} \times \frac{3}{4}) = n$

Tip

To choose between choices A and B, you will first need to decide which is greater, $\frac{5}{8}$ or $\frac{3}{4}$.

---

2 Erik estimated that $\frac{3}{4}$ of the students in his school think they have too much homework. He took a survey and found that $\frac{1}{4}$ of the 240 students disagreed with this opinion. The rest agreed. How many students agreed with his opinion?

A. 100
B. 150
C. 180
D. 200

Tip

Use Logical Reasoning for this problem. Since $\frac{1}{4}$ of the 240 students *disagreed* with Erik's opinion, then $\frac{3}{4}$ of the students must have *agreed* with it.

---

3 The Parks Department plans to plant a tree every 0.3 mile along certain sections of highway. Each tree will take about 15 minutes to plant. How many trees will they plant along one side of a section that is 2.4 miles long if they plant a tree at each end?

A. 8
B. 9
C. 72
D. 80

Tip

The strategy, *Make a Diagram*, can be used to solve this problem.

4 Jake drew squares as part of a pattern for a rug design. The sides of the first four squares, in inches, were $2\frac{1}{4}$, $2\frac{7}{8}$, $3\frac{1}{2}$, and $4\frac{1}{8}$. If Jake continues this pattern, what will be the lengths of the sides for the next three squares?

A. $4\frac{1}{2}$ in., $5\frac{1}{8}$ in., $5\frac{1}{2}$ in.

B. $4\frac{5}{8}$ in., 5 in., $5\frac{3}{8}$ in.

C. $4\frac{3}{4}$ in., $5\frac{3}{8}$ in., 6 in.

D. $4\frac{7}{8}$ in., $5\frac{1}{2}$ in., $5\frac{7}{8}$ in.

5 Paul needs 27 in. of silver braid for a hat band. Which length of braid should Paul buy if he does not want any braid left over?

A. $\frac{7}{8}$ yd   **C.** $\frac{2}{3}$ yd

B. $\frac{3}{4}$ yd   **D.** $\frac{1}{2}$ yd

6 In a three-week period, a pet supply store had weekly sales totals of $7,950; $4,062; and $6,875. Which is the best estimate of the total sales for the period?

A. Less than $16,000
B. Between $16,000 and $17,000
C. Between $17,000 and $19,000
D. More than $19,000

7 What is the area of the shaded triangle in square units?

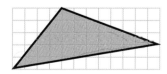

A. 20 sq units   **D.** 36 sq units
B. 26 sq units   **E.** Not Here
C. 30 sq units

8 Marge's mother was 26 years old when Marge was born. Marge's father is 4 years younger than her mother. The sum of their ages now is 80. How old is Marge's mother?

A. 34 yr   **D.** 46 yr
B. 38 yr   **E.** Not Here
C. 42 yr

9 In a survey, students at the Jefferson School were asked whether they wanted to go to the zoo or the science museum for their field trip. The graph shows the results of the survey.

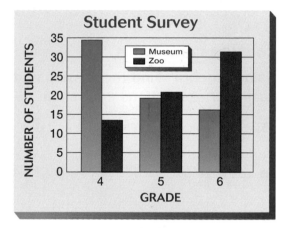

Which are the best estimates of the results of the survey?

A. Museum, 60; Zoo, 70
B. Museum, 75; Zoo, 75
C. Museum, 70; Zoo, 65
D. Museum, 75; Zoo, 60

10 José is older than Kara but younger than Luis. Carlos is younger than Amy but older than Luis. Which of these is a reasonable conclusion?

A. José is the oldest.
B. Amy is the oldest.
C. Luis is the youngest.
D. Carlos is the youngest.
E. Kara is older than Luis.

✓ Checkpoint

Fractions in Different Forms

Vocabulary

Match each word with its definition.

1. A fraction in which the numerator is greater than or equal to the denominator.

2. A number that is a factor of two or more given numbers.

3. Fractions that name the same number.

4. A number written as a whole number and a fraction.

Word Bank

common factor
equivalent fractions
improper fractions
mixed number

Concepts and Skills

Using Algebra Find the missing number that will make each pair of fractions equivalent. (pages 352–355)

5. $\frac{3}{4} = \frac{\blacksquare}{12}$

6. $\frac{5}{25} = \frac{1}{\blacksquare}$

7. $\frac{2}{5} = \frac{\blacksquare}{15}$

8. $\frac{\blacksquare}{6} = \frac{9}{18}$

9. $\frac{14}{49} = \frac{2}{\blacksquare}$

10. $\frac{3}{4} = \frac{\blacksquare}{100}$

11. $\frac{10}{12} = \frac{\blacksquare}{6}$

12. $\frac{24}{64} = \frac{\blacksquare}{8}$

Write each fraction in simplest form. (pages 356–357)

13. $\frac{8}{10}$

14. $\frac{15}{18}$

15. $\frac{7}{14}$

16. $\frac{18}{36}$

Compare. Write >, <, or = for each ●. (pages 358–361)

17. $\frac{2}{3}$ ● $\frac{8}{13}$

18. $\frac{4}{14}$ ● $\frac{2}{7}$

19. $\frac{8}{9}$ ● $\frac{15}{16}$

20. $\frac{4}{3}$ ● $\frac{5}{4}$

21. $\frac{4}{15}$ ● $\frac{8}{30}$

22. $\frac{9}{8}$ ● $\frac{17}{26}$

23. $\frac{8}{18}$ ● $\frac{4}{9}$

24. $\frac{20}{12}$ ● $\frac{3}{5}$

Mixed Practice

Using Algebra Find each missing number.

25. $\frac{3}{8} = \frac{\blacksquare}{72}$

26. $\frac{6}{24} = \frac{1}{\blacksquare}$

27. $\frac{2}{3} = \frac{\blacksquare}{60}$

28. $\frac{5}{100} = \frac{\blacksquare}{20}$

29. $\frac{8}{5} = 1\frac{\blacksquare}{5}$

30. $\frac{27}{4} = 6\frac{\blacksquare}{4}$

31. $\frac{59}{7} = 8\frac{\blacksquare}{7}$

32. $\frac{41}{9} = 4\frac{\blacksquare}{9}$

Problem Solving

33. Five twelfths of the performers in Scene I are ready to go on stage. Is this more or less than one half of the performers? Explain.

34. A group of fifth graders measured their hand spans with a ruler and then put the measurements in order from greatest to least. How did they list these measurements: $5\frac{3}{4}$ in., $6\frac{1}{2}$ in., $5\frac{1}{2}$ in., $6\frac{3}{8}$ in., $5\frac{1}{8}$ in., and $6\frac{3}{4}$ in.?

35. Does an advertisement that is $\frac{6}{8}$ of a page take up more or less of the page than an advertisement that is $\frac{3}{4}$ of the same page? Why?

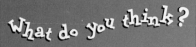
What do you think?

Are there more than 10 fractions equivalent to $\frac{1}{2}$? Explain why or why not.

Journal Idea

Sometimes it is helpful to use equivalent fractions to compare fractions with unlike denominators. Give an example of two fractions that you would need to change before you could compare them.

You Decide

Activity

Schoolyard Fun

Here's a chance for you and four partners to design a schoolyard.

First, draw the outline of your ideal schoolyard on grid paper. Next decide on the fractional parts each of the following areas will have: basketball court, picnic tables, and any others you would like. Label each area.

Describe your schoolyard by telling what fractional part of the yard each area makes up.

You might wish to include this work in your portfolio.

Extra Practice

Set A (pages 336–337)

Write the factors for the numbers in each set. Then find the GCF.

1. 7, 21　　**2.** 6, 9　　**3.** 5, 8　　**4.** 9, 21　　**5.** 18, 24　　**6.** 2, 5, 6

7. There are 16 jazz dancers and 24 tap dancers on the stage at once. Equal groups will be formed, but jazz and tap dancers will not be combined. What is the largest size group into which both kinds of dancers can be divided? Explain your answer.

Set B (pages 338–339)

Write the first six multiples for the numbers in each pair. Then find the LCM.

1. 6, 12　　**2.** 3, 4　　**3.** 2, 5　　**4.** 9, 12　　**5.** 5, 15　　**6.** 10, 12

7. **Using Mental Math** It takes 3 yards of fabric to make two costumes. How many costumes can be made from 12 yards? from 24 yards?

8. **Analyze** One student can sew three costumes for the school play in 5 hours. How many costumes can eight students sew if they all work for 15 hours?

Set C (pages 342–343)

Write the fractions and decimals that name the shaded portion and the portion not shaded.

1. 　　**2.** 　　**3.** 　　**4.**

Copy and complete the chart.

5.	Decimal Notation	0.3	■	0.13	0.8	■	■
6.	Fraction Notation	■	$\frac{9}{10}$	■	■	$\frac{69}{100}$	$\frac{20}{100}$ or $\frac{5}{25}$

Extra Practice

Set D (pages 346–347)

Compare. Write >, <, or = for each ⬤ .

1. $\frac{2}{3}$ ⬤ 1

2. $\frac{8}{6}$ ⬤ 1

3. $\frac{5}{5}$ ⬤ 1

4. $\frac{3}{7}$ ⬤ 1

5. $\frac{1}{4}$ ⬤ 1

6. $\frac{1}{2}$ ⬤ 1

7. $\frac{1}{2}$ ⬤ $\frac{2}{2}$

8. $\frac{6}{8}$ ⬤ $\frac{8}{6}$

Write each mixed number as an improper fraction. Write each improper fraction as a mixed number.

9. $2\frac{1}{3}$

10. $8\frac{2}{7}$

11. $5\frac{8}{9}$

12. $5\frac{1}{2}$

13. $9\frac{2}{5}$

14. $6\frac{3}{4}$

15. $\frac{11}{8}$

16. $\frac{17}{5}$

17. $\frac{10}{9}$

18. $\frac{9}{2}$

19. $\frac{25}{13}$

20. $\frac{19}{9}$

21. **Analyze** Martin and Sheila want to represent the total amount shaded below. Martin wants to write it as $\frac{9}{7}$, but Sheila wants to write it as $1\frac{2}{7}$. Explain each person's reasoning and tell who is correct.

Set E (pages 352–355)

Using Algebra Replace each ▰ with a number that will make the fractions equivalent.

1. $\frac{2}{3} = \frac{▰}{6}$

2. $\frac{1}{4} = \frac{▰}{16}$

3. $\frac{5}{8} = \frac{▰}{40}$

4. $\frac{7}{14} = \frac{▰}{2}$

5. $\frac{15}{25} = \frac{▰}{5}$

6. $\frac{10}{100} = \frac{▰}{50}$

7. $\frac{9}{36} = \frac{▰}{12}$

8. $\frac{16}{36} = \frac{▰}{9}$

9. $\frac{1}{2} = \frac{▰}{70}$

10. $\frac{4}{5} = \frac{▰}{25}$

11. Each page of the playbill for the school play can hold eight ads. If $\frac{3}{4}$ of one page is full, what is the greatest number of ads that can still fit on the page?

12. Jenny's school day is divided into 6 classes. If Jenny has completed 4 classes, is she more than or less than halfway through the day? Use a drawing to explain your answer.

Extra Practice

Using Mental Math Tell whether each fraction is in simplest form. Write *yes* or *no*. If *yes*, explain your reasoning. If *no*, simplify the fraction.

1. $\frac{3}{5}$
2. $\frac{9}{18}$
3. $\frac{6}{8}$
4. $\frac{9}{12}$
5. $\frac{7}{11}$
6. $\frac{8}{15}$

7. $\frac{1}{2}$
8. $\frac{4}{20}$
9. $\frac{7}{9}$
10. $\frac{5}{25}$
11. $\frac{16}{36}$
12. $\frac{21}{42}$

Write each fraction in simplest form.

13. $\frac{12}{15}$
14. $\frac{10}{18}$
15. $\frac{10}{25}$
16. $\frac{8}{28}$
17. $\frac{14}{42}$
18. $\frac{16}{64}$

19. $\frac{12}{24}$
20. $\frac{8}{12}$
21. $\frac{3}{18}$
22. $\frac{7}{21}$
23. $\frac{18}{4}$
24. $\frac{25}{5}$

25. On Friday nights, one fifth of the audience at the local theater is students who are 12 years old. If 25 people are in the audience, how many are 12 years old? Draw a diagram to show your answer.

26. **Explain** Tell how you know whether a fraction is in simplest form. Use an example in your explanation.

Compare. Write >, <, or = for each ⬤.

1. $\frac{1}{3}$ ⬤ $\frac{3}{7}$
2. $\frac{3}{6}$ ⬤ $\frac{1}{2}$
3. $\frac{5}{6}$ ⬤ $\frac{7}{18}$
4. $\frac{3}{10}$ ⬤ $\frac{2}{5}$
5. $\frac{10}{90}$ ⬤ $\frac{2}{9}$

6. $\frac{8}{5}$ ⬤ $\frac{9}{10}$
7. $\frac{9}{18}$ ⬤ $\frac{5}{10}$
8. $2\frac{7}{9}$ ⬤ $2\frac{2}{3}$
9. $\frac{18}{3}$ ⬤ $\frac{36}{6}$
10. $3\frac{1}{4}$ ⬤ $3\frac{1}{5}$

11. Students cut ribbon to decorate hats. The pieces are $7\frac{1}{2}$ in., $7\frac{1}{8}$ in., $6\frac{1}{2}$ in., $6\frac{7}{8}$ in., 7 in., $7\frac{3}{8}$ in., and $6\frac{5}{8}$ in. Students placed the pieces in order from shortest to longest. In what order were they placed?

Chapter Test

Use grid paper for Exercise 1.

1. Use drawings to show how you know if a number is prime or composite. Then explain your drawing.

Find the GCF and the LCM for each pair of numbers.

2. 9, 15   **3.** 10, 25

Write a fraction and a decimal for each shaded part.

4.   **5.**

Compare. Write >, <, or = for each ●.

6. $\frac{2}{3}$ ● $\frac{1}{4}$ **7.** $\frac{4}{5}$ ● $\frac{7}{8}$ **8.** $1\frac{1}{3}$ ● $1\frac{2}{6}$

Write each mixed number as an improper fraction.

9. $2\frac{1}{3}$ **10.** $4\frac{5}{7}$

11. $1\frac{7}{8}$ **12.** $9\frac{2}{5}$

Write each improper fraction as a mixed number.

13. $\frac{21}{6}$ **14.** $\frac{19}{3}$

15. $\frac{33}{2}$ **16.** $\frac{74}{8}$

Replace each ■ with a number that will make the fractions equivalent.

17. $\frac{2}{3} = \frac{■}{6}$ **18.** $\frac{1}{5} = \frac{■}{15}$

19. $\frac{5}{9} = \frac{20}{■}$ **20.** $\frac{12}{5} = \frac{24}{■}$

Write each fraction in simplest form. Write *yes* if the fraction is already in simplest form.

21. $\frac{4}{12}$ **22.** $\frac{15}{25}$ **23.** $\frac{8}{15}$

Solve.

24. Mrs. Tamar's fifth-grade class spends $\frac{3}{8}$ of math time going over homework and $\frac{1}{2}$ of the time using fraction pieces. Is there any time left for classwork? Explain.

25. During the months before the school play, the cast uses the stage every third day, the scenery crew uses the stage every sixth day, and the costume crew uses the stage every eighth day. On which day will the cast and the scenery crew both be on the stage? the cast and the costume crew? all three?

 Self-Check

Look back at Exercises 21–23. Did you check to be sure your answers are in simplest form?

Performance Assessment

Show What You Know About Fraction Concepts

1 Use the pictures to answer the questions below.

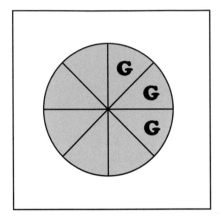 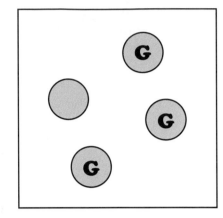

a. Write a fraction showing the number of spaces containing a G for each picture.

b. Which fraction is greater? Explain how you know.

c. Create Your Own Write a problem using one whole number and one fraction. Tell how you would solve it.

Self-Check Did you remember to compare fractions and decide which fraction is greater?

2 Use the table. What fraction of the band is made up of the instruments shown in the categories listed in a, b, and c below? Write an equivalent fraction for each. Using fraction pieces may be helpful.

a. trumpets

b. flutes and trumpets

c. clarinets, trumpets, and cymbals

Self-Check Did you remember to find an equivalent fraction for each answer?

School Band	
Instrument	**Number of Players**
Clarinet	12
Drum	2
Trumpet	14
Cymbal	2
Flute	4
Trombone	2

For Your Portfolio

You might wish to include this work in your portfolio.

Extension

Exploring Prime Factorization and Factor Trees

▶ Every whole number greater than one can be expressed as a product of prime numbers. This is called a **prime factorization**.

$15 = 3 \times 5$ — These numbers are prime, so 3 and 5 are the prime factors of 15.

▶ If a number only has a few factors, it is easy to find its prime factorization. The primes are usually written from least to greatest.

$4 = 2 \times 2$ $6 = 2 \times 3$ $10 = 2 \times 5$

▶ If a number has many factors, it can be difficult to find its prime factorization. A factor tree can help you. At the right is a factor tree for the prime factorization of 18.

When all the branches end in prime numbers, you can write the prime factorization.

$18 = 2 \times 3 \times 3 = 2 \times 3^2$

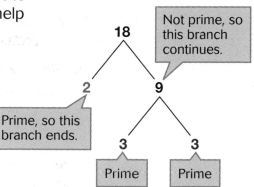

18 — Not prime, so this branch continues.

2 — Prime, so this branch ends.   9

3 — Prime   3 — Prime

exponent↘
base → 3^2 means 3×3

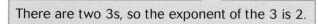

There are two 3s, so the exponent of the 3 is 2.

Another Example

$1{,}125 = 3 \times 3 \times 5 \times 5 \times 5 = 3^2 \times 5^3$

Use factor trees to find the prime factorization of each number. Use exponents to write the prime factorization.

1. 45   **2.** 24   **3.** 17   **4.** 81   **5.** 16

6. 35   **7.** 88   **8.** 21   **9.** 72   **10.** 48

11. Explain how 3×4 and 3^4 are different.

12. What is 10^1? 10^2? 10^3? 10^4? Compare your answers to the exponents. Describe any pattern you see.

Using Math in Science

*Use **counting** and **multiplication** to **estimate** from a sample the number of pine trees in a forest.*

Seeing the Forest and the Trees

Suppose you are a forest ranger who has been asked to estimate how many pine trees are growing in a 10,000 m² area of the forest. How could you estimate this number without counting every tree?

What You Need

For each pair:
calculator (optional)

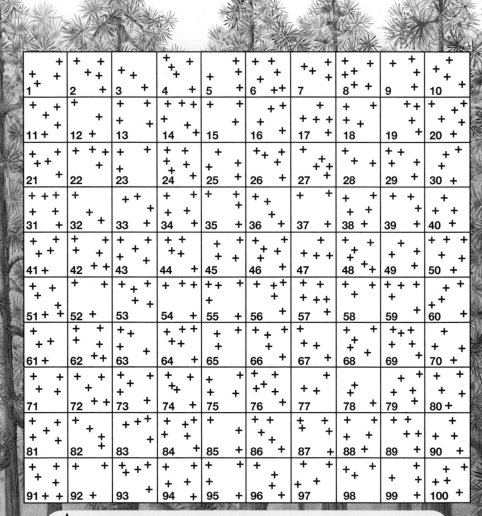

▲ This grid represents a forest with an area of 10,000 m². Each square represents an area of 100 m². Each + represents a tree.

Explore

Step 1 Make a chart like the one shown below. Provide ten lines for recording your data.

Numbered Squares Chosen	Trees Counted

Total Trees Counted: _____
Average: _____
Estimated Tree Population for Forest: _____

Step 2 Randomly pick 10 numbered squares from the grid on page 372. In the first column of the chart, record the numbers of the squares you select.

Step 3 Count the number of trees in each of the squares you selected. Record this information in the second column of your chart and then find the total.

Step 4 Find the average number of trees in the 10 squares by dividing the total by 10. Record this average.

Step 5 Multiply the average number of trees in one square by the total number of squares (100). Record this number as your estimated tree population.

Analyze

1. Why should you find the average number of trees in ten sections before finding the total estimated tree population?

2. Compare your results with those of other students. What might have caused any differences?

For Your Portfolio

Write about what you discovered. Explain how you can use a sample to estimate the total number of objects. Describe how the size of the sample affects data.

Explore Further!

Predict How might changing the sample size (number of squares counted) affect the estimates for the entire forest? Find out by repeating the activity using 5 squares, 15 squares, and 20 squares.

Cumulative Review

★★★★★★ **Preparing for Tests**

Choose the correct letter for each answer.

Number Concepts	Probability and Statistics

1. Which of these numbers is 350 when rounded to the nearest ten and 300 when rounded to the nearest hundred?

   A. 341   **C.** 347
   B. 344   **D.** 353

2. Which set of numbers is in order from *greatest* to *least*?

   A. 0.788 0.087 0.898 0.888
   B. 0.898 0.888 0.087 0.788
   C. 0.087 0.788 0.888 0.898
   D. 0.898 0.888 0.788 0.087

3. Yesterday, Frank wrote 4 pages of his 10-page report. What fraction of his report did he complete?

   A. $\frac{4}{5}$ **C.** $\frac{2}{3}$
   B. $\frac{3}{4}$ **D.** $\frac{2}{5}$

4. Which number sentence represents the models shown?

   A. $\frac{3}{5} = \frac{5}{7}$
   B. $\frac{2}{5} < \frac{2}{7}$
   C. $\frac{5}{7} > \frac{3}{5}$
   D. $\frac{2}{5} = \frac{2}{7}$

5. Will's 6 bowling scores were 93, 105, 115, 120, 105, and 98. What was his mean (average) score?

   A. 100   **C.** 106
   B. 105   **D.** 117

6. There are 4 green marbles, 6 blue marbles, 3 white marbles, and 5 red marbles in a bag. If you choose 1 marble without looking, what is the probability that it will be either a green or a blue marble?

   A. $\frac{1}{10}$ **C.** $\frac{4}{9}$
   B. $\frac{2}{5}$ **D.** $\frac{5}{9}$

7. If you spin the spinner 100 times, on which 2 colors is the spinner *least* likely to stop?

   A. Green or yellow
   B. Red or blue
   C. Yellow or red
   D. Blue or green

8. Marsha, Ruth, and Ellen are sisters. In how many different ways can they stand in a row for a family picture?

   A. 3
   B. 6
   C. 12
   D. 18

Patterns, Relationships, and Algebraic Thinking	Measurement

9. Which expression is equivalent to $7 \times (8 - 6)$?

A. $(7 \times 8) - (7 \times 6)$
B. $15 - 13$
C. $(7 + 8) - (7 + 6)$
D. $56 - 6$

10. One magazine costs $1.50. Two cost $3.00. Three cost $4.50. At this rate, how much would a dozen magazines cost?

A. $9.00
B. $11.50
C. $16.50
D. $18.00
E. $21.50

11. Which letter best represents $4\frac{3}{8}$ on the number line?

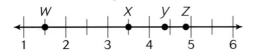

A. W
B. X
C. Y
D. Z

12. Dean practiced the guitar for 11 minutes Wednesday, 13 minutes Thursday, 16 minutes Friday, and 20 minutes Saturday. If he continues with this pattern but does not practice on Sunday, how many minutes will he practice on Tuesday?

A. 22 min
B. 25 min
C. 31 min
D. 33 min

13. Melissa is 5 feet 2 inches tall. Her sister is 5 feet $4\frac{1}{2}$ inches tall. Her mother is 5 feet 7 inches tall. How much shorter is Melissa than her mother?

A. $2\frac{1}{2}$ in.
B. 3 in.
C. 5 in.
D. 1 foot 5 in.

14. The circumference of a circle is about 3.14 times its diameter. The radius of the bottom of a soda can is about 1 inch. What is the approximate *circumference* of the bottom of the can?

A. 1.57 in.
B. 3.14 in.
C. 4.71 in.
D. 6.28 in.

15. The *perimeter* of a rectangular playing field is 290 yards. If the length of the field is 120 yards, how many *feet* wide is the field? [1 yard = 3 feet]

A. 50 ft
B. 65 ft
C. 75 ft
D. 150 ft
E. 175 ft

16. What is the *volume* of this carton?

A. 8 cm³
B. 16 cm³
C. 28 cm³
D. 32 cm³
E. 64 cm³

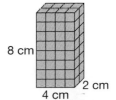

8 cm
2 cm
4 cm

Chapter 10

Working With Fractions

Chapter Theme: FOOD

·······Real Facts··········

The young chefs in the photograph on the right are using math as they make cupcakes. They measure the amount they need of each ingredient, using both whole units and fractions. Here is the recipe they are using.

Bonnie Butter Cupcakes (makes 24 cupcakes)	
$\frac{2}{3}$ cup butter	$1\frac{1}{2}$ teaspoons vanilla
$1\frac{3}{4}$ cups sugar	$2\frac{1}{2}$ teaspoons baking powder
$2\frac{3}{4}$ cups flour	1 teaspoon salt
1 to 2 eggs	$1\frac{1}{4}$ cups milk

- If the chefs wanted to make 48 cupcakes (twice the recipe), how much butter would they need?

- If they wanted to make 12 cupcakes ($\frac{1}{2}$ the recipe), how much salt would they need?

- Suppose the chefs made a batch of cupcakes large enough to require $5\frac{1}{4}$ cups of sugar. How many cupcakes would they make?

·······Real People··········

Meet David Liu. As a pastry chef he makes and decorates cakes, pies, and other desserts at a New York restaurant. His dazzling creations are both beautiful and delicious! Like the young chefs in the picture, Mr. Liu's interest in baking started when he was a child.

Pick Your Pizza!

A model can help you understand how to add fractions.

Learning About It

Less than 50 years ago, most Americans had never heard of pizza. Today nearly everyone has heard of pizza. Pizzas can be ordered with just a cheese topping or they can be ordered with many choices of extra toppings. What part of this pizza has extra toppings?

To find out, add $\frac{2}{8} + \frac{4}{8}$.

THERE'S ALWAYS A WAY!

● **One way** is to use a model.

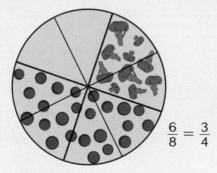

$\frac{6}{8} = \frac{3}{4}$

● **Another way** is to use paper and pencil.

$$\begin{array}{r} \frac{2}{8} \\ + \frac{4}{8} \\ \hline \frac{6}{8} \end{array}$$

Add the numerators, 2 and 4. Use the common denominator, 8. Simplify, if possible.

$\frac{6}{8} = \frac{6 \div 2}{8 \div 2} = \frac{3}{4}$

Three fourths of the pizza has extra toppings.

More Examples

A.

$$\begin{array}{r} \frac{5}{10} \\ + \frac{3}{10} \\ \hline \frac{8}{10} \end{array} = \frac{8 \div 2}{10 \div 2} = \frac{4}{5}$$

B.

$$\begin{array}{r} \frac{4}{9} \\ + \frac{5}{9} \\ \hline \frac{9}{9} \end{array} = 1$$

C. $\frac{3}{12} + \frac{4}{12} = \frac{7}{12}$

Connecting Ideas

Adding mixed numbers is just like adding fractions with an extra step—you have to add the whole numbers as well as the fractions.

The Smith family ate $1\frac{2}{3}$ pizzas and the Khadder family ate $2\frac{2}{3}$ pizzas. How much pizza was eaten altogether?

To find out, add $1\frac{2}{3} + 2\frac{2}{3}$.

One way to add mixed numbers is to draw a diagram.

$= 3\frac{4}{3} = 4\frac{1}{3}$

Another way is to use paper and pencil.

Step 1 Add the fractions.	**Step 2** Add the whole numbers.	**Step 3** Simplify the sum, if possible.
$\begin{array}{r} 1\frac{2}{3} \\ + 2\frac{2}{3} \\ \hline \frac{4}{3} \end{array}$	$\begin{array}{r} 1\frac{2}{3} \\ + 2\frac{2}{3} \\ \hline 3\frac{4}{3} \end{array}$	$\begin{array}{r} 1\frac{2}{3} \\ + 2\frac{2}{3} \\ \hline 3\frac{4}{3} = 3 + 1\frac{1}{3} = 4\frac{1}{3} \end{array}$

$4\frac{1}{3}$ pizzas were eaten.

More Examples

A. $4\frac{2}{5} + 3\frac{4}{5} = 7\frac{6}{5} = 7 + 1\frac{1}{5} = 8\frac{1}{5}$

$\frac{6}{5} = 1 + \frac{1}{5} = 1\frac{1}{5}$

B. $\begin{array}{r} 1\frac{5}{6} \\ + 1\frac{5}{6} \\ \hline 2\frac{10}{6} = 2 + 1\frac{4}{6} = 3\frac{4}{6} = 3\frac{2}{3} \end{array}$

Remember to write the answer in simplest form.

Think and Discuss Will the sum of $\frac{5}{8}$ and $\frac{4}{8}$ be greater than or less than 1? How do you know without finding the exact sum?

Try It Out

Add. Write each answer in simplest form.

1. $\frac{5}{8} + \frac{2}{8}$
2. $\frac{3}{5} + \frac{2}{5}$
3. $\frac{1}{6} + \frac{3}{6}$
4. $\frac{1}{4} + \frac{3}{4}$
5. $\frac{2}{3} + \frac{3}{3}$

6. $1\frac{4}{11}$
$+ 3\frac{5}{11}$

7. $6\frac{3}{8}$
$+ 1\frac{7}{8}$

8. $7\frac{2}{5}$
$+ 9\frac{4}{5}$

9. $6\frac{2}{3}$
$+ 8\frac{1}{3}$

10. $3\frac{5}{8}$
$+ 2\frac{7}{8}$

For each pizza write a number sentence that shows how much of the pizza has extra toppings.

11.

12.

13.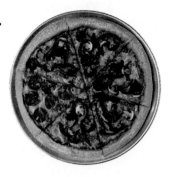

Practice

Add. Write each answer in simplest form.

14. $\frac{5}{7} + \frac{1}{7}$
15. $\frac{5}{9} + \frac{4}{9}$
16. $\frac{8}{15} + \frac{2}{15}$
17. $\frac{6}{13} + \frac{4}{13}$

18. $5\frac{4}{8} + 2\frac{3}{8}$
19. $\frac{5}{12} + \frac{11}{12}$
20. $1\frac{3}{4} + 1\frac{3}{4}$
21. $\frac{9}{10} + \frac{3}{10}$

22. $\frac{9}{10}$
$+ \frac{5}{10}$

23. $\frac{3}{8}$
$+ \frac{7}{8}$

24. $3\frac{2}{4}$
$+ 2\frac{3}{4}$

25. $7\frac{5}{6}$
$+ 5\frac{4}{6}$

26. $4\frac{2}{4}$
$+ 5\frac{3}{4}$

27. $\frac{5}{5}$
$+ \frac{3}{5}$

28. $\frac{6}{7}$
$+ \frac{1}{7}$

29. $2\frac{1}{2}$
$+ 1\frac{1}{2}$

30. $7\frac{3}{4}$
$+ 4\frac{3}{4}$

31. $\frac{5}{16}$
$+ \frac{10}{16}$

Create Your Own For Exercises 32–34, draw each pizza described with two different toppings. Write a number sentence that shows what part of each has extra toppings.

32. a pizza with 6 equal pieces

33. a pizza with 8 equal pieces

34. a pizza with 12 equal pieces

Social Studies Connection
Today, many different styles of
pizza are enjoyed all over the world.
These students attend one of the
many culinary schools established
in the United States to learn the art
of cooking. ➤

Problem Solving

35. Steve delivers pizzas. He traveled
$1\frac{1}{10}$ miles to the first stop. His next
stop was $1\frac{5}{10}$ miles from his first
stop. If it was 3 miles back to the
pizza parlor, how far did he travel to
make these two deliveries?

36. Nina ordered a pizza that had eight
equal slices. Four slices were
topped with sausage and two other
slices were topped with vegetables.
What part of the pie was plain
cheese?

37. Explain A waiter took an order for
a pizza with $\frac{5}{8}$ of the pizza topped
with mushrooms and $\frac{5}{8}$ of it topped
with onions. What's wrong with the
pizza order?

38. What If? Suppose you order two
pizzas, each with eight slices. One
is $\frac{5}{8}$ mushrooms, and the other is $\frac{5}{8}$
peppers. How many slices are
plain?

39. Journal Idea Draw a circle and
divide it into 8 equal parts. Then try
to divide another circle into 9 equal
parts. Explain which drawing was
easier and why.

40. Analyze Suppose you ordered $\frac{3}{8}$ of
a pizza with extra cheese $\frac{3}{8}$ with
sausage, $\frac{4}{8}$ with vegetables, and $\frac{6}{8}$
plain. How many whole pies would
you get?

Review and Remember

Choose a Method Use paper and pencil or a calculator to
find each answer. Tell why you chose the method you did.

41.   36.8
      + 24.7

42.   4,825
      − 1,999

43.   16,549
      ×   6.7

44.   2.15
      × 0.06

45.   427
      × 5.9

46.   98.67
      − 19.68

47.   98,657
      + 65,197

48.   166.5
      − 77.68

49. 75$)\overline{26,850}$

50. 34$)\overline{39,304}$

51. 325 + 1,678 + 4,597 + 965

That's Some Cookie!

Knowing how to add fractions and mixed numbers can help you subtract fractions and mixed numbers.

Learning About It

Five sixths of a giant oatmeal-raisin cookie was left over from dinner on Monday. After school on Tuesday, you decided to eat two of the five pieces. What part of the cookie is left now?

To find out, subtract $\frac{5}{6} - \frac{2}{6}$.

THERE'S ALWAYS A WAY!

● **One way** is to use a model.

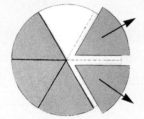

● **Another way** is to use paper and pencil.

Step 1 Subtract the numerators. Use the common denominator.

$$\begin{array}{r} \frac{5}{6} \\ -\frac{2}{6} \\ \hline \frac{3}{6} \end{array}$$

Think: 5 − 2 = 3. The denominator, 6, is the same.

Step 2 Simplify, if possible.

$$\begin{array}{r} \frac{5}{6} \\ -\frac{2}{6} \\ \hline \frac{3}{6} = \frac{3 \div 3}{6 \div 3} = \frac{1}{2} \end{array}$$

There is $\frac{1}{2}$ of the giant cookie left.

More Examples

A. $\frac{7}{8} - \frac{2}{8} = \frac{7-2}{8} = \frac{5}{8}$

B. $\frac{7}{12} - \frac{3}{12} = \frac{4}{12}$

$\frac{4}{12} = \frac{4 \div 4}{12 \div 4} = \frac{1}{3}$

Connecting Ideas

Subtracting mixed numbers is just like subtracting fractions, except that you have to subtract the whole numbers as well as the fractions.

A baker measures $4\frac{1}{8}$ pounds of flour to bake two kinds of muffins. If he uses $1\frac{5}{8}$ pounds for apple muffins, how much is left for blueberry muffins?

To find out, subtract $4\frac{1}{8} - 1\frac{5}{8}$.

THERE'S ALWAYS A WAY!

● **One way** is to draw a diagram.

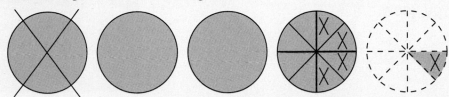

$$4\frac{1}{8} - 1\frac{5}{8} = 2\frac{4}{8} = 2\frac{1}{2}$$

Think: Take away 1 whole and 5 eighths.

● **Another way** is to use paper and pencil.

Step 1 You need to rename before you subtract, since $\frac{1}{8} < \frac{5}{8}$.	**Step 2** Subtract the fractions and the whole numbers.	**Step 3** Simplify, if possible.

$$\begin{array}{l} 4\frac{1}{8} - \boxed{3\frac{8}{8} + \frac{1}{8}} \rightarrow -3\frac{9}{8} \\ -1\frac{5}{8} = \hspace{2.5cm} -1\frac{5}{8} \\ \hline \end{array}$$

$$\begin{array}{r} 3\frac{9}{8} \\ -1\frac{5}{8} \\ \hline 2\frac{4}{8} \end{array}$$

$$\begin{array}{r} 3\frac{9}{8} \\ -1\frac{5}{8} \\ \hline 2\frac{4}{8} = 2\frac{1}{2} \end{array}$$

There are $2\frac{1}{2}$ pounds of flour left for blueberry muffins.

More Examples

A.
$$\begin{array}{l} 9\frac{2}{5} = \boxed{8\frac{5}{5} + \frac{2}{5}} = 8\frac{7}{5} \\ -7\frac{3}{5} \hspace{2.5cm} -7\frac{3}{5} \\ \hline \hspace{3cm} 1\frac{4}{5} \end{array}$$

B.
$$\begin{array}{l} 3\frac{7}{12} = \boxed{2\frac{12}{12} + \frac{7}{12}} = 2\frac{19}{12} \\ -2\frac{11}{12} \hspace{2.5cm} -2\frac{11}{12} \\ \hline \hspace{3cm} \frac{8}{12} = \frac{2}{3} \end{array}$$

Think and Discuss How is renaming for subtraction with mixed numbers similar to regrouping for subtraction with whole numbers?

Try It Out

Subtract. Simplify each difference, if possible.

1. $\dfrac{7}{9}$
   $- \dfrac{2}{9}$

2. $\dfrac{11}{12}$
   $- \dfrac{5}{12}$

3. $4\dfrac{3}{8}$
   $- 1\dfrac{5}{8}$

4. $10\dfrac{1}{3}$
   $- 8\dfrac{2}{3}$

5. $6\dfrac{1}{4}$
   $- 2\dfrac{3}{4}$

6. **Explain** When Charlie's family sat down to eat, $\dfrac{7}{12}$ of a pan of muffins was on the table. When the family finished eating, only $\dfrac{1}{12}$ of the pan of muffins was left. What part of the original number of muffins did Charlie's family eat? Tell how you know.

Practice

Subtract. Write each answer in simplest form.

7. $\dfrac{5}{8} - \dfrac{5}{8}$

8. $\dfrac{3}{5} - \dfrac{2}{5}$

9. $\dfrac{9}{10} - \dfrac{6}{10}$

10. $\dfrac{6}{7} - \dfrac{1}{7}$

11. $\dfrac{8}{9} - \dfrac{2}{9}$

12. $\dfrac{7}{12} - \dfrac{3}{12}$

13. $\dfrac{7}{10} - \dfrac{7}{10}$

14. $\dfrac{5}{5} - \dfrac{3}{5}$

15. $\dfrac{8}{11} - \dfrac{3}{11}$

16. $\dfrac{13}{15} - \dfrac{8}{15}$

17. $7\dfrac{8}{9} - 4\dfrac{4}{9}$

18. $5\dfrac{3}{12} - 4\dfrac{2}{12}$

19. $8\dfrac{3}{11}$
    $- 5\dfrac{5}{11}$

20. $4\dfrac{3}{4}$
    $- 1\dfrac{1}{4}$

21. $6\dfrac{2}{5}$
    $- 1\dfrac{4}{5}$

22. $5\dfrac{2}{7}$
    $- 3\dfrac{6}{7}$

Write the correct letter for each answer.

23. $6\dfrac{4}{5} - 3\dfrac{3}{5}$
   a. $3\dfrac{2}{5}$ b. $2\dfrac{1}{5}$ c. $3\dfrac{1}{5}$ d. $2\dfrac{2}{5}$

24. $9\dfrac{2}{7} - 7\dfrac{5}{7}$
   a. $2\dfrac{3}{7}$ b. $1\dfrac{4}{7}$ c. $2\dfrac{7}{7}$ d. $16\dfrac{3}{7}$

25. $4\dfrac{3}{4} - 2\dfrac{1}{4}$
   a. $2\dfrac{1}{4}$ b. $6\dfrac{2}{4}$ c. $2\dfrac{1}{2}$ d. $1\dfrac{2}{4}$

26. $6\dfrac{3}{8} - 4\dfrac{5}{8}$
   a. $1\dfrac{3}{4}$ b. 2 c. $1\dfrac{2}{8}$ d. $2\dfrac{1}{4}$

Problem Solving

27. Explain It takes $2\frac{1}{4}$ c of sugar to bake one loaf of bread and $1\frac{3}{4}$ c to bake another loaf. Is 5 c enough to bake both loaves? Explain.

28. At noon the cash register at a bakery held $385.50. If sales that morning were $265.25, how much was in the register at the start of the day?

29. It took a baker $2\frac{2}{3}$ h to make 15 loaves of pumpkin bread. It took her $3\frac{1}{3}$ h to bake 20 loaves of cinnamon bread. How much longer did it take her to bake cinnamon bread than pumpkin bread?

30. Analyze Bill made a sweet potato pie. His wife ate one slice, his son ate two slices, and his daughter ate three slices. If $\frac{1}{4}$ of the pie is left, how many slices had the pie been cut into?

▲ Sweet potatoes are a vegetable used to make sweet potato pie.

Review and Remember

Using Algebra Find each *n*.

31. $789 + n = 1{,}443$

32. $n - 991 = 18$

33. $198 \times n = 17{,}226$

34. $1{,}782 \div 42 = n$

35. $n \div 23 = 30$

36. $751 \times 68 = n$

Time for Technology

Using the Calculator

Keying in Fractions

You can use a fraction calculator to add $3\frac{1}{8} + 2\frac{5}{8}$.

Press: (3) (Unit) (1) (/) (8) (+) (2) (Unit) (5) (/) (8) (=)

Display: (5 ∪ 6/8)   You can also simplify the answer.

Press: (Simp) (=)   Display: (5 ∪ 3/4)

Try these using a calculator. Remember to simplify.

1. $\frac{1}{6} + \frac{3}{6}$
2. $\frac{4}{9} + \frac{2}{9}$
3. $2\frac{3}{7} + 1\frac{4}{7}$
4. $3\frac{4}{5} + 2\frac{4}{5}$
5. $1\frac{2}{3} + 2\frac{2}{3}$

For Extra Practice, see Set B, page 416.

Developing Skills for Problem Solving

First read for understanding and then focus on deciding which information you need to solve a problem.

READ FOR UNDERSTANDING

A mother and her son are planning a picnic with friends. Their picnic basket will be packed with plastic glasses, plastic plates, a thermos of juice, $1\frac{1}{2}$ lb of apples, $\frac{1}{2}$ lb of raisins, and some sandwiches. The picnic area is $17\frac{1}{2}$ miles away, and they will drive about 35 mph to get there. In the past year their car has traveled 8,344 miles.

1 How many sandwiches will be packed?

2 How many miles away is the picnic area?

THINK AND DISCUSS

Too Much or Too Little Information
Sometimes you have too much information to solve a problem. At other times you have too little information. You must decide exactly what information you need to solve a problem.

Reread the paragraph at the top of the page. For Problems 3–5, tell whether there is too little or too much information.

3 What information do you need to find out if enough glasses, plates, and sandwiches will be packed?

4 What information do you need to calculate how long it will take to get to the park?

5 Patrice and Sarah are planning to leave their home at 11:00 A.M. At what time will they arrive for the picnic? Can you solve this problem? Explain.

Show What You learned

Answer each question. Give a reason for your choice.

Ken and Sandy plan to spend two hours at the park. Before leaving, Ken made a snack of $\frac{2}{3}$ pound of walnuts, $\frac{2}{3}$ pound of raisins, and $\frac{1}{3}$ pound of sunflower seeds. The walnuts, raisins, and seeds cost $5.76.

1 What information is needed to help find the weight of the snack?

  a. Ken and Sandy plan to spend two hours at the park.

  b. Ken bought $\frac{2}{3}$ pound of walnuts.

  c. The snack cost $5.76.

2 What information is *not* needed to find the weight of the snack?

  a. Ken bought $\frac{2}{3}$ pound of raisins.

  b. Ken bought $\frac{1}{3}$ pound of sunflower seeds.

  c. The snack cost $5.76.

3 Which of the following tells how to find the total weight of the snack?

  a. Multiply the weight of the walnuts by 2.

  b. Divide the total cost of the snack by the number of foods in the snack.

  c. Add the weights of the walnuts, raisins, and sunflower seeds.

4 Which number sentence can be used to find the total weight of the snack?

  a. $\frac{2}{3} + \frac{2}{3} + \frac{1}{3} = 1\frac{2}{3}$

  b. $5.76 \div 3 = 1.92$

  c. $\frac{2}{3} \div 2 = \frac{1}{3}$

For each problem decide if there is too much or too little information. Then solve the problem or tell what information is missing.

Ken is making pasta salad. The recipe calls for pasta, 4 stewed tomatoes, and 2 sliced carrots. Ken needs enough pasta salad for only two people, so he will make $\frac{1}{2}$ of the recipe.

5 How much pasta should Ken use to make the pasta salad?

6 **Explain** How many people does a whole recipe serve? If the problem can be solved, tell how you solved it.

Soup's On!

Using a number line can help you estimate with mixed numbers.

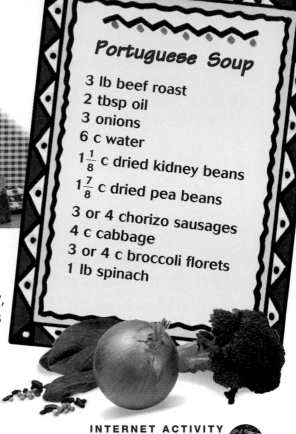

Portuguese Soup

3 lb beef roast
2 tbsp oil
3 onions
6 c water
$1\frac{1}{8}$ c dried kidney beans
$1\frac{7}{8}$ c dried pea beans
3 or 4 chorizo sausages
4 c cabbage
3 or 4 c broccoli florets
1 lb spinach

Learning About It

Lourdes wants to learn to cook Portuguese soup. Her grandmother said that chorizos—spicy, Spanish sausages—are the secret to making this soup. Chorizos can be bought at markets that have Spanish or Latin American foods.

About how many cups of beans are needed for Portuguese soup?

Estimate $1\frac{1}{8} + 1\frac{7}{8}$ by rounding each mixed number to the nearest whole number. Use the number line to help you.

INTERNET ACTIVITY
www.sbgmath.com

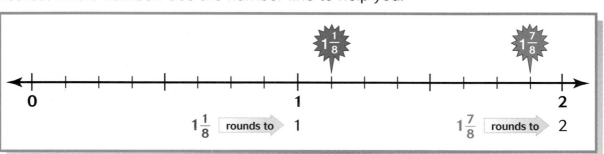

$1\frac{1}{8}$ rounds to 1 $1\frac{7}{8}$ rounds to 2

Since $1 + 2 = 3$, about 3 cups of beans are needed.

More Examples

A. $5\frac{11}{12} - 3\frac{5}{12}$ rounds to $6 - 3 = 3$ **B.** $4\frac{3}{7} + 5\frac{6}{7}$ rounds to $4 + 6 = 10$

Think and Discuss How does looking at a number line help you round fractions?

Try It Out

Estimate each sum or difference.

1. $2\frac{3}{4}$
$+ 5\frac{1}{4}$

2. $8\frac{3}{12}$
$+ 5\frac{11}{12}$

3. $2\frac{5}{6}$
$+ 5\frac{5}{6}$

4. $9\frac{7}{8}$
$- 2\frac{3}{8}$

5. $8\frac{5}{6}$
$- 2\frac{1}{6}$

Practice

Estimate each sum or difference.

6. $5\frac{3}{5}$
$- 2\frac{4}{5}$

7. $5\frac{3}{7}$
$+ 4\frac{5}{7}$

8. $8\frac{7}{12}$
$- 5\frac{5}{12}$

9. 5
$+ 3\frac{5}{6}$

10. 9
$- 1\frac{1}{5}$

11. $5\frac{3}{10} - 2$

12. $4\frac{6}{7} + 5\frac{4}{7}$

13. $5\frac{4}{5} + 9\frac{2}{5}$

14. $12\frac{3}{7} - 5\frac{6}{7}$

15. $7 - 3\frac{2}{8}$

16. $5\frac{1}{6} - 4\frac{5}{6}$

17. $7\frac{8}{12} - 3\frac{2}{12}$

18. $7\frac{1}{8} - 3\frac{1}{8}$

Problem Solving

**Estimate or find an exact answer to solve each problem.
For Problems 19 and 20, use the recipe at the right.**

19. **Explain** Will two cucumbers be enough to make three batches of gazpacho? Tell how you know.

20. While shopping for the ingredients for gazpacho, you bought onions, tomatoes, and a green pepper. How many individual items did you buy?

21. Claudia spent $10.93 on ingredients for her grandmother's *arroz con pollo* dinner. The chicken was on sale for $3.99 a pound. If she bought 2 pounds of chicken, how much of her money was spent on other ingredients?

22. **Analyze** Will $2\frac{3}{4}$ pints of water and $3\frac{5}{8}$ pints of juice fit into a 4-pint container? Explain.

Gazpacho

6 green onions
6 ripe tomatoes
$\frac{1}{2}$ cucumber
1 clove of garlic
1 green pepper
1 slice of bread
2 tbsp olive oil
2 tbsp lemon juice
pinch of salt and pepper
$\frac{1}{2}$ c cold water

Review and Remember

Using Algebra Find each *s*.

23. $\$1.09 \times 7 = s$

24. $8.01 + 10.1 = s$

25. $2.24 \div 8 = s$

26. $4.05 - 0.99 = s$

Fraction Action

*Using fraction pieces can help you understand
adding and subtracting fractions with unlike denominators.*

Learning About It

Work with a group. Explore adding and subtracting
fractions with unlike denominators.

Step 1 Use fraction pieces to find $\frac{2}{3} + \frac{1}{4}$.

- Place two $\frac{1}{3}$ pieces and one $\frac{1}{4}$ piece underneath
  a 1-whole piece.

What You Need

*For each group:
  fraction pieces*

- Then find like fraction pieces that fit exactly
  underneath the sum of $\frac{2}{3} + \frac{1}{4}$. Use the picture at
  the right to help you.

- How many twelfths did you use to fit exactly under
  $\frac{2}{3}$? under $\frac{1}{4}$? Write a number sentence that shows
  what you did.

$$
\begin{array}{r}
\frac{2}{3} = \frac{\blacksquare}{12} \\
+\ \frac{1}{4} = +\ \frac{\blacksquare}{12} \\
\hline
\frac{\blacksquare}{12}
\end{array}
$$

Step 2 Now use fraction pieces to find $\frac{3}{4} - \frac{2}{3}$.

- Place three $\frac{1}{4}$ pieces under the 1-whole piece.

- Place two $\frac{1}{3}$ pieces under the $\frac{1}{4}$ pieces.

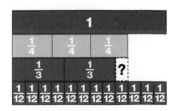

- Look for like fraction pieces that allow you to make $\frac{2}{3}$ and $\frac{3}{4}$. Then place one or more pieces next to the two $\frac{1}{3}$ pieces to fill the space exactly under $\frac{3}{4}$.

- What did you place next to the two $\frac{1}{3}$ pieces to equal $\frac{3}{4}$? Write an example that shows what you did.

$$\frac{3}{4} = \frac{9}{12}$$
$$-\frac{2}{3} = -\frac{8}{12}$$
$$\frac{\blacksquare}{12}$$

Step 3 Use fraction pieces to help you find each missing numerator and denominator.

a.
$$\frac{3}{6} = \frac{6}{\blacksquare}$$
$$+\frac{1}{12} = +\frac{1}{\blacksquare}$$
$$\frac{\blacksquare}{\blacksquare}$$

b.
$$\frac{1}{6} = \frac{2}{\blacksquare}$$
$$+\frac{3}{4} = +\frac{\blacksquare}{12}$$
$$\frac{\blacksquare}{\blacksquare}$$

c.
$$\frac{7}{8} = \frac{7}{\blacksquare}$$
$$-\frac{1}{4} = -\frac{2}{8}$$
$$\frac{5}{\blacksquare}$$

Think and Discuss When you found the sum of $\frac{2}{3}$ and $\frac{1}{4}$, you used a common denominator of 12. What do you think would be a common denominator for $\frac{1}{3} + \frac{5}{6}$? Tell why.

Practice

Use fraction pieces or draw diagrams to find each answer. Write a number sentence for each to show what you did.

1. $\frac{3}{8} + \frac{1}{2}$

2. $\frac{3}{4} - \frac{1}{3}$

3. $\frac{5}{6} + \frac{2}{3}$

4. $\frac{7}{8} - \frac{3}{4}$

5. $\frac{4}{5} - \frac{7}{10}$

6. $\frac{2}{3} + \frac{1}{4}$

7. $\frac{7}{8} - \frac{1}{2}$

8. $\frac{1}{6} + \frac{1}{2}$

9. $\frac{7}{12} - \frac{1}{4}$

10. $\frac{11}{12} + \frac{5}{6}$

Use a, b, and c below to answer Exercises 11–13. Think about trading fraction pieces.

11. Which one involves no trading?

12. Which one involves trading only one piece?

13. Which one involves trading for pieces different from either addend?

14. **Journal Idea** Explain how using fraction pieces shows how to add and subtract fractions with unlike denominators.

a. $\frac{1}{2} + \frac{3}{8}$

b. $\frac{3}{8} + \frac{3}{8}$

c. $\frac{1}{3} + \frac{3}{4}$

Dressing the Salad

You can use what you have learned about common denominators to add fractions with unlike denominators.

Learning About It

Paul likes to mix his own salad dressing. He adds $\frac{5}{6}$ cup of olive oil and $\frac{1}{4}$ cup of vinegar to the contents of a packet of seasoning to complete the mixture. How much liquid does Paul add?

To find out, add $\frac{5}{6} + \frac{1}{4}$.

THERE'S ALWAYS A WAY!

• **One way** is to use a model.

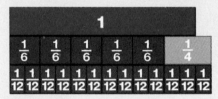

• **Another way** is to use paper and pencil.

Step 1 Find the least common denominator (LCD). Remember that the LCD is the least common multiple of 6 and 4.

$$\frac{5}{6}$$
Multiples of 6: 6, 12, 18, ...

$$+\frac{1}{4}$$
Multiples of 4: 4, 8, 12, ...

Step 2 Write the equivalent fractions, using the LCD, 12.

$$\frac{5}{6} = \frac{5 \times 2}{6 \times 2} = \frac{10}{12}$$

$$+\frac{1}{4} = \frac{1 \times 3}{4 \times 3} = +\frac{3}{12}$$

Step 3 Add. Simplify the sum, if possible.

$$\frac{5}{6} = \frac{10}{12}$$

$$+\frac{1}{4} = +\frac{3}{12}$$

$$\frac{13}{12} = 1\frac{1}{12}$$

Paul adds $1\frac{1}{12}$ cups of liquid.

Think and Discuss How is trading with fraction pieces similar to using the least common denominator when adding two fractions?

Try It Out

Add. Simplify each sum, if possible.

1. $\frac{2}{5} + \frac{1}{2}$　　**2.** $\frac{2}{7} + \frac{3}{5}$　　**3.** $\frac{5}{6} + \frac{1}{4}$　　**4.** $\frac{3}{8} + \frac{3}{4}$　　**5.** $\frac{1}{2} + \frac{3}{10}$

Practice

Add. Simplify each sum, if possible.

6. $\begin{array}{r} \frac{7}{10} \\ + \frac{1}{5} \\ \hline \end{array}$　　**7.** $\begin{array}{r} \frac{9}{10} \\ + \frac{1}{4} \\ \hline \end{array}$　　**8.** $\begin{array}{r} \frac{4}{5} \\ + \frac{3}{4} \\ \hline \end{array}$　　**9.** $\begin{array}{r} \frac{4}{5} \\ + \frac{2}{3} \\ \hline \end{array}$　　**10.** $\begin{array}{r} \frac{3}{8} \\ + \frac{1}{2} \\ \hline \end{array}$

11. $\frac{2}{3} + \frac{1}{9}$　　**12.** $\frac{5}{8} + \frac{1}{2}$　　**13.** $\frac{5}{6} + \frac{5}{8}$　　**14.** $\frac{3}{10} + \frac{1}{4}$　　**15.** $\frac{5}{7} + \frac{1}{3}$

16. $\frac{1}{2} + \frac{3}{8}$　　**17.** $\frac{1}{8} + \frac{3}{4}$　　**18.** $\frac{2}{5} + \frac{2}{3}$　　**19.** $\frac{1}{3} + \frac{5}{6}$　　**20.** $\frac{1}{3} + \frac{3}{6} + \frac{1}{4}$

Problem Solving

21. Paul spent $10.32 on the ingredients for a chef's salad. If two items cost $1.29 each, what was the cost of the other items?

22. Cindy likes to make a blend of juices to sell. At the end of the day, Cindy has $\frac{1}{4}$ can of tropical juice concentrate and $\frac{5}{6}$ can of orange juice concentrate left. If the cans are the same size, how much concentrate does she have left?

23. Using Estimation Paul spent $\frac{3}{4}$ hour shopping for supplies at the supermarket. It took him $\frac{1}{4}$ hour to walk each way. Did Paul's trip take him more than, less than, or about 1 hour? Explain.

Review and Remember

Write the place of each underlined digit. Then round to that place.

24. 1<u>2</u>4.49　　**25.** <u>1</u>75.9　　**26.** 0.9<u>9</u>8

27. 8<u>0</u>5.03　　**28.** 0.5<u>7</u>9　　**29.** 3.26<u>4</u>7

▲ **Health and Fitness Connection**
One of the ingredients that enhances the flavor of a salad is garlic. Garlic is believed by some people to fight off coughs and colds and to keep your heart healthy.

For Extra Practice, see Set D, page 417.

For the Sport of It

Find common denominators to subtract fractions with unlike denominators.

Learning About It

Judy pours a sports drink for herself before going on a long bike ride. She fills the container at 8:00 A.M. At 10:00 A.M., there is $\frac{2}{3}$ of the drink left in the container. By noon there is only $\frac{1}{4}$ left. How much of the sports drink did she drink between 10 o'clock and noon?

To find out, subtract $\frac{2}{3} - \frac{1}{4}$.

THERE'S ALWAYS A WAY!

- **One way** is to use a model.

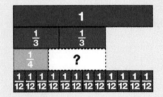

1	
$\frac{1}{3}$	$\frac{1}{3}$

$\frac{1}{4}$	?

$\frac{1}{12}$ $\frac{1}{12}$ $\frac{1}{12}$ $\frac{1}{12}$ $\frac{1}{12}$ $\frac{1}{12}$ $\frac{1}{12}$ $\frac{1}{12}$ $\frac{1}{12}$ $\frac{1}{12}$ $\frac{1}{12}$ $\frac{1}{12}$

- **Another way** is to subtract.

Step 1 Find the LCD.

$$\frac{2}{3}$$ Multiples of 3:
3, 6, 9, **12**, 15,…

$$-\frac{1}{4}$$ Multiples of 4:
4, 8, **12**, 16,…

Step 2 Write equivalent fractions, using the LCD.

$$\frac{2}{3} = \frac{2 \times 4}{3 \times 4} = \frac{8}{12}$$

$$-\frac{1}{4} = \frac{1 \times 3}{4 \times 3} = -\frac{3}{12}$$

Step 3 Subtract. Simplify, if possible.

$$\frac{2}{3} = \frac{8}{12}$$

$$-\frac{1}{4} = -\frac{3}{12}$$

$$\frac{5}{12}$$

Judy drank $\frac{5}{12}$ of the sports drink.

More Examples

A. $\frac{5}{6} - \frac{1}{2} = \frac{5}{6} - \frac{3}{6} = \frac{2}{6} = \frac{1}{3}$

B. $\frac{5}{6} - \frac{1}{4} = \frac{10}{12} - \frac{3}{12} = \frac{7}{12}$

Think and Discuss In Example B above, why is 12 the denominator in the answer?

Try It Out

Subtract. Simplify each difference, if possible.

1. $\frac{5}{8} - \frac{3}{8}$

2. $\frac{3}{8} - \frac{1}{4}$

3. $\frac{7}{10} - \frac{2}{5}$

4. $\frac{3}{4} - \frac{2}{3}$

5. $\frac{1}{2} - \frac{1}{8}$

6. $\frac{5}{6} - \frac{5}{12}$

7. $\frac{5}{9} - \frac{1}{3}$

8. $\frac{2}{3} - \frac{3}{8}$

9. $\frac{4}{5} - \frac{1}{2}$

10. $\frac{6}{7} - \frac{1}{5}$

Practice

Subtract. Simplify, if possible.

11. $\frac{6}{7} - \frac{1}{2}$

12. $\frac{3}{5} - \frac{1}{4}$

13. $\frac{3}{6} - \frac{1}{9}$

14. $\frac{2}{3} - \frac{5}{9}$

15. $\frac{3}{4} - \frac{1}{2}$

16. $\frac{4}{5} - \frac{2}{3}$

17. $\frac{7}{8} - \frac{3}{4}$

18. $\frac{1}{2} - \frac{3}{10}$

19. $\frac{5}{10} - \frac{1}{4}$

20. $\frac{3}{5} - \frac{1}{3}$

21. $\frac{6}{8} - \frac{1}{3}$

22. $\frac{5}{12} - \frac{1}{3}$

23. $\frac{13}{18} - \frac{2}{9}$

24. $\frac{7}{12} - \frac{1}{4}$

25. $\frac{11}{12} - \frac{2}{3}$

26. $\frac{3}{5} - \frac{2}{5}$

Problem Solving

27. **Using Algebra** The answers for Exercises 23–26 follow a pattern. Write the next three fractions in the pattern. Then write a number sentence whose answer would be the ninth term in the pattern.

28. Stephen drank $\frac{1}{6}$ of his bottle of Exer-ade. Sarah drank $\frac{1}{8}$ of her bottle of Exer-ade. How much more of his bottle of Exer-ade did Stephen drink?

29. **Analyze** Judy's regular sports drink costs $1.98 for two bottles. A new brand of sports drink costs $1.29 for one bottle. How much would Judy pay for 12 bottles of her regular sports drink? the new brand? Which is more expensive?

2 for $1.98

Review and Remember

Find each answer.

30. 67×126

31. $0.17 + 1.34$

32. $\$1.28 \times 61$

33. $57,672 \div 81$

34. $34.98 - 20$

35. $\$19.01 \times 18$

36. $2,783 \div 23$

37. 0.03×215

For Extra Practice, see Set E, page 417.

It's Nutty!

You need to find common denominators to add mixed numbers with unlike denominators.

Learning About It

At P.J.'s Nut House you can buy any combination of nuts. Lynn ordered $1\frac{2}{3}$ lb of peanuts, $3\frac{1}{4}$ lb of pistachios, and $1\frac{1}{6}$ lb of cashews. How many pounds of nuts did Lynn order?

$$1\frac{2}{3} + 3\frac{1}{4} + 1\frac{1}{6} = n$$

Estimate first: $2 + 3 + 1 = 6$

Then find the exact answer.

pistachios $3\frac{1}{4}$ lb

cashews $1\frac{1}{6}$ lb

Step 1 Find the LCD.	**Step 2** Write equivalent fractions, using the LCD 12.	**Step 3** Add. Then simplify the sum.
$1\frac{2}{3}$ Multiples of 3: 3, 6, 9, 12, … $3\frac{1}{4}$ Multiples of 4: 4, 8, 12, … $+\,1\frac{1}{6}$ Multiples of 6: 6, 12, …	$1\frac{2}{3} = \quad 1\frac{8}{12}$ $3\frac{1}{4} = \quad 3\frac{3}{12}$ $+\,1\frac{1}{6} = +\,1\frac{2}{12}$	$1\frac{2}{3} = \quad 1\frac{8}{12}$ $3\frac{1}{4} = \quad 3\frac{3}{12}$ $+\,1\frac{1}{6} = +\,1\frac{2}{12}$ $= \quad 5\frac{13}{12} = 6\frac{1}{12}$ $5 + 1\frac{1}{12} = 6\frac{1}{12}$

Lynn ordered $6\frac{1}{12}$ lb of nuts. The answer is close to the estimate.

Another Example

$$2\frac{1}{4} + 4\frac{3}{8} = 2\frac{2}{8} + 4\frac{3}{8} = 6\frac{5}{8}$$

Think and Discuss Describe how fraction pieces could model $3\frac{7}{8} + 2\frac{3}{4}$.

Try It Out

Estimate first. Then find the exact sum.

1. $3\frac{2}{3} + 5\frac{1}{6}$ **2.** $2\frac{7}{8} + 1\frac{1}{4}$ **3.** $9\frac{3}{5} + 5\frac{3}{4}$ **4.** $8\frac{7}{10} + 5\frac{3}{5}$ **5.** $2\frac{3}{7} + 5\frac{1}{3}$

Practice

Add. Simplify each sum, if possible. Estimate to check if your answer is reasonable.

6. $3\frac{5}{8}$ **7.** $4\frac{6}{7}$ **8.** $8\frac{3}{5}$ **9.** $9\frac{7}{8}$ **10.** $2\frac{3}{8}$

    $+\ 2\frac{2}{3}$ $+\ 1\frac{1}{2}$ $+\ 2\frac{1}{3}$ $+\ 2\frac{1}{4}$ $+\ 1\frac{5}{6}$

11. $2\frac{3}{4} + 1\frac{3}{5}$ **12.** $6\frac{2}{5} + 1\frac{3}{7}$ **13.** $4\frac{8}{9} + 2\frac{1}{2}$ **14.** $3\frac{6}{7} + 1\frac{2}{3}$ **15.** $5\frac{2}{5} + 3\frac{1}{3}$

16. $5\frac{2}{9} + 3\frac{2}{3}$ **17.** $3\frac{2}{9} + 5\frac{5}{6}$ **18.** $2\frac{4}{5} + 5\frac{3}{8}$ **19.** $8 + 2\frac{3}{4}$ **20.** $9\frac{6}{7} + 3\frac{1}{2}$

Problem Solving

21. P.J. puts $1\frac{3}{4}$ lb of peanuts and $\frac{5}{8}$ lb of cashews in a small decorative tin. How many pounds of nuts does P.J. put in the tin?

22. What If? Suppose P.J. adds $\frac{1}{4}$ lb of walnuts to the other nuts in the tin. Now how many pounds of nuts are in the tin?

23. In a super-sized party tin, P.J. puts $3\frac{1}{8}$ lb of pistachios, $3\frac{3}{16}$ lb of peanuts, and $2\frac{1}{4}$ lb of walnuts. The weight of the tin when it is empty is $1\frac{1}{2}$ lb. What is the total weight of this package of mixed nuts?

24. Using Mental Math P.J. has to make a package of 10 lb of mixed nuts. He decides to use $3\frac{2}{4}$ lb of cashews, $4\frac{1}{2}$ lb of peanuts, and 2 lb of pistachios. Is this enough? Explain your reasoning.

25. You Decide P.J. has asked you to make up a gift package containing 5 lb of mixed nuts. In your mixture, you may include peanuts, pistachios, cashews, or walnuts. Each type of nut may be in any quantity you choose. Describe your mixture.

Review and Remember

Write three equivalent fractions for each fraction.

26. $\frac{6}{7}$ **27.** $\frac{1}{6}$ **28.** $\frac{1}{2}$ **29.** $\frac{8}{10}$ **30.** $\frac{10}{12}$ **31.** $\frac{2}{3}$

My Hero

Subtracting mixed numbers is like adding mixed numbers.
You need a common denominator to both add and subtract.

Learning About It

Mr. Hope's fifth-grade class ordered a 6-ft-long submarine sandwich for lunch. When the sandwich arrived, it was actually $6\frac{1}{2}$ ft long! After the students finished lunch, there were $1\frac{3}{4}$ ft left. How many feet of the sub did the class eat?

$$6\frac{1}{2} - 1\frac{3}{4} = n$$

Estimate first: $7 - 2 = 5$

▲ **Language Arts Connection**
A submarine sandwich is sometimes called a sub, a hero, a poor boy, a hoagie, or a grinder!

Then find the exact answer.

Step 1 Write equivalent fractions, using the LCD.	**Step 2** Rename before you subtract, since $\frac{3}{4} > \frac{2}{4}$.	**Step 3** Subtract the fractions and the whole numbers. Simplify, if possible.
$6\frac{1}{2} = 6\frac{2}{4}$ $-1\frac{3}{4} = -1\frac{3}{4}$	$6\frac{2}{4} = \boxed{5\frac{4}{4} + \frac{2}{4}} = 5\frac{6}{4}$ $-1\frac{3}{4}$ $-1\frac{3}{4}$	$5\frac{6}{4}$ $-1\frac{3}{4}$ $4\frac{3}{4}$

Mr. Hope's class ate $4\frac{3}{4}$ ft of the sub sandwich. The answer $4\frac{3}{4}$ is close to the estimate of 5.

More Examples

A.

$$6 = 5\frac{8}{8}$$
$$-4\frac{2}{8} = -4\frac{2}{8}$$
$$1\frac{6}{8} = 1\frac{3}{4}$$

B.

$$12\frac{2}{5} = 12\frac{4}{10} = 11\frac{14}{10}$$
$$-6\frac{1}{2} = -6\frac{5}{10} = -6\frac{5}{10}$$
$$5\frac{9}{10}$$

Think and Discuss Look back at Example A. Why is it necessary to rename 6 as $5\frac{8}{8}$?

Try It Out

Estimate. Then find each difference. Simplify, if possible.

1. $5\frac{1}{2}$
   $-\,2\frac{2}{5}$

2. $7\frac{1}{8}$
   $-\,4\frac{1}{4}$

3. $5\frac{3}{10}$
   $-\,2\frac{1}{2}$

4. $2\frac{4}{7}$
   $-\,1\frac{1}{2}$

5. 8
   $-\,5\frac{3}{4}$

$2\frac{1}{2}$　　3　　$3\frac{1}{2}$　　4　　$4\frac{1}{2}$　　5　　$5\frac{1}{2}$　　6

$6\frac{1}{2}$ ft

Practice

Subtract. Simplify, if possible.

6. $8\frac{3}{5}$
   $-\,5\frac{3}{10}$

7. $14\frac{2}{3}$
   $-\,3\frac{1}{6}$

8. $9\frac{7}{8}$
   $-\,2\frac{3}{4}$

9. $5\frac{3}{8}$
   $-\,1\frac{1}{2}$

10. $7\frac{3}{7}$
    $-\,4\frac{2}{3}$

11. $9 - 5\frac{2}{3}$

12. $18\frac{3}{7} - 3\frac{1}{7}$

13. $6\frac{3}{8} - 2\frac{1}{4}$

14. $2\frac{3}{5} - \frac{7}{10}$

15. $9\frac{1}{4} - 6\frac{3}{4}$

16. $8\frac{2}{7} - 4\frac{3}{14}$

17. $7 - 3\frac{5}{8}$

18. $8\frac{4}{5} - 6$

Problem Solving

19. **Analyze** Three classes each ordered a 6-ft sub. Each sub was actually $6\frac{1}{2}$ ft! If each class ate $5\frac{3}{4}$ ft of its sub, what was the total amount left?

20. The sub shop needs to make 8 feet of super sub sandwiches. The baker delivered one $3\frac{2}{3}$ ft-long roll and one $4\frac{1}{4}$ ft-long roll. Are the rolls long enough to make the sandwiches?

Did You Know?

John Montague, the fourth Earl of Sandwich (in Wiltshire, England), is said to have been the first to place cold meat between two pieces of bread.

Review and Remember

Find each answer.

21. $23.1 \div 3$

22. 3.1×2.5

23. $34.1 + 2.03$

24. 7.45×4.9

25. $5.09 - 4.23$

26. $96.18 \div 2$

27. 4.5×0.2

28. $89.1 - 41.01$

For Extra Practice, see Set G, page 418.

✔ Checkpoint

Adding and Subtracting Fractions and Mixed Numbers

Add. Simplify, if possible. (pages 376–379)

1. $\frac{4}{7} + \frac{2}{7}$

2. $\frac{3}{8} + \frac{5}{8}$

3. $1\frac{1}{8} + 1\frac{5}{8}$

4. $8\frac{5}{12} + 4\frac{7}{12}$

Subtract. Simplify, if possible. (pages 380–383)

5. $\frac{7}{9} - \frac{5}{9}$

6. $\frac{5}{8} - \frac{3}{8}$

7. $\frac{9}{15} - \frac{3}{15}$

8. $\begin{array}{r} 2\frac{1}{8} \\ -\ 1\frac{4}{8} \\ \hline \end{array}$

9. $\begin{array}{r} 4\frac{5}{9} \\ -\ 2\frac{4}{9} \\ \hline \end{array}$

10. $\begin{array}{r} 5\frac{3}{12} \\ -\ 1\frac{5}{12} \\ \hline \end{array}$

> ### What do you think?
>
> How can you tell if you need to rename when subtracting mixed numbers?

Estimate each sum or difference. (pages 386–387)

11. $4\frac{3}{5} + 1\frac{1}{5}$

12. $7\frac{5}{16} + 8\frac{7}{16}$

13. $3\frac{2}{5} - 1\frac{4}{5}$

14. $5\frac{3}{7} - 4$

Find each sum. Simplify, if possible. (pages 390–391)

15. $\frac{1}{2} + \frac{1}{3}$

16. $\frac{5}{12} + \frac{3}{8}$

17. $\frac{2}{5} + \frac{4}{15}$

18. $\frac{5}{6} + \frac{5}{18}$

Find each difference. Simplify, if possible. (pages 392–393)

19. $\frac{3}{4} - \frac{1}{3}$

20. $\frac{2}{3} - \frac{1}{6}$

21. $\frac{5}{8} - \frac{1}{2}$

22. $\frac{3}{16} - \frac{1}{8}$

23. $\frac{5}{15} - \frac{1}{3}$

24. $\frac{7}{10} - \frac{1}{2}$

25. $\frac{8}{9} - \frac{5}{6}$

26. $\frac{2}{3} - \frac{4}{7}$

Estimate. Then add. Simplify, if possible. (pages 394–395)

27. $\begin{array}{r} 5\frac{1}{8} \\ +\ 4\frac{1}{2} \\ \hline \end{array}$

28. $\begin{array}{r} 2\frac{3}{10} \\ +\ 1\frac{1}{5} \\ \hline \end{array}$

29. $\begin{array}{r} 3\frac{5}{16} \\ +\ 1\frac{3}{4} \\ \hline \end{array}$

30. $\begin{array}{r} 8\frac{2}{5} \\ +\ 6\frac{6}{15} \\ \hline \end{array}$

Estimate. Then subtract. Simplify, if possible. (pages 396–397)

31. $\begin{array}{r} 7\frac{3}{4} \\ -\ 6\frac{2}{5} \\ \hline \end{array}$

32. $\begin{array}{r} 15\frac{3}{8} \\ -\ 4\frac{9}{16} \\ \hline \end{array}$

33. $\begin{array}{r} 9\frac{27}{28} \\ -\ 5 \\ \hline \end{array}$

34. $\begin{array}{r} 10 \\ -\ 4\frac{5}{8} \\ \hline \end{array}$

Mixed Practice

Add or subtract. Simplify, if possible.

35. $2\frac{3}{5}$
$+\ 1\frac{1}{5}$

36. $5\frac{7}{12}$
$-\ 4\frac{5}{12}$

37. $\frac{5}{8}$
$-\ \frac{3}{16}$

38. $7\frac{4}{9}$
$+\ 6\frac{2}{3}$

39. $3\frac{4}{7} - 2\frac{1}{3}$

40. $6\frac{3}{10} + 4\frac{1}{3}$

41. $8\frac{11}{12} - 4\frac{5}{6}$

42. $9 - 3\frac{3}{10}$

Problem Solving

43. Using Estimation Ms. Barth needs about $2\frac{1}{2}$ lb of plant food for her corn and about $1\frac{1}{3}$ lb for her green vegetables. About how many pounds of plant food does she need?

44. Carole has a recipe for bread that requires 1 packet of dry yeast and $3\frac{2}{3}$ cups of flour. She wants to double the recipe. How much flour does she need?

45. It took Chef Anita $2\frac{1}{2}$ h to prepare a pot of vegetable-beef soup and $1\frac{3}{4}$ h to prepare a pot of lentil soup. The vegetable-beef soup was put on the stove to simmer when she started to prepare the lentil soup. If both soups simmered for 2 hours, how long did it take, from start until the soups finished simmering, to make both soups?

Journal Idea

Write about one way you use fractions or mixed numbers in your everyday life.

Critical Thinking Corner

Visual Thinking

Fractured Fractions

Look at the picture of a garden. Write the fraction that tells what part of the garden is planted with corn.

| Green Beans $\frac{1}{6}$ | Tomatoes $\frac{1}{3}$ |
| Radishes $\frac{1}{8}$ | Corn ? |

Problem Solving
Solve a Simpler Problem

Sometimes solving a simpler problem can help you find the solution to a more difficult problem.

Paul is in the fruit-and-vegetable aisle. He likes 6 different kinds of vegetables. Paul wants to choose 2 different kinds of vegetables for his dinner. In how many ways can he choose 2 vegetables?

 ## UNDERSTAND

What do you need to find?

You need to find the number of different ways Paul can choose 2 vegetables from 6 vegetables.

 ## PLAN

How can you solve the problem?

You can begin by **solving a simpler problem**. Think about how many ways Paul can choose 2 vegetables if the store sells 2, then 3, and then 4 vegetables.

 ## SOLVE

If only 2 vegetables are sold, there is only 1 way to choose them. If 3 vegetables are sold, there are 3 ways. If 4 vegetables are sold, there are 6 ways.

Organize your results in a table. Then look for a pattern. The number of ways to choose 2 vegetables increases by 2, then by 3, and then by 4. When 6 vegetables are sold, the number of ways will increase by 5.

There are 15 different ways Paul can choose 2 vegetables.

Number of Vegetables Sold	Number of Ways to Choose 2 Vegetables
2	1
3	3
4	6
5	10
6	?

 ## LOOK BACK

Look for another pattern in the table. Does the pattern give the same results for 6 vegetables?

Using the Strategy

Use a simpler problem to help you solve each problem.

1 A fruit display has 6 rows of oranges. It has 1 orange in the first row, 3 in the second row, and 5 in the third row. If this pattern continues, how many oranges are in the display?

2 A fruit tree grew 3 branches in the first year after it was planted. If it grows 2 new branches every year after that, how many branches will it have after ten years?

3 Pints of strawberries are labeled on the top and front side of each pint. How many labels can you see if there are 6 rows of 4 pints?

4 Boxes of grapes are labeled on each of the four sides of a box. How many labels can you see when 18 boxes are lined up side by side?

5 Eight people buy potatoes. The first customer buys 1 pound. After the second customer leaves, 4 pounds have been sold in all. After the third customer leaves, a total of 9 pounds have been sold. After the fourth customer leaves, 16 pounds have been sold. If this pattern continues, how many pounds are sold in all?

Mixed Strategy Review

Try these or other strategies to solve each problem. Tell which strategy you used.

Problem Solving Strategies

- *Work Backwards*
- *Find a Pattern*
- *Write an Equation*
- *Make a Table*

6 One bottle of fruit juice blend contains $4\frac{5}{8}$ c of orange juice, $2\frac{1}{4}$ c of lemon juice, and $1\frac{3}{8}$ c of lime juice. How many cups of juice will there be in four bottles?

7 A grapefruit, a tangerine, and an orange together weigh $3\frac{3}{8}$ lb. The grapefruit weighs $1\frac{1}{2}$ lb. The orange weighs $1\frac{1}{8}$ lb. What is the weight of the tangerine?

8 Use the picture at the right. Ms. Kane lives $9\frac{1}{2}$ miles from Sunset Grove and $6\frac{7}{10}$ miles from Golden Grove. How much closer to her house is Golden Grove than Sunset Grove?

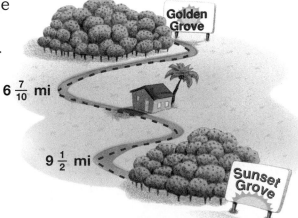

Golden Grove

$6\frac{7}{10}$ mi

$9\frac{1}{2}$ mi

Sunset Grove

Taco Mania

You can find a fraction of a whole number by multiplying.

Learning About It

Kenneth, his sister, and his dad made one dozen tacos. Kenneth and his sister made $\frac{1}{4}$ of the tacos and their dad made the last $\frac{3}{4}$. How many tacos did Dad make?

To find out, multiply $\frac{3}{4} \times 12$.

Step 1 Multiply the numerators. Then multiply the denominators.	**Step 2** Write the product in simplest form.
$\frac{3}{4} \times 12 = \frac{3}{4} \times \frac{12}{1} = \frac{3 \times 12}{4 \times 1} = \frac{36}{4}$ The whole number can be written as a fraction. $12 = \frac{12}{1}$	$\frac{36}{4} = \frac{36 \div 4}{4 \div 4} = \frac{9}{1} = 9$

Kenneth's dad made 9 tacos.

More Examples

A. $\frac{2}{3} \times 18 = \frac{2}{3} \times \frac{18}{1}$

$= \frac{2 \times 18}{3 \times 1} = \frac{36}{3} = \frac{12}{1} = 12$

B. $6 \times \frac{3}{4} = \frac{6}{1} \times \frac{3}{4}$

$= \frac{6}{1} \times \frac{3}{4} = \frac{18}{4} = \frac{9}{2} = 4\frac{1}{2}$

Think and Discuss $\frac{3}{4}$ of 16 tomatoes are red. How many are not red? Explain your thinking.

Try It Out

Multiply. Simplify, if possible.

1. $\frac{5}{8} \times 8$ **2.** $14 \times \frac{3}{7}$ **3.** $22 \times \frac{9}{10}$ **4.** $\frac{5}{6} \times 4$

Practice

Multiply. Simplify each product, if possible.

5. $\frac{5}{9} \times 6$ **6.** $\frac{1}{7} \times 6$ **7.** $7 \times \frac{6}{7}$ **8.** $12 \times \frac{1}{2}$

9. $\frac{1}{2} \times 28$ **10.** $20 \times \frac{4}{5}$ **11.** $\frac{1}{10} \times 14$ **12.** $\frac{5}{12} \times 9$

13. $\frac{5}{6} \times 24$ **14.** $25 \times \frac{2}{3}$ **15.** $\frac{3}{8} \times 16$ **16.** $7 \times \frac{7}{9}$

17. $\frac{2}{5} \times 3$ **18.** $12 \times \frac{2}{3}$ **19.** $\frac{5}{6} \times 30$ **20.** $\frac{4}{5} \times 40$

Problem Solving

21. Look at the circle graph at the right. If a total of 80 sets of napkins were sold, how many of each color were sold?

22. Create Your Own Write a multiplication problem about 24 tacos that has 4 tacos as an answer.

Napkins Sold

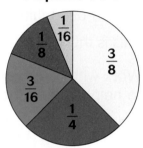

Review and Remember

Using Algebra Evaluate each expression. Then write >, <, or = for each ⬤.

23. $138 \div 23$ ⬤ $384 \div 64$ **24.** $1,750 - 989$ ⬤ $301 + 412$

25. 745×92 ⬤ $13,902 + 84,287$ **26.** 162×58 ⬤ $56,370 \div 6$

27. 252×15 ⬤ $5825 - 2866$ **28.** 136×2 ⬤ $554 \div 2$

Critical Thinking Corner

Logical Thinking

What's Wrong?

Analyze. Explain what is wrong in each example.

1. I have 640 acres of land. 320 acres are planted in corn. Soon I'll plant the other $\frac{2}{3}$.

2. This bulletin just in: Nearly $\frac{2}{3}$ of the city is without electricity. The other half may lose power soon.

For Extra Practice, see Set H, page 418.

EXPLORE: Modeling Fraction Multiplication

Baking Baklava

Diagrams can help you understand multiplication with fractions.

Learning About It

Sophia and her father baked several pans of baklava for their family reunion. After the reunion, $\frac{3}{4}$ of one pan of baklava was leftover. On Monday, Sophia's family ate $\frac{1}{2}$ of the leftover baklava. What part of the entire pan of baklava did Sophia's family eat on Monday?

To find out, multiply $\frac{1}{2} \times \frac{3}{4}$.

This is the same as finding $\frac{1}{2}$ of $\frac{3}{4}$.

Work with your partner. You can use a diagram to help you find the product.

Step 1 Draw a rectangle to represent a whole pan of baklava.

Step 2 Divide the rectangle into 4 equal sections. Shade 3 of the 4 sections. This is $\frac{3}{4}$ of the whole rectangle.

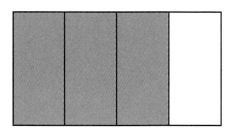

Step 3 Divide the rectangle in half in the other direction. With a different color, draw slanted lines across $\frac{1}{2}$ of the $\frac{3}{4}$ that has been shaded.

▼ Baklava is a Greek dessert made of thin layers of pastry, nuts, and honey.

What You Need

For each pair:
   crayons or colored pencils

Step 4 What part of the whole rectangle has both shading and lines? This is the product of $\frac{1}{2} \times \frac{3}{4}$. Record your results in a chart like the one shown in Step 5.

Since $\frac{1}{2} \times \frac{3}{4} = \frac{3}{8}$, Sophia's family ate $\frac{3}{8}$ of one pan of baklava.

Step 5 Follow Steps 1–4 to find the product of each pair of fractions in the chart. Remember to record your work.

First Fraction	Second Fraction	Diagram	Number Sentence
$\frac{1}{2}$	$\frac{3}{4}$		$\frac{1}{2} \times \frac{3}{4} = \frac{\blacksquare}{8}$
$\frac{3}{8}$	$\frac{1}{2}$		
$\frac{5}{6}$	$\frac{1}{4}$		
$\frac{2}{5}$	$\frac{2}{3}$		

Think and Discuss Look at your chart.

- Compare the numerators of the factors with the numerators of the products. How are they related?

- Compare the denominators.

- Try writing a rule for multiplying two fractions.

Practice

1. **Predict** What is the product of $\frac{2}{3} \times \frac{3}{5}$? Make a diagram to check your prediction.

2. Which diagram shows $\frac{5}{7} \times \frac{1}{2}$? $\frac{3}{4} \times \frac{3}{7}$? $\frac{5}{7} \times \frac{2}{3}$? Write the product represented by each diagram.

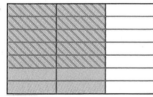 a.

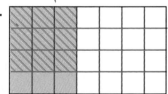 b.

 c.

Find each product. Make a diagram or use your rule.

3. $\frac{1}{8} \times \frac{2}{5}$ 　　4. $\frac{3}{8} \times \frac{1}{2}$ 　　5. $\frac{2}{3} \times \frac{1}{4}$ 　　6. $\frac{2}{3} \times \frac{3}{6}$ 　　7. $\frac{5}{7} \times \frac{2}{4}$

An Apple a Day

You know how to multiply a fraction by a whole number. Now you will learn to multiply a fraction by another fraction or by a mixed number.

Learning About It

The Dodd family received a crate of apples as a gift. They were happy to see that $\frac{3}{4}$ of the apples were the Delicious variety. If $\frac{2}{3}$ of the Delicious apples were Golden Delicious, what part of the crate held Golden Delicious apples?

To find $\frac{2}{3}$ of $\frac{3}{4}$, multiply $\frac{2}{3} \times \frac{3}{4}$.

THERE'S ALWAYS A WAY!

• **One way** to find the product is to draw a diagram.

Granny Smith

Red Delicious

Golden Delicious

• **Another way** to find $\frac{2}{3}$ of $\frac{3}{4}$ is to use paper and pencil.

- Multiply the numerators.

- Multiply the denominators.

- Write the product in simplest form, if possible.

$$\frac{2}{3} \times \frac{3}{4} = \frac{2 \times 3}{3 \times 4} = \frac{6}{12} = \frac{1}{2}$$

One half of the crate held Golden Delicious apples.

More Examples

A. $\frac{5}{8} \times \frac{2}{5} = \frac{5 \times 2}{8 \times 5} = \frac{10}{40} = \frac{1}{4}$

B. $\frac{9}{4} \times \frac{3}{4} = \frac{27}{16} = 1\frac{11}{16}$

C. $\frac{9}{7} \times \frac{7}{3} = \frac{63}{21} = 3$

Connecting Ideas

Before you can multiply mixed numbers, you need to change the mixed numbers to improper fractions.

INTERNET ACTIVITY
www.sbgmath.com

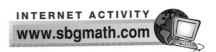

The Dodds read the card included with the crate of apples. It said that the apples weighed $10\frac{1}{2}$ lb in all. Two fifths of this weight was Granny Smith apples. How much did the Granny Smith apples weigh?

To find out, multiply $\frac{2}{5} \times 10\frac{1}{2}$.

Step 1 Write the mixed number as an improper fraction.

$$\frac{2}{5} \times 10\frac{1}{2} = \frac{2}{5} \times \frac{21}{2}$$

Step 2 Multiply. Write the product in simplest form.

$$\frac{2}{5} \times \frac{21}{2} = \frac{2 \times 21}{5 \times 2} = \frac{42}{10} = \frac{21}{5} = 4\frac{1}{5}$$

The Granny Smith apples weighed $4\frac{1}{5}$ lb.

More Examples

A. $5 \times 2\frac{2}{3} = \frac{5}{1} \times \frac{8}{3}$

$\qquad = \frac{5 \times 8}{1 \times 3}$

$\qquad = \frac{40}{3} = 13\frac{1}{3}$

B. $2\frac{1}{4} \times 1\frac{1}{3} = \frac{9}{4} \times \frac{4}{3}$

$\qquad = \frac{9 \times 4}{4 \times 3}$

$\qquad = \frac{36}{12} = \frac{3}{1} = 3$

Think and Discuss Describe a problem that could be solved by multiplying two mixed numbers.

Try It Out

Choose a Method Draw a diagram or use paper and pencil to multiply. Simplify the product, if possible.

1. $\frac{2}{5} \times \frac{1}{2}$

2. $\frac{3}{7} \times \frac{1}{2}$

3. $\frac{3}{7} \times \frac{7}{9}$

4. $\frac{1}{8} \times \frac{5}{6}$

5. $\frac{2}{3} \times 1\frac{4}{9}$

6. $1\frac{5}{8} \times 2\frac{4}{5}$

7. $1\frac{2}{3} \times \frac{2}{3}$

8. $2\frac{2}{3} \times 1\frac{3}{8}$

9. **Discuss** Can you think of two fractions less than 1 with a product greater than 1? Explain your answer.

Problem Solving
Representing Remainders

When dividing whole numbers, sometimes you must think about which way to express the remainder.

Forty-three apples are to be divided equally among 20 brown-bag lunches. How would you express the remainder to show how many apples will be left over?

 ## UNDERSTAND

What do you need to find?

You need to find the number of apples that will be left over after the apples are divided equally among the lunches.

 ## PLAN

How can you solve the problem?

You can divide 43 by 20. Then use the remainder to find out how many apples will be left over.

 ## SOLVE

There are three ways to express a remainder.

As a fraction	As a decimal	As a whole number
$2\frac{3}{20}$ $20\overline{)43}$ $\underline{-40}$ 3	2.15 $20\overline{)43.00}$ $\underline{-40}$ 30 $\underline{-20}$ 100 $\underline{-100}$ 0	2 R3 $20\overline{)43}$ $\underline{-40}$ 3

To find out how many apples are left over, it makes sense to write the remainder as a whole number. This remainder tells you that 3 apples will be left over.

 ## LOOK BACK

Why doesn't it make sense to use the fraction or the decimal remainder to solve this problem?

Show What You Learned

For each problem, decide how to express the remainder. Tell why you chose the method you did.

1. One Saturday, Amber and her friends were making 180 ham-and-cheese sandwiches. They used 450 slices of cheese. How many slices of cheese were placed in each sandwich?

2. Pat has 24 box lunches to transport. She has cartons that hold 10 lunches each. How many cartons does she need to transport all the lunches?

3. The cost of 24 box lunches is $84. What is the cost of one lunch if all lunches are the same price?

4. Amy's class is going on a field trip. The school is $82\frac{1}{2}$ miles from the state park and 95 miles from the zoo. How long will it take the students to get to the park from the school if they travel 55 miles per hour?

▲ **Kid Connection** Amber Coffman and her friends make and pack hundreds of lunches for homeless people each week. In 1993, Amber formed Happy Helpers for the Homeless in Glen Burnie, Maryland.

5. A bag of raisins must be divided equally among 24 box lunches. The bag contains 42 ounces of raisins. How many ounces of raisins will there be in each lunch?

6. A carton of box lunches weighs 25 pounds. One carton holds 10 box lunches. How much does one box lunch weigh?

7. A bag of dried apricots weighing 27 ounces must be equally divided among 15 students' lunches. How many ounces will each student receive?

8. **Analyze** Jerry can deliver 30 cartons of lunches in one trip. How many trips does he have to make to deliver 250 cartons of lunches?

9. **Explain** A box lunch is 5 in. wide. How many box lunches will fit across a picnic table that is 27 in. wide? Tell how you decided.

10. **Create Your Own** Write a problem about traveling that requires dividing by $2\frac{1}{2}$ to solve.

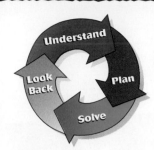

Problem Solving

★★★★★ **Preparing for Tests**

Practice What You Learned

Choose the correct letter for each answer.

1 Greg planted two rows of rosebushes, with 24 bushes in each row. For the first row he used the color pattern RWW, RWW, and so on. For the second row, he used the pattern WYYY, WYYY, and so on. How often was a white rosebush (W) planted behind a red rosebush (R)?

- **A.** Every fourth bush
- **B.** Every fifth bush
- **C.** Every seventh bush
- **D.** Every ninth bush
- **E.** Every twelfth bush

Tip

Use the *Draw a Diagram* strategy to help you solve this problem.

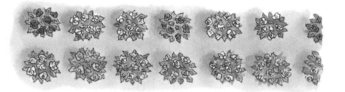

2 Salmon costs $0.75 cents more per pound than tuna. If $\frac{3}{4}$ lb of salmon costs $8.97, which is a reasonable estimate of the price of salmon per pound?

- **A.** $7.50
- **B.** $12.00
- **C.** $14.00
- **D.** $15.00

Tip

Use one of the strategies to solve this problem.
- *Guess and Check*
- *Draw a Diagram*
- *Solve a Simpler Problem*

3 The pictograph shows the number of registered voters in a neighborhood. How many fewer voters live on Pine and Oak than live on Elm and Park?

- **A.** 75
- **B.** 100
- **C.** 125
- **D.** 150
- **E.** Not Here

Tip

Start by making sure you understand the key for the graph.

Registered Voters	
Street	**Number of People**
Pine	⬤⬤⬤⬤⬤
Oak	⬤⬤⬤⬤⬤◗
Elm	⬤⬤⬤⬤⬤⬤⬤◔
Park	⬤⬤⬤◗
	⬤ = 100 people

4 For a fruit salad, Wally used about half of a 3-lb bag of nuts. He also used $\frac{3}{4}$ of a 2-lb bag of cherries. In the salad, which weighed more, the nuts or the cherries, and how much more?

A. Nuts; $\frac{1}{4}$ lb

B. Nuts; $\frac{1}{8}$ lb

C. Cherries; $\frac{1}{4}$ lb

D. Cherries; $\frac{1}{8}$ lb

E. They weighed the same.

5 Wendy mailed 3 packages. The heaviest weighed $4\frac{1}{2}$ lb. The lightest weighed $\frac{7}{8}$ lb. Two of the packages weighed the same. Which is reasonable for the total weight of the packages?

A. Between $\frac{7}{8}$ lb and 10 lb

B. Between $3\frac{1}{2}$ lb and 12 lb

C. Between 4 lb and $12\frac{1}{2}$ lb

D. Between 6 lb and 10 lb

6 Salita had an average of 92 in math. On 3 science tests, she got scores of 90, 75, and 85. What score must she get on the next science test to have an average of at least 85 in science?

A. At least 75   **C.** At least 85
B. At least 80   **D.** At least 90

7 How many 2-in. pieces can Rose cut from a strip of ribbon $3\frac{2}{3}$ ft long?

A. 20   **C.** 22
B. 21   **D.** 24

8 Hal bought 3 sweaters for $14 each and 2 hats for $8 each. Which equation could you use to find *n*, the total amount Hal spent?

A. $(2 + 3) \times (8 + 14) = n$
B. $(3 \times 14) \times (2 \times 8) = n$
C. $(3 \times 14) + (2 \times 8) = n$
D. $(3 \times 14) - (2 \times 8) = n$

9 The graph shows the results of an election. Who won the election, and by about how many votes?

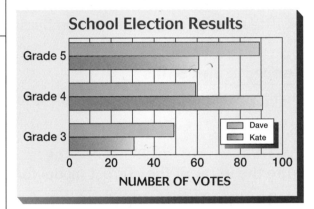

A. Dave; by about 10 votes.
B. Dave; by about 20 votes.
C. Kate; by about 10 votes.
D. Kate; by about 20 votes.

10 Kim drew this design for a brick patio. What is the *area* of the white part of the design?

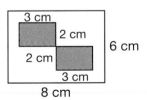

A. 12 cm²
B. 36 cm²
C. 42 cm²
D. 48 cm²
E. Not Here

Checkpoint

Multiplying and Dividing by Fractions and Mixed Numbers

Vocabulary

Write the missing words that complete each sentence.

1. The number above the fraction bar is the ___?___ .

2. A fraction is in ___?___ when the greatest common factor of the numerator and denominator is 1.

3. A ___?___ names part of a whole.

4. The number below the fraction bar is the ___?___ .

Word Bank

fraction
numerator
denominator
simplest form

Concepts and Skills

Multiply. Write the answer in simplest form. (pages 402–403)

5. $4 \times \frac{3}{4}$ **6.** $16 \times \frac{5}{8}$ **7.** $2 \times \frac{7}{10}$ **8.** $3 \times \frac{4}{5}$ **9.** $27 \times \frac{3}{9}$

Write the letter of the correct model for each. (pages 404–405)

10. $\frac{2}{3} \times \frac{1}{5} = \frac{2}{15}$

11. $\frac{1}{2} \times \frac{1}{2} = \frac{1}{4}$

12. $\frac{5}{3} \times \frac{1}{2} = \frac{1}{3}$

a.   **b.** 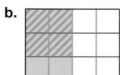 **c.**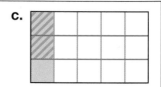

Multiply. Simplify, if possible. (pages 406–409)

13. $\frac{3}{4} \times \frac{1}{3}$ **14.** $\frac{1}{2} \times \frac{2}{3}$ **15.** $\frac{2}{3} \times \frac{7}{9}$ **16.** $\frac{1}{2} \times \frac{3}{4}$

17. $3\frac{1}{4} \times 1\frac{1}{2}$ **18.** $2\frac{5}{6} \times 8$ **19.** $1\frac{3}{4} \times 11$ **20.** $10 \times 4\frac{1}{2}$

Write the letter of the correct number sentence for the model shown. (pages 410–411)

21.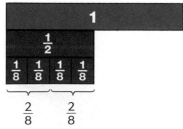

a. $\frac{2}{8} \div \frac{1}{2} = \frac{2}{4}$ **b.** $\frac{1}{2} \div \frac{2}{8} = 2$ **c.** $1 \div \frac{1}{2} = 2$

Problem Solving

22. **Analyze** Sandra is using sugar cubes to make the floor of a gingerbread house. She arranges the cubes in a 3-by-4 array, and she smoothes icing on the top and sides of the floor. How many sides of the sugar cubes have icing on them? What strategy can you use to solve the problem?

What do you think?

How is multiplying by $\frac{1}{3}$ like dividing by 3?

23. Amy's grandparents sent her family a box of 24 oranges and grapefruit from Florida. If $\frac{3}{8}$ of the box is grapefruit, how many grapefruit are in the box?

24. **Explain** A container holds a dozen eggs. If a transport company needs to ship 835 eggs, how many of these containers does it need? Explain your answer.

25. Mr. Lee has $10\frac{1}{2}$ bushels of vegetables. He sells $\frac{3}{4}$ of them. How many bushels are left?

Journal Idea

Use a model to show $\frac{2}{3}$ of 9. Then describe how your model shows $\frac{2}{3} \times 9$.

You Decide

Activity

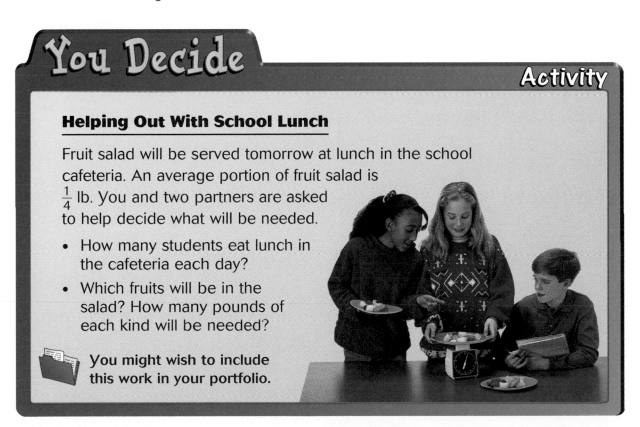

Helping Out With School Lunch

Fruit salad will be served tomorrow at lunch in the school cafeteria. An average portion of fruit salad is $\frac{1}{4}$ lb. You and two partners are asked to help decide what will be needed.

- How many students eat lunch in the cafeteria each day?

- Which fruits will be in the salad? How many pounds of each kind will be needed?

You might wish to include this work in your portfolio.

Extra Practice

Set A (pages 376–379)

Add. Simplify each sum, if possible.

1. $\frac{3}{5} + \frac{1}{5}$

2. $\frac{7}{12} + \frac{5}{12}$

3. $\frac{5}{11} + \frac{3}{11}$

4. $\frac{3}{10} + \frac{2}{10}$

5. $2\frac{1}{8} + 1\frac{5}{8}$

6. $5\frac{3}{8} + 4\frac{5}{8}$

7. $9\frac{7}{8} + 6\frac{3}{8}$

8. $9 + 4\frac{3}{4}$

9. One out of eight slices of a pizza has sausage topping. Three out of eight slices of a second pizza has sausage topping. What fraction of the two pizzas is topped with sausage?

Set B (pages 380–383)

Subtract. Simplify each difference, if possible.

1. $\frac{2}{3} - \frac{1}{3}$

2. $\frac{5}{16} - \frac{3}{16}$

3. $\frac{7}{12} - \frac{5}{12}$

4. $\frac{6}{13} - \frac{5}{13}$

5. $\frac{7}{12} - \frac{1}{12}$

6. $\begin{array}{r} 7\frac{1}{8} \\ -\ 4\frac{1}{4} \\ \hline \end{array}$

7. $\begin{array}{r} 5\frac{5}{9} \\ -\ 1\frac{4}{9} \\ \hline \end{array}$

8. $\begin{array}{r} 7\frac{3}{9} \\ -\ 3\frac{4}{9} \\ \hline \end{array}$

9. $\begin{array}{r} 8\frac{5}{12} \\ -\ 4\frac{7}{12} \\ \hline \end{array}$

10. $\begin{array}{r} 6\frac{3}{4} \\ -\ 5\frac{7}{8} \\ \hline \end{array}$

11. If there are $2\frac{2}{3}$ boxes of cereal in your cupboard and you eat $\frac{1}{3}$ of a box, how much cereal is left over?

Set C (pages 386–387)

Estimate each sum or difference.

1. $4\frac{3}{5} + 2\frac{1}{5}$

2. $3\frac{2}{11} + 1\frac{7}{11}$

3. $6\frac{1}{8} + 2\frac{5}{8}$

4. $3\frac{5}{12} + 7\frac{1}{12}$

5. $2\frac{2}{3} - 1\frac{2}{3}$

6. $4\frac{8}{10} - 1\frac{7}{10}$

7. $6 - 5\frac{1}{4}$

8. $8\frac{6}{7} - 3\frac{6}{7}$

9. A recipe calls for $2\frac{3}{4}$ teaspoons of garlic powder and $\frac{1}{8}$ teaspoon of salt. About how many teaspoons of seasonings are needed for this recipe?

Extra Practice

Set D (pages 390–391)

Add. Simplify each sum, if possible.

1. $\frac{1}{2} + \frac{3}{4}$ 2. $\frac{1}{2} + \frac{1}{3}$ 3. $\frac{5}{12} + \frac{1}{4}$ 4. $\frac{2}{3} + \frac{4}{9}$ 5. $\frac{1}{3} + \frac{2}{7}$

6. $\frac{7}{10} + \frac{1}{5}$ 7. $\frac{4}{5} + \frac{1}{6}$ 8. $\frac{3}{7} + \frac{3}{4}$ 9. $\frac{1}{6} + \frac{3}{4}$ 10. $\frac{3}{8} + \frac{2}{4}$

11. A recipe for punch for the school dance calls for $\frac{3}{4}$ qt of ginger ale, 1 qt cranberry juice, and $\frac{1}{2}$ qt lemonade. How much punch will the recipe make?

Set E (pages 392–393)

Subtract. Simplify each difference, if possible.

1. $\frac{3}{4} - \frac{3}{8}$ 2. $\frac{4}{5} - \frac{3}{10}$ 3. $\frac{16}{21} - \frac{2}{7}$ 4. $\frac{5}{6} - \frac{3}{8}$ 5. $\frac{21}{24} - \frac{5}{8}$

6. $\frac{1}{2} - \frac{1}{4}$ 7. $\frac{7}{12} - \frac{11}{24}$ 8. $\frac{3}{4} - \frac{2}{5}$ 9. $\frac{7}{12} - \frac{1}{3}$ 10. $\frac{7}{9} - \frac{2}{3}$

11. What is the difference between $\frac{7}{12}$ and $\frac{1}{9}$?

Set F (pages 394–395)

Add. Simplify each sum, if possible.

1. $2\frac{7}{10}$ $+ 5\frac{3}{5}$ 2. $4\frac{2}{5}$ $+ 3\frac{1}{4}$ 3. $6\frac{2}{7}$ $+ 2\frac{1}{3}$ 4. $4\frac{4}{9}$ $+ 1\frac{5}{6}$ 5. $3\frac{1}{3}$ $+ 4\frac{3}{4}$

6. $7 + 3\frac{2}{5}$ 7. $8\frac{5}{6} + 2\frac{3}{8}$ 8. $4\frac{1}{4} + \frac{3}{5}$ 9. $5 + 2\frac{7}{8}$

10. Maryanne's mother paid for 6 feet of sub sandwiches at the local sub shop. If the shop gave her a sub $2\frac{1}{3}$ feet long and a sub $2\frac{3}{4}$ feet long, was she charged correctly? Explain your answer.

Extra Practice

Set G (pages 396–397)

Subtract. Simplify each difference, if possible.

1. $5\frac{5}{9} - 1\frac{1}{3}$

2. $2\frac{4}{5} - 1\frac{1}{2}$

3. $3\frac{7}{8} - 3\frac{1}{16}$

4. $4\frac{2}{3} - 3\frac{1}{7}$

5. $7\frac{7}{12} - 2\frac{1}{3}$

6. $4\frac{5}{8} - 2\frac{1}{6}$

7. $5 - 3\frac{1}{3}$

8. $7 - 6\frac{2}{5}$

9. It took Samuel $3\frac{2}{3}$ hours to bake 5 dozen cookies. It took John $1\frac{1}{4}$ hours to bake the same number of cookies. How much longer did it take Samuel to bake his cookies?

Set H (pages 402–403)

Multiply. Simplify each product, if possible.

1. $\frac{3}{5} \times 40$

2. $16 \times \frac{3}{4}$

3. $\frac{5}{7} \times 21$

4. $\frac{5}{6} \times 18$

5. $20 \times \frac{3}{10}$

6. $\frac{7}{9} \times 36$

7. $\frac{4}{5} \times 5$

8. $\frac{5}{8} \times 56$

9. What is $\frac{2}{3}$ of 27?

10. What is $\frac{3}{8}$ of 16?

11. What is $\frac{2}{6}$ of 12?

12. What is $\frac{1}{9}$ of 81?

13. What is $\frac{1}{2}$ of 250?

14. What is $\frac{5}{7}$ of 49?

Set I (pages 406-409)

Multiply. Simplify each product, if possible.

1. $\frac{3}{5} \times \frac{1}{2}$

2. $\frac{2}{7} \times \frac{3}{8}$

3. $\frac{2}{3} \times \frac{3}{5}$

4. $\frac{2}{5} \times \frac{1}{3}$

5. $2\frac{1}{3} \times \frac{3}{5}$

6. $4\frac{5}{8} \times \frac{2}{7}$

7. $3\frac{1}{6} \times 4$

8. $\frac{5}{8} \times 2\frac{1}{3}$

9. Mary helped cook dinner by breading $\frac{1}{2}$ of the chicken. If Mary ate $\frac{1}{3}$ of the chicken she breaded, how much of the chicken did she eat?

Chapter Test

Estimate, then add or subtract. Write each answer in simplest form.

1. $\frac{3}{8} + \frac{3}{8}$

2. $\frac{4}{5} + \frac{3}{5}$

3. $\frac{7}{8} - \frac{3}{8}$

4. $\frac{2}{9} - \frac{1}{9}$

5. $\frac{5}{6} + \frac{2}{3}$

6. $\frac{7}{10} + \frac{3}{5}$

7. $\frac{3}{4} - \frac{3}{8}$

8. $\frac{7}{8} - \frac{1}{6}$

9. $1\frac{2}{3} + 1\frac{1}{3}$

10. $2\frac{3}{7} + 3\frac{4}{7}$

11. $3\frac{2}{5} - 1\frac{4}{5}$

12. $2\frac{7}{8} - 1\frac{3}{8}$

13. $3\frac{1}{2} + \frac{5}{14}$

14. $7\frac{3}{8} + 5\frac{3}{4}$

15. $5 - 1\frac{1}{4}$

16. $5\frac{3}{8} - 1\frac{3}{4}$

Match each multiplication example to its diagram. Write the product in simplest form.

17. $\frac{1}{2} \times \frac{3}{4}$

18. $\frac{1}{2} \times \frac{1}{3}$

19. $\frac{1}{2} \times \frac{3}{5}$

  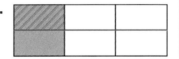

Multiply. Write each answer in simplest form.

20. $\frac{3}{5} \times \frac{1}{2}$

21. $\frac{5}{6} \times \frac{1}{3}$

22. $\frac{3}{5} \times 5$

23. $\frac{3}{4} \times 4\frac{1}{2}$

Solve.

24. Ralph uses $\frac{3}{4}$ cup of milk in a muffin recipe. Alex uses $\frac{1}{2}$ that amount in her muffin recipe. How much milk does Alex use to make muffins?

25. Joanne's cake weighs $7\frac{1}{2}$ ounces more than Lydia's cake. If Joanne's cake weighs $18\frac{3}{4}$ ounces, how much does Lydia's cake weigh?

 Self-Check

For Exercises 1–23, did you write your answers in simplest form?

Performance Assessment

Show What You Know About Fractions

1 Suppose you need to make 6 pounds of fruit salad.

a. You already have $2\frac{1}{4}$ pounds of strawberries, melon, and grapes. How much more fruit do you need?

b. You decide to buy blueberries, kiwi, and raspberries. You buy $1\frac{1}{2}$ pounds of blueberries and $\frac{3}{4}$ pounds of kiwi. How many pounds of raspberries do you need to buy?

c. You want to double the recipe. How much will you have of each kind of fruit?

Self-Check Did you remember to rename the 6 before subtracting $2\frac{1}{4}$?

2 Use the square below. Fraction pieces may be helpful.

a. What fraction is shown by the shaded region?

b. **Analyze** Without multiplying, tell whether the product $\frac{1}{2} \times \frac{3}{4}$ is less than or greater than 1. Explain.

Self-Check Did you realize that the square is divided into 4 equal parts for Question 2a?

 For Your Portfolio

You might wish to include this work in your portfolio.

Extension

Estimating a Fraction of a Number

Stevens Forest Elementary School has 97 fifth graders. If $\frac{1}{4}$ of them are in Mr. Ortega's class, about how many students are in his class?

You can estimate $\frac{1}{4}$ of 97 by thinking of a compatible number close to 97 that is divisible by 4.

Think 97 is very close to 100. $\frac{1}{4}$ of 100 is 25. This estimate is close to $\frac{1}{4}$ of 97, so there are about 25 students in Mr. Ortega's class.

> **Math Note**
>
> Did you remember that compatible numbers are numbers that are easy to compute with?

More Examples

Three fifths of the fifth-grade students ride buses. About how many students ride buses?

Think $\frac{1}{5}$ of 100 is 20.

$\frac{2}{5}$ would be $2 \times 20 = 40$.

$\frac{3}{5}$ would be $3 \times 20 = 60$.

$\frac{3}{5}$ of 97 is about 60.

There are about 60 students who ride buses.

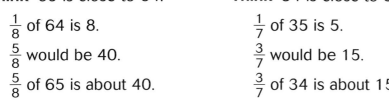

Estimate $\frac{5}{8}$ of 65.

Think 65 is close to 64.

$\frac{1}{8}$ of 64 is 8.

$\frac{5}{8}$ would be 40.

$\frac{5}{8}$ of 65 is about 40.

Estimate $\frac{3}{7}$ of 34.

Think 34 is close to 35.

$\frac{1}{7}$ of 35 is 5.

$\frac{3}{7}$ would be 15.

$\frac{3}{7}$ of 34 is about 15.

Try It Out

Estimate. Tell what compatible number you used.

1. $\frac{1}{4}$ of 25
2. $\frac{1}{5}$ of 27
3. $\frac{2}{3}$ of 14
4. $\frac{1}{2}$ of 51
5. $\frac{3}{10}$ of 102
6. $\frac{1}{8}$ of 43

7. One third of the fifth graders are in the band. About how many students are in the band?

Cumulative Review

Choose the correct letter for each answer.

Number Concepts	Operations

1. Which expression shows 56 as a product of prime factors?

    A. 7×8
    B. 2×28
    C. $2 \times 4 \times 7$
    D. $2 \times 2 \times 2 \times 7$

2. Maria got a hit 6 out of 10 times at bat. What fraction of her times at bat did she get a hit?

    A. $\frac{1}{4}$ **C.** $\frac{3}{5}$
    B. $\frac{2}{5}$ **D.** $\frac{5}{6}$

3. Which number sentence is **NOT** true?

    A. $0.567 > 0.0674$
    B. $0.45 = 0.450$
    C. $0.234 < 0.245$
    D. $0.036 < 0.033$

4. A recipe calls for $1\frac{1}{2}$ teaspoons of oil, $\frac{2}{3}$ teaspoon of vanilla, $\frac{3}{8}$ teaspoon of baking soda, and $1\frac{3}{4}$ teaspoons of water. How should these amounts be ordered from *least* to *greatest*?

    A. $\frac{3}{8}, \frac{2}{3}, 1\frac{1}{2}, 1\frac{3}{4}$

    B. $\frac{3}{8}, \frac{2}{3}, 1\frac{3}{4}, 1\frac{1}{2}$

    C. $1\frac{3}{4}, 1\frac{1}{2}, \frac{2}{3}, \frac{3}{8}$

    D. $\frac{2}{3}, \frac{3}{8}, 1\frac{1}{2}, 1\frac{3}{4}$

5. Katie sold 45 tickets to the Youth Club car wash. Ryan sold 67 tickets, including 7 tickets to his family. How many more tickets need to be sold to break the club record of 200 tickets?

    A. 155   **C.** 89
    B. 133   **D.** 88

6. There are 100 chairs set up in the gym. If the first 12 rows have 8 chairs each, how many chairs does the last row have?

    A. 10   **C.** 6
    B. 8   **D.** 4

7. Bo borrowed $50 from his brother Ken. He paid half of it back the first month. Then he paid back $10 more. How much does Bo still owe Ken?

    A. $25   **D.** $10
    B. $15   **E.** Not Here
    C. $12.50

8. Jackie and Brenda each bought a bag of 1,500 beads to make bracelets. It takes 50 beads to make a bracelet. If the girls made a total of 23 bracelets, about how many beads did they use?

    A. 500   **D.** 2,000
    B. 1,000   **E.** 3,000
    C. 1,500

Measurement	**Probability and Statistics**

9. Which expression can be used to find the **_area_** in square units of the section that is **NOT** shaded?

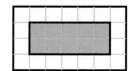

- **A.** 7 × 4
- **B.** (2 × 7) + (2 × 4)
- **C.** (7 × 4) − (5 × 2)
- **D.** 2 × (7 + 2)

10. How many meters are in the **_perimeter_** of this figure? (1 m = 100 cm)

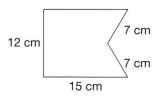

12 cm
7 cm
7 cm
15 cm

- **A.** 0.56 m
- **C.** 1.05 m
- **B.** 0.85 m
- **D.** 1.80 m

11. In Maria's science experiment, Frog A weighed 350 grams, and Frog B weighed 425 grams. Frog A then gained 125 grams, while Frog B stayed the same weight. How much more does Frog A now weigh than Frog B?

- **A.** 25 g
- **C.** 475 g
- **B.** 50 g
- **D.** 550 g

12. The **_perimeter_** of a rectangular dock is 90 feet. If the dock is 5 feet wide and rises 4 feet above the water, how long is it?

- **A.** 85 ft
- **B.** 70 ft
- **C.** 38 ft
- **D.** 40 ft

13. In a total of 500 spins, on which number will the spinner probably land the greatest number of times?

- **A.** 0
- **B.** 2
- **C.** 4
- **D.** 6

14. Amy has 4 beanbag animals to arrange in a row on one shelf. In how many different orders can she arrange the animals?

- **A.** 8
- **C.** 16
- **B.** 12
- **D.** 24

15. Dave's baseball team played 15 games this season. Dave struck out 1, 9, 3, 6, and 6 batters in the 5 games he pitched. What was the mean (average) number of batters he struck out per game?

- **A.** 5
- **C.** 7
- **B.** 6
- **D.** 9

16. Which is the best estimate of the difference between the high and low water levels in 1992?

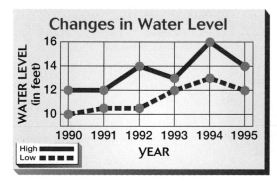

- **A.** 1 foot
- **C.** $2\frac{1}{2}$ feet
- **B.** 2 feet
- **D.** $3\frac{1}{2}$ feet

Chapter 11 Measurement

Chapter Theme: CONTAINERS

Real Facts

Pets come in all sizes, and so do their carriers and cages! The students in the picture on the right have brought their pets to school in containers specifically designed for each type of pet. The chart below shows the measurements for some pet containers.

Dimensions of Animal Cages/Carriers at Petmart			
Animal	Length (in.)	Width (in.)	Height (in.)
Small Dog	36	23	24
Cat	21	16	15
Gerbil	11	9	9
Bird	11	12	15

- A cat carrier needs to be long enough for a cat to comfortably lie down. Suppose your cat is $1\frac{1}{2}$ feet long lying down. Would you buy the cat carrier listed in the chart? Explain.

- How many gerbil cages could you completely fit end-to-end on a 3-foot by 1-foot table? Explain.

Real People

Meet Wendy Glancy, a merchandising supervisor. She plans how products are packaged and displayed in stores. Her displays are designed to fit exactly in a planned space and to show off a product in the best way possible. When her company needed a display case for back-to-school materials, she made it look like a yellow school bus. That really caught the customer's eye!

A Drip in Time

You can use what you know about telling time to change units and to find out how much time has passed.

Learning About It

What time is it? The ancient Egyptians told time with a water clock. Today, you simply look at your watch. But sometimes you need to change certain units of time to other units of time.

> **Word Bank**
>
> elapsed time

◄ **Social Studies Connection**
This clepsydra, or water clock, was filled with water. Water dripped through a hole in the bottom. Time was kept by noting the changing water level.

To change from a larger unit to a smaller unit, multiply.	To change from a smaller unit to a larger unit, divide.
2 d = ■ h (1 d = 24 h) 2 × 24 = 48 2 d = 48 h	78 wk = ■ yr (52 wk = 1 yr) $78 \div 52 = 1\frac{1}{2}$ $78 \text{ wk} = 1\frac{1}{2} \text{ yr}$

More Examples

A. 6 h 15 min = ■ min   (1 h = 60 min)
(6 × 60) + 15 = 360 + 15
6 h 15 min = 375 min

B. 35 d = ■ wk   (7 d = 1 wk)
35 ÷ 7 = 5
35 d = 5 wk

Connecting Ideas

Once you know how to change units of time, you can use addition and subtraction to find elapsed time.

It took from 8:30 A.M. until 12:15 P.M. to have a watch repaired. How long did the repair take? To find out, subtract. The difference between the two times is called **elapsed time**.

> **Units of Time**
>
> 60 seconds (s) = 1 minute (min)
> 60 minutes = 1 hour (h)
> 24 hours = 1 day (d)
> 7 days = 1 week (wk)
> 12 months (mo) = 1 year (yr)
> 52 weeks = 1 year
> 365 days = 1 year
> 366 days = 1 leap year

● **One way** to find elapsed time is to use a number line.

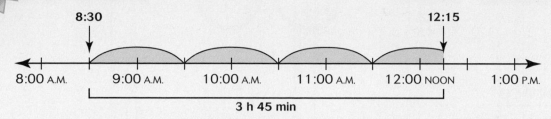

3 h 45 min

● **Another way** is to subtract.

11 h 75 min
~~12~~ h ~~15~~ min
− 8 h 30 min
─────────────
3 h 45 min

Rename 12 h 15 min
as 11 h 75 min, since
1 h = 60 min

It takes 3 h 45 min to repair the watch.

More Examples

1 h 90 min
A. ~~2~~ h ~~30~~ min
− 1 h 45 min
─────────
45 min

B. 3 h 45 min
+ 4 h 50 min
───
7 h **95 min** = 7 h + 1 h + 35 min = 8 h 35 min

Think and Discuss Samantha made a model of an Egyptian water clock. She filled the model at 9:35 A.M. The model was empty at 12:05 P.M. How much time had elapsed? Explain how you found the answer.

Try It Out

Choose a Method Use paper and pencil or a calculator to complete. Tell which method you chose and why.

1. 48 h = ■ d   **2.** 5 min = ■ s   **3.** 245 d = ■ wk   **4.** 2 yr = ■ wk

5. 26 wk = ■ yr   **6.** 36 h = ■ d   **7.** 7,200 s = ■ h   **8.** 91 d = ■ wk

Add or subtract.

9.   3 h 20 min
+ 2 h 35 min

10.   7 h 55 min
− 2 h 45 min

11.   5 h 7 min 18 s
+ 3 h 4 min 15 s

12.   4 h 12 min
− 2 h 22 min

Find each elapsed time.

13.
A.M.　　　　P.M.

14.
A.M.　　　　P.M.

15.
A.M.　　　　P.M.

Practice

Choose a Method Use paper and pencil or a calculator to complete. Tell which method you chose and why.

16. 1 d = ▇ min

17. 2 yr = ▇ d

18. 60 mo = ▇ yr

19. 2 h 35 min = ▇ min

20. 240 s = ▇ min

21. 108 h = ▇ d ▇ h

Add or subtract.

22.　　5 h 10 min
　　　+ 2 h 20 min

23.　　6 h 12 min
　　　− 2 h 15 min

24.　　8 h 45 min
　　　+ 6 h 50 min

25.　　17 h
　　　−　5 h 20 min

26.　　3 h 15 min
　　　+ 4 h 50 min

27.　　6 h 32 min
　　　− 5 h 40 min

28.　　9 h 12 min
　　　+ 7 h 52 min

29.　　36 h
　　　−　4 h 25 min

Find each elapsed time.

30. 5:00 A.M. to 7:17 A.M.

31. 2:20 P.M. to 1:50 A.M.

32. 11:15 A.M. to 6:10 P.M.

33. 7:45 A.M. to 5:15 P.M.

34. 8:10 P.M. to 12:35 A.M.

35. 10:20 A.M. to 3:35 P.M.

Problem Solving

36. Carolyn put her cake batter in the oven at 7:15 A.M. and set the timer for 50 minutes. What time was it when the timer buzzed?

37. At a bottling plant, 6,000 bottles are filled with spring water each hour. Would it be reasonable to say that 100 bottles are filled each minute?

38. Mrs. Van Ness's class rehearsed the show *Time After Time,* beginning at 9:15 A.M. If the rehearsal lasted 1 h 25 min, at what time did it end?

39. Analyze There was a power outage in Cynthia's neighborhood at 9:47 A.M. It lasted for 1 h 45 min. At what time was the power restored?

▲ **Social Studies Connection** The egg timer on the right is similar to the English sandglass on the left.

40. Journal Idea Suppose you are a space scientist preparing to travel to a planet where a day is 20 Earth hours long. Design a clock that divides such a day into hours that have 60 minutes each.

Review and Remember

Find each answer.

41. $\frac{7}{10} + \frac{1}{4}$ **42.** $\frac{3}{8} + \frac{1}{5}$ **43.** $\frac{5}{6} - \frac{2}{3}$ **44.** $5\frac{1}{8} - 2\frac{3}{8}$ **45.** $3\frac{2}{3} + 2\frac{1}{4}$

46. $18 + 6\frac{1}{2}$ **47.** $3\frac{1}{3} - \frac{2}{3}$ **48.** $4\frac{2}{3} - 1\frac{3}{4}$ **49.** $3\frac{7}{8} + 8\frac{5}{16}$ **50.** $5\frac{5}{8} + 4\frac{13}{16}$

51. $2.5 + 8.7$ **52.** 82×38 **53.** $62\overline{)3{,}857}$ **54.** 0.5×0.08 **55.** $8.41 - 0.526$

Critical Thinking Corner
Visual Thinking

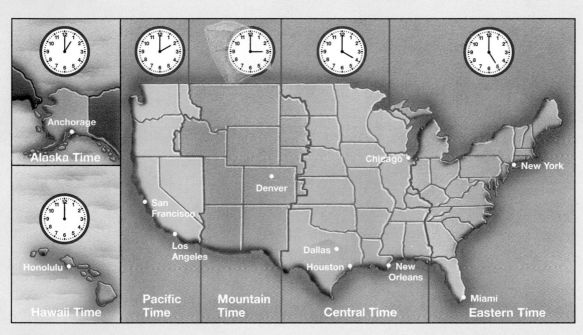

Pacific Time | Mountain Time | Central Time | Eastern Time

Time Zones

The U.S. swimming competition was held at 5:00 P.M. in San Francisco. It was broadcast live throughout the United States. The broadcast lasted 3 hours and 30 minutes.

1. What time did the broadcast begin in Dallas? in Honolulu?

2. When did the broadcast end in San Francisco? in Honolulu?

Will It Fit?

The length of an object can be measured in customary units.

Learning About It

Suppose you are buying a miniature model car. You want to know if it will fit in the storage box you have. You need to measure the box. Look at the ruler below. To the nearest $\frac{1}{16}$ inch, the box is $2\frac{1}{16}$ inches wide and $3\frac{1}{16}$ inches long. The model car will fit inside the box.

What You Need

For each student:
   inch ruler

Length: $2\frac{7}{8}$ in.
Width: $1\frac{3}{16}$ in.

$3\frac{1}{16}$ in.

inches

Estimate and then measure some things in your classroom.

- To the nearest inch, what is the length of your desk?

- To the nearest $\frac{1}{2}$ in., what is the width of your mathematics book?

- To the nearest $\frac{1}{4}$ in., how thick is your mathematics book?

- To the nearest $\frac{1}{8}$ in., how long is your pencil?

- To the nearest $\frac{1}{16}$ in., how wide is a paper clip?

Sometimes you need to change units of length. What would be the length of your desk in feet and inches?

> **Customary Units of Length**
>
> 12 inches (in.) = 1 foot (ft)
> 36 inches = 3 feet, or 1 yard (yd)
> 5,280 feet = 1 mile (mi)

To change from a larger unit to a smaller unit, multiply.	To change from a smaller unit to a larger unit, divide.

2 ft 3 in. = ■ in.   (1 ft = 12 in.)
$(2 \times 12) + 3 = 24 + 3$
2 ft 3 in. = 27 in.

27 in. = ■ ft   (12 in. = 1 ft)
$27 \div 12 = 2$ R3
27 in. = 2 ft 3 in.

Another Example

63 in. = ■ yd ■ ft ■ in.   (36 in. = 1 yd / 12 in. = 1 ft)
$63 \div 36 = 1$ yd 27 in.
$27 \div 12 = 2$ ft 3 in.
63 in. = 1 yd 2 ft 3 in.

Connecting Ideas

You can change units of length to larger or smaller units to add and subtract measurements.

Your class decides to organize the class supplies in boxes and keep them on a shelf. To find out how wide the shelf space must be to store the boxes, you can add.

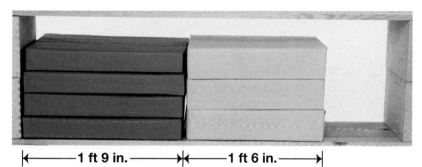

|← 1 ft 9 in. →|← 1 ft 6 in. →|

  1 ft 9 in.
+ 1 ft 6 in.
—————————
2 ft 15 in. = 2 ft + 1 ft + 3 in. = 3 ft 3 in.   (Rename 15 in. as 1 ft + 3 in.)

The shelf space needs to be at least 3 ft 3 in. wide.

Another Example

   3 ft 15 in.
   4̶ ft 3̶ in.   (Rename 4 ft 3 in. as 3 ft 15 in.)
 − 2 ft 6 in.
—————————
   1 ft 9 in.

Think and Discuss What unit of measure would you use to measure your shoe? a fence around a vegetable garden? the distance to a friend's house in another city?

Try It Out

Estimate each length. Then measure each to the nearest $\frac{1}{4}$ inch, nearest $\frac{1}{8}$ inch, and nearest $\frac{1}{16}$ inch.

1.

2.

3.

Complete.

4. 5 yd = ▓ ft

5. 84 ft = ▓ yd

6. 32 in. = ▓ ft ▓ in.

7. 10 mi = ▓ ft

8. 156 ft = ▓ yd

9. 86 in. = ▓ ft ▓ in.

Add or subtract. Change to a larger unit when possible.

10. 6 yd 2 ft
     + 7 yd 1 ft

11. 5 ft 1 in.
     − 2 ft 10 in.

12. 4 mi 7 ft
     + 3 mi 9 ft

13. 10 yd 6 ft 5 in.
     − 3 yd 7 ft 3 in.

Practice

Measure the length of the box to each unit given.

14. nearest $\frac{1}{2}$ in.

15. nearest $\frac{1}{4}$ in.

16. nearest $\frac{1}{8}$ in.

17. nearest $\frac{1}{16}$ in.

Complete.

18. 18 yd = ▓ in.

19. 25 ft = ▓ yd

20. 56 in. = ▓ ft ▓ in.

Add or subtract. Change to a larger unit when possible.

21. 14 yd 1 ft
     + 8 yd 1 ft

22. 8 ft 10 in.
     + 9 ft 9 in.

23. 3 mi 150 ft
     − 2 mi 55 ft

24. 32 yd 2 ft 1 in.
     − 13 yd 1 ft 7 in.

25. 8 ft 7 in.
     − 2 ft 11 in.

26. 2 yd 9 in.
     + 1 yd 2 in.

27. 21 ft 5 in.
     − 5 ft 9 in.

28. 15 mi 13 yd 2 ft
     + 8 mi 12 yd 1 ft

29. 1mi 2,000 ft
     +1mi 3,380 ft

30. 6 yd 2 ft
     − 2 yd 3 ft

31. 36 ft 7 in.
     − 21 ft 9 in.

32. 27 yd 2ft 11in.
     + 46 yd 2ft 9in.

Problem Solving

33. Using Estimation A box is $3\frac{3}{8}$ in. wide. Would five boxes fit side by side in a 20-in. wide container? Tell how you decided.

34. Analyze Suppose you fit the four boxes described below inside each other as shown here. What would be the width and length of Box D?

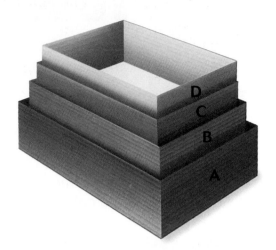

- Box A: 7 in. wide by 10 in. long

- Box B: 1 inch smaller in each dimension than Box A

- Box C: $\frac{1}{2}$ inch smaller in each dimension than Box B

- Box D: $\frac{1}{4}$ inch smaller in each dimension than Box C

Review and Remember

Round each number to the underlined place.

35. 1.3<u>0</u>2   **36.** <u>0</u>.514   **37.** 256,4<u>9</u>5   **38.** 6,<u>4</u>68,920   **39.** 26.1<u>9</u>3

40. 2<u>3</u>.65   **41.** 9,1<u>5</u>8   **42.** 782,<u>7</u>60   **43.** 6,279,<u>0</u>99   **44.** 138.2<u>7</u>

Time for Technology

Surf the Net

Changing Units of Measure

Many times you need to change one unit of measure to another unit, such as changing inches to yards or meters to kilometers.

There are sites on the Internet that can help you with measurement conversions. Explore the sites below and then share your findings.

www.vol.it/mirror/meascon/

Developing Skills for Problem Solving

First read for understanding and then focus on deciding if an estimate is enough to solve a problem.

READ FOR UNDERSTANDING

Last summer Anne earned a total of $55 raking leaves. She decided to spend some of her money to buy *The Big Box of Games* from a catalog store. After placing her order, Anne received the confirmation slip shown below.

TOTALLY GAMES				
Item Number	Description	Cost of Item	Shipping and Handling	Delivery Date
18114	The Big Box of Games	$41.98	$7.35	May 12–May 15

1 What is the cost of *The Big Box of Games*?

2 What is the cost of shipping and handling?

THINK AND DISCUSS

 MATH FOCUS

Is an Estimate Enough? Whether or not an estimate or an exact answer is needed depends upon the situation. Some problems can be solved by finding an estimate. Others require an exact answer.

Reread the paragraph at the top of the page.

3 Is an estimate all Anne needs to find if she has enough money to pay for *The Big Box of Games*? Why or why not?

4 How much will Anne have to pay in all for her order? Did you find an exact answer or an estimate? Why?

5 Write a problem that needs to be solved by finding an exact answer and another problem that can be solved by estimating.

Show What You Learned

Answer each question. Explain your choice.

Totally Games sells over 700 sets of The Big Box of Games each year. This year The Big Box of Games costs $41.98. That is a $2.26 increase over last year's price.

1 Which is true about the number of games sold?

   a. At least 700 were sold.

   b. Less than 700 were sold.

   c. Exactly 700 were sold.

2 Which is true about the price increase?

   a. It was less than $2.26.

   b. It was more than $2.26.

   c. It was exactly $2.26.

3 Which represents the cost of The Big Box of Games last year?

   a. The sum of the price this year and the increase in price

   b. The difference between the price this year and the increase in price

   c. The difference between the number sold and the price this year

4 Which expression gives the cost of The Big Box of Games last year?

   a. $41.98 + $2.26 = $44.24

   b. $700 − $41.98 = $658.02

   c. $41.98 − $2.26 = $39.72

Mr. Cook has $200 to spend on wooden shelves for the classroom. Use the information on the catalog page at the right for Problems 5–6.

5 Mr. Cook would like to buy three shelves. Does he need an exact answer or can he estimate to see if he has enough money? Explain your choice.

6 Mr. Cook decides to buy two wooden shelves. If the cost of shipping and handling is $12.49, what is the total cost? Tell how you found your answer. Is it exact or an estimate?

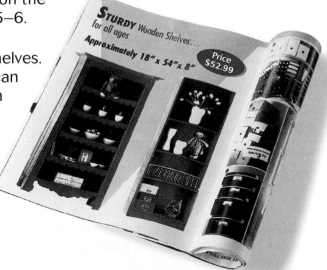

STURDY Wooden Shelves...
for all ages
Approximately 18" x 54" x 8"
Price $52.99

Fill It Up!

Customary units of capacity tell how much containers hold.

Learning About It

Capacity is the amount of liquid a container can hold. The conversion table below shows how different units of capacity are related to each other.

Customary Units of Capacity

8 fluid ounces (fl oz) = 1 cup (c)
2 cups = 1 pint (pt)
2 pints = 1 quart (qt)
4 quarts = 1 gallon (gal)

| 1 gal | 4 qt = 1 gal | 8 pt = 1 gal | 16 c = 1 gal |

Connecting Ideas

Use the relationships shown in the table above when you change from one unit to another.

To change from a larger unit to a smaller unit, multiply.	To change from a smaller unit to a larger unit, divide.

5 gal = ■ qt   (1 gal = 4 qt)
5 x 4 = 20
5 gal = 20 qt

16 c = ■ pt   (2 c = 1 pt)
16 ÷ 2 = 8
16 c = 8 pt

More Examples

A. 6 gal = ■ pt   (1 gal = 8 pt)
    6 × 8 = 48
    6 gal = 48 pt

B. 48 fl oz = ■ c   (8 fl oz = 1 c)
    48 ÷ 8 = 6
    48 fl oz = 6 c

Think and Discuss Find a combination of standard-sized containers that will hold one gallon of water.

Try It Out

Complete.

1. 6 gal = ■ qt

2. 14 qt = ■ c

3. 6 c = ■ fl oz

4. 3 pt = ■ qt

Practice

Complete.

5. 5 qt = ■ pt

6. 9 gal = ■ pt

7. 8 c = ■ pt

8. 32 fl oz = ■ c

9. 18 c = ■ pt

10. 20 qt = ■ gal

11. 12 pt = ■ c

12. 8 gal = ■ qt

13. $9\frac{1}{2}$ gal = ■ qt

14. 8 c = ■ fl oz

15. $1\frac{1}{2}$ qt = ■ pt

16. 160 fl oz = ■ pt

17. 2 gal = ■ pt

18. 8 qt = ■ c

19. 11 qt = ■ gal

20. 9 c = ■ pt

Problem Solving

For Problems 21–24, write a customary unit of capacity that is reasonable.

21. The gas tank was filled with 15 __?__ of gas.

22. The thirsty boy drank 16 __?__ of water after running the race.

23. The recipe called for 1 __?__ of flour.

24. The store was out of gallons, so he had to buy 4 __?__ of milk.

25. You Decide You need exactly $1\frac{3}{4}$ gallons of water. You have a gallon jug, a few quart containers, and a few pint containers. List a combination of containers to equal $1\frac{3}{4}$ gallons.

26. About how many fluid ounces of water are needed to fill one of the containers shown in the photograph?

▲ This Moroccan man is carrying water to be sold to thirsty people. Each container holds about $1\frac{1}{2}$ cups of water.

Review and Remember

Compare. Write >, <, or = for each ●.

27. $\frac{2}{3}$ ● $\frac{2}{7}$

28. $\frac{1}{3}$ ● $\frac{1}{5}$

29. $\frac{2}{4}$ ● $\frac{3}{6}$

30. $\frac{4}{8}$ ● $\frac{5}{6}$

31. $\frac{1}{3}$ ● $\frac{4}{5}$

32. $\frac{3}{4}$ ● $\frac{7}{8}$

33. $\frac{2}{3}$ ● $\frac{2}{6}$

34. $\frac{7}{12}$ ● $\frac{1}{2}$

35. $2\frac{3}{8}$ ● $2\frac{3}{4}$

36. $4\frac{5}{6}$ ● $4\frac{7}{8}$

37. $1\frac{2}{3}$ ● $1\frac{3}{4}$

38. $\frac{3}{24}$ ● $\frac{1}{8}$

For Extra Practice, see Set C, page 467.

Pack It Up!

Tons, pounds, and ounces are customary units of weight.

Learning About It

You have two boxes to mail. One is brass, and one is wood. The cost to mail a box depends on its weight. How much heavier is one than the other?

1 lb 4 oz

15 oz

Customary Units of Weight

16 ounces (oz) = 1 pound (lb)
2,000 pounds = 1 ton (T)

You can compare the weights of two objects by using the same units to express their weights.

To change from a larger unit to a smaller unit, multiply.	To change from a smaller unit to a larger unit, divide.

1 lb 4 oz = ■ oz   (1 lb = 16 oz)

(1 × 16) + 4 = 20

1 lb 4 oz = 20 oz

2,500 lb = ■ T ■ lb   (2,000 lb = 1 T)

2,500 ÷ 2,000 = 1 R500

2,500 lb = 1 T 500 lb

Since 1 lb 4 oz = 20 oz and 20 − 15 = 5, the brass box weighs 5 oz more than the wood box.

Think and Discuss How could you write the answer to 20 oz ÷ 16 oz so that the answer would show only pounds?

Try It Out

Complete each statement.

1. 5 lb = ■ oz

2. 26 oz = ■ lb ■ oz

3. 100 oz = ■ lb ■ oz

4. 8 lb 2 oz = ■ oz

5. 3 T = ■ lb

6. 1,000 lb = ■ T

The illustrations below represent real containers.
For each, write a reasonable unit of weight.

7.

can of peas

8.

crate of apples

9.

packet of sugar

10.

cement mixer

Practice

Complete each statement.

11. 48 oz = ▇ lb

12. 36 oz = ▇ lb ▇ oz

13. 9 lb = ▇ oz

14. 5,000 lb = ▇ T ▇ lb

15. 46 oz = ▇ lb ▇ oz

16. 4 T = ▇ lb

17. 92 oz = ▇ lb

18. 10,000 lb = ▇ T

19. 7 lb 9 oz = ▇ oz

20. 8 T 30 lb = ▇ lb

21. 8,750 lb = ▇ T ▇ lb

22. 9 lb 4 oz = ▇ oz

For each, list two objects whose weights are measured in
the unit listed. Then estimate each object's weight.

23. ounces

24. pounds

25. tons

Problem Solving

26. How many 1-oz servings of cereal are in a giant
5 lb 4 oz box?

27. A store received a shipment of 20 backpacks
weighing 21 lb. If a large backpack weighs
20 oz and a small backpack weighs 12 oz, how
many of each size were in the shipment? Tell
what strategy you used to solve the problem.

28. Mary used a circular basket, much like the one
at the right, to carry 85 oz of rice. If the basket
weighed 2 lb 2 oz, what was the total weight of
the rice and basket?

▲ **Social Studies Connection**
This circular basket, which weighs
about 2 pounds, was made in
China during the late sixteenth
century. Made of wood and
woven materials, it was used
for carrying food.

Review and Remember

Using Algebra Write a rule for each input/output table.

29.

Input	Output
1.65	2.05
6.02	6.42

30.

Input	Output
1,550	2,600
4,265	5,315

31.

Input	Output
10.68	10.63
0.72	0.67

For Extra Practice, see Set D, page 467.

Around the World

You have learned to use customary measurements.
Now you will learn to use the metric system of measurement.

Learning About It

The metric system is officially called the International System of Units because it is used around the world. The term *metric* comes from the Latin word for measure, *metricus*. In the metric system, the basic unit of length is the **meter**.

What You Need

For each student:
  metric ruler
  large paper clip

Word Bank

meter

Metric Units of Length

1,000 millimeters (mm) = 1 meter (m)
100 centimeters (cm) = 1 meter
10 decimeters (dm) = 1 meter
1 kilometer (km) = 1,000 meters

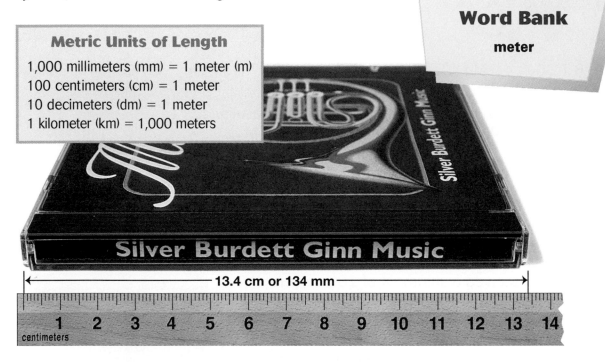

13.4 cm or 134 mm

Estimate, then measure some things in your classroom.

- To the nearest centimeter, what is the width of a jumbo paper clip?

- To the nearest millimeter, what is the thickness of eight sheets of notebook paper?

- To the nearest decimeter, what is the width of your desk?

- To the nearest centimeter, what is the length of an unsharpened pencil?

- To the nearest millimeter, what is the width of an eraser?

Connecting Ideas

Notice that the width of the CD jewel case on page 438 is 13.4 cm or 134 mm. Here is how you change from one unit of measure to another.

Since the metric system is based on 10s, it is easy to change from one unit to another.

The table below shows the relationships among metric units of length.

Metric Units of Length

1 kilometer 1,000.0 m	1 hectometer 100.0 m	1 dekameter 10.0 m	1 meter	1 decimeter 0.1 m	1 centimeter 0.01 m	1 millimeter 0.001 m

Changing from one unit to another is like moving from one place-value position to another.

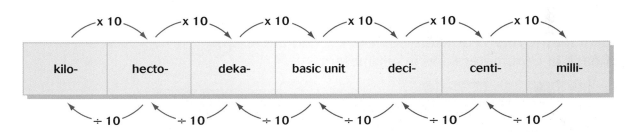

To change from a larger unit to a smaller unit, multiply.	To change from a smaller unit to a larger unit, divide.

1.03 m = ■ cm   (1 m = 100 cm)
1.03 × 100 = 103
1.03 m = 103 cm

39 m = ■ km   (1 km = 1,000 m)
39 ÷ 1,000 = 0.039
39 m = 0.039 km

More Examples

A. 88 km = ■ m   (1 km = 1,000 m)
88 × 1,000 = 88,000
88 km = 88,000 m

B. 27 cm = ■ m   (100 cm = 1 m)
27 ÷ 100 = 0.27
27 cm = 0.27 m

Think and Discuss What metric unit would be the best to use for measuring the length of a shoelace? the width of your classroom? the distance to another state?

Try It Out

Choose a reasonable metric unit for each item listed.
Then estimate and measure each item.

1. width of classroom   **2.** length of chalk   **3.** thickness of math book

Choose a Method Use mental math or paper and pencil
to complete. Tell which method you chose and why.

4. 1.8 km = ▦ m   **5.** 750 m = ▦ km   **6.** 95.8 cm = ▦ mm   **7.** 197 cm = ▦ m

Practice

Complete each sentence with a metric unit of length that
is reasonable.

8. A dime is only 1 ▦ thick.   **9.** A large paper clip is about 5 ▦ long.

10. John's arm is 63 ▦ long.   **11.** Bob ran 42.195 ▦ in a marathon.

12. New York City is about 4,800 ▦
from Los Angeles.   **13.** A computer disk is about 9 ▦ wide.

Use a metric ruler. For Exercises 14–19, find the length
of each in centimeters and in millimeters.

14.

15.

16.

17. ├────────┤   **18.** ├──┤   **19.** ├──────────┤

Using Mental Math Complete each statement.

20. 8 km = ▦ m   **21.** 3.8 cm = ▦ mm   **22.** 9,875 m = ▦ km

23. 7.29 mm = ▦ cm   **24.** 52 m = ▦ dm   **25.** 94 mm = ▦ cm

26. 25,450 m = ▦ km   **27.** 37 dm = ▦ m   **28.** 520 mm = ▦ m

29. 14.5 mm = ▦ cm   **30.** 234 cm = ▦ m   **31.** 35 km = ▦ m

Problem Solving

Use the picture of the cassette storage tower for Problems 32–34.

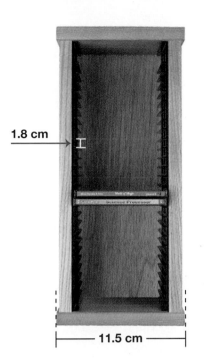

1.8 cm

11.5 cm

32. If three CD storage towers are placed side by side, what will be the overall width in cm?

33. From center-to-center, the height of a CD slot is 1.8 cm. If a tower holds 30 CDs, what is the height inside the tower in cm?

34. What If? Suppose you bought a CD tower that had an inside height of 81 cm. How many CDs would it hold?

35. Analyze One CD tower costs $29.95. If you paid $95.25 for three towers, how much sales tax did you pay?

Review and Remember

Find each answer.

36. 9×0.875

37. 5×13.5

38. $88.5 - 7$

39. 92.6×8

40. $28.56 + 3$

41. $42.50 - 7.43$

42. $14.4 \div 9$

43. $57.9 \div 6$

Money $ense

Postage Paid

At the Send and Save shipping service, shipping charges are based on weight. A customer shipped the following 3 items:

- an envelope weighing 0.6 oz

- an envelope weighing 3 oz

- a package weighing 4 pounds.

The customer sent the envelopes by regular service and the package by express service. She gave the clerk a ten-dollar bill. What were the total charges, and how much change did she get back?

Regular Service	
First Ounce (or less)	$0.32
Each Additional Ounce	$0.23
Over 11 ounces (See Express Service)	

Express Service	
Up to 2 Pounds	$3.00
Each Additional pound	$1.00

For Extra Practice, see Set E, page 467.

Hold Everything

*What you know about metric units of length can
help you understand metric units of capacity.*

Learning About It

Just how much is a liter? Compare the capacities of
several different containers to that of a 1-liter bottle.
Which hold more than a liter? Which hold less?

What You Need

For each group:
    *numbered containers of
        different sizes*
    two 1-L bottles of water
    metric measuring cup

Metric Units of Capacity

1 liter (L) = 1,000 milliliters (mL)

Step 1 Work with your group. Estimate
the capacity of each container to the
nearest 100 mL. Record your estimates
in a chart like the one shown.

Step 2 Use the measuring cup to find
the capacity of each container. Record
your measurements in the chart.
Compare your estimates with the
actual capacities.

Container	Estimated Capacity	Actual Capacity
1		
2		

To change from a larger unit
to a smaller unit, multiply.

8 L = ■ mL   (1 L = 1,000 mL)
8 × 1,000 = 8,000
8 L = 8,000 mL

To change from a smaller unit
to a larger unit, divide.

5,500 mL = ■ L   (1,000 mL = 1 L)
5,500 ÷ 1,000 = 5.5
5,500 mL = 5.5 L

Think and Discuss Look around your classroom.
What other containers hold about 1 liter of liquid?

Try It Out

Select a reasonable metric unit of capacity for each item. Use *mL* or *L*.

1. a fuel tank   **2.** a dose of medicine   **3.** a glass of water   **4.** water in a bathtub

Complete.

5. 50 L = ■ mL   **6.** 5.8 L = ■ mL   **7.** 1,500 mL = ■ L   **8.** 6,000 mL = ■ L

Practice

Select a reasonable metric unit of capacity for each. Use *mL* or *L*.

9. a teapot

10. an aquarium

11. a mug

12. Her car gets 20 km to a ■ of gas.

13. The test requires the nurse to take 10 ■ of blood.

14. The spring water came in a 1-■ bottle.

Complete.

15. 23 L = ■ mL

16. 500 mL = ■ L

17. 10,500 mL = ■ L

18. 5,250 mL = ■ L

19. 25 L = ■ mL

20. 1.55 L = ■ mL

21. 7,300 mL = ■ L

22. 0.5 L = ■ mL

23. 250 mL = ■ L

Problem Solving

24. Using Estimation You buy seven 1-liter bottles of a sports drink. Each bottle costs $0.98. A glass holds about 235 mL.

    a. About how many glasses can you fill?

    b. About how much does each glass cost?

25. Alison wants to drink 2 L of water a day. She has already had four 250 mL glasses. How many more glasses of water should she drink?

$\frac{2}{3}$ water $\frac{1}{2}$ water

▲Health and Fitness Connection
About two thirds of a man's body and little more than half of a woman's body are made up of water. The average man has about 47.3 L of water in his body, and the average woman, about 31.2 L.

Review and Remember

Find each answer.

26. 3.1 × 6.4

27. 52.5 − 36.28

28. 30.4 ÷ 8

29. 854 + 765.9

For Extra Practice, see Set F, page 467.

Balancing Act

You will learn more about measuring mass by comparing the masses of different objects.

Learning About It

In the metric system, the basic unit of **mass** is the **gram**. A 1-inch-long paper clip has a mass of about 1 gram. In this activity you will find the masses of familiar objects.

Step 1 Work with your group. Compare the objects in the paper bag by holding each in your hand. Arrange the objects from lightest to heaviest.

> **Word Bank**
>
> **mass**
> **gram**

What You Need

For each group:
  large paper bag of
    assorted objects
  pan balance
  gram masses

Step 2 Estimate the mass of each object. Record your estimates.

Step 3 Find the mass of the object you think is the lightest. Use a pan balance to find the actual mass. How close was your estimate?

Step 4 Repeat the process above for each object. Did your estimates get closer with each try?

> **Metric Units of Mass**
>
> 1 kilogram (kg) = 1,000 grams (g)
> 1 g = 1,000 milligrams (mg)

To change from a larger unit to a smaller unit, multiply.	To change from a smaller unit to a larger unit, divide.
3.4 kg = ▉ g (1 kg = 1,000 g)	250 mg = ▉ g (1,000 mg = 1 g)
3.4 × 1,000 = 3,400	250 ÷ 1,000 = 0.25
3.4 kg = 3,400 g	250 mg = 0.25 g

More Examples

A. 2.5 g = ■ mg   1 g = 1,000 mg
2.5 × 1,000 = 2,500
2.5 g = 2,500 mg

B. 45.3 g = ■ kg   1,000 g = 1 kg
45.3 ÷ 1,000 = 0.0453
45.3 g = 0.0453 kg

Think and Discuss A milligram is 0.001 gram. What might be measured in milligrams?

> ### Did You Know?
> The mass of one raisin is about 0.3 grams, the mass of one nickel is about 5 grams, and the mass of two chalkboard erasers is about 100 grams.

Try It Out

Complete each statement.

1. 42 kg = ■ g
2. 9,000 g = ■ kg
3. 25 g = ■ mg
4. 450 mg = ■ g

Practice

For each, choose *kg*, *g*, or *mg*.

5. a pickup truck
6. a cereal box
7. a grand piano
8. a box of tissues
9. a toothpick
10. a pen

Using Mental Math Complete each statement.

11. 83 kg = ■ g
12. 6,000 g = ■ kg
13. 15 kg = ■ g
14. 0.8 kg = ■ g
15. 9,700 mg = ■ g
16. 8,345 g = ■ kg
17. 1.98 g = ■ mg
18. 700 g = ■ kg
19. 20,000 g = ■ kg

Problem Solving

20. **Analyze** Which has a greater mass—one hundred 49-g boxes of pasta or ten 0.49-kg boxes of pasta?

21. You are buying boxes of pasta, and the contents of each box has a mass of 450 g. How many boxes must you buy if you want to cook at least 1 kg of pasta?

22. Jill bought 36 hamburger patties. If each patty has a mass of 100 g and contains about 28 g of fat, about how many kg of fat are in the 36 patties?

Review and Remember

Write each fraction as a decimal.

23. $\frac{3}{4}$
24. $\frac{2}{5}$
25. $\frac{1}{10}$
26. $\frac{3}{100}$
27. $\frac{4}{5}$
28. $\frac{1}{4}$

For Extra Practice, see Set G, page 467.

Cool It!

You are probably more familiar with the Fahrenheit scale than with the Celsius scale.

Learning About It

In the metric system, temperature is read in Celsius degrees. In the customary system, it is read in Fahrenheit degrees.

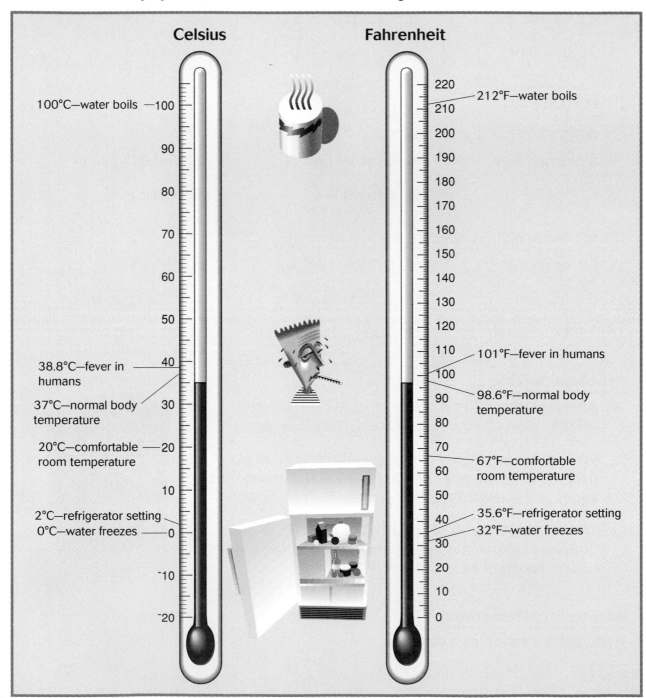

Celsius

100°C—water boils —100
90
80
70
60
50
38.8°C—fever in humans —40
37°C—normal body temperature —30
20°C—comfortable room temperature —20
10
2°C—refrigerator setting
0°C—water freezes —0
⁻10
⁻20

Fahrenheit

220
212°F—water boils
210
200
190
180
170
160
150
140
130
120
110
101°F—fever in humans
100
90 — 98.6°F—normal body temperature
80
70
67°F—comfortable room temperature
60
50
40 — 35.6°F—refrigerator setting
30 — 32°F—water freezes
20
10
0

Think and Discuss Describe the clothes you would wear if the temperature were ⁻5°C, 20°C, and 36°C.

Try It Out

For each thermometer, write the temperature and an appropriate outdoor activity for that temperature.

1.
°C

2.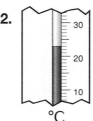
°C

3.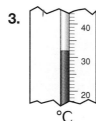
°C

4.
°F

5.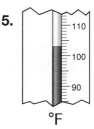
°F

Practice

Write the temperature for each thermometer. Then tell which one represents water boiling.

6.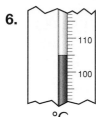
°C

7.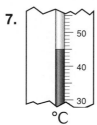
°C

8.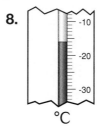
°C

9.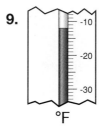
°F

10.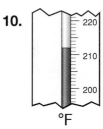
°F

Problem Solving

INTERNET ACTIVITY
www.sbgmath.com

Use the bar graph to answer Problems 11–13.

11. Social Studies Connection What is the difference in the average temperature between Tirunelveli and Djibouti?

12. How much colder is the average temperature in Norilsk, Russia, than the average temperature in Yakutsk, Russia?

13. Analyze How much hotter is the average temperature in Djibouti than in Norilsk?

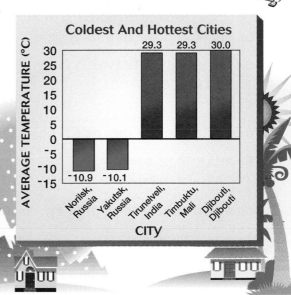

Review and Remember

Find each answer.

14. $\frac{3}{4} \times 20$ **15.** $1\frac{1}{8} + \frac{3}{4}$ **16.** $15 \times \frac{3}{5}$ **17.** $40 - \frac{5}{8}$ **18.** $\frac{2}{3} \times 21$

✓ Checkpoint
Time and Measurement

Find each elapsed time. (pages 424–427)

1. Start: 4:40 P.M.
Finish: 6:25 P.M.

2. Start: 10:10 A.M.
Finish: 12:50 P.M.

3. Start: 8:30 A.M.
Finish: 1:15 P.M.

Add or subtract. (pages 424–427)

4. 5 h 25 min
+ 2 h 15 min

5. 14 h
− 6 h 25 min

6. 20 min 17 s
− 6 min 30 s

Add or subtract. Change to a larger unit when possible. (pages 428–431)

7. 45 yd 7 ft 2 in.
− 16 yd 6 ft 8 in.

8. 17 mi 12 yd 2 ft
+ 9 mi 13 yd 3 ft

9. 33 ft 4 in.
+ 6 ft 10 in.

Complete each statement. (pages 434–435)

10. 3 qt = ■ pt

11. 3 c = ■ fl oz

12. 5 c = ■ pt

Complete each statement. (pages 436–437)

13. 108 oz = ■ lb ■ oz

14. 15,000 lb = ■ T ■ lb

15. $2\frac{1}{2}$ lb = ■ oz

For each, choose *mm, cm, m,* or *km*. (pages 438–441)

16. the distance between New York and Chicago

17. the length of your kitchen table

For each, choose *mL,* or *L*. (pages 442–443)

18. a bottle of soda

19. a sample of blood

20. a dose of cough syrup

For each, choose *mg, g,* or *kg*. (pages 444–445)

21. a vitamin pill

22. an adult woman

23. a can of peaches

What happens to water at each of these temperatures?
(pages 446–447)

24. 0°C

25. 100°C

26. 212°F

27. 32°F

Problem Solving

28. On Friday morning, when the school bell rang, all the electric clocks read 6:22 A.M.. The school bell usually rings at 8:15 A.M.. How long was the electricity probably off?

29. You have pint and quart containers. What are some combinations of containers for collecting 1 gallon?

30. The temperature at 6 A.M. was 15°F. By noon it had risen 22°, and by 6:00 P.M. it had dropped 12°. What was the temperature at 6:00 P.M.?

What do you think?

Which system of measurement—customary or metric—is easier to use? Give a reason for your answer.

Journal Idea

Use examples to explain why you multiply to change hours into minutes and why you divide to change minutes into hours.

Critical Thinking Corner

Visual Thinking

Optical Illusions

Compare line segments $\overline{AB}$ and $\overline{BC}$. Are they the same length or different lengths? Tell what you think. Then measure both segments. Do your measurements agree with your first reaction? Give a reason for the result.

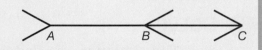

Compare line segments $\overline{MN}$ and $\overline{OP}$. Are they the same length or different lengths? Measure the two segments. How can you account for the way they appear?

These two drawings are optical illusions. You see the lines, but you usually do not accurately judge what you are seeing. Try making your own optical illusion and share it with a classmate.

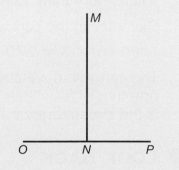

Problem-Solving Strategy

Problem Solving
Use a Simulation

*Sometimes using a simulation can help
you see mathematical relationships.*

How far will the cart in the picture move
with one turn of its wheels? This distance
is equal to the **circumference** of 1 wheel.

 UNDERSTAND

What do you need to find?

You need to find the distance the cart
will travel in one turn of its wheels
without actually moving the cart.

 PLAN

How can you solve the problem?

You can **use a simulation**, or model, of a
moving cart. Try rolling a quarter to simulate the
rolling cart wheels. Think of what you know
about the diameter and circumference of a circle
to find out how far the wheels would move.

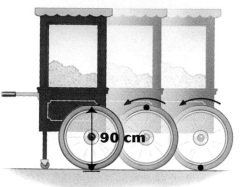

 SOLVE

By rolling a quarter, you find that the distance of
one roll is a little more than 3 times the length of the
coin's diameter. In one turn the cart will travel
a little more than 3 times the diameter of one wheel.

Diameter of the cart wheel = 90 cm

90 cm × 3 = 270 cm

The cart will move about 270 cm in
one turn of its wheels. This distance
is the circumference of the wheel.

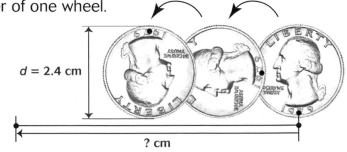

$d = 2.4$ cm

? cm

 LOOK BACK

Why could you also use a circular plate as a model
to simulate finding the circumference of a cart wheel?

▲ The circumference of any
circle is about 3 times
the length of its diameter.
What is the approximate
circumference of a quarter?

Using the Strategy

Use a simulation to solve Problems 1–4.

1 José and Elaine painted a fence. In an hour, José painted $\frac{1}{4}$ of his side, and Elaine painted $\frac{1}{3}$ of her side. At the same rate, how long will it take José to paint his side? Elaine to paint her side?

2 Don cut out a cardboard circle with a diameter of 12 inches. He will display earrings around the edge of the circle. Each pair takes up 2 in. on the circumference of the circle. About how many pairs can he fit?

3 A school plans to place flags on every post of the 300-foot fence in front of the school. There are posts at each end and every 6 feet apart. How many flags are needed?

4 Phyllis wants to roll her cart straight ahead 14 ft. The diameter of each wheel on her cart is 28 in. About how many turns of the wheel will it take to move the cart 14 ft?

▲ The students' drawings simulate painting a fence.

Mixed Strategy Review

Try these or other strategies to solve each problem.
Tell which strategy you used.

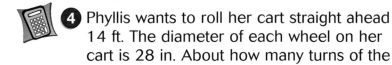

Problem Solving Strategies

THERE'S ALWAYS A WAY!

● *Draw a Diagram*   ● *Write an Equation*   ● *Guess and Check*

5 **Using Algebra** Tama has $2.25 in quarters, dimes, and nickels. She has one more nickel than quarters and twice as many dimes as nickels. How many of each kind of coin does she have?

6 **Analyze** In one section of a mall, there is a vendor's cart in each of four corners. Carpeted pathways connect each cart to every other cart. How many pathways are there?

7 Amanda will be buying 300 beads at $0.06 per bead, 150 beads at $0.04 per bead, 3 rolls of wire at $1.59 per roll, and 4 tubes of glue at $2.25 per tube. What will be the cost of her purchases?

Using Algebra

Around the Pool

Finding the perimeter tells you the distance around any figure.

Learning About It

You can find the **perimeter** of a swimming pool or any polygon by adding the lengths of its sides.

9.3 m
5.4 m
6 m
5.4 m
7.6 m
4 m

Estimate first: $6 + 9 + 5 + 5 + 4 + 8 = 37$ m
$6 + 9.3 + 5.4 + 5.4 + 4 + 7.6 = 37.7$ m

The perimeter of the pool pictured above is 37.7 m.

Connecting Ideas

When polygons have two or more sides the same length, you can use a **formula** to find the perimeter.

Find the perimeter of a rectangle.

51 m
32 m   32 m
51 m

$P = (2 \times l) + (2 \times w)$
$P = (2 \times 51) + (2 \times 32)$
$P = 102 + 64 = 166$ m

l = length
w = width

Find the perimeter of a square.

3 m
3 m   3 m
3 m

Since the sides of a square are equal,
$P = 4 \times s$
$P = 4 \times 3 = 12$ m

s = side

Think and Discuss Write a formula to find the perimeter of an equilateral triangle. Use P for perimeter and s for each length of a side. Explain why your formula works.

Try It Out

Estimate and then find the perimeter of each figure.

1.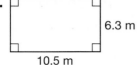
6.3 m
10.5 m

2.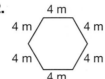
4 m
4 m   4 m
4 m   4 m
4 m

3.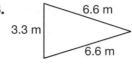
6.6 m
3.3 m
6.6 m

4.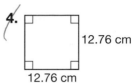
12.76 cm
12.76 cm

Practice

Find the perimeter of each figure.

5.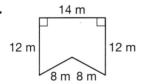
14 m
12 m   12 m
8 m 8 m

6.
12 cm
5 cm

7.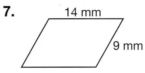
14 mm
9 mm

8.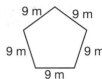
9 m   9 m
9 m   9 m
9 m

Analyze Find each missing measurement.

9.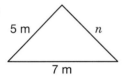
5 m   n
7 m

$P = 17$ m
$n = $ ▨

10.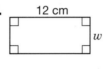
12 cm
w

$P = 38$ cm
$w = $ ▨

11.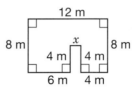
12 m
8 m   x   8 m
4 m 4 m
6 m   4 m

$x = $ ▨
$P = $ ▨

12.
s

$P = 80$ cm
$s = $ ▨

Problem Solving

13. How much fencing is needed to enclose a rectangle 75 m × 40 m? Explain whether you would need more or less fencing to enclose a square 60 m on a side.

15. Analyze Van wants to frame a painting 80 cm by 50 cm. It costs $0.25 for each centimeter of framing. How much will it cost to frame Van's painting?

14. Generalize Complete the chart below for rectangles with the measurements given. What happens to the perimeter when both the length and width are doubled?

l	w	P
2 cm	3 cm	
4 cm	6 cm	
8 cm	12 cm	
16 cm	24 cm	

Review and Remember

Find each answer.

16. 378
       × 24

17. 2,752
       + 1,698

18. 72.54
       − 8.658

19. 0.08
       × 0.06

20. 3)31.8

For Extra Practice, see Set I, page 468.

Don't Kick the Can!

Using Algebra

Finding the area can tell you how much surface a figure covers.

Word Bank

area

Each quart covers 75 square feet.

RED

8 ft

5 $\frac{3}{4}$ ft

BLUE

5 ft

5 ft

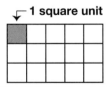

Learning About It

Fifth graders are painting the backdrop for the arts fair. Do the cans contain enough red paint and blue paint?

Area is the number of square units a figure covers. 15 square units are shown.

1 square unit

Find the area of the rectangle.

$A = l \times w$

l = length
w = width

$A = 8$ ft $\times$ 5$\frac{3}{4}$ ft

$A = 46$ square feet (ft²)

Since 46 ft² < 75 ft², there is enough red paint.

Find the area of the square.

$A = s \times s$

s = side

$A = 5$ ft $\times$ 5 ft

$A = 25$ square feet (ft²)

Since 25 ft² < 75 ft², there is enough blue paint.

Think and Discuss Do you need to find the exact area of the rectangle and square or is an estimate enough?

Try It Out

Estimate. Then find the area of each figure.

1.
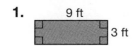
9 ft
3 ft

2.
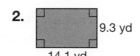
9.3 yd
14.1 yd

3.
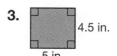
4.5 in.
5 in.

4.
7.1 ft
7.1 ft

5. Choose a rectangular object in your classroom. Estimate the area in square inches. Then measure the length and width and find the area. Does your answer make sense?

Practice

Find each missing measurement. Draw a diagram, if necessary.

6. $s = 12\frac{1}{2}$ yd
$A = $ ▨

7. $s = 3\frac{2}{5}$ ft
$A = $ ▨

8. $s = 5.9$ mi
$A = $ ▨

9. $s = 25$ ft
$A = $ ▨

10. $l = 1.6$ ft
$w = 3$ ft
$A = $ ▨

11. $l = 17$ in.
$w = 25$ in.
$A = $ ▨

12. $l = 234$ yd
$w = 199$ yd
$A = $ ▨

13. $l = 2.34$ in.
$w = 10.2$ in.
$A = $ ▨

14. $A = 31.0$ in.²
$w = 5$ in.
$l = $ ▨

15. $A = 420$ in.²
$l = 30$ in.
$w = $ ▨

16. $A = 16$ ft²
$s = $ ▨

17. $A = 25$ yd²
$s = $ ▨

Problem Solving

18. Analyze How many square feet are in a square yard? Draw a diagram to show how you know.

19. Create Your Own Write your own problem on finding the area of a rectangle.

20. Students are painting a 14 ft by 19 ft wall. If a can of paint covers 75 square feet, would 3 cans be a reasonable amount of paint to buy? Explain.

Review and Remember

Write each improper fraction as a mixed number. Write each mixed number as an improper fraction. Simplify if possible.

21. $\frac{46}{9}$

22. $\frac{68}{10}$

23. $5\frac{3}{8}$

24. $\frac{22}{6}$

25. $2\frac{3}{5}$

26. $7\frac{5}{8}$

27. $\frac{44}{8}$

28. $6\frac{2}{5}$

29. $10\frac{4}{5}$

30. $7\frac{3}{16}$

Diorama Dilemma

Using
Algebra

You can use what you know about the area of rectangles to find the area of parallelograms and triangles.

Learning About It

Anna wants to cut up leftover felt to cover the back of her diorama. The felt is in the shape of a parallelogram. If Anna can find the area of the felt, she will know if she has enough.

Word Bank
base
height

What You Need

For each pair:
grid paper
scissors

Work with your partner. Find the area of a parallelogram.

Step 1 Use grid paper. Cut out a rectangle that is 6 units by 12 units as shown at the right. Find the area.

Step 2 Draw a line segment to form a triangle as shown below. Shade the triangle. Cut along the line segment. Tape the triangle to the other side of the rectangle to form a parallelogram.

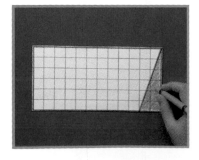

Notice that the **base (*b*)** is 12 units, the **height (*h*)** is 6 units, and the area is still 72 square units.

Area of a parallelogram: $A = b \times h$

Since you have not added or taken anything away, the areas of the parallelogram and the rectangle are the same. Anna's felt will fit the diorama.

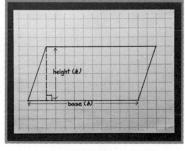

▲ The height is perpendicular to the base.

Connecting Ideas

You can use what you know about parallelograms to find the area of a triangle.

Follow these steps to find the area of a triangle.

Step 1 Draw and cut out a parallelogram like the one shown at the right. Find the area.

Step 2 Draw a diagonal line segment as shown in the figure below. Cut the parallelogram in half by cutting along the line segment.

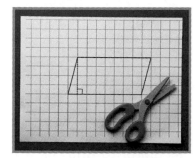

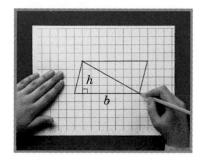

You now have two congruent triangles whose areas are each half of the area of the parallelogram.

Area of a triangle: $A = \frac{1}{2} \times b \times h$

More Examples

A. $A = 9 \times 6$

$A = 54 \text{ ft}^2$

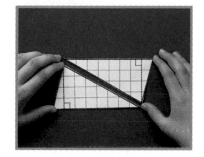

6 ft

9 ft

B. $A = \frac{1}{2} \times 5 \times 6$

$A = \frac{1}{2} \times 30$

$A = 15 \text{ yd}^2$

6 yd

5 yd

Think and Discuss What kind of triangles do you think you would form if you cut a rectangle diagonally from vertex to vertex? Tell why.

Try It Out

Find the area of each figure.

1.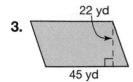
6.7 ft
4.1 ft

2.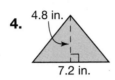
2.4 in.
5 in.

Remember to use these formulas:
Area of a parallelogram: $A = b \times h$
Area of a triangle: $A = \frac{1}{2} \times b \times h$

INTERNET ACTIVITY
www.sbgmath.com

3.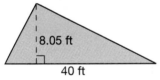
22 yd
45 yd

4.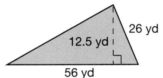
4.8 in.
7.2 in.

5. Explain Which has the greater area, a triangle with a base of 4 units and a height of 5 units or a parallelogram with a base of 3 units and a height of 4 units? Explain.

Practice

Choose a Method Use mental math, paper and pencil, or a calculator to find the area of each figure.

6.
8.05 ft
40 ft

7.
26 yd
12.5 yd
56 yd

8.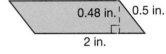
0.48 in. 0.5 in.
2 in.

Find each missing measurement.

9. triangle
$b = 6$ in.
$h = 6$ in.
$A = \blacksquare$

10. parallelogram
$b = 12$ ft
$h = 20$ ft
$A = \blacksquare$

11. parallelogram
$b = 8$ ft
$h = 3$ ft
$A = \blacksquare$

12. triangle
$b = 7$ yd
$h = 10$ yd
$A = \blacksquare$

13. parallelogram
$b = 155$ ft
$h = 6$ ft
$A = \blacksquare$

14. triangle
$b = 4$ in.
$h = 3$ in.
$A = \blacksquare$

15. parallelogram
$b = 16$ in.
$h = \blacksquare$
$A = 224$ in.^{2}

16. triangle
$b = 9$ ft
$h = \blacksquare$
$A = 27$ ft^2

17. triangle
$b = \blacksquare$
$h = 20$ in.
$A = 90$ in.^{2}

Problem Solving

18. The area of a parallelogram is 24 ft^2. The height is 6 ft. What is the base?

19. A triangular piece of felt has a base of 3.4 in. and a height of 6.7 in. What area will it cover?

20. Two parallelograms, each with a base of 5 in. and a height of 4 in., are sewn together with no overlap. What is the combined area of the figure formed from the parallelograms? Explain how you know.

22. Journal Idea Explain how it is possible for two rectangles to have the same perimeters but different areas. You may wish to draw a diagram to help illustrate your explanation.

21. Analyze The bottom of a triangular package has a base of 3 ft and a height of 2 ft. What is its area? How could the manufacturer change the dimensions to double the area of the bottom of the package? Explain.

23. Susan knows that the area of a triangle is 10 in². She also knows that the base is 4 in. How can she find the height of the triangle? What is the height?

Review and Remember

Find each average.

24. 72, 74, 84, 78

25. $10.97, $9.75, $10.98, $9.34

26. 31, 35, 32, 37, 30

27. 97, 74, 76, 69, 70, 73, 73

28. 131, 116, 143, 129, 136

29. $1.97, $3.63, $5.89, $0.91

Critical Thinking Corner

Logical Thinking

Finding Surface Area

Surface area is the sum of the areas of all of the faces of a space figure.

Find the areas of Figures A–E in this triangular prism. Then find the surface area. Explain what you did.

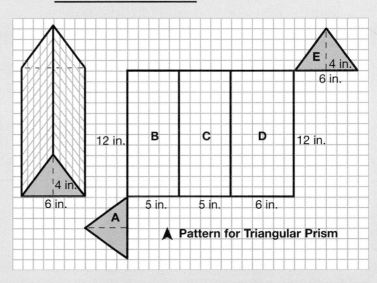

Pattern for Triangular Prism

Problem Solving
Area of Irregular Polygons

You can find the area of an irregular polygon by breaking it into smaller, familiar polygons.

Jo is making a jewelry box like the one shown. After assembling and painting the box, she will line the bottom of the box with red velvet. How many square centimeters of red velvet will Jo need?

 ### UNDERSTAND

What do you need to find?

You need to find the area of the bottom of the box.

 ### PLAN

How can you solve the problem?

You can draw a diagram of the bottom of the box. Then break up the irregular shape into familiar polygons and find those areas.

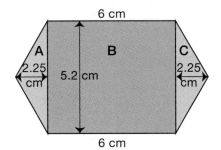

 ### SOLVE

Break the hexagon into two triangles and one rectangle. Find the area of each figure. Then find the sum of the areas.

Triangle A: $A = \frac{1}{2} \times 5.2 \text{ cm} \times 2.25 \text{ cm} = 5.85 \text{ cm}^2$

Rectangle B: $A = 6 \text{ cm} \times 5.2 \text{ cm} = 31.2 \text{ cm}^2$

Triangle C is congruent to Triangle A, so its area is also 5.85 cm².

Now add the areas.

5.85 cm² + 5.85 cm² + 31.2 cm² = 42.9 cm²

So, Jo needs 42.9 cm² of red velvet.

Remember:
Area of a triangle:
$A = \frac{1}{2} \times b \times h$
Area of a rectangle:
$A = b \times h$

 ### LOOK BACK

How could you use grid paper to find the area of an irregular polygon?

Show What You Learned

Break the polygons into familiar figures to find the area of each blue region.

1
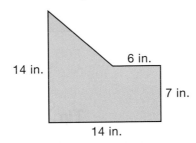

2
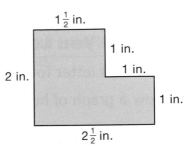

3
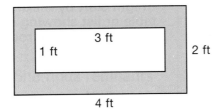

4
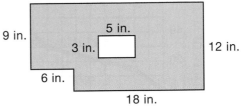

Solve by using the drawing next to each problem.

5 Doug is making a model of one hole of a miniature golf course. He wants to cover the green with outdoor carpet. How much carpeting does he need?

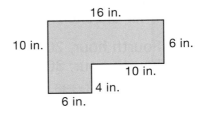

6 Sharon bought a wooden box to store sewing supplies. She wants to line the bottom of the box with black felt. How many square inches of black felt does she need?

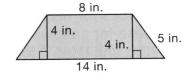

7 A large sheet of plastic is used to cover a sandbox. The size and shape of the sandbox are shown to the right. What is the area of the plastic needed to cover the sandbox?

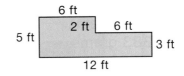

8 Beverly is buying clear plastic to cover her seedlings. She is growing them in a framed area that is the size and shape shown to the right. How much plastic does she need?

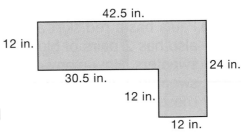

9 **Create Your Own** Draw an irregular shape and label the dimensions. Write how you would find the area of the shape. Have a classmate solve your problem. Then compare your methods and your answers.

Time in a Box

Using Algebra

Finding the volume can tell you how much a container can hold.

Learning About It

Mrs. Litton's class is making a time capsule to bury in the schoolyard. The students want to know how much space they will have to store their items.

Word Bank

volume

What You Need

For each pair:
  centimeter cubes

The **volume** of a container is the number of unit cubes needed to fill the container. Volume is expressed in cubic units (units³). What is the volume of the time capsule?

Step 1 Work with your partner. Use centimeter cubes to explore the volume of a rectangular prism. First make a model, such as the one shown here.

- Arrange 12 centimeter cubes in a rectangular shape 3 cm wide and 4 cm long.

- Add 3 more layers.

Step 2 Estimate, then count the number of cubic centimeters (cm³) in your prism. Record your results in a chart like the one shown.

Length (*l*)	Width (*w*)	Height (*h*)	Volume (*V*)
4 cm	3 cm	4 cm	■ cm³

Step 3 Use the 48 centimeter cubes. Make three more prisms by changing the dimensions. Record your work.

Step 4 Use 30 cubes to create as many prisms as you can. Record the dimensions and volume of each prism.

Think and Discuss Which formula below represents the volume of a rectangular prism? Explain. Find the volume of the time capsule on page 462.

a. $V = l \times w$ **b.** $V = l + w + h$ **c.** $V = l \times w \times h$

Practice

Choose a Method Use a calculator or paper and pencil to find each missing measurement.

1. $l = 6$ m
$w = 4$ m
$h = 2$ m
$V = \blacksquare$

2. $l = 4.5$ cm
$w = 3.25$ cm
$h = 8$ cm
$V = \blacksquare$

3. $l = 6.3$ m
$w = 5.2$ m
$h = 1.7$ m
$V = \blacksquare$

4. $l = 1.4$ mm
$w = 1.7$ mm
$h = 2.1$ mm
$V = \blacksquare$

5. $l = 2$ dm
$w = 1$ dm
$h = 5$ dm
$V = \blacksquare$

6. $l = 10$ mm
$w = 5$ mm
$h = 2$ mm
$V = \blacksquare$

7. $l = \blacksquare$
$w = 2$ cm
$h = 10$ cm
$V = 60$ cm³

8. $l = \blacksquare$
$w = 9$ dm
$h = 3$ dm
$V = 135$ dm³

9. $l = \blacksquare$
$w = 9$ cm
$h = 9$ cm
$V = 729$ cm³

10. $l = 11$ cm
$w = 8$ cm
$h = \blacksquare$
$V = 440$ cm³

11. $l = 6$ m
$w = 3.2$ m
$h = 4$ m
$V = \blacksquare$

12. $l = 5.8$ m
$w = 3.4$ m
$h = 2.0$ m
$V = \blacksquare$

13. A box 12 in. long and 2 in. high has a volume of 288 in.³ Will it fit in a space 13 in. wide? Explain.

14. Analyze How many prisms can you make with 15 centimeter cubes if the length, width, and height are never 1? Explain.

15. What If? You want to bury the time capsule on page 462 so that its base is 50 cm below the surface. The hole must be 10 cm wider and 10 cm longer than the capsule. How can you find the volume of the hole?

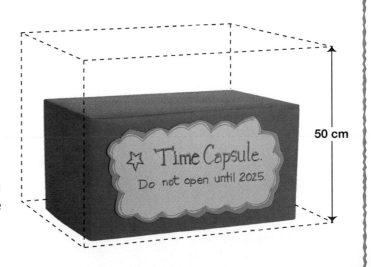

50 cm

☆ Time Capsule.
Do not open until 2025.

✓ Checkpoint

Perimeter, Area, and Volume

Vocabulary

Tell the word that each phrase describes.

1. the distance around a polygon

2. the distance around a circle

3. the amount of space a figure takes up

4. the number of square units a figure covers

Concepts and Skills

Using Algebra Find the missing measurement for each figure. (pages 452–453)

5.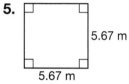

$P = \blacksquare$

6.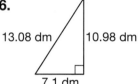

13.08 dm   10.98 dm

7.1 dm

$P = \blacksquare$

7.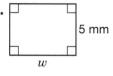

5 mm

w

$w = \blacksquare$
$P = 24 \text{ mm}$

8.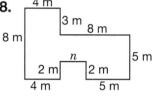

$n = \blacksquare$
$P = \blacksquare$

Using Algebra Find each missing measurement. (pages 454–455)

9. rectangle
$l = 35.9 \text{ cm}$
$w = 22 \text{ cm}$
$A = \blacksquare$

10. square
$s = 7.8 \text{ m}$
$A = \blacksquare$

11. rectangle
$l = \blacksquare$
$w = 16 \text{ km}$
$A = 400 \text{ km}^2$

12. square
$s = \blacksquare$
$A = 25 \text{ m}^2$

Using Algebra Find the missing measurement for each triangle or parallelogram. (pages 456–459)

13.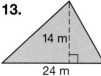

14 m

24 m

$A = \blacksquare$

14.

h

10 mm

$A = 60 \text{ mm}^2$
$h = \blacksquare$

15.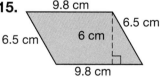

9.8 cm   6.5 cm
6.5 cm   6 cm
9.8 cm

$A = \blacksquare$

16.

9 m

b

$A = 63 \text{ m}^2$
$b = \blacksquare$

Using Algebra Find the missing measurement for each prism. (pages 462–463)

17. $l = 4.5 \text{ m}$
$w = 5 \text{ m}$
$h = 2 \text{ m}$
$V = \blacksquare$

18. $l = 1\frac{1}{4} \text{ m}$
$w = 2\frac{1}{2} \text{ m}$
$h = 2\frac{1}{3} \text{ m}$
$V = \blacksquare$

19. $l = 7.8 \text{ km}$
$w = 3.1 \text{ km}$
$h = 2.2 \text{ km}$
$V = \blacksquare$

20. $l = 3 \text{ m}$
$w = 5 \text{ m}$
$h = \blacksquare$
$V = 60 \text{ m}^3$

Problem Solving

21. Maddie bought a gallon of paint to paint a fence with her dad. One gallon covers about 90 square feet. If the fence is 6 ft high, about what length of fence can she paint?

22. You want to cover the bottom of your fish tank with a 2-in. layer of stones. If the tank is 18 in. long and 12 in. wide, how many cubic inches of stones do you need?

23. Ron is planning to build a patio that is 8 ft by 10 ft. It will take 5 bricks to complete one square foot. Is 600 a reasonable number of bricks for Ron to buy to build his patio? Explain.

24. A cereal company wants to pack 10 boxes in one carton for shipping. Each cereal box is 6 in. × 9 in. × 12 in. What size carton, by volume, does the company need?

25. A container with a circular opening has a diameter of 8 cm. Find the circumference of the lid that fits on top of this container. How did you find it?

Journal Idea

Write a paragraph about a situation where it would be useful to know an object's perimeter, area, or volume.

What do you think?

Why would knowing the area of the base of a rectangular prism be helpful in finding the volume?

You Decide

Activity

Shoes to Show

Design a display for 2 shelves of shoes. Each shelf is 5 ft long and 1 ft wide. Arrange shoes, toe to heel, in rows. Draw and label a diagram of your arrangements.

Men's	Women's	Length
5½	6½	10.08 in.
6	7	10.25 in.
6½	7½	10.42 in.
7	8	?

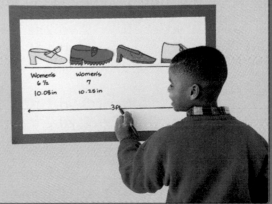

 You might wish to include this work in your portfolio.

Extra Practice

Set A (pages 424–427)

Use mental math or paper and pencil to complete.

1. 4 yr = ■ mo   **2.** 6 d = ■ h   **3.** 2 yr = ■ wk   **4.** 2 yr = ■ h

Add or subtract. Simplify if possible.

5. 3 h 10 min
     + 1 h 30 min

6. 6 h 5 min
     − 2 h 50 min

7. 2 h 15 min
     + 3 h 25 min

8. 10 h 10 min
     − 6 h 50 min

9. 5 h 50 min
     + 2 h 20 min

10. 6 h 48 min
      − 3 h 30 min

11. 7 h 30 min
      + 3 h 45 min

12. 10 h 25 min
      − 5 h 30 min

13. 6 h 10 min
      − 3 h 38 min

14. 7 h 29 min
      + 2 h 42 min

15. 9 h
      − 5 h 15 min

16. 18 h 30 min
      + 12 h 35 min

17. Ron arrived at his baby-sitting job at 2:30 P.M. and worked until 7:45 P.M. For how many hours should he be paid?

Set B (pages 428–431)

Measure the width of the frame to each unit given.

1. nearest $\frac{1}{2}$ inch   **2.** nearest $\frac{1}{4}$ inch

3. nearest $\frac{1}{8}$ inch   **4.** nearest $\frac{1}{16}$ inch

Add or subtract. Change to a larger unit when possible.

5. 3 mi 1 yd
     + 2 mi 1 yd

6. 2 yd 2 ft
     − 1 yd 1 ft

7. 4 ft 1 in.
     − 1 ft 2 in.

8. 2 yd 2 ft 8 in.
     + 2 yd 2 ft 8 in.

9. 8 yd 2 in.
     + 5 yd 2 in.

10. 3 yd 1 ft
      − 2 yd 2 ft

11. 4 yd 1 ft
      + 6 yd 2 ft

12. 3 yd 2 ft 4 in.
      − 1 yd 1 ft 9 in.

13. A football player ran 11 yards on the first play and 13 yards on the second. How many feet did he run altogether?

Extra Practice

Set C (pages 434–435)

Complete each statement.

1. 7 qt = ■ pt   **2.** 2 gal = ■ pt   **3.** 16 c = ■ pt

4. 12 c = ■ pt   **5.** 20 qt = ■ gal   **6.** 5 qt = ■ pt

7. 12 c = ■ fl oz   **8.** 16 c = ■ gal   **9.** 12 gal = ■ qt

Set D (pages 436–437)

Complete each statement.

1. 32 oz = ■ lb   **2.** 50 oz = ■ lb ■ oz   **3.** 8,000 lb = ■ T

4. 3 lb 4 oz = ■ oz   **5.** 5 T = ■ lb   **6.** 10 lb 6 oz = ■ oz

7. 5 lb = ■ oz   **8.** 7 lb 3 oz = ■ oz   **9.** 128 oz = ■ lb

Set E (pages 438–441)

Choose a Method Use mental math or paper and pencil to complete each statement.

1. 30 m = ■ km   **2.** 4.5 m = ■ cm   **3.** 4,569 m = ■ km

4. 16.5 cm = ■ mm   **5.** 377 cm = ■ m   **6.** 2.6 km = ■ m

7. 4.5 m = ■ km   **8.** 3.2 mm = ■ cm   **9.** 130 m = ■ mm

Set F (pages 442–443)

Complete each statement.

1. 45 L = ■ mL   **2.** 7.6 L = ■ mL   **3.** 3,000 mL = ■ L   **4.** 75 L = ■ mL

5. Joan's measuring cup can hold 225 mL. How many times would she be able to fill up the cup with a 2 L bottle of juice?

Set G (pages 444–445)

Complete each statement.

1. 50 kg = ■ g   **2.** 650 g = ■ kg   **3.** 254 g = ■ kg   **4.** 11,000 mg = ■ g

5. 3.5 kg = ■ g   **6.** 3.3 g = ■ kg   **7.** 73.1 kg = ■ g   **8.** 66 g = ■ mg

Extra Practice

Set H (pages 446–447)

Write an appropriate outdoor activity for each temperature.

1. 10°C

2. 85°F

3. ⁻10°C

4. 25°F

5. 37°C

6. 0°C

Set I (pages 452–453)

Estimate. Then find the perimeter of each figure.

1.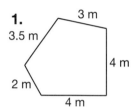
3 m, 3.5 m, 4 m, 2 m, 4 m

2.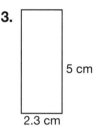
12.5 m, 6 m, 7 m

3.
5 cm

2.3 cm

4.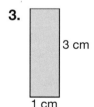
4.1 m, 3 m, 2 m, 2 m, 2 m, 2 m, 3 m, 4.1 m

Set J (pages 454–455)

Using Algebra Find the area of each figure.

1.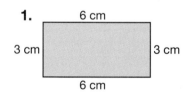
6 cm, 3 cm, 3 cm, 6 cm

2.
5 cm, 5 cm

3.
3 cm, 1 cm

4.
6 cm, 6 cm, 6 cm, 6 cm

5. Bill needs to carry brownies to school for a class party. If each brownie is 6 cm on a side, how many brownies can he fit in one layer in a box that is 30 cm by 48 cm?

Set K (pages 456–459)

Using Algebra Find the area of each figure.

1.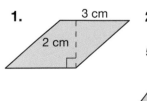
3 cm, 2 cm

2.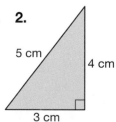
5 cm, 4 cm, 3 cm

3.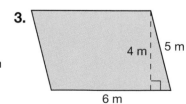
4 m, 5 m, 6 m

4.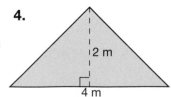
2 m, 4 m

 **Chapter Test**

Add or subtract. Simplify if possible.

1.   2 h 30 min
    + 1 h 10 min

2.   4 h 7 min
    + 2 h 58 min

3.   10 h 10 min
    − 5 h 50 min

Write an appropriate outdoor activity for each temperature.

4. 35°C   **5.** 27°F   **6.** 98°F   **7.** ⁻2°C

Complete each statement.

8. 5 cm = ■ mm

9. 5,000 g = ■ kg

10. 1,100 mL = ■ L

11. 5.5 m = ■ cm

12. 8 ft = ■ in.

13. 2 lb = ■ oz

14. 34 oz = ■ lb ■ oz

15. 9 qt = ■ gal ■ qt

16. 2 mi = ■ ft

Find the perimeter and area of each polygon.

17. [rectangle: 4 cm, 8 cm]

18. [square: 2 cm, 2 cm]

19. [parallelogram: 5 cm, 4 cm, 3.5 cm, 4 cm, 5 cm]

20. [triangle: 8 cm, 10 cm, 6 cm]

Find the volume of each rectangular prism.

21. $l = 8$ m
$w = 4$ m
$h = 3$ m

22. $l = 2.3$ cm
$w = 2.0$ cm
$h = 6.2$ cm

23. $l = 5$ dm
$w = 3$ dm
$h = 4\frac{1}{4}$ dm

Solve.

24. Mr. Hunt started to hike up a mountain trail at 10:15 A.M. He reached the observatory at 1:00 P.M. How long did it take Mr. Hunt to reach the observatory?

25. Use the picture to the right. About how far will a marble roll if it rolls once around the green track?

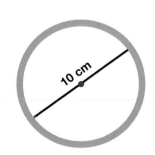

10 cm

 Self-Check

Look back at Exercises 17–23. Are your units of measure written correctly?

Performance Assessment

Show What You Know About Measurement

Use the container at the right for Questions 1 and 2.

1 Find the measurements of the edges *a* and *b* to the nearest $\frac{1}{8}$ in. and to the nearest mm.

Self-Check Did you remember to find the measurement in both inches and millimeters?

2 An aquarium measures 2 feet 4 inches long, 1 foot wide, and 1 foot 3 inches high.

a. What is the perimeter of the bottom of the tank?

b. What is the area of the bottom?

c. How would you change the dimensions of the bottom of the aquarium to produce an area of 1,344 in.²?

1 ft 3 in.

2 ft 4 in.

1 ft

Self-Check For Question 2b, did you remember to change the measurements so that they were all expressed in the same units?

 For Your Portfolio
You might wish to include this work in your portfolio.

Extension

Exploring Integers

You can use a thermometer to understand **negative numbers** and **positive numbers**.

Temperatures that are below zero can be expressed as negative numbers.

Temperatures above zero can be expressed as positive numbers.

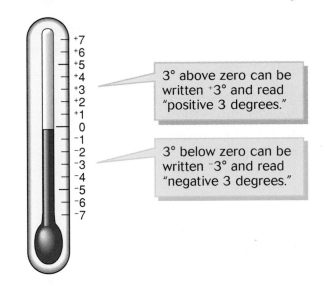

3° above zero can be written ⁺3° and read "positive 3 degrees."

3° below zero can be written ⁻3° and read "negative 3 degrees."

A number line can help you understand negative and positive numbers. This number line shows a set of **integers**.

Negative integers are less than zero.

Zero is not positive or negative.

Positive integers are greater than zero.

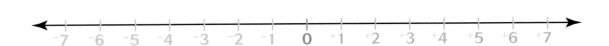

Write each integer that represents the temperature described.

1. 10 degrees below zero   2. 2 degrees above zero

3. 9 degrees above zero   4. 7 degrees below zero

Write the letter that locates each point on the number line.

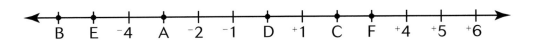

5. ⁻3   6. ⁺2   7. 0   8. ⁻6   9. ⁺3   10. ⁻5

Draw a number line. Then label each point.

11. ⁺8   12. 0   13. ⁻1   14. ⁺6   15. ⁺3   16. ⁻6

Cumulative Review

★★★★★ **Preparing for Tests**

Choose the correct letter for each answer.

Number Concepts	Geometry and Spatial Reasoning

1. Which of these numbers is 50 when rounded to the nearest ten and 53 when rounded to the nearest one?

A. 50.1
B. 52.4
C. 53.1
D. 53.5

2. Which shaded region does NOT represent $\frac{1}{3}$ of the figure?

A.   **C.**

B.   **D.**

3. Minnie cut a sheet cake into 24 pieces for the 12 members of her family. Her family ate 8 pieces for dessert. Which fraction shows how much of the cake they ate?

A. $\frac{1}{6}$ **C.** $\frac{2}{5}$

B. $\frac{1}{3}$ **D.** $\frac{3}{4}$

4. Which product is equal to 75?

A. $3 \times 3 \times 5$
B. $15 \times 2 \times 2$
C. $5 \times 2 \times 3$
D. $3 \times 5 \times 5$

5. *EFGH* is a parallelogram. Which statement is true?

A. $\angle E$ is congruent to $\angle F$
B. $\angle E$ is congruent to $\angle G$
C. $\angle F$ is congruent to $\angle G$
D. $\angle G$ is congruent to $\angle H$

6. Which figures appear to be congruent?

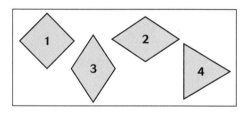

A. 3 and 4   **C.** 2 and 3
B. 1 and 2   **D.** 1 and 4

7. If you dipped the shape shown below in paint and rolled it in a straight line along a piece of paper, what shape would you make?

A. Rectangle
B. Circle
C. Triangle
D. Square

8. How many lines of symmetry does a square have?

A. 1   **C.** 3
B. 2   **D.** 4

Patterns, Relationships, and Algebraic Thinking	Measurement

9. Which expression is equivalent to $(4 \times 3) + (4 \times 6)$?

  A. $4 + (3 \times 6)$
  B. $7 + 10$
  C. 12×10
  D. $4 \times (3 + 6)$

10. There were 6 rows of flowers in a garden. The back row had 35 plants; the next—32; the fourth—28; and the third—23. If this pattern continued, how many plants would be in the **first** row?

  A. 16   **C.** 10
  B. 14   **D.** 8

Use the graph below to answer Questions 11 and 12.

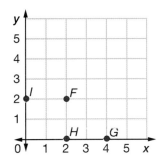

11. Which point best represents the ordered pair (2, 2)?

  A. *F*   **C.** *H*
  B. *G*   **D.** *I*

12. Which ordered pair names the point you would reach if you moved two units vertically down from point *I*?

  A. (1, 1)
  B. (0, 1)
  C. (1, 2)
  D. (0, 0)

13. A tree in Henry's yard is 33.4 m tall and 2.2 m in diameter. The top of Henry's house is 16 m high. How much taller is the tree than the house?

  A. 21.2 meters
  B. 18.2 meters
  C. 17.4 meters
  D. 13.8 meters

14. What is the **area** in square centimeters of the triangle?

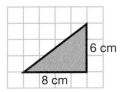

  A. 48 cm²   **C.** 14 cm²
  B. 24 cm²   **D.** 7 cm²

15. This is a diagram of a new pool being built. What is its **perimeter**?

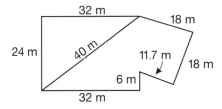

  A. 141.7 meters
  B. 161.7 meters
  C. 171.7 meters
  D. 181.7 meters

16. Jim bought 6 liters of a sports drink for $1.09 a liter. His glass holds about 120 milliliters. Which is reasonable for the number of glasses he can fill with the sports drink? (1 L = 1,000 mL)

  A. 500   **C.** 40
  B. 50   **D.** 30

Chapter 12

Ratio, Percent, and Probability

Chapter Theme: CRAFTS AND GAMES

Real-World Math

.............Real Facts.................

Making pottery is a hobby for all ages! After a piece of pottery is shaped, it has to be glazed and fired before it is ready to use. The graph below is posted at The Pottery People ceramic studio to show the cost of firing pottery.

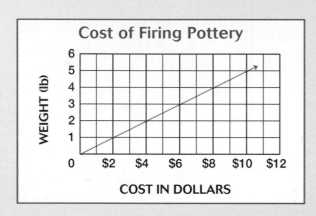

Cost of Firing Pottery

WEIGHT (lb) / COST IN DOLLARS

- How much is charged at The Pottery People for firing 1 pound of pottery?

- Compare the number of pounds to the cost of firing for several different weights. Write these comparisons as fractions in simplest form.

............Real People.................

Meet Gladys Remde, a potter. She uses clay to make many different things, including beautiful vases and ornate chess sets that are sold around the world!

In the picture at the right, Gladys adds water to correct the ratio of water to clay, while a young student shapes a pot.

String Along

A ratio describes a relationship between two quantities.

Learning About It

People first began stringing beads thousands of years ago. Early beads were made from pebbles, shells, animal bones, and berries. Today beads also are made from metal, glass, cork, wood, plastic, and other materials.

A **ratio** is often used to compare two quantities. The necklace at the right uses three round beads for every seven long beads. The ratio of round beads to long beads is 3 to 7. There are four different ways to write the ratio.

three to seven   3 to 7   3:7 $\frac{3}{7}$

On the whole necklace, there are 18 round beads and 42 long beads. What are four ways to write this ratio?

Think and Discuss If the total number of beads is 60, what is the ratio of long beads to total beads?

Word Bank

ratio

Try It Out

Write each ratio in two different ways.

1. 4:7   **2.** $\frac{10}{3}$ **3.** 2 to 3   **4.** one to nine   **5.** 8 to 4

6. 2:5   **7.** $\frac{16}{5}$ **8.** 3 to 5   **9.** two to seven   **10.** 10 to 5

Use the pin at the right to write each ratio for Exercises 11–13.

11. turquoise stones to red stones

12. red stones to teardrop-shaped stones

13. turquoise stones to total stones

Practice

Write two different ratios for each string of beads.
Tell what your ratios represent.

14.    **15.**

Make a drawing for each ratio in Exercises 16–27.

⭐ Hint ⭐ Use color, shape, or size to show the ratio.

16. $\frac{4}{3}$ **17.** $\frac{3}{4}$ **18.** 1:2   **19.** 3 to 8   **20.** $\frac{4}{5}$ **21.** 4:10

22. 5:2   **23.** 12:8   **24.** 6:3   **25.** 1 to 7   **26.** 5:3   **27.** 7:2

Problem Solving

28. Draw a string of 27 beads so that the ratio of black beads to red beads is 4:5. Tell how many of each color bead are in the string.

29. Analyze Karen and Kate looked at a collection of stones. Karen said the ratio 2:3 represented the stones. Kate said the ratio 2:5 represented the stones. They were both right. Explain why.

30. Create Your Own Use the table at the right to choose beads for your own string of beads. Label the colors and sizes of the beads. Then exchange drawings with a classmate and write as many ratios as you can for the string of beads.

Did You Know?

The Navajo people make cylinder-shaped beads called heishi. The beads are made from polished shells or semiprecious stones and strung in necklaces.

Number and Kinds of Beads

	Red	Yellow	Blue
Small	20	30	25
Medium	10	15	20
Large	4	5	6

Review and Remember

Find each answer. Write each fraction in simplest form.

31. $4 - \frac{3}{4}$ **32.** $8 \times 2\frac{2}{3}$ **33.** $\frac{5}{8} + \frac{1}{3}$ **34.** $2\frac{1}{4} - 1\frac{2}{5}$

35. $3\frac{7}{8} \times 5$ **36.** $2\frac{2}{9} + 3\frac{4}{5}$ **37.** $\frac{7}{16} \times \frac{2}{3}$ **38.** $1\frac{2}{5} + 3\frac{1}{4}$

39. $28 - 9.7$ **40.** $32.5 + 0.02$ **41.** $12.9 \div 3$ **42.** 3.68×0.9

Using Algebra

Origami

The same relationship can be expressed by several ratios.

Learning About It

Origami is the Japanese art of paper folding. Suppose it takes two cranes and five walruses to make one mobile. It takes ten cranes for five mobiles. How many walruses are needed for five mobiles?

$$\frac{2 \text{ cranes}}{5 \text{ walruses}} = \frac{10 \text{ cranes}}{? \text{ walruses}}$$

How many walruses?

Word Bank

ratio table
equivalent ratio

THERE'S ALWAYS A WAY!

● **One way** to find out is to use a **ratio table**.

	×1	×2	×3	×4	×5
Number of cranes	2	4	6	8	10
Number of walruses	5	10	15	20	25

The ratios 2:5, 4:10, 6:15, 8:20, and 10:25 express the same relationship. They are **equivalent ratios**.

● **Another way** is to multiply or divide each number in the ratio by the same nonzero number.

$$\frac{\text{Number of cranes}}{\text{Number of walruses}} = \frac{2}{5} \xrightarrow{\times 5} \frac{10}{25}$$

Multiply each term by 5.

It takes 25 walruses to make five mobiles.

Think and Discuss Are $\frac{24}{36}$ and $\frac{4}{6}$ equivalent ratios? Tell how you know.

Try It Out

Copy and complete each ratio table.

1.

4	8	■	■	■	■
9	■	27	36	■	54

2.

3	■	9	■	■	18
7	14	■	■	■	■

Use equivalent ratios to find each missing number.

3. $\dfrac{1}{5} = \dfrac{■}{10}$ **4.** $\dfrac{3}{5} = \dfrac{■}{20}$ **5.** $\dfrac{10}{16} = \dfrac{5}{■}$ **6.** 2:■ = 4:6 **7.** 18 to ■ and 6 to 9

Practice

Copy and complete each ratio table.

8.

3	6	■	12	15	■
4	■	12	■	■	24

9.

■	6	9	■	15	■
8	■	24	32	■	48

Write three ratios that are equivalent to each given ratio.

10. $\dfrac{1}{6}$ **11.** 3:5 **12.** $\dfrac{28}{140}$ **13.** 16 to 24

14. 1:4 **15.** 8 to 12 **16.** 3 to 9 **17.** 20:30

18. $\dfrac{7}{8}$ **19.** $\dfrac{2}{5}$ **20.** 12:36 **21.** 5 to 6

Problem Solving

Use the photograph at the right for Problems 22–24.

22. There are 18 red cranes in six centerpieces. How many patterned cranes are there?

23. If there are 16 patterned cranes, how many red cranes are there? Tell how you know.

24. If a total of 72 red cranes were made for centerpieces over three weeks, how many patterned cranes needed to be made during the same time?

▲ **Social Studies Connection**
The crane, the most popular of the animal forms in origami, is a Japanese symbol of good fortune.

Review and Remember

Find each answer.

25. 6.02 × 8 **26.** 8.95 + 5.4 **27.** 0.06 × 0.12 **28.** 33.6 ÷ 4 **29.** 9.1 − 6.25

Using
Algebra

Berry Nice!

You can use equivalent ratios to understand scale.

Learning About It

A photograph usually is not the same size as the actual object. **Scale** is a ratio that compares the size of an object in a photograph or drawing to the size of an actual object.

The strawberries shown above are actual size. Every inch in the photograph at the right represents two inches of the actual strawberries. If the photograph is 2 inches wide, what is the actual width of the strawberries?

Scale: 1 in. represents 2 in.

THERE'S
ALWAYS
A WAY!

● **One way** to figure out the actual width is to make a ratio table.

Photograph size	1 in.	2 in.	3 in.	4 in.
Actual size	2 in.	4 in.	6 in.	8 in.

● **Another way** is to find an equivalent ratio.

The numerator is multiplied by 2, so the denominator also should be multiplied by 2.

$$\frac{1}{2} = \frac{2}{4}$$

×2

×2

← Photograph size
← Actual size

The actual width of the strawberries is 4 inches.

Connecting Ideas

The small photograph on page 478 is a reduction of the actual fruit. Just as scale helps you reduce an object, it also helps you to enlarge an object.

The small photograph on page 478

The relationship between the dimensions of Camera A and Camera B is a ratio. Camera B is an enlargement of Camera A.

$$\frac{\text{Camera A}}{\text{Camera B}} = \frac{1}{2}$$

Camera A

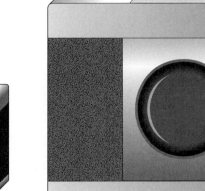

Camera B

What You Need

For each pair:
ruler or tape measure

Work with a partner. Follow the steps below to learn more about enlargements.

Step 1 Make a chart like the one shown. Measure each part of Camera A and record it on your chart. Then measure Camera B or calculate the measurement.

Part	Camera A	Camera B	Your Camera
Camera width	$1\frac{1}{2}$ in.		
Camera height			
Lens diameter			
Button width			
Button height			

Step 2 Now create your own enlargement. The ratio of Camera A to your camera should be 1:3. This means that each measurement for your camera should be 3 times the measurement for Camera A. Find the measurement of each part of your camera. Record each measurement on your chart.

Step 3 Use the measurements on the chart to make a scale drawing of your camera.

Think and Discuss If a scale drawing did not show the scale, how might you estimate the scale?

Try It Out

Find the missing measurement.

1.

Photograph width	3 in.	6 in.	■
Actual width	9 in.	■	27 in.

2.

Scale drawing	4 in.	8 in.	■
Height of building	40 ft	■	120 ft

3. $\dfrac{16 \text{ ft}}{32 \text{ ft}} = \dfrac{\text{model size}}{16 \text{ ft}}$

4. $\dfrac{\text{model size}}{8 \text{ ft}} = \dfrac{12 \text{ in.}}{32 \text{ ft}}$

5. $\dfrac{7 \text{ ft}}{5 \text{ in.}} = \dfrac{56 \text{ ft}}{\text{actual size}}$

Practice

Find each missing measurement.

6.

Photograph height	2 in.	■	■
Actual height	10 ft	20 ft	30 ft

7.

Scale drawing	2 cm	4 cm	■
Microorganism	0.15 mm	■	0.45 mm

8.

Scale drawing	6 in.	■	18 in.
Length of insect	$\frac{1}{2}$ in.	1 in.	■

9.

Scale drawing	6.4 in.	12.8 in.	19.2 in.
Length of snake	3.2 in.	■	■

10. $\dfrac{3 \text{ in.}}{16 \text{ ft}} = \dfrac{\text{model size}}{48 \text{ ft}}$

11. $\dfrac{5 \text{ ft}}{9 \text{ ft}} = \dfrac{30 \text{ ft}}{\text{actual size}}$

12. $\dfrac{\text{actual size}}{15 \text{ in.}} = \dfrac{21 \text{ ft}}{45 \text{ in.}}$

13. $\dfrac{\text{model size}}{27 \text{ cm}} = \dfrac{1 \text{ cm}}{9 \text{ cm}}$

14. $\dfrac{2 \text{ ft}}{5 \text{ ft}} = \dfrac{24 \text{ ft}}{\text{actual size}}$

15. $\dfrac{4.9 \text{ cm}}{2.1 \text{ m}} = \dfrac{\text{actual size}}{8.4 \text{ m}}$

16. Analyze In the equivalent ratio $\dfrac{12}{36} = \dfrac{9}{h}$, is it reasonable to say that h is greater than 9? Why or why not?

Problem Solving

A store sells model railroad cars. They are all made to a scale of 1 in. representing 87 in. Use the scale to complete the chart. Round each answer to the nearest hundredth.

Actual boxcar = 44 feet

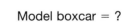

Model boxcar = ?

Actual and Model Railroad Car Lengths			
Railroad Car	**Actual Feet**	**Actual Inches**	**HO Scale Model**
Pullman sleeper	80 ft	960 in.	11.03 in.
17. Tank car	50 ft	600 in.	■
18. Boxcar	44 ft	528 in.	■
19. Refrigerator car	60 ft	■	■

20. A mural is 20 inches long in a scale drawing. The scale is 2 in. represents 3 ft. What is the actual length of the mural?

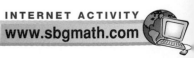

Choose a Method Use mental math or paper and pencil. Use the scale and the blueprint for Problems 21–24.

21. What is the actual length of the house?

22. What is the actual length of the living room? actual width of the living room?

23. How many feet wider is the dining room than the kitchen?

24. **Create Your Own** Use the blueprint to write a problem for a classmate to solve.

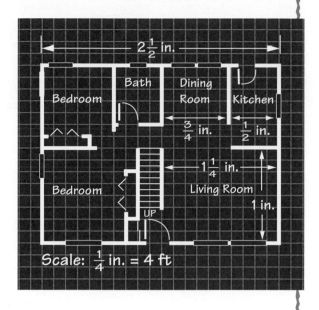

Review and Remember

Add or subtract.

25. $4\frac{5}{8} - 2\frac{3}{8}$

26. $16\frac{3}{4} + 5\frac{7}{8}$

27. $8\frac{1}{3} - 4\frac{2}{3}$

28. $2\frac{5}{6} - \frac{11}{12}$

Critical Thinking Corner

Visual Thinking

Map Scales

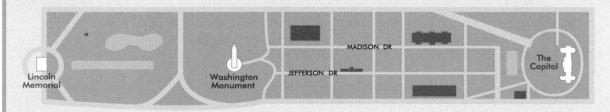

Social Studies Connection A map has a scale to show how many inches represent an actual distance. To find the actual distance, first measure the distance on the map. Then use the scale to compute the actual distance.

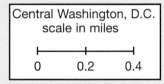

1. Find the shortest distance from the Washington Monument to the Lincoln Memorial.

2. What is the shortest distance between the Capitol and the Lincoln Memorial?

3. What is the scale of this map?

4. Find the shortest distance from the Washington Monument to the Capitol.

Using Algebra

Rate It Right

Rate can help you compare things that have different units.

Learning About It

As a hobby, Dan puts kites together. He can put together 6 kites in 2 hours.

▶ A **rate** such as *6 kites in 2 hours* is a kind of ratio that compares different units. The rate *6 kites in 2 hours* compares the number of kites made to the number of hours worked.

Word Bank
rate
unit price

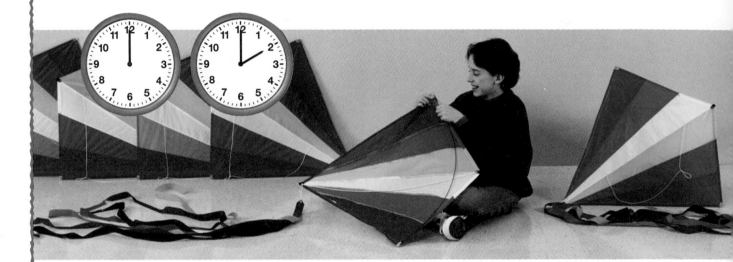

If Dan can put together 6 kites in 2 hours, how many kites can he put together in 8 hours?

To find out, you can find an equivalent ratio.

$$\frac{\text{number of kites}}{\text{number of hours}} = \frac{6 \text{ kites}}{2 \text{ hours}} = \frac{24 \text{ kites}}{8 \text{ hours}}$$

Dan can put together 24 kites in 8 hours.

▶ **Unit price** is a rate that tells the price for one part, or unit. If 12 paint jars sell for $24, what is the cost, or the unit price, of one jar?

12 jars of paint for $24 ($24 ÷ 12 = $2)
  1 jar of paint for $2

Think and Discuss How could you use equivalent ratios to find the unit price in the example above?

Try It Out

Use equivalent ratios or division to complete.

1. 2 ounces of paint for $1.90
1 ounce of paint for __?__

2. 12 bagels for $4.20
1 bagel for __?__

3. 96 jars in 8 boxes
__?__ jars in 4 boxes

4. 485 miles in 4 days
__?__ miles in 1 day

Practice

Use equivalent ratios or division to complete.

5. 8 kites painted in 2 hours
__?__ kites painted in 6 hours

6. 56 kite tails made in 7 hours
__?__ kite tails made in 1 hour

7. 2 craft books for $49.96
1 craft book for __?__

8. 6 rubber stamps for $32.94
1 rubber stamp for __?__

9. 5 sticks of gum for $0.50
1 stick of gum for __?__

10. 24 cakes in 8 hours
6 cakes in __?__

Problem Solving

Use the signs to answer Problems 11–12.

11. Analyze Which shop has the better buy on beads? Explain.

12. Describe What is the cost of 27 beads at Carol's Crafts? Tell how you found it.

13. Jan can string a dozen beads in 5 minutes. How many beads can she string in an hour?

14. Journal Idea A rate is always a ratio but is a ratio always a rate? Give an example to prove your answer is correct.

Carol's Crafts
Beads—18 for $7.20

Ben's Hobbies
Beads —12 for $4.32

15. If 48 handmade birdhouses sell for a total of $576, what is the unit price for a birdhouse?

Review and Remember

Write the value of each underlined digit.

16. 0.3<u>7</u>2

17. 10<u>9</u>,837

18. <u>2</u>3,984,746

19. 83.8<u>4</u>7

20. 6<u>4</u>7,823

21. 5,<u>6</u>56,388

22. <u>4</u>,372,258,927

23. 282.73<u>6</u>

Developing Skills for Problem Solving

First read for understanding and then focus on choosing which operation to use.

READ FOR UNDERSTANDING

Denise wants to make six wall decorations and nine jigsaw puzzles to sell at the school's art-and-crafts fair. She made the list at the right of all the materials and their prices. She has $35 to spend for materials.

Item	Cost per Unit
1/4 sheet plywood	$7.80 per sheet
2 wood strips, each 8 feet long	$0.50 per foot
Glue, 1 bottle	$3.79 per bottle
Varnish, 1 bottle	$4.50 per bottle
9 pictures for jigsaw puzzles	$1.75 each

1 How much money does Denise have to spend?

2 What is the cost of one sheet of plywood? one foot of wood strip? one picture for a jigsaw puzzle?

THINK AND DISCUSS

MATH FOCUS

Choose the Operation Clues in a problem can help you decide what operation to use. You add to combine groups, subtract to compare groups, multiply to combine equal groups, and divide to separate into equal groups.

Reread the paragraph at the top of the page.

3 Which operation would you use to find the total cost of the plywood? Why?

4 Which operation would you use to find the total cost of the wood strips? the nine puzzle pictures? Why?

5 Does Denise have enough money to buy all the materials? Which operations did you use to find out?

6 Why might it be difficult to know which operation to use?

Show What You Learned

Answer each question. Give a reason for your choice.

Marta made 20 potholders to sell for $1.25 each at the fair. She bought 5 bags of loops at $1.59 each to make the potholders. She sold 17 potholders at the fair.

1 Which sentence describes how to find the amount of money that Marta earned at the fair?

  a. Multiply the price of the potholders by the number sold.

  b. Divide the price of the potholders by the number sold.

  c. Add the cost of a potholder and the cost of a bag of loops.

2 Which expression describes the amount of money Marta earned?

  a. $1.25 × 17

  b. $1.25 + $1.59

  c. $1.25 ÷ 17

3 Which sentence describes how to find the amount that Marta spent on loops?

  a. Multiply the cost per bag by 20.

  b. Multiply the cost per bag by the number of bags she bought.

  c. Multiply the cost per bag by the number of potholders Marta made.

4 Which expression describes the amount that Marta spent on loops?

  a. $1.59 × 4

  b. $1.59 × 20

  c. $1.59 × 5

5 Profit is the amount of money earned less the expenses. Which sentence describes how to find Marta's profit?

  a. Subtract the money earned from the money spent on materials.

  b. Add the cost of materials and the price of potholders.

  c. Subtract the money spent on materials from the money earned.

6 Which expression describes the amount of profit Marta made?

  a. ($1.25 × 17) − ($1.59 × 5)

  b. ($1.59 × 5) − ($1.25 × 17)

  c. ($1.59 × 5) + ($1.25 × 5)

Tabitha is making 4 pillows like the one at the right. She is using 2 kinds of fabric. For the front of each pillow, she makes a patchwork pattern, using 20 squares.

7 How would she find the number of squares of each fabric needed for 4 pillows? Explain.

Quilt Designs

You can use what you know about ratios to learn about percents.

Word Bank

percent

◄ **Fine Arts Connection**
This quilt block is called a Log Cabin Variation. The red center stands for the hearth. The dark side of the block represents the difficult parts of life; the light side represents the happy times.

Learning About It

Quilts usually are made from pieces of fabric that are stitched together in interesting patterns. The quilt block shown above has 100 squares. Four of the squares are red, 44 are blue, and 52 are yellow.

Work with a partner. Make your own quilt design.

Step 1 On grid paper, mark off 10 rows with 10 squares in each row.

Step 2 Make a red, yellow, and blue design on the 100-square grid.

- Color whole squares, not parts of squares.

- Use only one color in each square.

- Choose a name for your quilt design.

Step 3 Use your quilt design to answer each question.

- How many blue squares does your quilt have? What is the ratio of blue squares to the total number of squares?

- What is the ratio of yellow squares to the total number of squares?

- What is the ratio of red squares to the total number of squares?

What You Need

For each pair:
1-cm grid paper
crayons or colored pencils

▶ A ratio that shows the relationship between a number and 100 is called a **percent**. *Percent* means "per hundred." The percent symbol is %.

- Look at the quilt on page 486. The ratio $\frac{44}{100}$ tells how many of the total squares are blue. The ratio $\frac{44}{100}$ can be written as 44%. 44% is read "44 percent."

$$44\% = \frac{44 \div 4}{100 \div 4} = \frac{11}{25} \leftarrow \text{ simplest form}$$

- The fraction $\frac{11}{25}$ represents 44%.

Step 4 Look at the quilt design you made. What percent of the squares are blue? red? yellow?

Think and Discuss Use what you know about equivalent fractions to express the ratio $\frac{7}{25}$ as a percent. Tell what you did.

▲ Modern quilters often use old patterns, such as this variation of a Log Cabin pattern.

INTERNET ACTIVITY
www.sbgmath.com

Practice

Tell what percent of each grid is shaded.

1. 　**2.** 　**3.** 　**4.**

Write each percent as a ratio. For Exercises 9–12, write the ratio in simplest form.

5. 60%　　**6.** 40%　　**7.** 50%　　**8.** 55%

9. 32%　　**10.** 64%　　**11.** 90%　　**12.** 6%

Write each ratio as a percent. Use grid paper, if you wish.

13. $\frac{27}{100}$　**14.** 45 out of 100　**15.** $\frac{1}{2}$　**16.** $\frac{35}{50}$

17. $\frac{9}{10}$　**18.** 1 out of 4　**19.** $\frac{3}{25}$　**20.** $\frac{20}{20}$

21. Analyze The quilt block at the right is called Ozark Trail. What percent of the block is green? yellow?

Stamp and Wrap

Just as ratios can be expressed as percents, percents can be expressed as decimals.

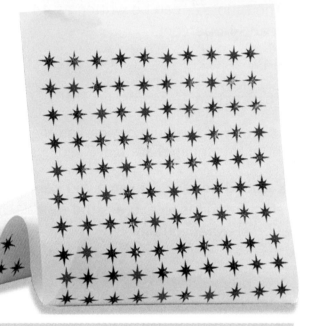

Learning About It

Have you ever put your creativity to work to design something useful? Some people like to make their own designs for things such as greeting cards and wrapping paper.

This wrapping-paper design was made with rubber stamps. A piece with 100 stamp prints will be cut off. Twenty out of 100 prints are red. What part of the 100 prints is red?

THERE'S ALWAYS A WAY!

You can express 20 out of 100 in three different ways.

- **As a fraction** $\frac{20}{100}$

- **As a percent** 20%

Remember: percent means "per 100."

- **As a decimal** 0.20

So, 20 out of 100 = $\frac{20}{100}$ = 20% = 0.20 of the prints are red.

Another Example

80 out of 100 can be expressed in three ways.

- As a fraction

$\frac{80}{100}$

- As a percent

$\frac{80}{100} = 80\%$

- As a decimal

$\frac{80}{100} = 0.80$

Think and Discuss How can you write 0.35 as a percent? as a fraction? as a fraction in simplest form?

Try It Out

Write each expression in two other ways.

1. 3% **2.** $\frac{17}{100}$ **3.** 4% **4.** $\frac{7}{10}$ **5.** 0.6 **6.** 51%

Practice

Write each percent as a decimal and as a fraction in simplest form.

7. 40% **8.** 9% **9.** 72% **10.** 64% **11.** 55% **12.** 90%

13. 5% **14.** 88% **15.** 65% **16.** 78% **17.** 1% **18.** 85%

19. 2% **20.** 125% **21.** 15% **22.** 33% **23.** 200% **24.** 150%

Express each shaded part as a decimal, a percent, and a fraction in simplest form.

25.   **26.**   **27.**   **28.**

Problem Solving

29. Draw a 10 by 10 grid. Shade 48% of the squares. What percent is not shaded?

30. Analyze A design has 100 tiles. 30% of the tiles are either blue or yellow. 70% are red. There are two more yellow tiles than blue tiles. How many blue tiles are there? Tell what strategy you used to solve the problem.

31. Using Algebra The pattern at the right continues downward for a total of ten rows. How many dark tiles are in the tenth row? What percent of all the tiles in the ten-row pattern are dark?

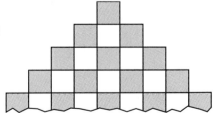

Review and Remember

Find each answer.

32. 4 ft 3 in.
  + 2 ft 7 in.

33. 9 ft 4 in.
  − 5 ft 11 in.

34. 7 yd 2 ft 8 in.
  + 4 yd   10 in.

35. 38.2 × 9 **36.** 182.5 − 1.68 **37.** 5,246 + 8.21 + 6.5

✔ Checkpoint

Understanding Ratio and Percent

Write each ratio in two different ways. (pages 474–475)

1. 4 to 5

2. 9:8

3. 3:7

4. 8 to 4

Using Algebra   Find each *n*. (pages 476–477)

5. $\dfrac{5}{9} = \dfrac{25}{n}$

6. $\dfrac{n}{15} = \dfrac{24}{30}$

7. $\dfrac{4}{11} = \dfrac{12}{n}$

8. $\dfrac{18}{n} = \dfrac{9}{5}$

9. $\dfrac{16}{23} = \dfrac{n}{46}$

10. $\dfrac{25}{100} = \dfrac{1}{n}$

11. $\dfrac{8}{n} = \dfrac{64}{8}$

12. $\dfrac{15}{n} = \dfrac{45}{51}$

Using Algebra   Find each missing measurement. (pages 478–481)

13. $\dfrac{1 \text{ m}}{8 \text{ m}} = \dfrac{\text{scale model}}{56 \text{ m}}$

14. $\dfrac{10 \text{ cm}}{\text{actual size}} = \dfrac{40 \text{ cm}}{48 \text{ cm}}$

15. $\dfrac{11 \text{ m}}{25 \text{ mm}} = \dfrac{44 \text{ m}}{\text{scale model}}$

16. $\dfrac{5 \text{ mm}}{18 \text{ m}} = \dfrac{\text{actual size}}{72 \text{ m}}$

17. $\dfrac{1 \text{ cm}}{\text{actual size}} = \dfrac{148 \text{ cm}}{296 \text{ m}}$

18. $\dfrac{\text{scale model}}{55 \text{ m}} = \dfrac{1 \text{ mm}}{5 \text{ m}}$

Use equivalent ratios or division to complete. (pages 482–483)

19. 15 silk flowers on 3 stems

  ___?___ flowers on 1 stem

20. 48 cans in 8 boxes

  ___?___ cans in 1 box

21. 18 ounces in 3 cans

  ___?___ ounces in 1 can

22. 35 invitations written in 2.5 hours

  ___?___ invitations written in 1 hour

23. 2 albums for $12.00

  1 album for ___?___

24. 4 pillows for $29.00

  1 pillow for ___?___

25. 3 canisters for $51.00

  1 canister for ___?___

26. 5 fabric frames for $12.50

  1 fabric frame for ___?___

Express the shaded part of each grid as a decimal, a percent, and a fraction in simplest form. (pages 488–489)

27.

28.

29.

30.

Problem Solving

Use the scale and the drawing of the model of the Boeing 747 at the right to answer Problems 31–33.

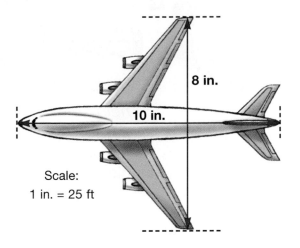

8 in.

10 in.

Scale:
1 in. = 25 ft

31. What is the actual wingspan? Tell how you found your answer.

32. How long is the actual plane? Tell how you found your answer.

33. If the actual length of the tail section is 75 ft, how long is the tail section on the model?

34. Alison is buying five sets of markers for each of her 12 art students. If each set of markers costs $5.75, how much will she spend on markers?

35. **Explain** A design has 20 tiles. 40% of them are white, and 50% are blue. The rest of the tiles are red. How many tiles are red? Explain how you found your answer.

Journal Idea

Explain why a percent is a ratio. Use an example in your explanation.

What do you think?

Describe how you can tell if 50% is greater than or less than $\frac{1}{3}$.

Critical Thinking Corner

Logical Thinking

What's Wrong?

At a local store there is a rack of sale items. Each week the price of everything on the rack is reduced by $\frac{1}{4}$. Joanne wants a jacket that was originally marked $100. She reasons that if she waits 4 weeks, she can get the jacket for free. What's wrong with her reasoning? What would it actually cost?

$100

Problem Solving
Use Logical Reasoning

You can use logical reasoning to help solve some types of problems.

Rosa is hanging four pictures in a row. Each picture has a frame of a different color. The green picture frame is to the left of the blue frame. The yellow frame is to the right of the blue frame. The red frame is between the green frame and the blue frame. From left to right, what is the order of the frames on the wall?

 UNDERSTAND

What do you need to find?

You need to find the order, from left to right, in which Rosa is hanging the picture frames.

 PLAN

How can you solve the problem?

You can **use logical reasoning** to find the order of the frames on the wall.

 SOLVE

green	blue

Green is to the left of blue.

green	blue	yellow

Yellow is to the right of blue.

green	red	blue	yellow

Red is between green and blue.

The order of the frames from left to right is green, red, blue, yellow.

 LOOK BACK

Check to be sure that the positions of the frames satisfy all the conditions.

Using the Strategy

Use logical reasoning to solve Problems 1–4.

1 The seats in art class are numbered from 1 to 30. Jill, Cheryl, and Terry are sitting in seats 11, 12, and 13. Jill is not in seat 11. Terry is sitting between Jill and Cheryl. Who is sitting in seat 13?

2 Al, Bob, Curt, and Don sit in the front four seats in their classroom. Al is not on either end. Bob is between Al and Curt. Don is not in the first seat. In what order are the four boys seated?

3 A cat, bird, and fish are owned by three students. Marie does not own a cat. Jack's pet has four legs. Paul's pet does not walk. Who owns which pet?

4 **Social Studies Connection** Allie, Tyrone, Stan, and Betina each live in a different state. The states are Maine, Texas, Florida, and Hawaii. Allie's state is not in the Southeast. Tyrone and Stan do not live in a state that borders Canada. Betina's state is Texas. Tyrone's state has volcanoes. In which state does each live? You may wish to use the chart.

	ME	TX	FL	HI
Allie				
Tyrone				
Stan				
Betina		X		

Mixed Strategy Review

Try these or other strategies to solve each problem.
Tell which strategy you used.

THERE'S ALWAYS A WAY!

Problem Solving Strategies

- *Make a Table*
- *Guess and Check*
- *Draw a Diagram*
- *Find a Pattern*
- *Write an Equation*
- *Make a List*

---

5 Study the pattern at the right. Draw the next five figures.

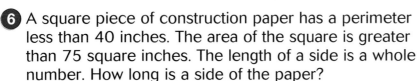

6 A square piece of construction paper has a perimeter less than 40 inches. The area of the square is greater than 75 square inches. The length of a side is a whole number. How long is a side of the paper?

7 **Explain** Ty is buying stickers and stars to put on six cards he is making. He puts 2 stickers and 5 stars on each card. The stickers cost $0.20 each and the stars cost $0.04 each. Ty has $4.00. Does he have enough money to buy stars and stickers for the cards? Explain.

Stickers 20¢ each

4¢ each

Probably So!

Making cards and picking them out of a bag can help you understand probability.

Learning About It

You are going to conduct an experiment on probability You will be looking at the chance of picking a card with either a triangle or square on it.

What You Need

For each group:
  8 blank index cards
  markers
  small paper bag

Work with a group.

Step 1 Draw a triangle on each of five index cards and a square on each of three index cards. Put one triangle card and one square card in the bag. Do you think the chance of picking a triangle is the same as the chance of picking a square? Explain.

Step 2 Make a frequency table like the one shown.

Frequency Table

Shape	Tally	Frequency
Triangle		
Square		

Step 3 Use the bag from Step 1 with two cards in it. Without looking, pick a card from the bag. Then make a tally mark in the *Tally* column, showing the kind of card you picked. Return the card to the bag. Shake the bag. Repeat 29 more times. Record your results in the chart.

Would you expect the results of other groups to be similar to yours? Compare and see if they are.

Step 4 Add 2 more triangle cards and 2 more square cards to the bag. Repeat Steps 2–3.

- Did you expect one shape to be picked more often than the other? Explain.

- Compare your results with those of other groups. What do you notice?

Step 5 Place 2 more triangle cards in the bag and remove 2 square cards. Repeat Steps 2–3. Did you expect the chance of choosing a triangle card would be greater than that of choosing a square card? Explain.

Think and Discuss How did the *Frequency* column change when you had 5 triangle cards and 1 square card?

Practice

1. You have 5 triangle cards, 5 square cards, and 2 circle cards. Which card is least likely to be picked? Why?

2. You have 10 triangle cards and 2 square cards in a bag.

   a. Describe your chances of picking a triangle card out of the bag.

   b. Describe your chances of picking a circle card out of the bag.

3. **Create Your Own** Make up an experiment using colored chips. Predict what you will be most likely to pick. Have a classmate test your prediction.

Critical Thinking Corner

Visual Thinking

Connect the Dots

Copy the array of dots. Then without lifting your pencil, connect the 9 dots with just 4 straight lines.

In a Spin!

You can use ratio to find the probability of an event.

Learning About It

Jeremy and Steffi made a spinner with six equal sections. What is the **probability** that the pointer will stop on the number 5?

In an experiment, such as spinning a spinner, each possible result is an **outcome**. If each result is as likely to occur as every other, they are **equally likely** outcomes.

$$\text{Probability} \text{ (of an event)} = \frac{\text{number of favorable outcomes}}{\text{number of possible outcomes}}$$

$$\text{Probability} \text{ (of spinning a 5)} = \frac{\text{sections with number 5}}{\text{total number of sections}} \text{ or } \frac{1}{6}$$

The probability that the pointer will stop on 5 is $\frac{1}{6}$.

The probability of an event is always 0, 1, or any number between 0 and 1.

An impossible event has a probability of 0. A certain event has a probability of 1.

Think and Discuss What is the probability that the pointer will stop on 10? land on a number?

> **Word Bank**
>
> probability
> outcome
> equally likely

Try It Out

Look at Jeremy and Steffi's spinner. What is the probability that the pointer will stop on each of the following?

1. blue
2. not yellow
3. section 4
4. not blue

5. not 4 or 5
6. an even number
7. section 2
8. green

9. **Discuss** All six sections of a spinner are green. What is the probability of the pointer stopping on green? What is the probability of the pointer stopping on red? Tell why.

Practice

A bag holds 26 cards, one with each letter of the alphabet. You pick a card out of the bag without looking. After you pick a card, you return it to the bag. Find each probability.

10. z

11. a vowel

12. a letter after m

13. a 6

14. p, q, r, s, t

15. a consonant

Problem Solving

16. Analyze A box contains 10 shirts. Suppose the probability of choosing a red shirt from the box is $\frac{3}{10}$. How many red shirts are in the box?

17. What If? Suppose the box in Problem 16 contains only red shirts. What is the probability of picking a red shirt? some other color?

18. Journal Idea Write a paragraph describing how probability is used in reporting the weather, sports, or some other everyday activity.

Review and Remember

Find each answer. Use a calculator to check your work.

19. 5.66×4.75

20. $36.85 \div 33.5$

21. $15.75 - 6.39$

22. $26.34 + 86.9$

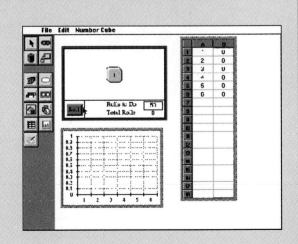

Time for Technology
Using the MathProcessor™ CD-ROM

Using Number Cubes

You can link number cubes, a spreadsheet, and a bar graph to explore probability.

- Click number cubes. Link it to a spreadsheet. Link the spreadsheet to a bar graph.

- Key 50 into Rolls to Do. Click Roll.

- Roll 100. Roll 500. Roll 1,000. Roll 2,500. Roll 10,000.

- Click writing space. Write about what you observed.

For Extra Practice, see Set F, page 510.

Play Fair!

In this lesson you will find out what makes a game fair or unfair.

Learning About It

How can you tell the difference between a fair game and an unfair game? A **fair game** is one in which all players have the same chance of winning. An **unfair game** is one in which players do not have the same chance of winning.

Jenna and Eric made up two coin-toss games. Do you think the games are fair or unfair?

Work with a partner to find out.

Step 1 For each game, make a chart of outcomes like the one shown.

Step 2 Play each game 30 times. Follow the rules and keep track of the number of times you play each game and the number of times each player wins.

Word Bank
fair game
unfair game

What You Need

For each pair:
   1 penny
   1 nickel

Jenna's Game
Penny Toss

How to play: Toss one penny.
If the penny lands heads up, Player A wins.
If the penny lands tails up, Player B wins.

Outcome	Player A Wins	Player B Wins
Heads (penny)		
Tails (penny)		

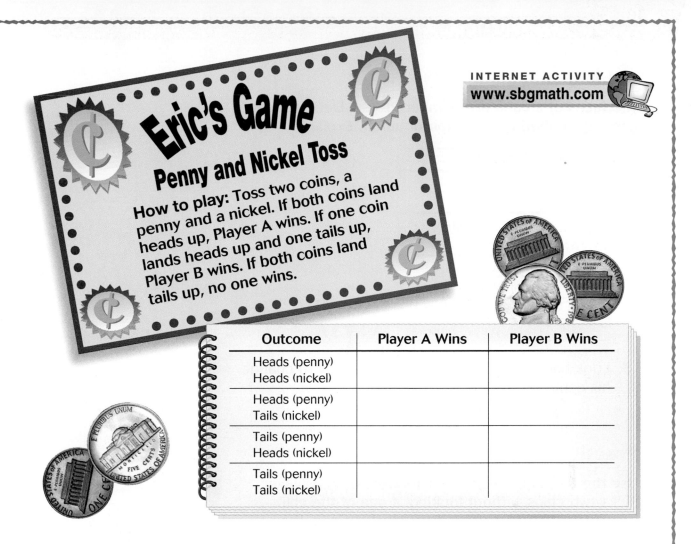

Eric's Game

Penny and Nickel Toss

How to play: Toss two coins, a penny and a nickel. If both coins land heads up, Player A wins. If one coin lands heads up and one tails up, Player B wins. If both coins land tails up, no one wins.

Outcome	Player A Wins	Player B Wins
Heads (penny) Heads (nickel)		
Heads (penny) Tails (nickel)		
Tails (penny) Heads (nickel)		
Tails (penny) Tails (nickel)		

Which game is fair? One way to find out if a game is fair is to look at the possible outcomes.

▶ In Jenna's Game, there are two possible outcomes: One is heads, and the other is tails.

Since winning is getting heads or getting tails, do you think Player A or Player B has a better chance of winning? Is Jenna's Game fair?

▶ In Eric's Game, there are four possible outcomes.

Heads (penny) and heads (nickel)
Heads (penny) and tails (nickel)
Tails (penny) and heads (nickel)
Tails (penny) and tails (nickel)

One outcome is both heads. One outcome is both tails. Two outcomes are heads and tails. Do Player A and Player B have the same chance of winning? Is Eric's Game fair?

Think and Discuss How does looking at possible outcomes help you decide if a game is fair or unfair?

Try It Out

The faces of a cube are numbered 1–6. Decide if each game described below is fair or unfair. Explain.

	Player	What Wins
1.	A	1, 2, 3
	B	4, 5, 6
2.	A	Odd numbers
	B	Even numbers
3.	A	Numbers < 4
	B	Numbers > 4
4.	A	Prime numbers
	B	Not prime numbers

5. Look back at Eric's Game. Is there a way to change his game to make it fair? Explain.

Practice

Use the bag at the right for Exercises 6–7. A player picks two chips without looking. If one of the chips is red, then Player A wins. If no chips are red, then Player B wins.

6. What are the possible outcomes?

7. Is the game fair? Explain.

Sid and Eileen played Spin-to-Win, using the spinner shown. Sid wins if the pointer stops on a prime number. Eileen wins if the pointer stops on a multiple of 4.

8. Why is the game unfair?

9. Change the rules of the game to make a fair game.

10. Check to see that the new rules make the game fair.

    a. What are the possible outcomes?

    b. Does each player have the same chance to win?

11. **Discuss** Choose a game that you and your friends often play. Review the game rules. Discuss whether the game is fair or unfair. Give a reason for your answer.

Problem Solving

12. Create Your Own Make up your own game, using colored chips. Set up the game so that it is fair. Explain the rules to some friends and play it.

13. Survey your class to find out how many different kinds of games are played by each student and his or her family. Organize the data in a bar graph. Use the bar graph to rank the games from most to least played.

14. You Decide You've been given $50 to buy board games, puzzles, and jump ropes.

• You must buy at least one of each item.

• Your must spend as much of the money as you can.

Tell what you will buy and how much change you will get.

Review and Remember

Find each answer.

15. 235 × 48	**16.** 7,998 + 299	**17.** 1,286 − 597	**18.** 3,097 − 898

19. 328 ÷ 10   **20.** 5.8 × 100   **21.** 42)‾3,192   **22.** 6,633 ÷ 67

23. 4,621 − 1,045   **24.** 53.61 × 52   **25.** 2,623 ÷ 43   **26.** 1,802 ÷ 53

 Money $ense

Shop 'Til You Drop

Blank cassettes can be purchased at three local stores.

• Music, Music offers 12 cassettes for $9.00.

• Bargains Galore is advertising 25% off the regular price of $1.00 each.

• The Sound Shop is giving 1 free when you buy 6 for $5.25.

Where would you shop? Which store has the lowest price?

Flowers and Bows

Tree diagrams can help you find all the possible outcomes.

Word Bank

tree diagram

Learning About It

Ginny is making party favors, using one bow and one flower. The pictures show the colors of the flowers and bows. How many different kinds of favors can she make?

THERE'S ALWAYS A WAY!

● **One way** is to make a tree diagram.

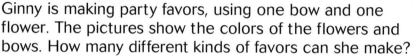

Bow Color Choices	Flower Color Choices	Possible Outcomes
	white	green, white
	yellow	green, yellow
	violet	green, violet
	white	blue, white
	yellow	blue, yellow
	violet	blue, violet

● **Another way** is to multiply.

bow colors × flower colors = number of outcomes
2 × 3 = 6 possible outcomes

Ginny can make 6 different kinds of favors.

Think and Discuss How can you use a tree diagram to help you find probability? Explain, using an example.

Try It Out

Use the pictures at the right for Exercises 1–3.

1. Make a tree diagram to show the possible outcomes of picking a bow and a flower.

2. What is the probability of choosing a gold bow and a pink flower?

3. What is the probability of choosing a gold bow and not a pink flower?

Practice

Use the tree diagram of earring beads below for Exercises 4–5.

Gold Bead Choices	Colored Bead Choices	Possible Outcomes
large gold	black red	large gold, black large gold, red
small gold	black red	small gold, black small gold, red

4. What is the probability that an earring will have a small gold bead and a red bead?

5. Find the probability of choosing a large gold bead and a blue bead.

6. **Discuss** Explain how the table at the right is like the tree diagram on page 502.

	White	Yellow	Violet
Green	green white	green yellow	green violet
Blue	blue white	blue yellow	blue violet

Problem Solving

7. **Analyze** Kayla bought a beaded necklace at a flea market for $1.29. She paid for the necklace with exactly 11 coins. What coins might she have used?

8. Centerpieces, such as the one shown at the right, were made with red, blue, green, and white candles and with white, orange, and purple bows. How many different kinds of centerpieces were possible?

Review and Remember

Using Algebra Compare. Write >, <, or = for each ⬤.

9. 3,400 ÷ 5 ⬤ 68 × 10

10. 2,550 × 6 ⬤ 500 × 3

11. 75.75 ÷ 3 ⬤ 110.10 ÷ 4

12. 145.66 + 1,045.66 ⬤ 595.5 × 2

For Extra Practice, see Set H, page 510.

Problem Solving
Using a Circle Graph

Sometimes you can use a circle graph to analyze data.

Magda makes and sells pottery, but she plans to make a fewer number of items next year. She wants to make only the three items that are the best sellers. She uses a circle graph to analyze her annual sales. Which three items should she make?

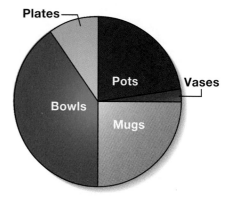

▲ **Fine Arts Connection**
A potter's spinning wheel is an important tool for a potter.

 ### UNDERSTAND

What do you need to find?

You need to find which three of Magda's pottery items are the best sellers.

 ### PLAN

How can you solve the problem?

A circle graph can be divided into sections, one for each item. You can use a circle graph to decide which three items are the best sellers.

 ### SOLVE

The whole circle represents 100% of Magda's annual sales.

The greatest sales are of bowls. They make up more than 25%, but less than 50%, of the graph.

The next greatest section is mugs. This section is about 25% of the circle graph. The section for pots is slightly less than 25%, but greater than the section for plates.

Magda should make bowls, mugs, and pots.

A circle graph represents 100%.

 ### LOOK BACK

Use logical reasoning to check your answer. If the sections for vases and plates are less than those for bowls, mugs, and pots, then the answer is reasonable.

Show What You Learned

Use the circle graphs below to solve Problems 1–5.

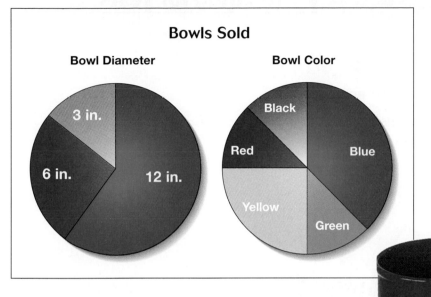

Bowls Sold

Bowl Diameter

3 in.

6 in.

12 in.

Bowl Color

Black

Red

Blue

Yellow

Green

1 Which size bowl was sold most often?
Which size bowl was sold least often?

2 About what percent of the bowls sold were
6 inches in diameter?

3 Which color bowl was the most popular?

4 **Describe** Compare the combined number of yellow
and green bowls sold to the number of blue bowls
sold. Tell how the numbers sold compare.

5 **Analyze** Was the number of 12-inch bowls sold more
than twice the number of 6-inch bowls sold? Tell how
you know.

6 At a school fund-raiser, students sold clay animal
figures they had made. They sold four dogs, four cats,
and eight rabbits. Draw a circle graph to show the sale
of these three kinds of figures.

7 Look back at Problem 6. What percent of the total
number of figures do the rabbits represent? What
percent do the dogs represent?

8 **Create Your Own** Write a problem that can be
answered by using any of the graphs from
Problems 1–7. Share the problem with your classmates.

Problem Solving

★★★★★ **Preparing for Tests**

Practice What You Learned

Choose the correct letter for each answer.

1 Jenny spent $1.50 on lemons and sugar to make lemonade. Then she used a gallon pitcher to fill $\frac{1}{4}$-pt glasses. Which equation could you use to find the number, n, of $\frac{1}{4}$-pt glasses she could fill?

(1 gal = 8 pt)

A. $4 \times \frac{1}{4} = n$

B. $4 \div \frac{1}{4} = n$

C. $8 \times \frac{1}{4} = n$

D. $8 \div \frac{1}{4} = n$

Tip

First change 1 gallon into pints. Then be sure to think about what would be a reasonable answer.

---

2 Anthony likes pizza more than he likes chicken but not as much as he likes lasagna. He likes shrimp more than he likes pizza. Which is a reasonable conclusion?

A. He prefers shrimp over lasagna.
B. He prefers pizza over lasagna.
C. He prefers shrimp over chicken.
D. He prefers chicken over shrimp.

Tip

Try the *Use a Simulation* strategy for this problem. Start by writing the name of a different food on each of 4 slips of paper.

---

3 Yoko arranged the plants in her garden in a series of 3 squares around a single plant in the middle. The innermost square had 2 plants on each side. The middle square had 3 plants on each side, and the outer square had 4 plants on each side. How many plants did she use?

A. 25
B. 30
C. 37
D. 40

Tip

Use one of these strategies to solve this problem.
• *Draw a Diagram*
• *Find a Pattern*
• *Make a Table*

4 The PTA sold 9,894 tickets for a drawing. If the PTA gives one prize for every 2,000 tickets sold, what is a reasonable number of prizes?

A. 5 prizes   **C.** 20 prizes
B. 10 prizes   **D.** 200 prizes

5 Based on the information in the graph, how many fewer students are in the math and science clubs than are in the other 3 clubs?

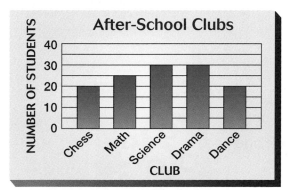

After-School Clubs

A. 15   **C.** 55
B. 20   **D.** 70

6 Amanda practiced the piano for $1\frac{1}{4}$ hours on Monday, $2\frac{1}{4}$ hours on Tuesday, and $\frac{3}{4}$ hours on Wednesday. If she plans to practice $7\frac{1}{2}$ hours this week, how many more hours does she need to practice?

A. $3\frac{1}{2}$ h   **C.** $4\frac{1}{4}$ h

B. $3\frac{1}{4}$ h   **D.** $4\frac{1}{2}$ h

7 In March, Ann sold $2,400 worth of merchandise. Her sales then increased 50% in April. How much did Ann sell in April?

A. $1,200   **D.** $4,800
B. $3,000   **E.** Not Here
C. $3,600

8 Based on the information in the graph, how many more artificial plants than live plants were sold in January and February?

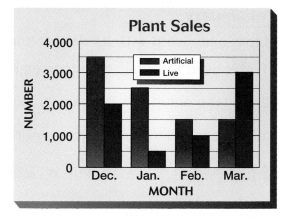

Plant Sales

A. 1,500
B. 2,500
C. 3,500
D. 4,000
E. Not Here

9 There are 1,597 students in a school, with about the same number of girls as boys. About 50% of the girls and 25% of the boys walk or bike to school. The rest of the students take the bus. How many students take the bus?

A. About 400
B. About 600
C. About 1,000
D. About 1,600

10 Jill can write up 14 orders in 2 hours. Sam can do 18 orders in 3 hours. Jill usually works 6 more hours than Sam does each week. How many more orders will Jill have completed than Sam after 8 hours?

A. 1   **D.** 12
B. 8   **E.** Not Here
C. 10

Checkpoint

Finding Probability

Vocabulary

Match each word with its description.

1. It is used to organize outcomes of an experiment.

2. It is the result in a probability experiment.

3. It is a comparison of two quantities.

4. It is a ratio whose second term is 100.

Word Bank

outcome
percent
ratio
tree diagram

Concepts and Skills

Use the bag of cards shown at the right for Exercises 5–6. (pages 494–495)

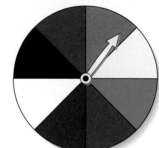

5. What are the possible outcomes if you pick one card at a time?

6. Suppose that two cards with squares were added to the bag. How would that affect the outcome?

Use the spinner shown for Exercises 7–10. Find the probability of the pointer stopping on each. (pages 496–497)

7. black

8. not black

9. blue or violet

10. red, orange, or green

11. **Analyze** A spinner has six sections of different sizes. Is each outcome equally likely? Explain.

Use the description below for Exercises 12–17. (pages 498–501)

In the game Toss It! a cube is labeled with the numbers 1–6. Player A wins when a 3 is tossed. Player B wins when an even number is tossed.

12. Describe the possible outcomes.

13. Is the game fair? Explain why or why not.

Find the probability of each outcome.

14. tossing a 3

15. not tossing a 3

16. tossing a 2 or 5

17. not tossing a 2 or 4

Problem Solving

Use the following description for Exercises 18–20.

Jaime is making decorations for a show with pictures of instruments and musical notes. The instruments are drums, piano, and guitar. The notes are eighth notes and quarter notes.

18. Draw a tree diagram to show all the possible outcomes of picking a picture of an instrument and a musical note.

19. What is the probability of picking a guitar and a sixteenth note? Explain.

20. Jacob, Susan, Brittany, and Dan were finishing crafts they had made for the school craft fair. Dan did not finish last. Brittany finished next after Jacob. Susan finished first. In what order did the students finish their crafts?

Journal Idea

Create Your Own Write the rules of a game. Then explain why the game is either fair or unfair.

What do you think?

Could a tree diagram be used for something besides solving a probability problem? Explain your answer.

You Decide

Activity

Enlargement Please

You and two partners select a small item you would like to enlarge, such as a pencil, coin, or your own hand.

Trace the selected object onto centimeter grid paper. Decide on a scale to use to enlarge your drawing.

• What ratio will you use for your enlargement?

Use your scale to draw an enlarged copy of your picture.

You might wish to include this work in your portfolio.

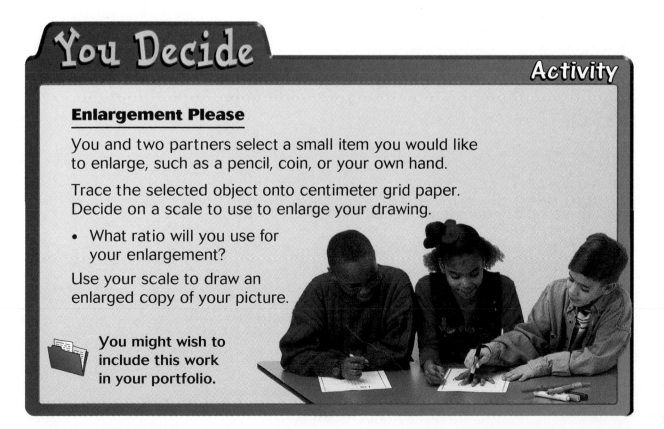

Extra Practice

Set A (pages 474–475)

Write each ratio in a different form.

1. 4 to 5   **2.** $\frac{3}{7}$ **3.** 7:9   **4.** 6:5   **5.** 9 to 13

Use the bead chain at the right to answer each question.

6. What is the ratio of red beads to blue-green beads?

7. What is the ratio of yellow beads to red beads?

8. Write the ratio of red beads to yellow beads in three different ways.

9. Is the ratio of yellow beads to red beads the same as the ratio of red beads to yellow beads? Explain.

Set B (pages 476–477)

Using Algebra Copy and complete each ratio table.

1.

4	8	▦	16	20
9	▦	27	▦	▦

2.

8	▦	▦	▦	40	48
15	30	45	60	▦	▦

Find each *n*.

3. $\frac{2}{5} = \frac{n}{20}$ **4.** $\frac{7}{8} = \frac{21}{n}$ **5.** $\frac{10}{15} = \frac{20}{n}$ **6.** $\frac{6}{7} = \frac{n}{56}$ **7.** $\frac{n}{16} = \frac{40}{64}$

Write three ratios equivalent to each ratio given.

8. 8 to 9   **9.** 30:40   **10.** 4:9

11. $\frac{6}{12}$ **12.** $\frac{2}{3}$ **13.** $\frac{7}{14}$

14. 12 to 7   **15.** 3 to 5   **16.** 20:50

17. In the time it takes Minna to make two origami pinwheels, Jen can make seven. If Minna makes 50 pinwheels, how many can Jen make?

Extra Practice

Set C (pages 478–481)

Using Algebra Find the model size or actual size of each object.

1.
Model size	3 in.	▨	9 in.	▨
Actual size	4 ft	8 ft	▨	▨

2.
Scale drawing	5 in.	▨	15 in.	20 in.
Length of vehicle	▨	14 ft	21 ft	▨

3.
Length of insect	1 in.	▨	▨	4 in.
Scale drawing	▨	22 in.	▨	44 in.

4.
Width of photograph	▨	4 in.	6 in.	▨
Actual width	8 ft	▨	24 in.	▨

5. $\dfrac{2 \text{ in.}}{5 \text{ ft}} = \dfrac{\text{model size}}{10 \text{ ft}}$

6. $\dfrac{1 \text{ in.}}{3 \text{ yd}} = \dfrac{7 \text{ in.}}{\text{actual size}}$

7. $\dfrac{\text{model size}}{12 \text{ in.}} = \dfrac{2 \text{ in.}}{3 \text{ in.}}$

8. $\dfrac{10 \text{ in.}}{\text{actual size}} = \dfrac{30 \text{ in.}}{60 \text{ yd}}$

9. $\dfrac{4 \text{ in.}}{7 \text{ ft}} = \dfrac{20 \text{ in.}}{\text{actual size}}$

10. $\dfrac{\text{model size}}{4 \text{ mi}} = \dfrac{9 \text{ ft}}{36 \text{ mi}}$

11. $\dfrac{3 \text{ in.}}{5 \text{ ft}} = \dfrac{\text{actual size}}{20 \text{ ft}}$

12. $\dfrac{1 \text{ ft}}{6 \text{ ft}} = \dfrac{\text{model size}}{36 \text{ ft}}$

13. $\dfrac{2 \text{ in.}}{\text{actual size}} = \dfrac{144 \text{ in.}}{216 \text{ ft}}$

Set D (pages 482–483)

Using Algebra Use equivalent ratios or division to complete.

1. 55 labels in 5 hours
   ___?___ labels in 1 hour

2. 25 push-ups in 25 seconds
   ___?___ push-ups in 5 seconds

3. 72 jars in 6 boxes
   ___?___ jars in 1 box

4. 45 yards of ribbon on 3 rolls
   ___?___ yards in 1 roll

5. 54 muffins in 18 bags
   ___?___ muffins in 3 bags

6. 240 miles in 4 hours
   ___?___ miles in 8 hours

7. 16 muffins for $8.00
   ___?___ for 1 muffin

8. 4 yards of fabric for $21.96
   ___?___ for 1 yard

9. 7 brushes for $29.33
   ___?___ for 1 brush

10. 19 marbles for $5.51
    ___?___ for 1 marble

11. Jennie can create 15 origami rabbits in 45 minutes.
    Archie can create 10 origami rabbits in 20 minutes.
    Who can create rabbits faster?

Extra Practice

Set E (pages 488–489)

Write each percent as a decimal and a fraction in simplest form. Write a percent for each decimal or fraction.

1. 50%   **2.** 18%   **3.** 76%   **4.** 90%   **5.** 16%   **6.** 75%

7. $\frac{89}{100}$ **8.** 0.32   **9.** $\frac{7}{10}$ **10.** 0.88   **11.** 0.3   **12.** $\frac{12}{50}$

13. A magazine ad says that 62 out of every 100 fifth graders will like Company A's colored pencils better than Company B's pencils. What percent is this?

Set F (pages 496–497)

Use the spinner. Find the probability that the pointer will stop on each section.

1. K   **2.** J   **3.** M   **4.** not L   **5.** not M   **6.** not L or M

Set G (pages 498–501)

A cube is numbered 1, 2, 3, 4, 5, 6. Decide if each game is fair or unfair. Give a reason for your decision.

1. Player A wins if an odd number is tossed.
Player B wins if an even number is tossed.

2. Player A wins if a number less than 6 is tossed.
Player B wins if a multiple of 1 is tossed.

Set H (pages 502–503)

Use the following description for Exercises 1–5. For Exercises 2–5, find the probability of each.

Beth is making paper decorations for each classroom door. Her first pick is from an apple or a pear. Her second pick is from a carrot, a radish, a tomato, or a cucumber.

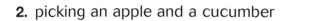

1. Make a tree diagram showing the possible combinations of paper decorations for each door.

2. picking an apple and a cucumber

3. picking a pear and a carrot

4. picking an apple but not a carrot

5. picking an apple and an artichoke

Chapter Test

Write each ratio in a different form.

1. $\frac{1}{2}$

2. 2:3

3. 5 to 3

Use a ratio table or equivalent ratios to find each *n*.

4. $\frac{3}{4} = \frac{n}{16}$

5. $\frac{5}{7} = \frac{40}{n}$

6. $\frac{1}{5} = \frac{13}{n}$

7. $\frac{12}{25} = \frac{n}{100}$

Complete each statement.

8. 15 play tickets for $45
   __?__ tickets for $9

9. 9 stickers for $0.63
   1 sticker for __?__

10. 235 students in 5 buses
    47 students in __?__ bus

Write each ratio as a decimal and then as a percent.

11. 37:100

12. 9 to 10

13. 4:25

14. 3 to 6

List the possible outcomes.

15. Tossing a number cube with the numbers 1–6

16. Picking a chip from a bag with 3 red and 2 blue chips

Use the bag of 16 chips. Find the probability of picking each color if you replace the chip after each pick.

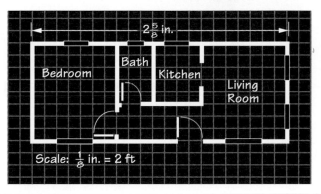

17. red

18. orange

Solve.

19. Use the blueprint at the right. What is the actual length of the house?

20. Marvin's parents pay $35 a month for cable television service. Sarah's parents pay $7 a week for their service. Is it cheaper to pay by the month or by the week for a year's worth of service?

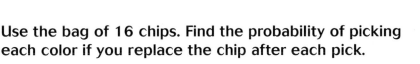

Bedroom Bath Kitchen Living Room

$2\frac{5}{8}$ in.

Scale: $\frac{1}{8}$ in. = 2 ft

Self-Check

Were the probabilities you found for Questions 17–18 between 0 and 1?

Performance Assessment

Show What You Know About Ratio, Percent, and Probability

① Use the spinner. What is the probability of each of the following?

a. A spinner stopping on 4

b. A spinner stopping on an odd number

c. A spinner stopping on a 2, 3, or 4

d. A spinner stopping on a 5

e. A spinner stopping on a number from 1 to 4

Self-Check Did you remember that the probability of an event ranges from 0 to 1?

What You Need

1 four-part spinner grid paper

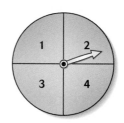

② Students at an art college specialize in different areas. This table shows the number of students studying art specialties.

Art Specialties	
Course	Number of Students
Painting	20
Graphic design	18
Sculpture	12
Advertising	24
Computer animation	26

a. What is the ratio of students in computer animation to those studying sculpture?

b. Explain Can you find a ratio equivalent to $\frac{3}{4}$? Explain your answer.

c. What is the ratio of students in painting to the total number of students? Write your ratio in simplest form.

Self-Check Did you remember that a ratio can be written as a to b, a:b, or $\frac{a}{b}$?

③ Use grid paper. Draw a 10 × 10 grid. Shade 32 percent of the grid. Then write the percent as a decimal.

Self-Check Did you carefully shade the correct number of squares?

For Your Portfolio

You might wish to include this work in your portfolio.

Extension

Estimating the Percent of a Number

Percents are used in many ways. Discounts on prices, sales tax, and tips can all be expressed as percents.

What you know about percents and equivalent fractions can help you find a percent of a number.

► **Some percents are easy to calculate mentally.**

Suppose a $40 art set is 50% off. If you buy it on sale, how much do you save?

What is 50% of $40?

Remember that 50% is the same as $\frac{1}{2}$. So 50% of $40 is half of $40, or $20. You would save $20.

► **Some other percents are also easy to use.**

$10\% = \frac{10}{100}$ or $\frac{1}{10}$ $25\% = \frac{25}{100}$ or $\frac{1}{4}$ $75\% = \frac{75}{100}$ or $\frac{3}{4}$

► **Some percents can be rounded before estimating.**

Art supplies cost $35 plus 8% tax. About what will the tax be?

8% rounds to 10%

$10\% = \frac{10}{100}$ or $\frac{1}{10}$

$\frac{1}{10} \times \$35 = \$3.50$

The tax is about $3.50.

Estimate each amount.

1. 25% of 400   **2.** 20% of 300   **3.** 32% of 10   **4.** 99% of 100

5. 10% of 250   **6.** 5% of 500   **7.** 50% of 86   **8.** 75% of 500

Cumulative Review

★ ★ ★ ★ ★ **Preparing for Tests**

Choose the correct letter for each answer.

Operations	**Geometry and Spatial Reasoning**

1. Over a 10-day period, 15,000 people went to the county fair. On Saturday, 5,673 people went. On Sunday, 6,190 went. How many people went on those 2 days?

   A. 3,137   **D.** 11,683
   B. 8,810   **E.** Not Here
   C. 9,327

2. Forty-seven skaters each rented skates for $4.50 a pair. There were 105 skaters at Skate World. How much did Skate World make in skate rentals?

   A. $211.50   **C.** $472.50
   B. $222.50   **D.** $493.50

3. Sid had $50. He bought 2 video games that cost $14 each. He also bought a poster for $5.69. How much money did he have left after his purchases?

   A. $33.69   **C.** $19.69
   B. $28.69   **D.** $16.31

4. A restaurant has 242 plates and 484 glasses. There are an equal number of plates on each of 11 tables. How many plates are there per table?

   A. 44   **D.** 11
   B. 40   **E.** Not Here
   C. 22

5. This lampshade is shaped most like which space figure?

   A. Triangular prism
   B. Cube
   C. Cylinder
   D. Cone

6. Which of the polygons listed has 6 sides and 6 angles?

   A. Quadrilateral
   B. Pentagon
   C. Hexagon
   D. Octagon

7. Which of the following shows an example of a reflection?

   A.   **C.**

   B.   **D.**

8. Which does **NOT** show a figure with a line of symmetry?

   A.

   B.

   C.

   D.

Probability and Statistics		**Patterns, Relationships, and Algebraic Thinking**

Probability and Statistics

9. A box contains 4 white tickets and 5 black tickets. What is the probability that Kit will draw a black ticket?

    A. $\frac{5}{9}$ **C.** $\frac{1}{4}$

    B. $\frac{4}{9}$ **D.** $\frac{1}{5}$

10. There are 4 red, 3 purple, 1 green, and 2 pink ribbons in a box. Which is a possible outcome if you choose 5 ribbons at random?

    A. 3 red, 2 green
    B. 2 purple, 1 green, 1 red
    C. 3 pink, 1 red, 1 blue
    D. 5 red

Use the graph for Questions 11 and 12.

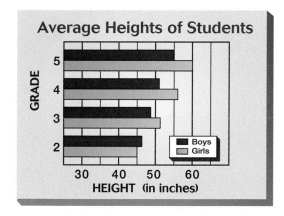

11. In what grade did the girls begin to be taller than the boys?

    A. 2   **C.** 4
    B. 3   **D.** 5

12. How much did the girls' average height change from Grade 2 to Grade 5?

    A. 15 inches   **C.** 8 inches
    B. 12 inches   **D.** 5 inches

Patterns, Relationships, and Algebraic Thinking

13. Read the input/output table. What is the rule?

Input	Output
4.50	7.25
5.25	8.00

    A. Add 2.75.
    B. Subtract 2.25.
    C. Multiply by 0.25.
    D. Add 3.25.

14. Which expression is equivalent to $(8 + 5) + 7$?

    A. $8 + 5 \times 7$
    B. $8 + (5 + 7)$
    C. $13 + 6$
    D. $(8 \times 7) + (5 \times 7)$

15. Which number best completes the input/output table?

Input	Output
47	35
690	678
121	■

    A. 109
    B. 111
    C. 123
    D. 133

16. Kevin put decorated eggs in cartons to store them. Each carton held 12 eggs. He then put 4 cartons in each crate. How many eggs did Kevin store if he completely filled 2 crates?

    A. 96
    B. 84
    C. 48
    D. 24

Additional
Resources

Tables

MEASURES

Customary

Length	Weight	Capacity
1 foot (ft) = 12 inches (in.)	1 pound (lb) = 16 ounces (oz)	1 cup (c) = 8 fluid ounces (fl oz)
1 yard (yd) = 3 feet, or 36 inches	1 ton (T) = 2,000 pounds	1 pint (pt) = 2 cups
1 mile = 5,280 feet, or 1,760 yards		1 quart (qt) = 2 pints
		1 gallon = 4 quarts

Metric

Length	Mass/Weight
1 meter (m) = 1,000 millimeters (mm)	1 gram (g) = 1,000 milligrams (mg)
1 meter = 100 centimeters (cm)	1 kilogram (kg) = 1,000 grams
1 meter = 10 decimeters (dm)	**Capacity**
1 centimeter = 10 millimeters	1 liter (L) = 1,000 milliliters (mL)
1 decimeter = 10 centimeters	
1 kilometer (km) = 1,000 meters	

Time

1 minute (min) = 60 seconds (s)	1 month (mo) = 28 to 31 days, or about 4 weeks
1 hour (h) = 60 minutes	1 year (yr) = 12 months (mo), or 52 weeks, or 365 days
1 day (d) = 24 hours	
1 week (wk) = 7 days	

SYMBOLS

=	is equal to	π	pi (approximately 3.14)	$\overleftrightarrow{AB}$	line AB
>	is greater than	°	degree	$\overline{AB}$	line segment AB
<	is less than	°C	degree Celsius	$\overrightarrow{AB}$	ray AB
≈	is approximately equal to	°F	degree Fahrenheit	$\angle ABC$	angle ABC
…	and so on, in the same manner	10^2	ten to the second power	$\triangle ABC$	triangle ABC
2:5	ratio of 2 to 5	‖	is parallel to	(3, 4)	ordered pair 3, 4
%	percent	⊥	is perpendicular to		

FORMULAS

$P = $ sum of all sides	Perimeter (general formula)	$A = s \times s$	Area of a square
		$A = b \times h$	Area of a parallelogram
$P = (2 \times l) + (2 \times w)$	Perimeter of a rectangle	$A = \frac{1}{2} \times b \times h$	Area of a triangle
$P = 4 \times s$	Perimeter of a square	$C = \pi \times d$	Circumference of a circle
$A = l \times w$	Area of a rectangle	$V = l \times w \times h$	Volume of a rectangular prism

Glossary

A

acute angle An angle with a measure less than 90°. (p. 250)

Example:

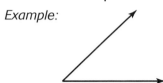

acute triangle A triangle with three acute angles. (p. 260)

algebra The branch of mathematics in which operations are performed that involve algebraic expressions. (p. 56)

algebraic expression An expression that contains at least one variable. (pp. 9, 18)

Example: $n + 5$

angle Two rays with a common endpoint called the vertex. (p. 250)

Example:

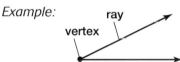

area The number of square units needed to cover a region. (p. 454)

array An arrangement of objects or numbers in rows and columns. (p. 130)

associative property of addition The way that addends are grouped does not change the sum. (p. 42)

Example: $(2 + 3) + 4 = 2 + (3 + 4)$

associative property of multiplication The way that factors are grouped does not change the product. (p. 130)

Example: $(2 \times 3) \times 4 = 2 \times (3 \times 4)$

average (mean) The sum of the addends divided by the number of addends. (p. 194)

axis Either the horizontal line (called x) or the vertical line (called y) that form the base lines of a graph. (p. 88)

Example:

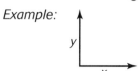

B

bar graph A graph with bars of different lengths. (p. 88)

base (in geometry) A face on which a figure rests. (pp. 282, 457)

Example:

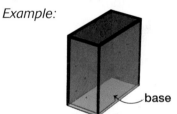

base (in arithmetic) The number that is multiplied by itself when raised to a power. (p. 371)

Example: In 5^3, 5 is the base.

C

capacity The amount a container can hold. (p. 434)

center The point from which all points on a circle are equally distant. (p. 280)

centimeter (cm) A unit of length in the metric system equal to 0.01 meter. (p. 438)

Glossary

chord A line segment with both endpoints on the circle. (p. 280)

circle A closed plane figure. All the points of a circle are the same distance from a point called the center. (p. 280)

Example:

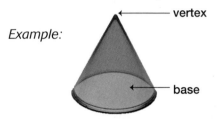

circle graph A graph that shows how a total amount has been divided into parts. (p. 125)

circumference The distance around a circle. (p. 450)

clustering An estimation method used when numbers are close to the same number. (p. 55)

common factor A number that is a factor of two or more given numbers. (p. 336)

Example: 1, 2, and 4 are common factors of 4 and 8.

common multiple A number that is a multiple of two or more given numbers. (p. 338)

Example: 6, is a common multiple of 2 and 3.

commutative (order) property of addition The order of the addends does not change the sum. (p. 42)

Example: $9 + 7 = 7 + 9$

commutative (order) property of multiplication The order of the factors does not change the product. (p. 130)

compatible numbers Numbers that are easy to compute mentally. (p. 44)

Example: $5 + 15 = 20$

compensation A mental math method in which numbers are adjusted up or down to make addition and subtraction easier. (p. 44)

composite number A whole number greater than one that has more than two factors. (p. 335)

cone A space figure with one circular base and one vertex. (p. 284)

Example:

congruent figures Figures that have the same size and shape. (p. 272)

coordinates Numbers used to locate a point on a line, on a surface, or in space. (p. 92)

cube A space figure with six congruent square faces. (p. 282)

cubic unit Unit used to measure volume. (p. 462)

Example: a cubic meter, m^3

customary system A system of weights and measures that measures length in inches, feet, yards, and miles; capacity in cups, pints, quarts, and gallons; weight in ounces, pounds, and tons; and temperature in degrees Fahrenheit. (p. 428)

cylinder A space figure with two parallel circular bases. (p. 284)

Example:

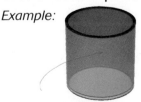

D

data Information, often numerical, that describes some situation. (p. 86)

decimal A number with one or more digits to the right of a decimal point. (p. 16)

Examples: 0.7, 1.8, 2.06, 0.175

degree (°) A unit for measuring angles. (p. 252)

degree Celsius (°C) A unit for measuring temperature in the metric system. (p. 446)

degree Fahrenheit (°F) A unit for measuring temperature in the customary system. (p. 446)

denominator The number below the fraction bar in a fraction. (p. 342)

Example: $\frac{2}{5}$ The denominator is 5.

diagonal A line segment that joins two vertices of a polygon but is not a side. (p. 457)

Example:

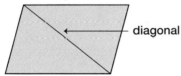

diameter A line segment that passes through the center of a circle and has both endpoints on the circle. (p. 280)

Example:

diameter

difference The answer for subtraction. (p. 50)

digit Any of the symbols used to write numbers: 0, 1, 2, 3, 4, 5, 6, 7, 8, and 9. (p. 5)

distributive property Multiplying a sum by a number is the same as multiplying each addend by the number and adding the products. (p. 130)

Example: $2 \times (3 + 4) = (2 \times 3) + (2 \times 4)$

dividend The number to be divided. (p. 185)

Example: $6\overline{)36}$ or $36 \div 6$
   The dividend is 36.

divisible A number is divisible by another number if the remainder is 0 after dividing. (p. 176)

divisor The number used to divide another number. (p. 184)

Example: $6\overline{)36}$ or $36 \div 6$
   The divisor is 6.

double bar graph A graph that uses pairs of bars to compare information. (p. 88)

E

edge A segment that is the intersection of two faces of a space figure. (p. 282)

Example:

edge

elapsed time An amount of time that has passed. (p. 424)

endpoint A point at the end of a line segment or ray. (p. 246)

Example: :

endpoint   endpoint
   X   Y

Glossary

equally likely outcomes Outcomes that have the same chance of occurring. (p. 496)

equation A number sentence with an equal sign. (pp. 56, 421)

equilateral triangle A triangle with all sides and angles equal. (p. 261)

Example:

equivalent fractions Fractions that name the same number. (p. 352)

equivalent ratios Ratios that represent the same rate or make the same comparison. (p. 476)

estimate An approximate rather than an exact answer. (p. 48)

expanded form A number written as the sum of the values of its digits. (p. 4)

Example: 500 + 50 + 5 is the expanded form for 555.

exponent A number that tells how many times the base is used as a factor. (p. 371)

Example: $10^3 = 10 \times 10 \times 10$
The exponent is 3 and the base is 10.

expression A mathematical phrase made up of a variable or combination of variables and/or numbers and operations. (p. 433)

Examples: $5n, 4x - 7, (5 \times 2) - \frac{6}{3}$

--- **F** ---

face A flat surface of a space figure. (p. 282)

factor tree A diagram used to show the prime factors of a number. (p. 371)

Example:

18
2 9
Prime
3 3
Prime Prime

factors The numbers that are multiplied to give a product. (p. 130)

Example: $3 \times 5 = 15$
The factors are 3 and 5.

fair game A game in which all players have the same chance of winning. (p. 498)

flip (reflection) A change in position that produces a mirror image of a figure. (p. 273)

Examples:

 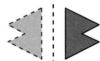

formula An equation that states a rule. (p. 452)

fraction A number that names part of a whole. (p. 342)

Examples: $\frac{1}{2}, \frac{2}{3}, \frac{6}{6}$

frequency table A table used to record and summarize the number of times something occurs. (p. 86)

front digit The digit in the place with the greatest value, used in front-end estimation. (p. 54)

front-end estimation A method of estimating sums, differences, products, and quotients using front digits. (p. 54)

gram (g) The basic unit of mass in the metric system. (p. 444)

graph A drawing used to show numerical information. (p. 30)

greatest common factor (GCF) The greatest number that is a factor of each of two or more numbers. (p. 336)
Example: The greatest common factor of 36 and 48 is 12.

grouping property See associative property of addition; associative property of multiplication. (pp. 42, 130)

height (of a geometric figure) The length of a perpendicular segment drawn from a vertex to the base. (p. 457)
Examples:

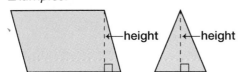

hexagon A polygon with 6 sides. (p. 256)

identity property
of addition The sum of any number and zero is that number. (p. 42)
of multiplication The product of any number and one is that number. (p.130)

improper fraction A fraction in which the numerator is greater than or equal to the denominator. (p. 346)
Examples: $\frac{4}{3}$, $\frac{6}{6}$

integer The numbers . . . −3, −2, −1, 0, +1, +2, +3, . . . (p. 471)

intersecting lines Lines that have exactly one point in common. (p. 247)

interval The distance between points on the scale of a graph. (p. 89)

inverse operations Two operations that have the opposite effect. Addition and subtraction are inverse operations. Multiplication and division are inverse operations. (p. 46)

isosceles triangle A triangle with two congruent sides. (p. 261)
Example:

kilogram (kg) A unit of mass in the metric system equal to 1,000 grams. 0.001 kg = 1 g. (p. 444)

kilometer (km) A unit of length in the metric system equal to 1,000 meters. 0.001 km = 1 m. (p. 438)

least common denominator (LCD) The least common multiple of the denominators of two or more fractions. (p. 358)

least common multiple (LCM) The least number, other than zero, that is a multiple of each of two or more numbers. (p. 338)

line An endless collection of points along a straight path. A line has no endpoints. (p. 246)

line graph A graph used to show changes over a period of time. (p. 98)

Glossary

line of symmetry A line that divides a figure, when folded along the lines into two congruent parts. (p. 278)

line plot A graphing method that shows each item of data on a number line. (p. 86)

line segment A part of a line having two endpoints. (p. 246)

logical reasoning Using logic to answer a question. (p. 492)

lowest terms A fraction is in lowest terms if the greatest common factor of the numerator and the denominator is 1. (p. 356)
Examples: $\frac{1}{4}$ and $\frac{3}{5}$ are in lowest terms.

mass The amount of matter an object contains that causes it to have weight. (p. 444)

mean The average of the numbers in a set of data. (p. 194)

median The middle number or average of the two middle numbers in a collection of data when the data are arranged in order. (p. 114)

memory key A calculator key that stores a product in the memory. Often it is used in multi-step problems. (p. 309)

mental math Performing a computation without the use of paper and pencil or a calculator. (p. 44)

meter (m) The basic unit of length in the metric system. (p. 438)

metric system A system of weights and measures that is based on the decimal system. The gram is the basic unit of mass; the meter is the basic unit of weight; and the liter is the basic unit of volume. (p. 438)

mixed number A number written as a whole number and a fraction. (p. 346)
Example: $2\frac{5}{6}$

mode The number or numbers that occur most often in a set of data. (p. 114)

multiple The product of a whole number and any other whole number. (p. 338)
Example: 0, 2, 4, 6, … are multiples of 2.

multiplication An operation on two or more numbers, called factors, to find a product. (p. 130)

negative number A number whose value is less than zero. (p. 471)
Examples: −5, −10, −456

number line A line that shows numbers in order. (p. 10)

number sentence An equation written in horizontal form. (p. 56)
Example: $3 \times 4 = 12$

numerator The number above the fraction bar in a fraction. (p. 342)
Example: $\frac{3}{4}$ The numerator is 3.

obtuse angle An angle with a measure greater than 90° but less than 180°. (p. 250)
Example:

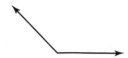

obtuse triangle A triangle with one obtuse angle. (p. 260)

octagon A polygon with eight sides. (p. 256)

Example:

optical illusion A misleading visual image. (p. 449)

order of operations The order in which operations are done in calculations. Work inside parentheses is done first. Then multiplication and division are done from left to right, and finally addition and subtraction are done from left to right. (p. 170)

ordered pair A pair of numbers often used to locate a point in a plane. (p. 92)

outcome A result in a probability experiment. (p. 496)

P

parallel lines Lines in the same plane that never intersect. (p. 247)

Example:

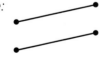

parallelogram A quadrilateral with each pair of opposite sides parallel and congruent. (p. 266)

Example:

partial product When multiplying two 2-digit numbers, the product after multiplying by ones or the product after multiplying by tens. (p. 146)

pentagon A polygon with five sides. (p. 256)

Example:

percent A ratio whose second term is 100. Percent means parts per hundred. (p. 487)

Example: 75% means 75 parts per hundred.

perimeter The distance around a polygon. (p. 452)

perpendicular lines Two lines that intersect at right angles. (p. 247)

Example:

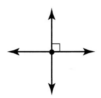

pictograph A graph that represents numerical data using pictures. (p. 74)

place value The value determined by the position of a digit in a number. (p. 4)

point An exact location in space. (p. 246)

polygon A closed plane figure with line segments as sides. (p. 256)

prime factorization Writing a number as the product of prime factors. (p. 371)

Example: $24 = 2 \times 2 \times 2 \times 3 = 2^3 \times 3$

prime number A whole number greater than 1 with only two factors—itself and 1. (p. 335)

Examples: 5, 7, and 11 are prime numbers.

Glossary

prism A space figure with two parallel and congruent bases that are polygons. (p. 282)

probability The ratio of the number of favorable outcomes to all outcomes of an experiment. (p. 496)

product The answer in multiplication. (p. 130)

proper fraction A fraction in which the numerator is less than the denominator. (p. 342)

Examples: $\frac{3}{4}$, $\frac{5}{8}$

protractor An instrument used to measure or draw angles. (p. 252)

pyramid A space figure whose base is a polygon and whose faces are triangles with a common vertex. (p. 282)

Example:

Q

quadrilateral A polygon with four sides. (p. 256)

quotient The answer in division. (p. 172)

R

radius A line segment with one endpoint on the circle and the other endpoint at the center. (p. 280)

Example:

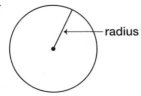

radius

range The difference between the greatest and least numbers in a set of data. (p. 114)

ratio A comparison of two quantities. (p. 474)

Example: 3 to 5, 3:5, $\frac{3}{5}$

ray A part of a line that has one endpoint and goes on and on in one direction. (p. 246)

Example:

rectangle A parallelogram with four right angles. (p. 266)

rectangular prism A space figure whose faces are all rectangles. (p. 282)

regular polygon A polygon with all sides congruent and all angles congruent. (p. 256)

Examples:

remainder The number that is left after dividing. (p. 176)

Example: $42 \div 8 = 5 \text{ R}2$
The remainder is 2.

rhombus A parallelogram with all sides congruent. (p. 266)

right angle An angle that measures 90°. (p. 251)

Example:

right triangle A triangle with one right angle. (p. 260)

Example:

Glossary

Roman numerals A numeration system using the symbols I, V, X, L, C, D, and M. It was first used by the Romans and is still used today on clocks and in dates. (p. 83)

round Replacing a number by expressing it to the nearest ten, hundred, thousand, and so on. (p. 10)

Example: 23 rounded to the nearest ten is 20.

scale The ratio of the measurements in a drawing, or model, to the measurements of the actual objects. (p. 478)

scalene triangle A triangle that has no congruent sides. (p. 261)

Example:

sequence A list of numbers that often follow a rule or a pattern. (p. 241)

set Any collection of things. (p. 198)

short division A method of dividing in which the multiplication and subtraction are performed mentally. (p. 188)

similar figures Figures that have the same shape but not necessarily the same size. (p. 276)

simplest form A fraction is in simplest form when the greatest common factor of the numerator and denominator is 1. Also, *lowest terms*. (p. 356)

simulation Representing the conditions of a problem using models, drawings, or a computer rather than actual objects or events. (p. 450)

slide (translation) A change in position that moves a figure up, down, or over. (p. 273)

Example:

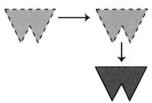

space figure A geometric figure whose points are in more than one plane. (p. 282)

sphere A space figure with all points an equal distance from the center. (p. 284)

spreadsheet Data arranged in rows and columns. It performs calculations with the recorded data. (p. 9)

square A rectangle with all sides congruent. (p. 266)

square number A whole number that is the product of 2 equal whole numbers. (p. 225)

Example: 25 is a square number since 25 = 5 × 5.

square unit A unit used to measure area. (p. 454)

Example: a square centimeter, cm²

standard form A number written with commas separating groups of three digits. (p. 4)

Example: 1,255,362

straight angle An angle that measures 180°. (p. 250)

sum The answer in addition. (p. 42)

surface area The sum of the areas of all the faces of a space figure. (p. 459)

survey To collect data to analyze some characteristic of a group. (p. 86)

Glossary

symmetry A figure is symmetric if it can be folded along a line so that the two resulting parts match exactly. (p. 278)

Example:

T
---

tessellation An arrangement of congruent figures in a plane in such a way that no figures overlap and there are no gaps. (p. 275)

transformation The turning, sliding, or flipping of a plane figure. (p. 273)

Examples:

trapezoid A quadrilateral with only one pair of opposite sides parallel. (p. 266)

Example:

tree diagram A diagram used to organize outcomes of an experiment. (p. 502)

triangle A polygon with three sides. (p. 256)

Example:

triangular prism A prism whose bases are triangles. (p. 283)

Example:

turn (rotation) A change of position that rotates a figure around a point. (p. 273)

Examples:

U
---

unfair game A game in which not all players have an equal chance of winning. (p. 498)

unit price The rate: price per unit of measure. (p. 482)

V
---

variable A letter, such as *n*, that stands for a number in an expression or equation. (p. 56)

Venn diagram A diagram that uses overlapping circles to show the relationships between groups of objects. (p. 337)

Example:

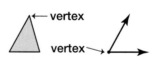

vertex The point of intersection of two sides of a polygon. The point of intersection of three edges of a space figure. (pp. 250, 282)

Examples:

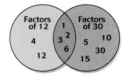

volume The number of cubic units that fit inside a space figure. (p. 462)

W
---

whole numbers The numbers in the set {0, 1, 2, 3, . . .}. (p. 10)

Z
---

zero property of multiplication The product of any number and 0 is 0. (p. 130)

Index

Index

Index

greater numbers, 196–197, 204, 228–231, 234–235

mean, median, and mode, 194–195, 198–199

by one-digit divisors, 184–187, 200–201, 203, 206

order of operations, 170–171, 202

patterns, 172–173, 180–181, 202, 210–211, 220–221, 236, 316–317, 328

performance assessment, 206, 240

relating multiplication to, 168–169, 202

remainders, 176–179, 180–181, 182–183, 207, 412–412A

short form, 188–189, 204

by two-digit divisors, 216–219, 220–221, 237, 240

two-digit quotients, 222–223, 224–225, 234–235, 237

zero in quotient, 190–191, 200–201, 204, 229

Double bar graph *See* Graph.

Draw a Diagram, 26–27

E

Edge, 282–283

Elapsed time, 424–427

Endpoint, 246

Equally likely outcomes, 496

Equation, 293

Equilateral triangle, 261–263

Equivalent fractions, 352–355, 364–365, 367

Equivalent ratio, 476–477

Estimation

adjusting estimate, 217

clustering, 55

data, 12–13, 432–433

dividing by two-digit numbers, 216–219, 220–221

and exact answers, 12–13, 48–49, 432–433

front-end, 54–55, 79

products, 138–139, 144–145, 300–301, 314–315

quotients, 174–175, 180–181, 203, 212–213, 216–219, 220–221, 236

by rounding, 50–53

sums and differences of mixed numbers, 386–387

two-digit quotients, 224–225

using, 11, 50–53, 54–55, 63, 69, 71, 76, 138–139, 141, 145, 155, 174–175, 187, 189, 201, 212–213, 219, 221, 225, 239, 254, 300–301, 308, 315, 321, 349, 357, 361, 386–387, 391, 399, 431, 443, 455

See also Decimals, Fractions, Whole numbers.

Event (probability), 496

Expanded form, 4, 14–15, 34

Explore lessons

adding and subtracting decimals, 64–65

circles, 280–281

classifying angles, 250–251

collecting data, 86–87

dividing by fractions, 410–411

finding averages, 194–195

investigating decimal division, 318–319

investigating decimal multiplication, 304–305

making line graphs, 102

modeling fraction multiplication, 404–405

primes and composites, 334–335

relating fractions to one half and one, 344–345

sum of the angles of a triangle, 264–265

two-digit quotients, 222–223

understanding one billion, 2–3

understanding partial products, 146–147

understanding percent, 486–487

understanding probability, 494–495

volume, 462–463

working with fractions with unlike denominators, 388–389

Exponent, 371

Extension

Chinese Remainder Problem, 207

Circle Graphs, 125

Equations, 293

Estimating a Fraction of a Number, 421

Integers, 471

Lattice Multiplication, 165

Mancala, 331

Percent of a Number, 513

Prime Factorization and Factor Trees, 371

Roman Numerals, 83

Sequences, 241

Writing a Check, 39

Extra Practice, 34–36, 78–80, 120–122, 160–162, 202–204, 236–238, 288–290, 326–328, 366–368, 416–418, 466–468, 508–510

F

Face, 282–285

Factor

common, 336–337, 348–349, 366

Index

Index

Index

Index

Credits

PHOTOGRAPHS

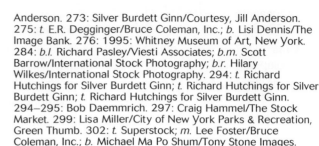

All photographs by Silver Burdett Ginn (SBG) unless otherwise noted.

Front cover: TRIAZZLE © 1995 Dan Gilbert, Inc.

viii: Eric Renard/Tony Stone Images. ix: Cliff Hollenbeck/International Stock Photography. x: Silver Burdett Ginn/Courtesy, Jill Anderson. 0: Ian Howarth for Silver Burdett Ginn. 0–1: Ian Howarth for Silver Burdett Ginn. 3: © Jerry Lodriguss/Photo Researchers, Inc. 5: Robert Frerck/Odyssey Productions. 7: Art Resource, NY. 13: The British Museum, London. 21: *t.* © Victor Englebert/Photo Researchers, Inc.; *b.* © Jany Sauvanet/Photo Researchers, Inc. 23: F. Scott Schafer/Outline Press Syndicate, Inc. 24: Randall Hyman for Silver Burdett Ginn. 28: Uniphoto. 29: NASA/AP/Wide World Photos. 40: Ken Redmond. 40–41: Bob Daemmrich/Stock Boston. 42: *bkgd.* Peter Pearson/Tony Stone Images. 43: Leverett Bradley/FPG International. 45: Arthur Tilley/FPG International. 52: © B & C Alexander/Photo Researchers, Inc. 60: Michael Yamashita/Corbis. 62: John Warden/Tony Stone Images. 65: David Madison. 70: Superstock. 73: Tom Stack for Silver Burdett Ginn. 83: Jessica Ehlers/Bruce Coleman, Inc. 84: *b.* Elliott Smith for Silver Burdett Ginn. 86: *m.* Robert Maier/Animals Animals. 88: *l.* Culver Pictures; *r.* Corbis-Bettmann. 89: *l.* Benn Mitchell/The Image Bank; *r.* Michael Chritton. 91: Richard Etchberger. 95: *t.,b.* The Western Reserve Historical Society. 97: *l.,m.,r.* Ron Kimball. 98: *t.* Smithsonian Institution Museum of American History; *m.* Bill Ray. 100: Paul Barton/The Stock Market. 101: Richard Hutchings for Silver Burdett Ginn. 107: Corbis-Bettmann. 112: *l.,m.* The Granger Collection, New York *r.* Dorey A. Cardinale/Parker/Boon Productions for Silver Burdett Ginn. 114: *r.* Donald Speker/Earth Scenes. 116A: *l.* Michael Holford; *r.* Superstock. 126: *l.* Rick Gayle/The Stock Market; *m.* David Young/Tom Stack & Associates; *r.* © David Parker/Photo Researchers, Inc.128: Walter Calahan. 128–129: Walter P. Calahan. 131: C. Prescott-Allen/Animals Animals. 132: *m.* Jack A. Barrie/Bruce Coleman, Inc.; *b.* Dr. Eckart Pott/Bruce Coleman, Inc. 133: Animals Animals. 135: *t.* Charles & Josette Lenars/Corbis; *b.* The Granger Collection, New York. 138: Frans Lanting/Minden Pictures. 139: *l.* Dan Williams for the Ward Museum of Wildfowl Art, Salisbury, MD; *r.* Connie Sines/Sines Studio. 140: Larry Lefever/Grant Heilman Photography. 141: Superstock. 142: © Tom McHugh/Photo Researchers, Inc. 151: Jonathan Blair/© National Geographic Image Collection. 152: Grenville Turner/Wildlight. 154: © Douglas Faulkner/Photo Researchers, Inc. 166–167: Richard Hutchings. 168: Michele Burgess/The Stock Market. 173: Eric Renard/Tony Stone Images. 174: D.E. Cox/Tony Stone Images. 178: Terje Rakke/The Image Bank. 179: Jose L. Pelaez/The Stock Market. 182: *t.* Kelly O'Neil Photography. 183: *t.,m.t.,m.b.,b.* Kelly O'Neil Photography. 185: Courtesy, Abercrombie & Kent International, Inc. 186: Tony Stone Images. 190: Wendell Metzen/Bruce Coleman, Inc. 196: *t.* Envision; *b.* Steven Needham/Envision. 197: Gerald Brimacombe/The Gamma Liaison Network. 198A: The Granger Collection, New York. 198: *t.* Kim Sayer/Corbis. 208: Michael A. Lorenz/Raul R. Rodriguez Design. 208–209: Ian Howarth. 210: Cliff Hollenbeck/International Stock Photography. 211: Cliff Hollenbeck/International Stock Photography. 216: *t.* © Renee Lynn/Photo Researchers, Inc. 218: Phil Schofield. 226: Superstock. 228: *t.* © Brenda Tharp/Photo Researchers, Inc. 229: *t.* Robert Holmes/Corbis. 230: *l.* Paul Natkin/Photo Reserve; *r.* John Bacchus for Silver Burdett Ginn. 240: Aaron Stevenson for Silver Burdett Ginn. 244: Valerie Santagto for Silver Burdett Ginn. 244–245: Leathers & Associates. 247: George Ancoma/International Stock Photography. 248: George Hunter/Tony Stone Images. 249: Jean Higgins/Envision. 254: Clifford Hausner/Leo de Wys. 256: *m.* Steve Solum/Bruce Coleman, Inc.; *b.l.* Chase Swift/Westlight; *b.m.* J.C. Carton/Bruce Coleman, Inc.; *b.r.* Bruce Coleman, Inc. 257: *t.l.* Sandy Felsenthal/Corbis; *t.m.l.* Richard Elkins/The Gamma Liaison Network; *t.r.* Valder/Tormey/International Stock Photography; *b.* Cesar Lucas/The Image Bank. 258: *t.r.* Superstock. 260: *t.* Courtesy, Dan Gilbert, Inc. 264: *t.* Uniphoto. 267: Dallas & John Heaton/Westlight. 272: *l.* Paul Chesley/Tony Stone Images; *r.* Silver Burdett Ginn/Courtesy, Jill Anderson. 273: Silver Burdett Ginn/Courtesy, Jill Anderson. 275: *t.* E.R. Degginger/Bruce Coleman, Inc.; *b.* Lisi Dennis/The Image Bank. 276: 1995: Whitney Museum of Art, New York. 284: *b.l.* Richard Pasley/Viesti Associates; *b.m.* Scott Barrow/International Stock Photography; *b.r.* Hilary Wilkes/International Stock Photography. 294: *t.* Richard Hutchings for Silver Burdett Ginn; *t.* Richard Hutchings for Silver Burdett Ginn; *t.* Richard Hutchings for Silver Burdett Ginn. 294–295: Bob Daemmrich. 297: Craig Hammel/The Stock Market. 299: Lisa Miller/City of New York Parks & Recreation, Green Thumb. 302: *t.* Superstock; *m.* Lee Foster/Bruce Coleman, Inc.; *b.* Michael Ma Po Shum/Tony Stone Images. 332: Courtesy, Steve McNicholas. 332–333: E. Patino/National Dance Institute. 335: Peter Cunningham/courtesy Mendola, Ltd. 343: Cameramann International Ltd. 347: Pat Lanza/Folio, Inc. 355: *t.,m.* Joseph Sohm/Chromosohm/Corbis. 357: *l.* Photofest; *m.* The Kobal Collection; *r.* Paramount Pictures/Photofest. 378: *t.* James A. Sugar/Black Star. 397: Archive Photos. 409: Scala/Art Resource, NY. 412A: Sam Kittner/© National Geographic Image Collection. 420: George Mattei/Envision. 422: Janet Century for Silver Burdett Ginn. 424: Michael Holford. 426: *l.* The Granger Collection, New York; *r.* Steven Needham/Envision. 435: Paul Kenward/Tony Stone Images. 437: Courtesy, Arthur M. Sackler Gallery, Smithsonian Institution, Washington, DC. 441: *b.* David Lassman/The Image Works Incorporated. 450: Robert Frerck/Odyssey Productions. 452: J.B. Grant/Leo de Wys. 480: *t.* Superstock. 484: *m.* Dorey A. Cardinale/Parker/Boon Productions for Silver Burdett Ginn.

ILLUSTRATIONS

2–3: Andy Levine. 4–6: Carlyn Iverson. 7: Ronda Henrichsen. 8: Stuart Zastrow. 9: Ronda Henrichsen. 12–13: Tom Powers. 20: Geo Systems. 22: Johnee Bee. 25: Stuart Zastrow. 26–27: Andy Levine. 28–29: Jim Salvaty. 30: Bernadette Hruby. 31: Tim Blough. 46: John Manders. 48–49: Larry Jost. 54–55: Diane Teske Harris. 56–57: Roger Roth. 59: Terry Sirrell. 60, 62–63: Dave Wherstein. 66–67: Robert Radigan. 69: Andrew Shiff. 70: Said Ramazan. 75: Pam Levy. 83: Jim Deigan. 88–89: Larry Jost. 89: Jackie Urbanovic. 92,94: Geo Systems. 98,101: Larry Jost. 102: Tim Blough. 103: Jackie Urbanovic. 108: Ronda Henrichsen. 112: Larry Jost. 114: Patrick Gnan. 117: Pam Levy. 126–127: Garry Colby. 131, 133–134,137: Patrick Gnan. 141: Dorothy Sullivan. 146: Patrick Gnan; Matt Zumbo. 148,151: Eldon Doty. 152: Skip Baker. 153: Eldon Doty. 154: Geo Systems; Larry Jost. 156: Patrick Gnan. 157: Pam Levy. 168: Geo Systems; Bill Vann. 171: Darryl Collins. 172: Bill Vann; Sarah Jane English. 174–175: Frank Riccio. 184: Larry Jost. 185: Bill Vann. 188–189: Garry Torrisi. 192: Garry Colby. 193: Garry Torrisi. 195: Bill Vann. 199: Jill Levy. 206: Rick Stromoski. 212–213: Roger Roth. 217: Andrew Shiff. 222: Andrew Shiff. 224: Robert Roper. 227: Dan Mcgowan. 228–230: Roger Roth. 231: Roger Roth; Robert Roper. 233: Jill Levy. 242–243: Bill Vann. 244: Gary Torrisi. 246: Don Baker. 247–248: Said Ramazan. 249: Susan Hunt Yule. 252–253: Lehner & Whyte. 256: Don Baker. 263: Stuart Zastrow. 264: Said Ramazan. 266: Don Baker. 267,272: Said Ramazan. 278–278A: Saul Rosenbaum. 281: John Francis. 282–283: Don Baker. 287: Susan Hunt Yule. 293: Lehner & Whyte. 302: Patrick Gnan. 307: Rod Thomas. 313: Eric Larson. 316: Garry Colby. 323: Gary Torrisi. 330: Patrick Gnan. 331: Rick Garica. 334: Fred Smith. 337: Marty Norman. 338: Linda Richards. 340: Roger Roth. 344,347: Felipe Galindo. 362: Fred Smith. 363: John Ellis. 372: Carlyn Iverson. 376: Gary Torrisi. 386–387: Burton Morris. 401: John Berg. 406: Matt Zumbo. 407: Eric Larson. 409: Garry Colby. 413,421: Andrew Shiff. 424: Angela Werneke. 427: Gary Torrisi. 431: Tim Bough. 437,441: Gary Torrisi. 446–447: Bob Berry, Sam Ward. 450: Larry Jost; Andrew Shiff. 451: Andrew Shiff. 471: Bob Berry. 481: Barbara Cousins. 491: Eric Larson. 493: Andrew Shiff. 494–495, 497: Dirk Wunderlich. 498–499: Sam Ward. 500: Dirk Wunderlich. 501: Mary Anne Ganley; Dirk Wunderlich. 502–503: Dirk Wunderlich. 505: Pam Levy. 507: Mary Anne Ganley. 510: Eric Larson. 511: Dirk Wunderlich. 513: Barbara Friedman. 539: Andrew Shiff. 541: Garry Colby. 542: Patrick Gnan. 544: Garry Colby.

Becoming a Better Test Taker

You've learned a lot of math skills this year! These skills will help you with your school work and with everyday activities outside of school. How can you show what you've learned in math? One way is by taking tests.

Did you know you could do better on tests just by knowing how to take a test? The test-taking strategies on these pages can help you become a better test taker. They might also help you think of test questions as a fun challenge! When you take a test, try to use these strategies to show all you know.

Multiple Choice Questions
Know Your ABCs!

For multiple choice questions, you are given several answer choices for a problem. Once you have solved the problem, you need to choose the right answer from the choices that are given.

1 Ⓐ Ⓑ Ⓒ Ⓓ Ⓔ
2 Ⓐ Ⓑ Ⓒ Ⓓ Ⓔ
3 Ⓐ Ⓑ Ⓒ Ⓓ Ⓔ

Example

$275 \div 5 = $ ▧

A 50   **B** 60   **C** 55   **D** 65   **E** Not Here

Think It Through

Read Did I read the problem carefully?
I need to divide 275 by 5.

Cross Out Are there any answers that are not reasonable?
50 is less than the estimated quotient, so I can cross out answer A.

Solve What is $275 \div 5$?
$275 \div 5 = 55$

Check Is there a way that I can check my answer?
I can multiply: $55 \times 5 = 275$.

Choose Which letter is next to my answer?
C is next to the answer 55.

Estimate whenever you can before you solve a problem. You can use an estimate to check whether your answer is reasonable or to identify answer choices that are not reasonable.

Reread the question and check your work before choosing "Not Here."

Make sure you fill in the letter on the answer sheet that matches your answer.

Try It!

❶ $6 \times 72 = $ ▧
A 420   **B** 422   **C** 432   **D** 490   **E** Not Here

❷ $4,000 \div 10 = $ ▧
A 4   **B** 14   **C** 40   **D** 400   **E** Not Here

❸ $420 \div 20 = $ ▧
A 21   **B** 210   **C** 400   **D** 440   **E** Not Here

❹ $600 \times 300 = $ ▧
A 18   **B** 180   **C** 1,800
D 18,000   **E** Not Here

Multistep Questions
One Step at a Time

Sometimes you need to do more than one step to answer a multiple choice question.

Example

There are 382 guests registered at a hotel. On Friday 218 guests check out and 426 check in. How many guests are registered at the hotel now?

A 644   **B** 590   **C** 426   **D** 382   **E** Not Here

▷ Always look at all of the answer choices that are listed.

▷ Even if you find your answer among the choices, check your work. Answers that come from making common mistakes are usually included in the choices!

▷ If you are having trouble answering a question, go on to the next question and come back to the more difficult question later.

Think It Through

Read
Did I read the problem carefully?
I need to find out how many guests are registered at the hotel after some check out and others check in.

Cross Out
Are there any answers that are not reasonable?
382 guests were registered before check out and check in. That figure will change, so I can cross out answer D.

Solve
How many guests are registered now?
382 − 218 = 164 and 164 + 426 = 590, so there are 590 guests registered now.

Check
Is there a way that I can check my answer?
382 − 218 + 426 = 590

Choose
Which letter is next to my answer?
B is next to the answer 590.

Try It!

1 A box contains 12 oranges. Each crate contains 24 boxes of oranges. How many oranges are in 30 crates?

A 233   **B** 864   **C** 4,680
D 8,640   **E** Not Here

2 Bea buys cheese for $2.49, milk for $2.19, and apples for $1.98. How much change does she receive from $20.00?

A $6.66   **B** $12.49   **C** $13.34
D $13.44   **E** Not Here

Measurement Questions
Measure Up!

Sometimes you will need to use a ruler to help you solve a multiple choice question.

Example

Martha was looking at a picture of a scale drawing of a flagpole. The scale is 1 inch represents 10 feet. Measure the height of the flagpole to the nearest half inch.

What is the actual height of the flagpole?

  A 15 feet   **B** 20 feet   **C** 25 feet   **D** 30 feet

Think It Through

Read — Did I read the problem carefully?
I need to use the inch side of the ruler.

Cross Out — Are there any answers that are not reasonable?
The drawing measures between 2 and 3 in. Since each in. represents 10 ft, I know that the actual flagpole is between 20 and 30 ft. So I can cross out answers A and D.

Solve — What can I do to solve the problem?
I will measure the length of the flagpole. It measures $2\frac{1}{2}$ inches.

Check — Is there a way to check my answer?
I can measure again.

Choose — Which letter is next to my answer?
The letter C is next to 25 feet.

Make sure you are using the correct side of the ruler when measuring.

Make sure you line up the 0 mark on the ruler with one end of the object you are going to measure.

Check to see how precisely you need to measure the object, such as to the nearest $\frac{1}{2}$ inch or the nearest $\frac{1}{4}$ inch.

Try It!

Bryan rode his bike from his house to the basketball court. How far did Bryan ride? Use the centimeter side of the ruler.

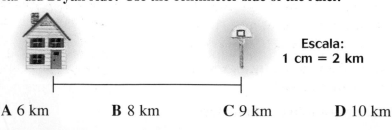

Escala:
1 cm = 2 km

  A 6 km   **B** 8 km   **C** 9 km   **D** 10 km

Short Answer Questions
The Write Stuff

Sometimes a test question asks you not only to *solve* a problem but to show *how* you solved the problem. For questions like these, you need to be able to write your thoughts on paper.

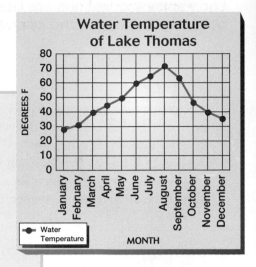

Water Temperature of Lake Thomas

Example

The line graph at the right shows the water temperatures of Lake Thomas.

You are helping to plan a trip to Lake Thomas with your family during summer vacation. If you want to be there when the water temperature is the warmest, when should you plan your trip? Explain.

Think It Through

Read   What am I being asked to write about?
I need to find when the water will be the warmest at Lake Thomas.

Plan   What can I do to solve the problem?
I can look at the line on the line graph to see when the water will be warmest.

Solve   What is the answer to the problem?
The water temperature will be warmest in August, so I would plan the trip for August.

Explain   How did I get my answer?
The highest point on the line graph is in August, so the water temperature is warmest in August.

Try It!

Use the line graph above to answer Questions 1–3. For each question, explain how you got your answer.

1 You are in charge of planning a trip for the skating club in your community. There is seasonal ice skating at Lake Thomas. When would be the best time to take this trip?

2 During which two months of the year does the greatest change in water temperature take place?

3 Which two months have the same water temperature?

Long Answer Questions
In Your Own Words

Long answer questions are like short answer questions, only they are longer and often have more than one step.

Example

Archaeologists on a dig have excavated two sites in an ancient city. Each site has different depths and has been divided into levels. Site A has 35 levels. Each is 12 inches deep. Site B has 41 levels. Each is 12 inches deep. A tunnel that is 3 feet deep has been found at the bottom of Site A. Which excavated site is deeper, including the tunnel?

▷ Remember to explain *how* you got your answer.

▷ When you're finished writing, read the question again to be sure you've answered it completely.

▷ Keep trying! If your first strategy doesn't work, try another one. You might get partial credit even if you can't find an answer.

▷ Long answer questions take longer to answer! Be patient, and take your time.

Think It Through

Read   What am I being asked to write about?
I need to compare the depths of two excavated sites.

Plan   What can I do to solve the problem?
I can find the total depth of each site and see which one is the deeper site.

Solve   What is the answer to the problem?
Site B is deeper than Site A.

Explain   How did I get my answer?
I found the depth of Site A first:
35 x 12 inches = 420 inches. Then I changed the tunnel depth from 3 feet to 36 inches:
420 + 36 = 456 inches. To find the depth of Site B, I multiplied 41 times 12 inches and got 492 inches. Site B is deeper than Site A.

Try It!

Answer Questions 1 and 2. Explain how you got your answers.

1. While on a trip, Ellen sent letters and postcards to her friends. She spent $2.16 on stamps. If stamps for her letters cost $0.32 and stamps for postcards cost $0.20, how many postcards and letters did Ellen send?

2. Karen went horseback riding on a trail. She rode 5 miles east and then 7 miles north. After she rested, she rode 6 miles south. How far is Karen from where she started?